Nyup nyup... Hello, Amélie here. We just moved. Wow, did she ever have it rough. Who's "she"? The lady at our house. I tell you, she is the minister of moving. The old guy just drew manga the whole time. What a jerk. I got pretty worn out myself... I'm going to take a little nap here with my cheese stick. *Nyup nyup...zzzzz...*

—*Yūki Tabata's dog, 2017*

YŪKI TABATA
was born in Fukuoka Prefecture and got his big break in the 2011 Shonen Jump Golden Future Cup with his winning entry, *Hungry Joker*. He started the magical fantasy series *Black Clover* in 2015.

BLACK CLOVER
VOLUME 12
SHONEN JUMP Manga Edition

Story and Art by YŪKI TABATA

Translation ✽ TAYLOR ENGEL, HC LANGUAGE SOLUTIONS, INC.
Touch-Up Art & Lettering ✽ ANNALIESE CHRISTMAN
Design ✽ SHAWN CARRICO
Editor ✽ ALEXIS KIRSCH

Printed in the U.S.A.

Published by VIZ Media, LLC
P.O. Box 77010
San Francisco, CA 94107

10 9 8 7 6 5 4 3 2 1
First printing, August 2018

ratings.viz.com
RATED T TEEN

PARENTAL ADVISORY
BLACK CLOVER is rated T for Teen and is recommended for ages 13 and up. This volume contains realistic and fantasy violence.

VIZ MEDIA
viz.com

SHONEN JUMP
shonenjump.com

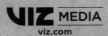

SHONEN JUMP MANGA

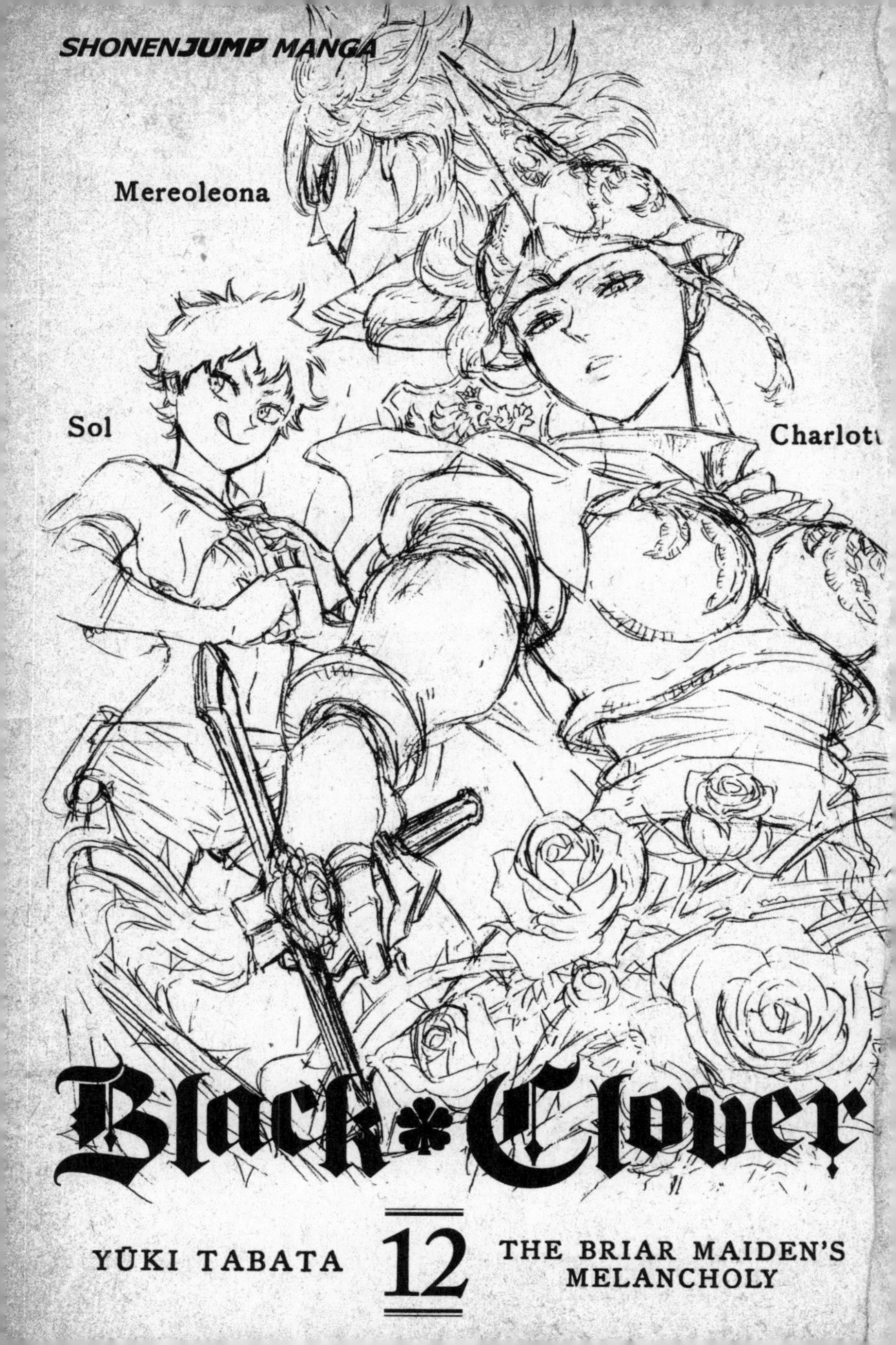
Mereoleona
Sol
Charlott

Black Clover

YŪKI TABATA

12

THE BRIAR MAIDEN'S MELANCHOLY

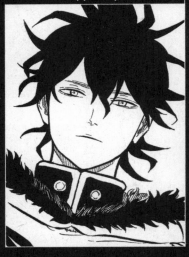

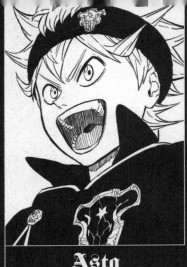

Asta

Member of: The Black Bulls
Magic: None (Anti-Magic)

He has no magic, but he's working to become the Wizard King through sheer guts and his well-trained body. He fights with an anti-magic sword.

Yuno

Member of: The Golden Dawn

Magic: Wind

Asta's best friend, and a good rival who's also been working to become the Wizard King. He controls Sylph, the spirit of wind.

Yami Sukehiro

Member of: The Black Bulls
Magic: Dark

A captain who looks fierce and has a hot temper, but is very popular with his brigade. A heavy smoker.

Noelle Silva

Member of: The Black Bulls
Magic: Water

A royal. She feels inferior to her brilliant siblings. Her latent abilities are an unknown quantity.

Finral Roulacase

Member of: The Black Bulls
Magic: Spatial

A flirt who immediately chats up any woman he sees. He can't attack, but he has

Vanessa Enoteca

Member of: The Black Bulls
Magic: Thread

She likes partying with everybody, and has an unparalleled love of liquor. She's someone important

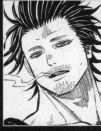

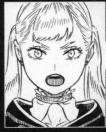

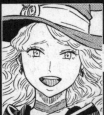

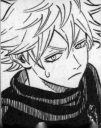

Fana

Magic: Fire

Mars's childhood friend. She was being controlled by the Eye of the Midnight Sun.

Mars

 Member of: The Diamond Kingdom
Magic: Mineral

One of the Eight Shining Generals. He previously encountered and fought Asta in a dungeon.

Charlotte Roselei

Member of: The Blue Rose Knights
Magic: Briar

Has a cool personality. As a rule, she doesn't like men, but she seems to make an exception for Yami…

Queen of Witches

Magic: Blood

The queen who rules the Forest of Witches. She'll do anything to achieve her ambition.

Leopold Vermilion

Member of: The Crimson Lion Kings
Magic: Flame

The younger brother of the brigade captain Fuegoleon. Considers Asta his rival.

Sol Marron

Member of: The Blue Rose Knights
Magic: Earth

Spirited, freewheeling and exceptionally energetic. Adores her captain and calls her "Sis."

STORY

In a world where magic is everything, Asta and Yuno are both found abandoned on the same day at a church in the remote village of Hage. Both dream of becoming the Wizard King, the highest of all mages, and they spend their days working toward that dream.

The year they turn 15, both receive grimoires, magic books that amplify their bearer's magic. They take the entrance exam for the Magic Knights, nine groups of mages under the direct control of the Wizard King. Yuno, whose magic is strong, joins the Golden Dawn, an elite group, while Asta, who has no magic at all, joins the Black Bulls, a group of misfits. With this, the two finally take their first step toward becoming the Wizard King…

During his battle with the Eye of the Midnight Sun and Ladros, Asta ends up in a nasty situation. Although he almost passes out, a new power awakes inside him, allowing him to defeat Ladros. While this is happening, the Witch Queen abruptly appears on the battlefield intent on making Vanessa hers. She tries to control Asta and make him kill his friends, but then something strange happens…

BLACK ✿ CLOVER

CONTENTS

BLACK ❁ CLOVER

12

Page 101: I'm Home

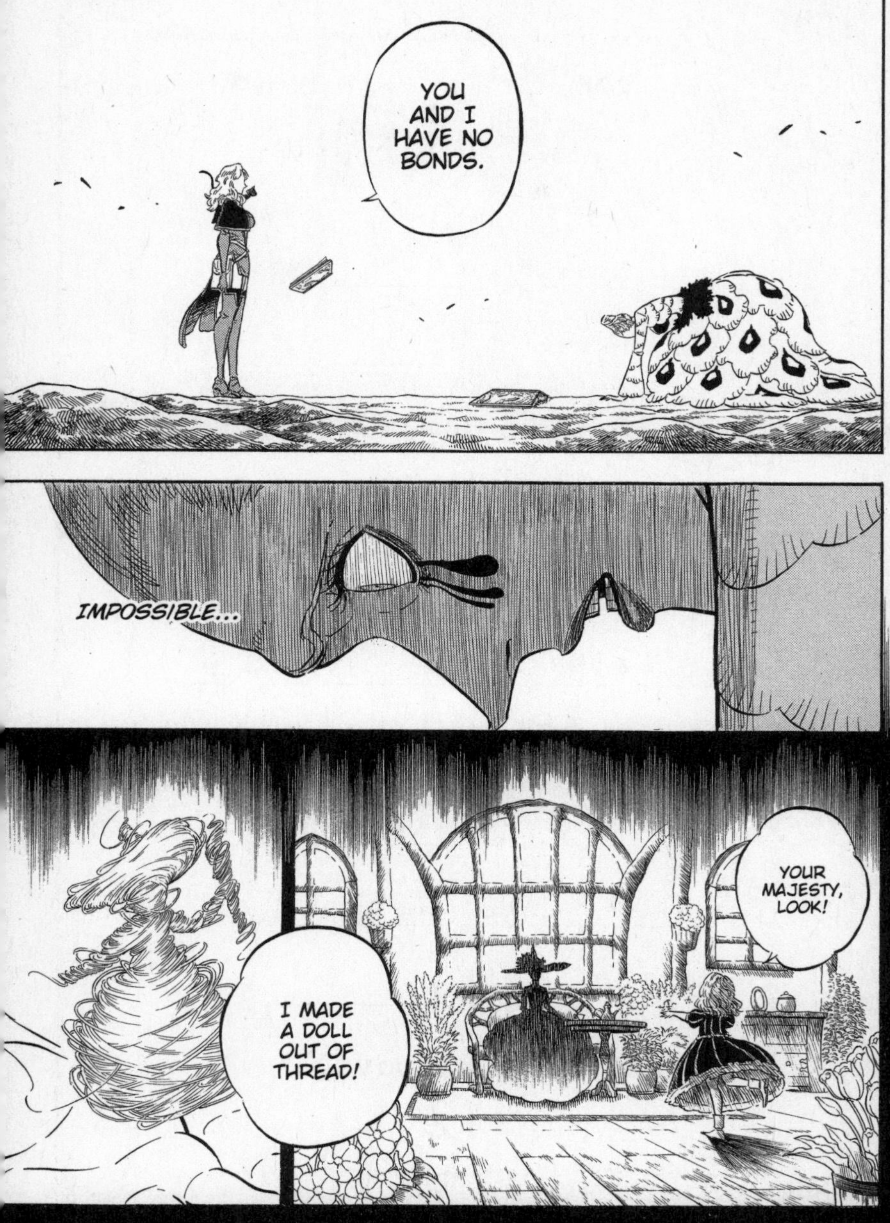
YOU AND I HAVE NO BONDS.
IMPOSSIBLE...
YOUR MAJESTY, LOOK!
I MADE A DOLL OUT OF THREAD!

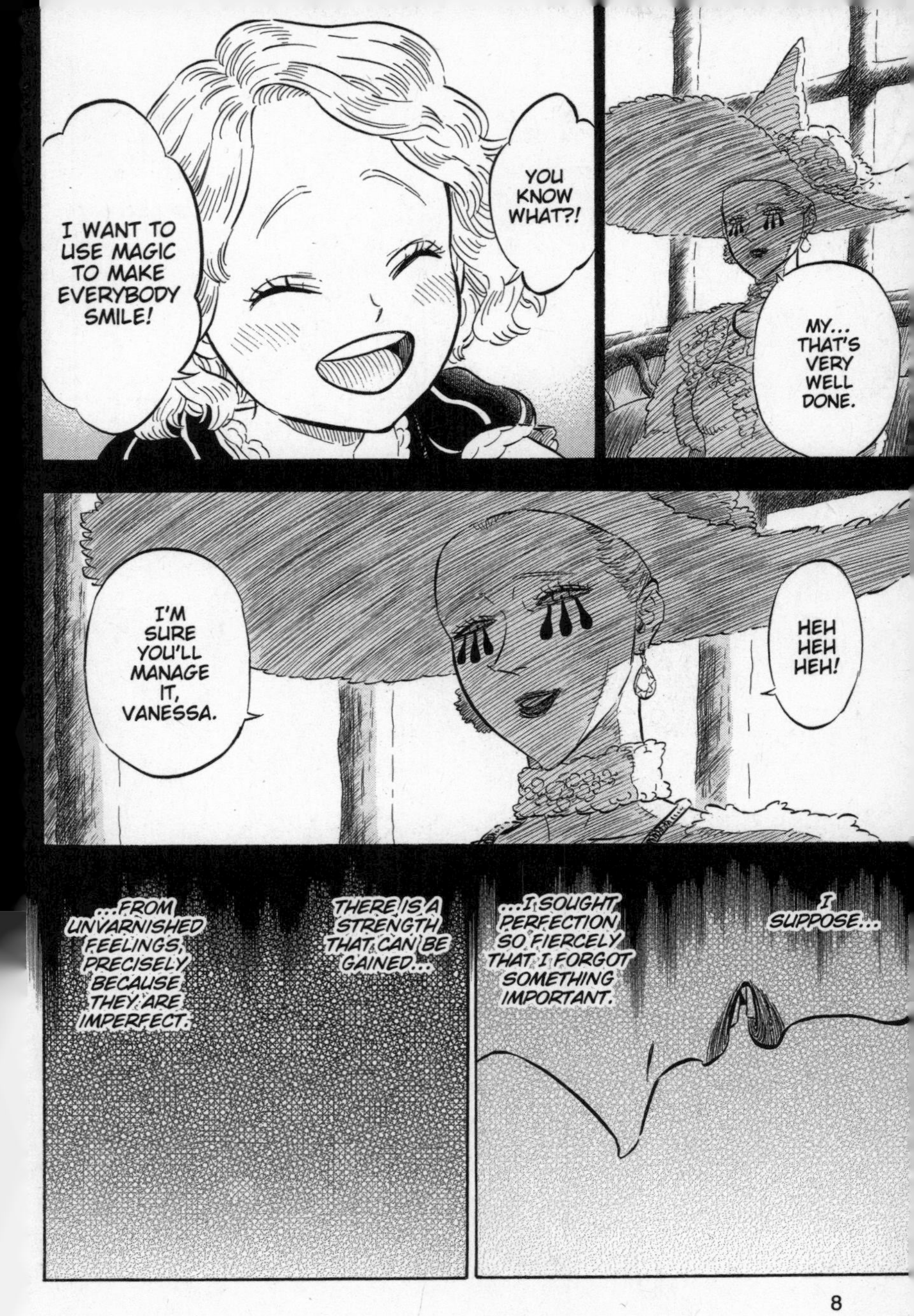
MY... THAT'S VERY WELL DONE.
YOU KNOW WHAT?!
I WANT TO USE MAGIC TO MAKE EVERYBODY SMILE!
HEH HEH HEH!
I'M SURE YOU'LL MANAGE IT, VANESSA.
I SUPPOSE...
...I SOUGHT PERFECTION SO FIERCELY THAT I FORGOT SOMETHING IMPORTANT.
THERE IS A STRENGTH THAT CAN BE GAINED...
...FROM UNVARNISHED FEELINGS, PRECISELY BECAUSE THEY ARE IMPERFECT.

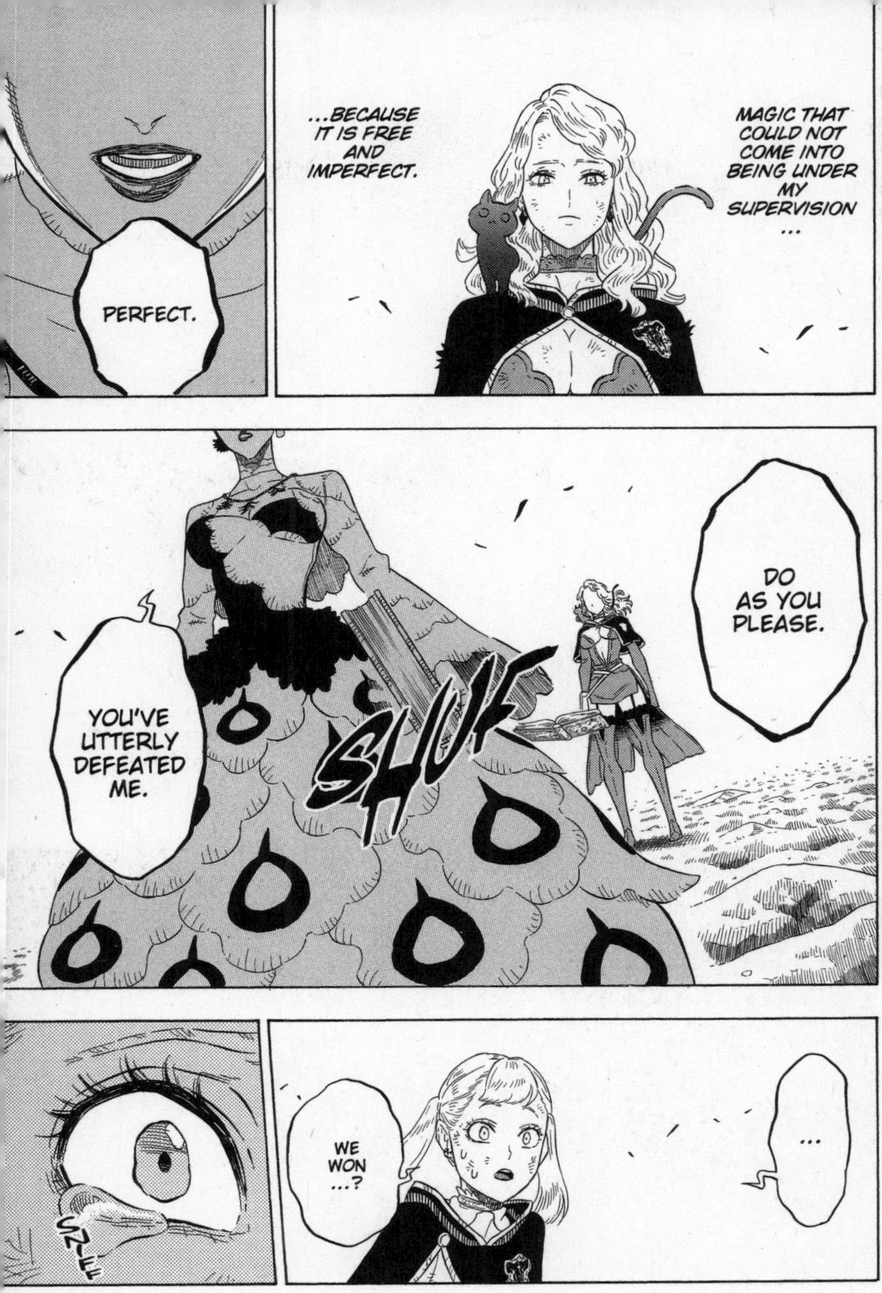
MAGIC THAT COULD NOT COME INTO BEING UNDER MY SUPERVISION ...
...BECAUSE IT IS FREE AND IMPERFECT.
PERFECT.
DO AS YOU PLEASE.
SHUF
YOU'VE UTTERLY DEFEATED ME.
...
WE WON ...?
SNIFF

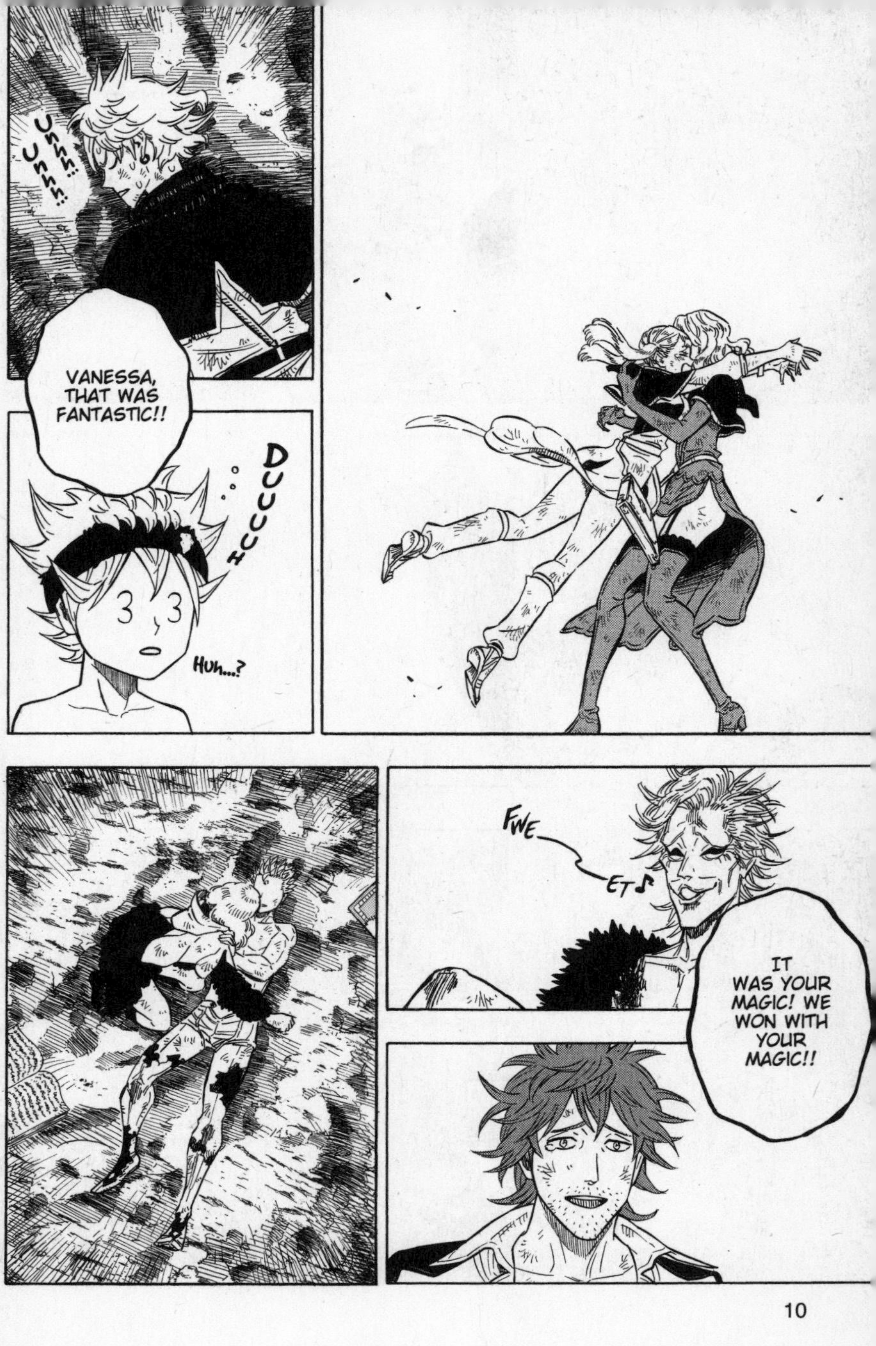
Unhh!! Unhh!!
VANESSA, THAT WAS FANTASTIC!!
DUUUUUH
Huh...?
FWEET♪
IT WAS YOUR MAGIC! WE WON WITH YOUR MAGIC!!

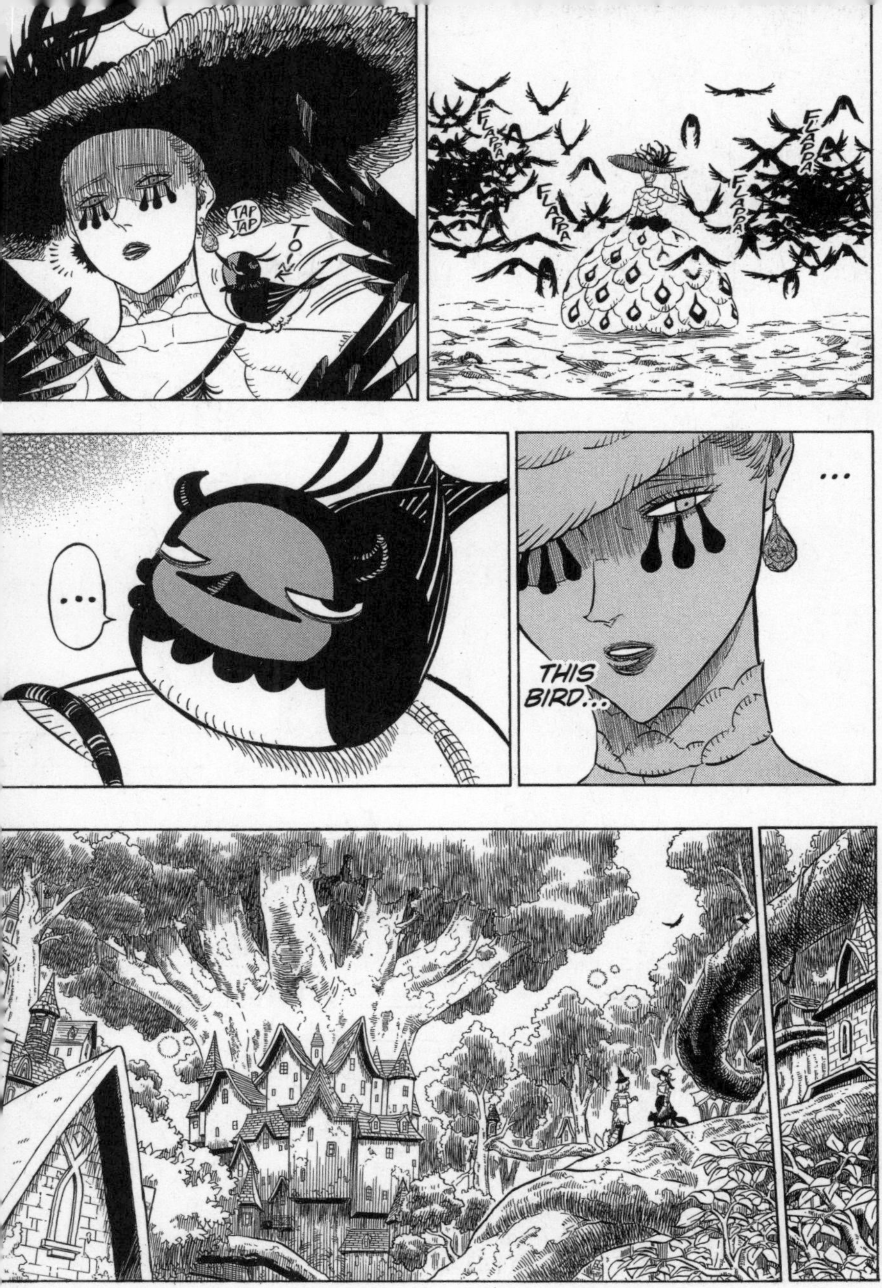
FLAPPA
FLAPPA
FLAPPA
FLAPPA
TAP TAP
TOINK
...
THIS BIRD...
...

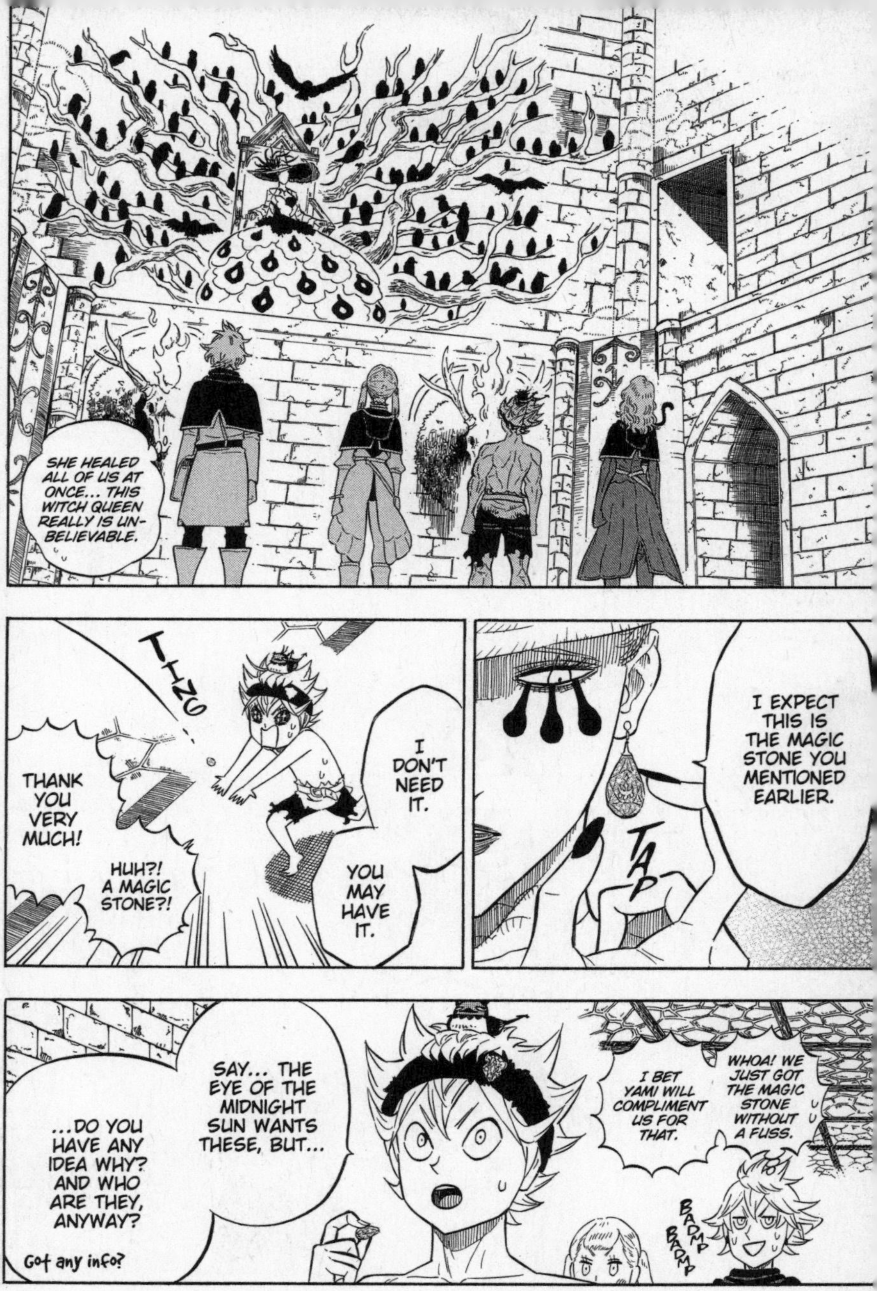
SHE HEALED ALL OF US AT ONCE... THIS WITCH QUEEN REALLY IS UNBELIEVABLE.
I EXPECT THIS IS THE MAGIC STONE YOU MENTIONED EARLIER.
TAP
I DON'T NEED IT.
YOU MAY HAVE IT.
TING
THANK YOU VERY MUCH!
HUH?! A MAGIC STONE?!
WHOA! WE JUST GOT THE MAGIC STONE WITHOUT A FUSS.
I BET YAMI WILL COMPLIMENT US FOR THAT.
BADMP BADMP
SAY... THE EYE OF THE MIDNIGHT SUN WANTS THESE, BUT...
...DO YOU HAVE ANY IDEA WHY? AND WHO ARE THEY, ANYWAY?
Got any info?

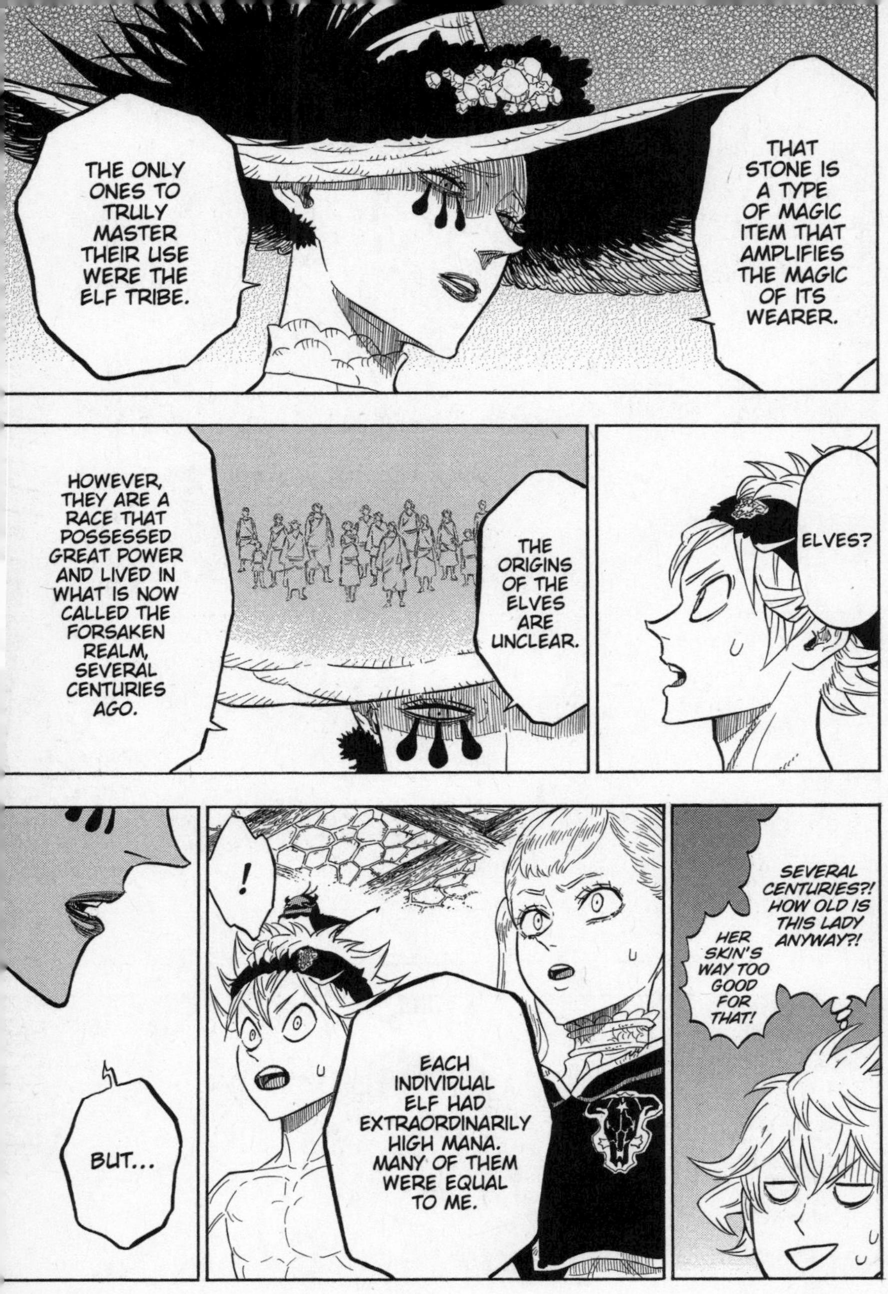
THAT STONE IS A TYPE OF MAGIC ITEM THAT AMPLIFIES THE MAGIC OF ITS WEARER.
THE ONLY ONES TO TRULY MASTER THEIR USE WERE THE ELF TRIBE.
ELVES?
THE ORIGINS OF THE ELVES ARE UNCLEAR.
HOWEVER, THEY ARE A RACE THAT POSSESSED GREAT POWER AND LIVED IN WHAT IS NOW CALLED THE FORSAKEN REALM, SEVERAL CENTURIES AGO.
SEVERAL CENTURIES?! HOW OLD IS THIS LADY ANYWAY?!
HER SKIN'S WAY TOO GOOD FOR THAT!
!
EACH INDIVIDUAL ELF HAD EXTRAORDINARILY HIGH MANA. MANY OF THEM WERE EQUAL TO ME.
BUT...

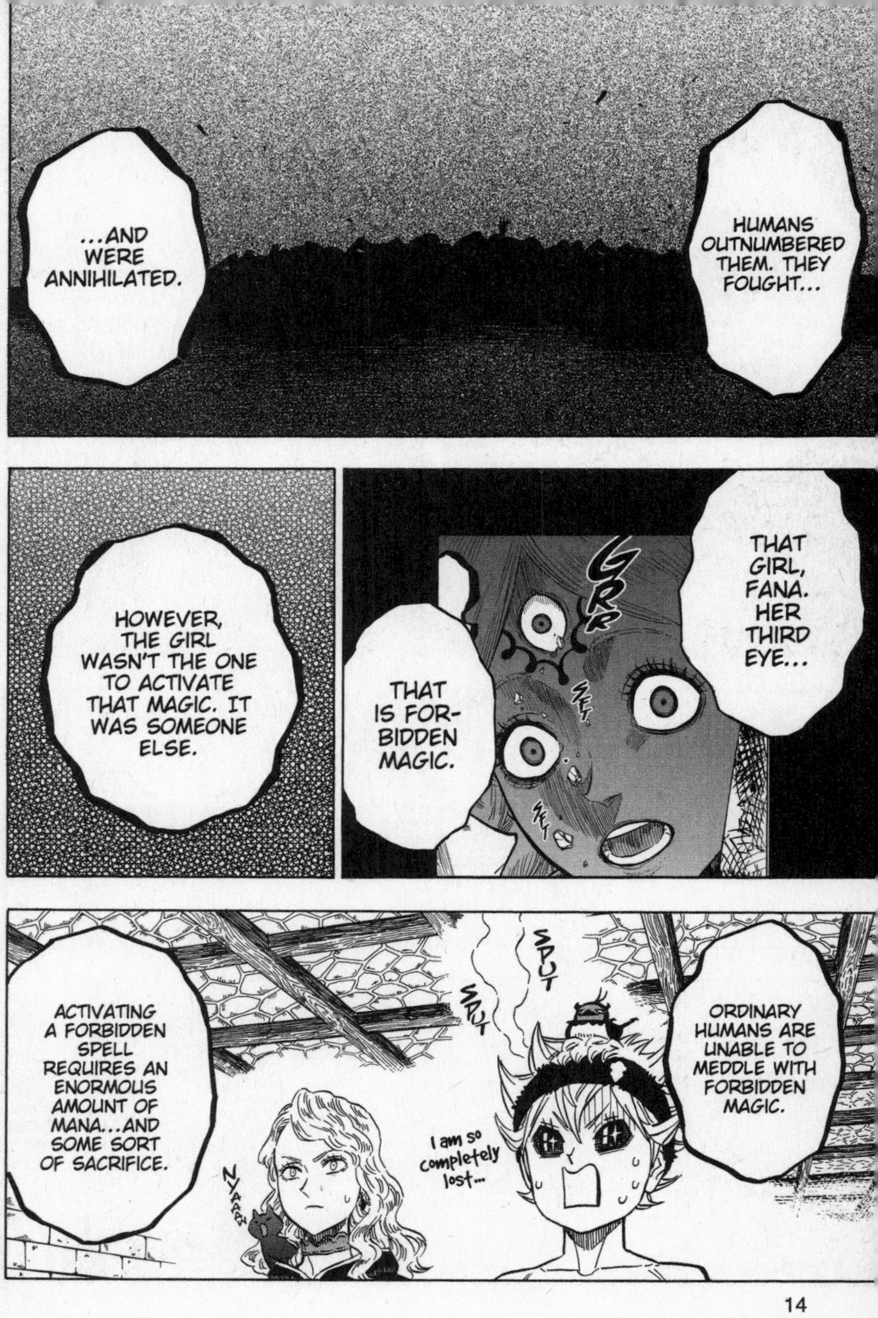
HUMANS OUTNUMBERED THEM. THEY FOUGHT...
...AND WERE ANNIHILATED.
THAT GIRL, FANA. HER THIRD EYE...
GRR
THAT IS FORBIDDEN MAGIC.
HOWEVER, THE GIRL WASN'T THE ONE TO ACTIVATE THAT MAGIC. IT WAS SOMEONE ELSE.
ORDINARY HUMANS ARE UNABLE TO MEDDLE WITH FORBIDDEN MAGIC.
SPUT
SPUT
I am so completely lost...
ACTIVATING A FORBIDDEN SPELL REQUIRES AN ENORMOUS AMOUNT OF MANA...AND SOME SORT OF SACRIFICE.

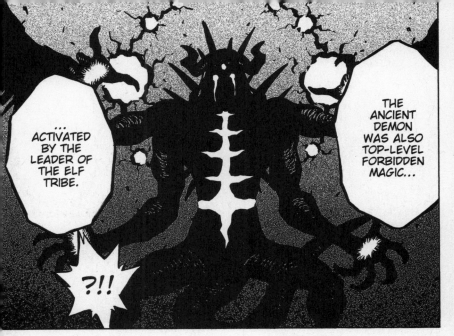

THE ANCIENT DEMON WAS ALSO TOP-LEVEL FORBIDDEN MAGIC...
...ACTIVATED BY THE LEADER OF THE ELF TRIBE.
?!!
THE EYE OF THE MIDNIGHT SUN...
...MAY BE DESCENDED FROM THAT TRIBE.
WE'RE GETTING A TON OF AMAZING NEW INTEL HERE!
Report time! I will become a reporting fiend!
SCRIT SCRIT
...
THOSE TWO SWORDS YOU BEAR.
AND, ASTA.

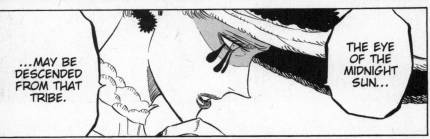

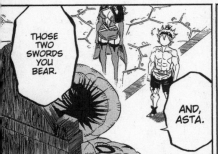

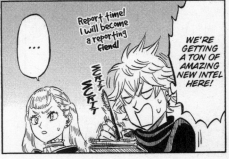

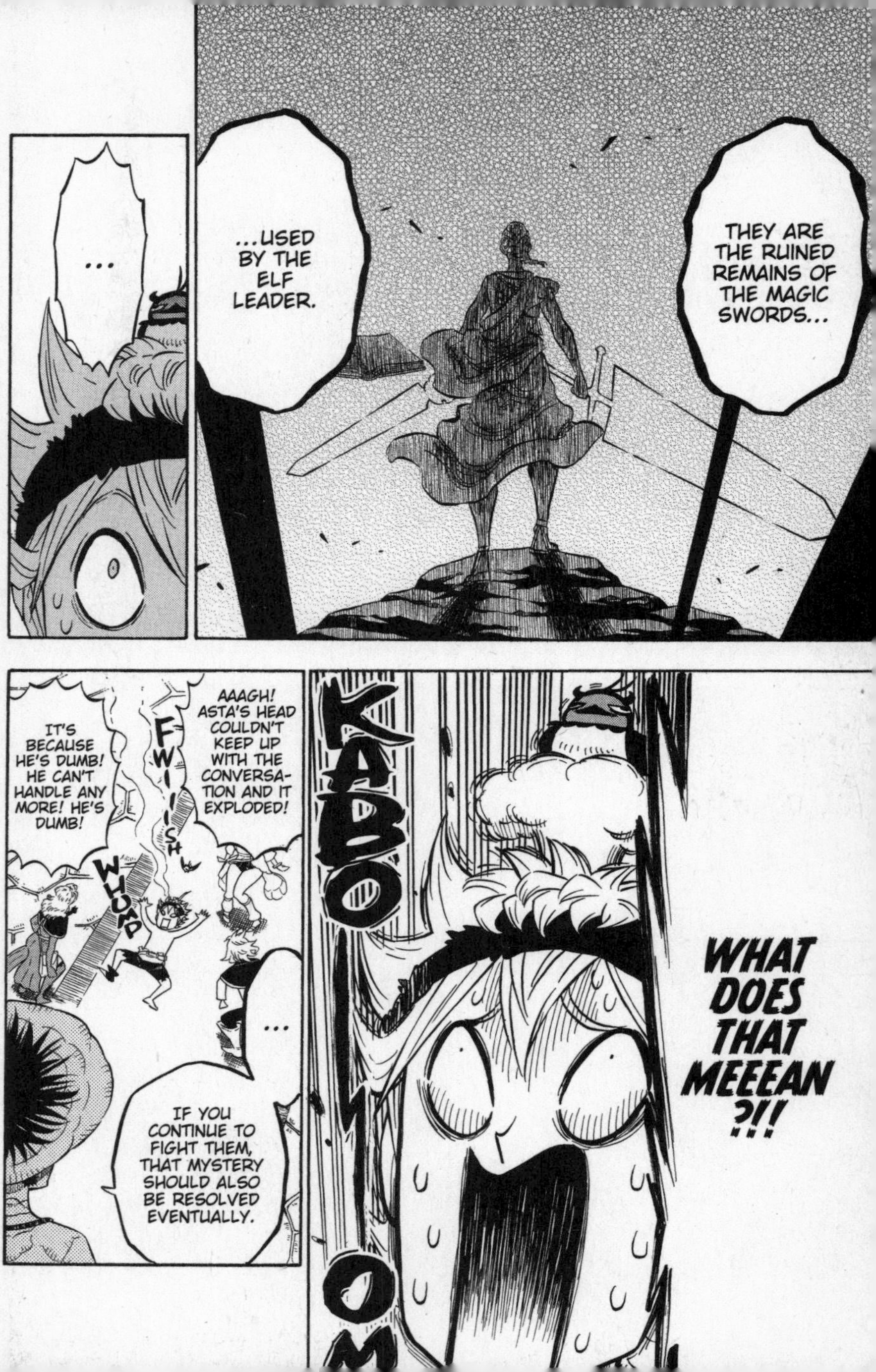
THEY ARE THE RUINED REMAINS OF THE MAGIC SWORDS...
...USED BY THE ELF LEADER.
...
KABOOM
WHAT DOES THAT MEEEAN?!!
AAAGH! ASTA'S HEAD COULDN'T KEEP UP WITH THE CONVERSATION AND IT EXPLODED!
IT'S BECAUSE HE'S DUMB! HE CAN'T HANDLE ANY MORE! HE'S DUMB!
FWIIISH
WHUMP
...
IF YOU CONTINUE TO FIGHT THEM, THAT MYSTERY SHOULD ALSO BE RESOLVED EVENTUALLY.

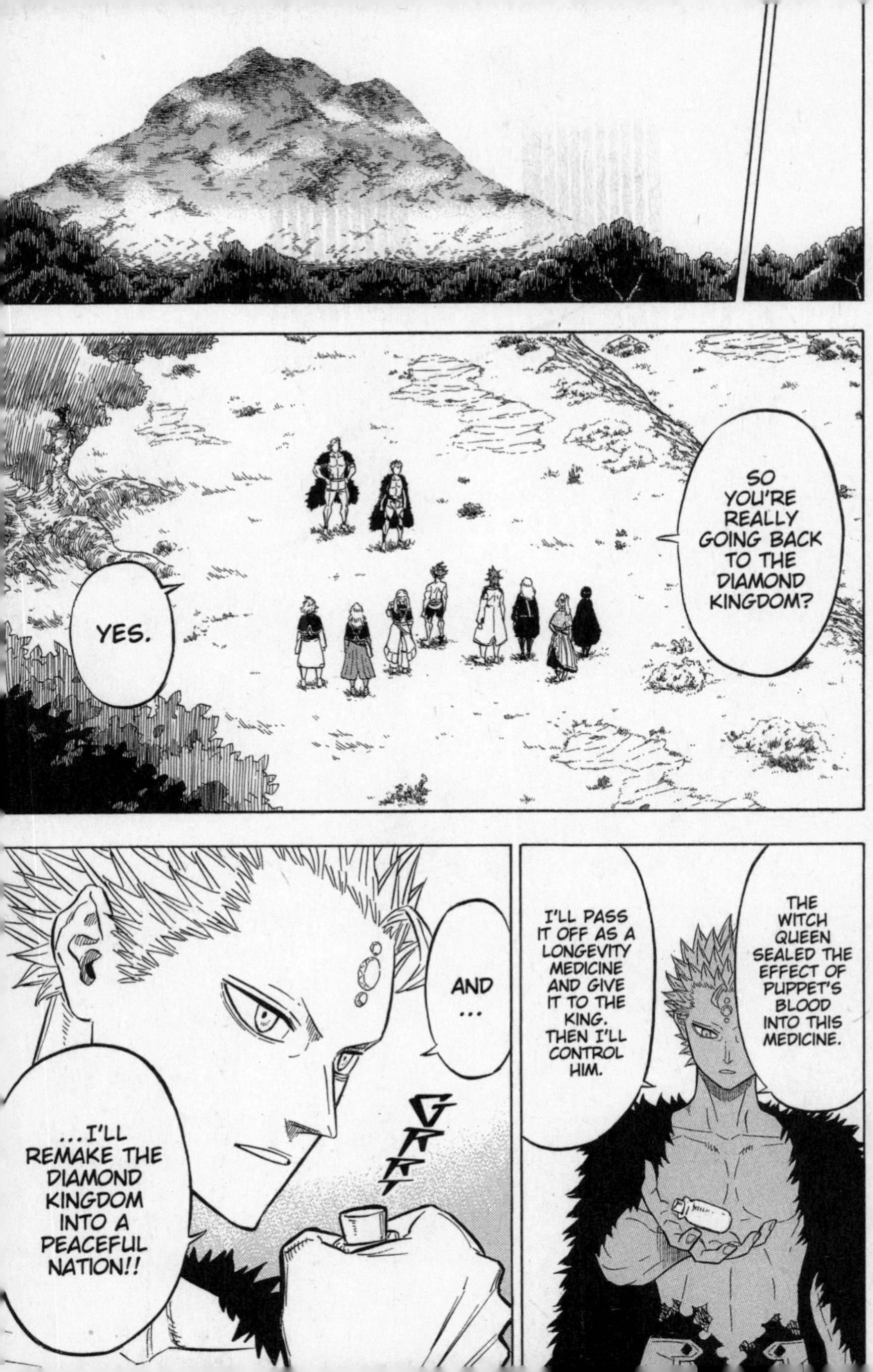
SO YOU'RE REALLY GOING BACK TO THE DIAMOND KINGDOM?
YES.
THE WITCH QUEEN SEALED THE EFFECT OF PUPPET'S BLOOD INTO THIS MEDICINE.
I'LL PASS IT OFF AS A LONGEVITY MEDICINE AND GIVE IT TO THE KING. THEN I'LL CONTROL HIM.
AND ...
GRRT
...I'LL REMAKE THE DIAMOND KINGDOM INTO A PEACEFUL NATION!!

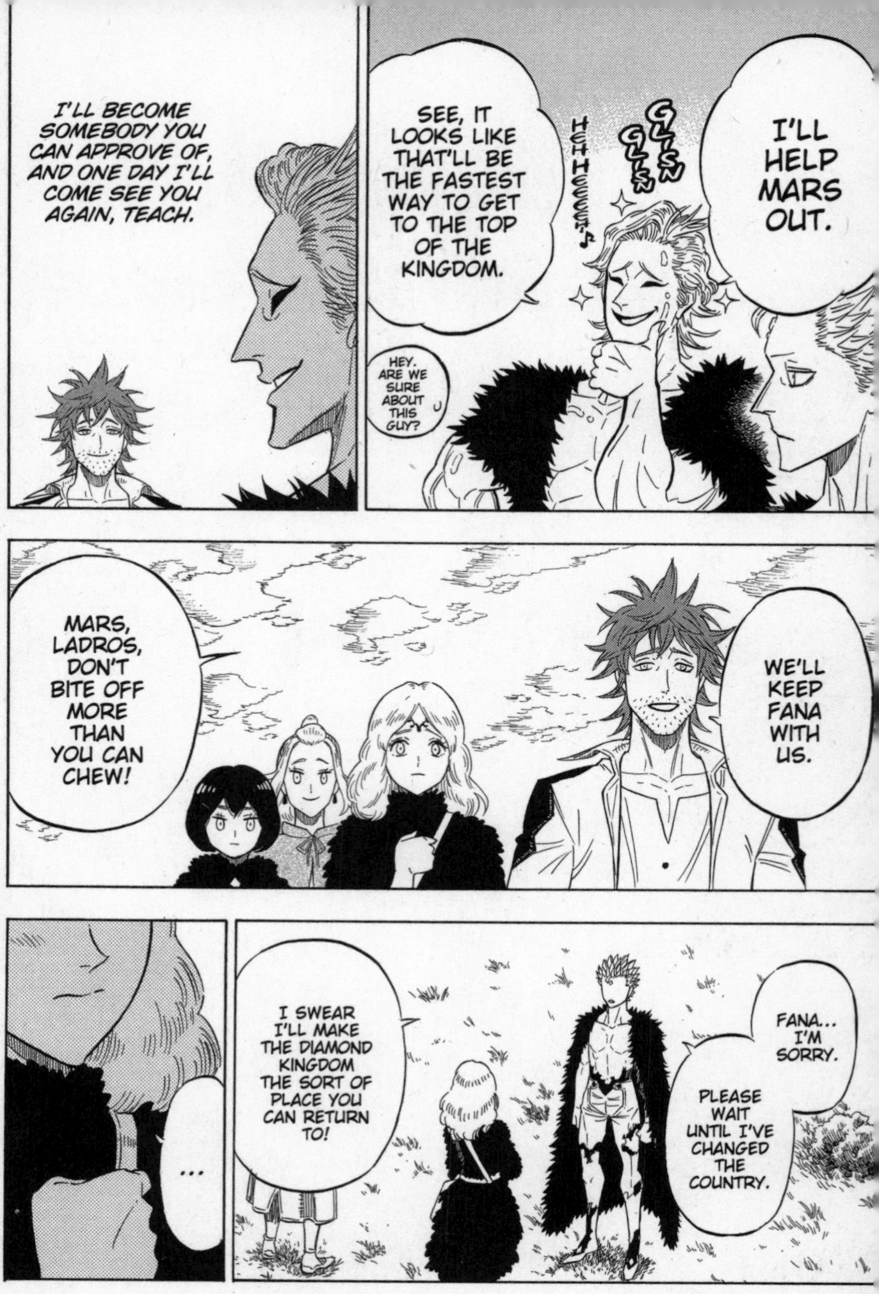
I'LL HELP MARS OUT.
GLISN GLISN
HEH HEEEEH♪
SEE, IT LOOKS LIKE THAT'LL BE THE FASTEST WAY TO GET TO THE TOP OF THE KINGDOM.
HEY. ARE WE SURE ABOUT THIS GUY?
I'LL BECOME SOMEBODY YOU CAN APPROVE OF, AND ONE DAY I'LL COME SEE YOU AGAIN, TEACH.
WE'LL KEEP FANA WITH US.
MARS, LADROS, DON'T BITE OFF MORE THAN YOU CAN CHEW!
FANA... I'M SORRY.
PLEASE WAIT UNTIL I'VE CHANGED THE COUNTRY.
I SWEAR I'LL MAKE THE DIAMOND KINGDOM THE SORT OF PLACE YOU CAN RETURN TO!
...

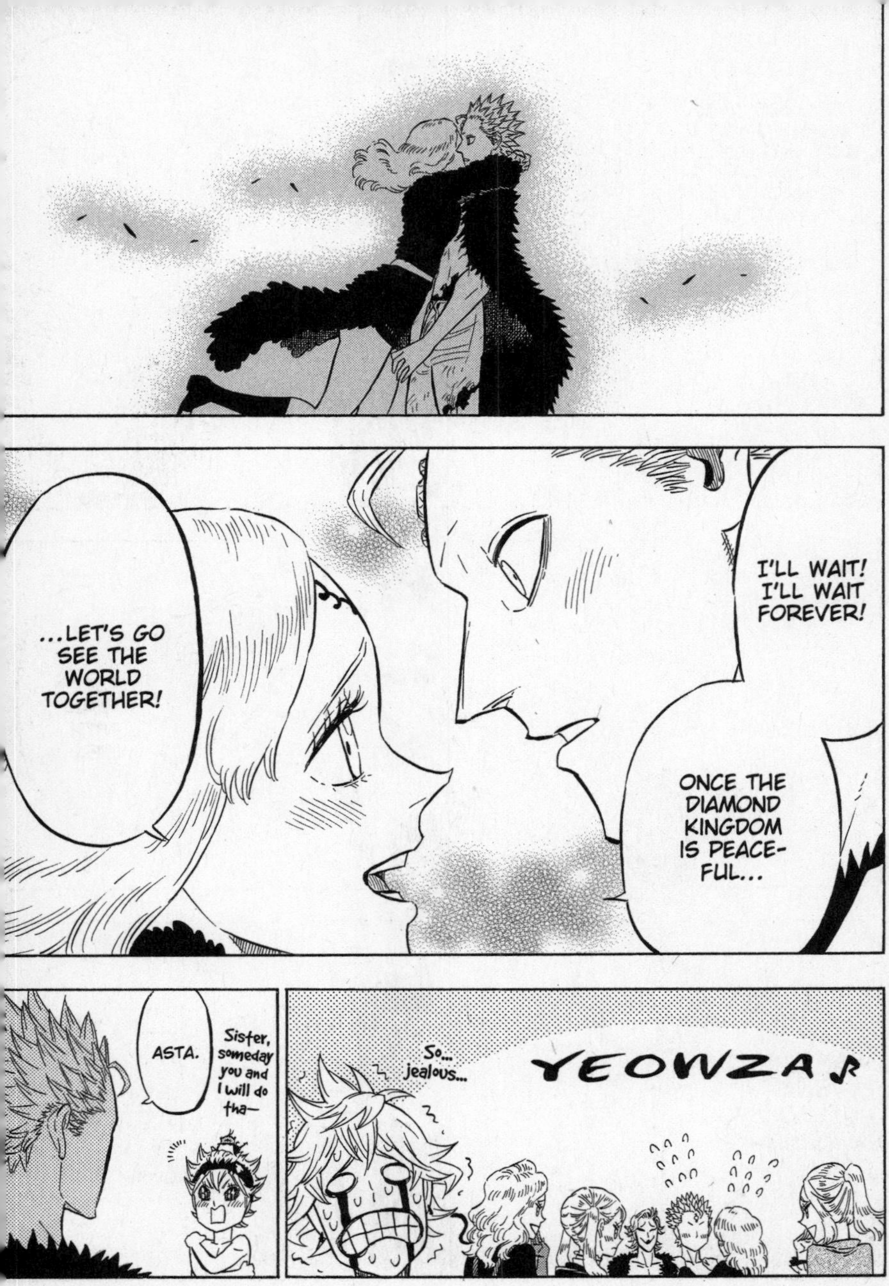
I'LL WAIT! I'LL WAIT FOREVER!
ONCE THE DIAMOND KINGDOM IS PEACE-FUL...
...LET'S GO SEE THE WORLD TOGETHER!
YEOWZA ♪
So... jealous...
Sister, someday you and I will do tha—
ASTA.

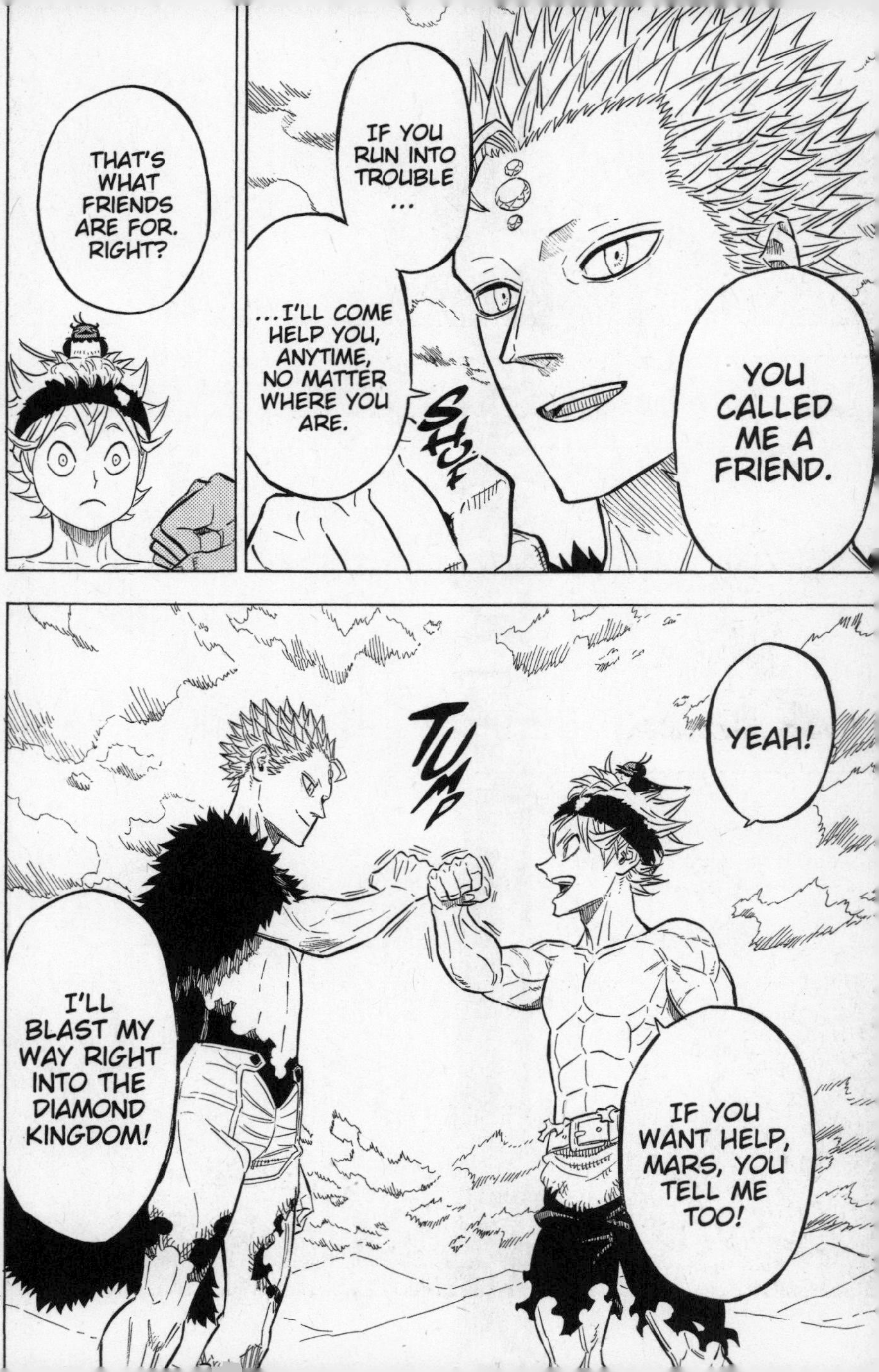
YOU CALLED ME A FRIEND.
IF YOU RUN INTO TROUBLE ...
...I'LL COME HELP YOU, ANYTIME, NO MATTER WHERE YOU ARE.
SHOK
THAT'S WHAT FRIENDS ARE FOR. RIGHT?
YEAH!
TUMP
IF YOU WANT HELP, MARS, YOU TELL ME TOO!
I'LL BLAST MY WAY RIGHT INTO THE DIAMOND KINGDOM!

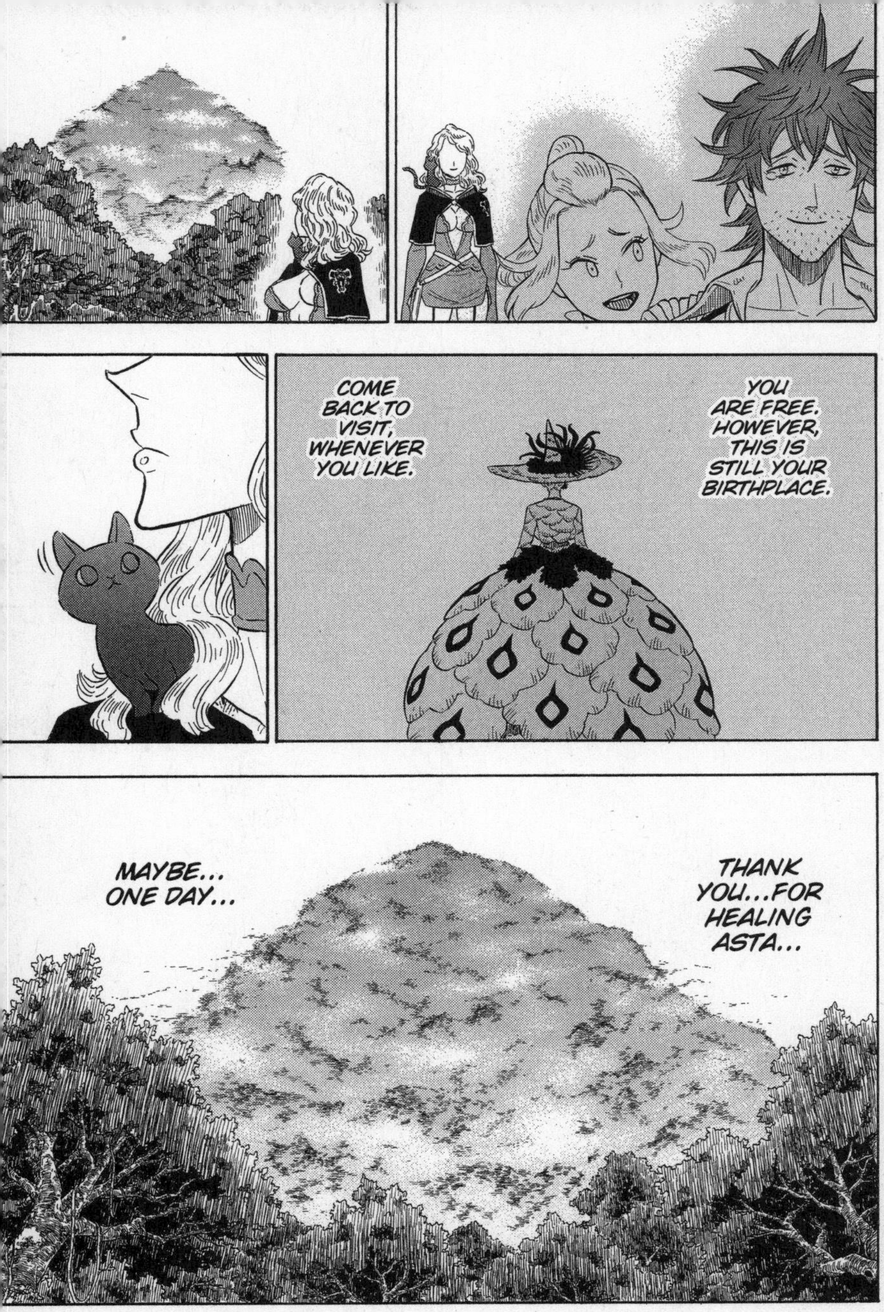
YOU ARE FREE. HOWEVER, THIS IS STILL YOUR BIRTHPLACE.
COME BACK TO VISIT, WHENEVER YOU LIKE.
THANK YOU...FOR HEALING ASTA...
MAYBE... ONE DAY...

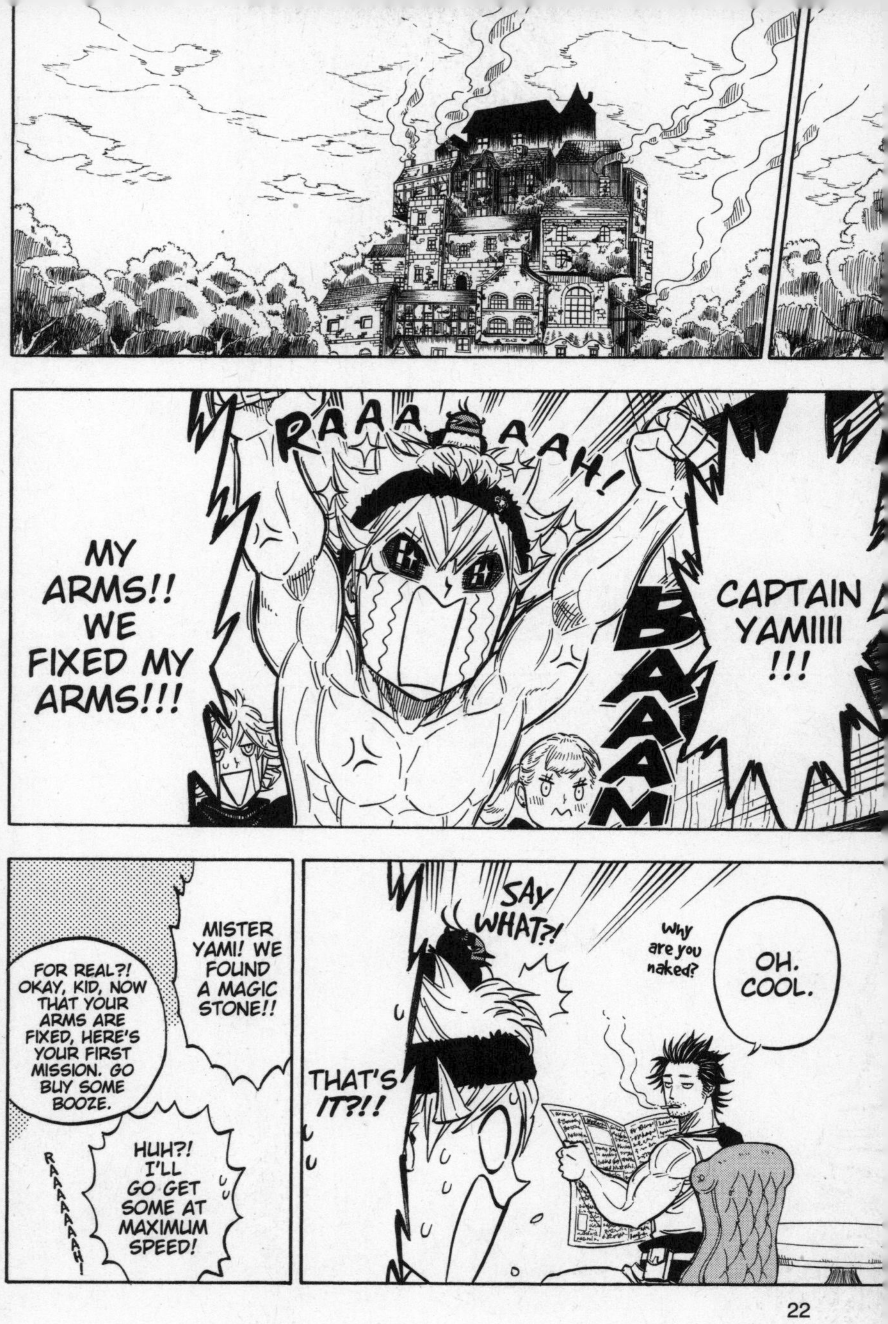
RAAA AAH!
CAPTAIN YAMIIII!!!
BAAAM
MY ARMS!! WE FIXED MY ARMS!!!
OH. COOL.
Why are you naked?
SAY WHAT?!
THAT'S IT?!!
MISTER YAMI! WE FOUND A MAGIC STONE!!
FOR REAL?! OKAY, KID, NOW THAT YOUR ARMS ARE FIXED, HERE'S YOUR FIRST MISSION. GO BUY SOME BOOZE.
HUH?! I'LL GO GET SOME AT MAXIMUM SPEED!
RAAAAAAAH!

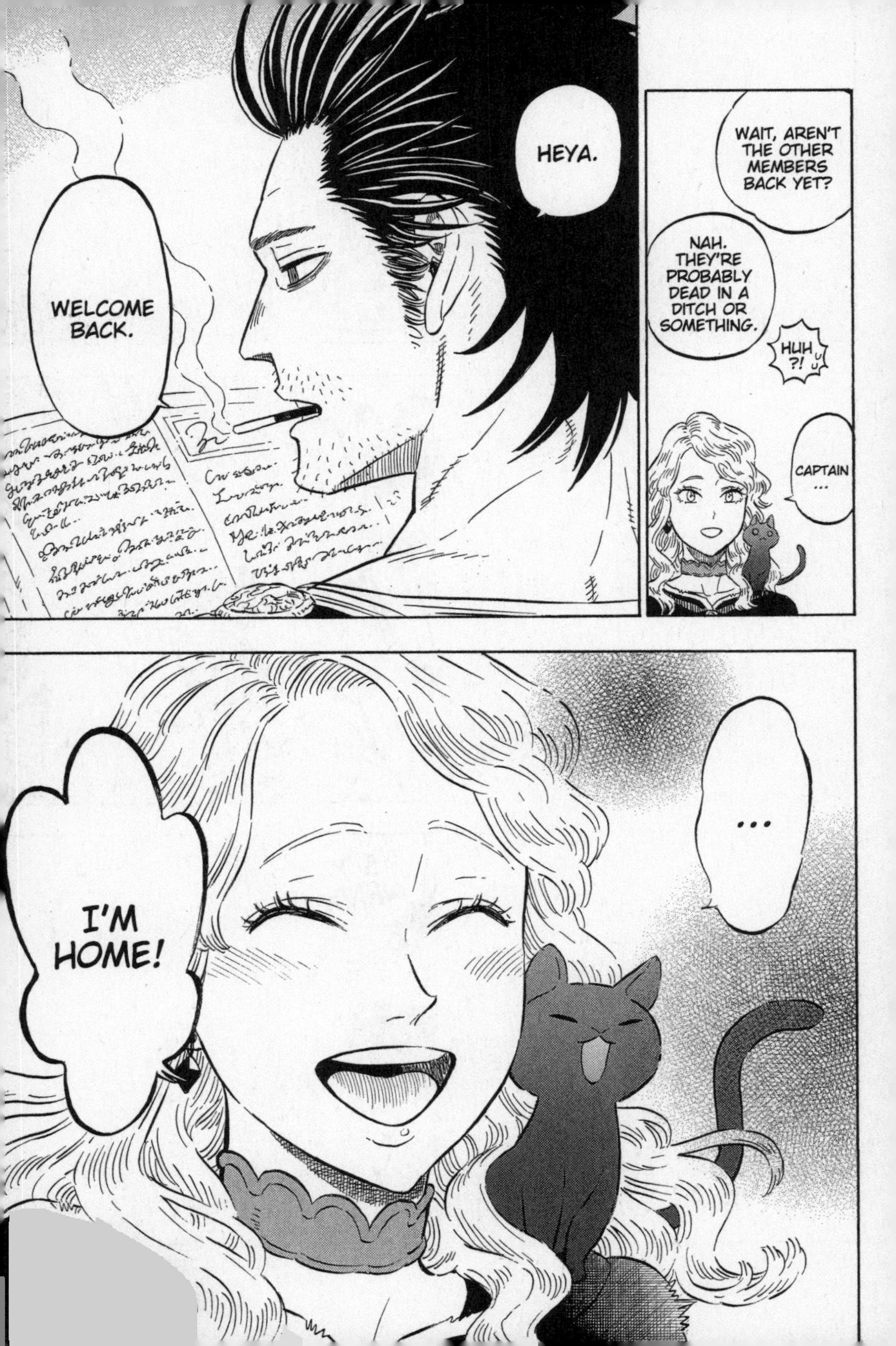
WAIT, AREN'T THE OTHER MEMBERS BACK YET?
NAH. THEY'RE PROBABLY DEAD IN A DITCH OR SOMETHING.
HUH ?!
CAPTAIN ...
HEYA.
WELCOME BACK.
...
I'M HOME!

Page 102: Asta's Day Off

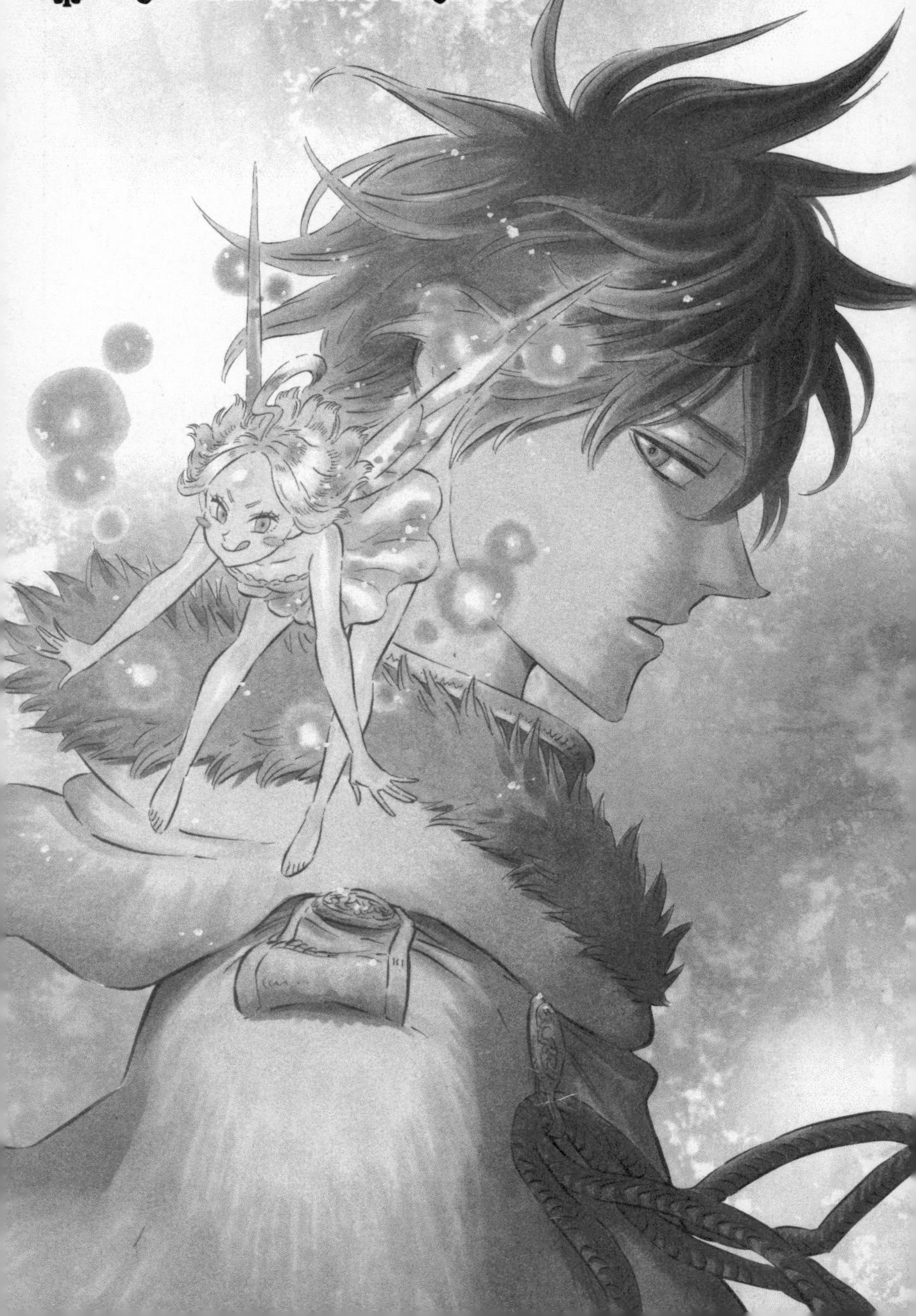

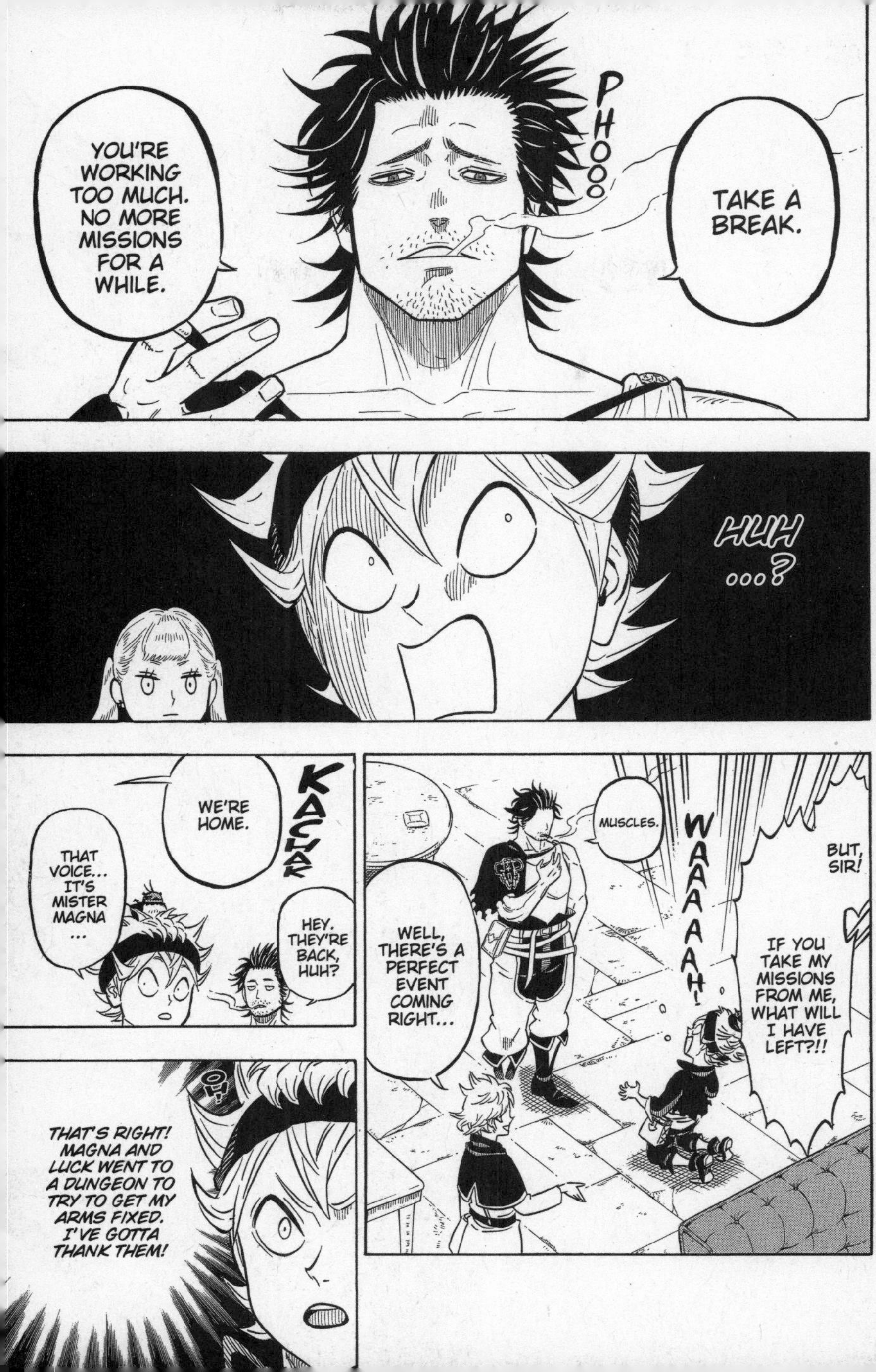
PHOOO
TAKE A BREAK.
YOU'RE WORKING TOO MUCH. NO MORE MISSIONS FOR A WHILE.
HUH ...?
BUT, SIR!
IF YOU TAKE MY MISSIONS FROM ME, WHAT WILL I HAVE LEFT?!!
WAAAAAH!
MUSCLES.
WELL, THERE'S A PERFECT EVENT COMING RIGHT...
KACHAK
WE'RE HOME.
HEY. THEY'RE BACK, HUH?
THAT VOICE... IT'S MISTER MAGNA ...
THAT'S RIGHT! MAGNA AND LUCK WENT TO A DUNGEON TO TRY TO GET MY ARMS FIXED. I'VE GOTTA THANK THEM!

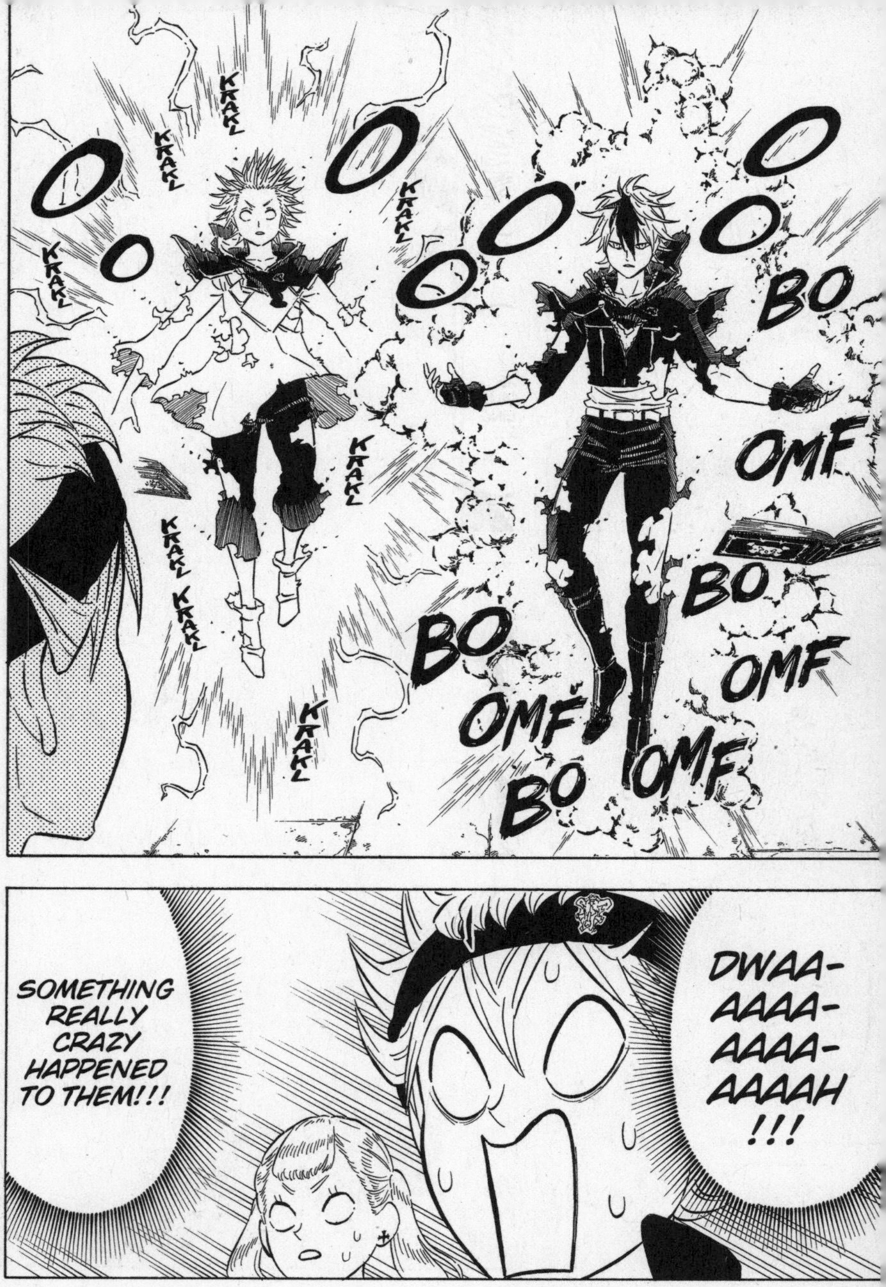
OOOOOOO
BO OMF
BO OMF
BO OMF
BO OMF
KRAKL
KRAKL
KRAKL
KRAKL
KRAKL
KRAKL
KRAKL
KRAKL
DWAA-AAAA-AAAA-AAAAH!!!
SOMETHING REALLY CRAZY HAPPENED TO THEM!!!

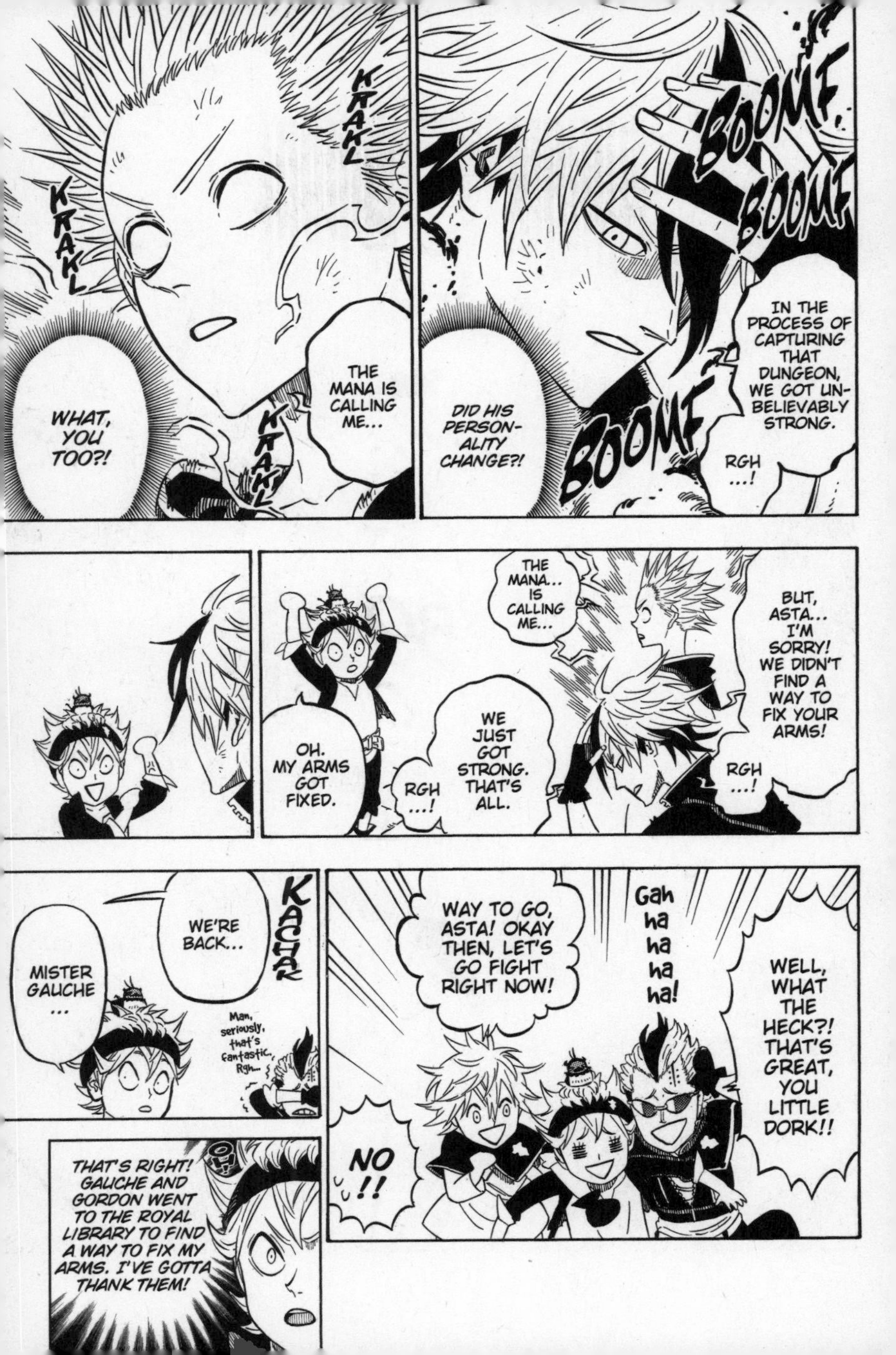
BOOMF
BOOMF
IN THE PROCESS OF CAPTURING THAT DUNGEON, WE GOT UNBELIEVABLY STRONG.
RGH ...!
BOOMF
DID HIS PERSONALITY CHANGE?!
KRAKL
THE MANA IS CALLING ME...
KRAKL
KRAKL
WHAT, YOU TOO?!
BUT, ASTA... I'M SORRY! WE DIDN'T FIND A WAY TO FIX YOUR ARMS!
RGH ...!
THE MANA... IS CALLING ME...
WE JUST GOT STRONG. THAT'S ALL.
RGH ...!
OH. MY ARMS GOT FIXED.
WELL, WHAT THE HECK?! THAT'S GREAT, YOU LITTLE DORK!!
Gah ha ha ha ha!
WAY TO GO, ASTA! OKAY THEN, LET'S GO FIGHT RIGHT NOW!
NO!!
KACHAK
WE'RE BACK...
Man, seriously, that's fantastic. Rgh...
MISTER GAUCHE ...
OH!
THAT'S RIGHT! GAUCHE AND GORDON WENT TO THE ROYAL LIBRARY TO FIND A WAY TO FIX MY ARMS. I'VE GOTTA THANK THEM!

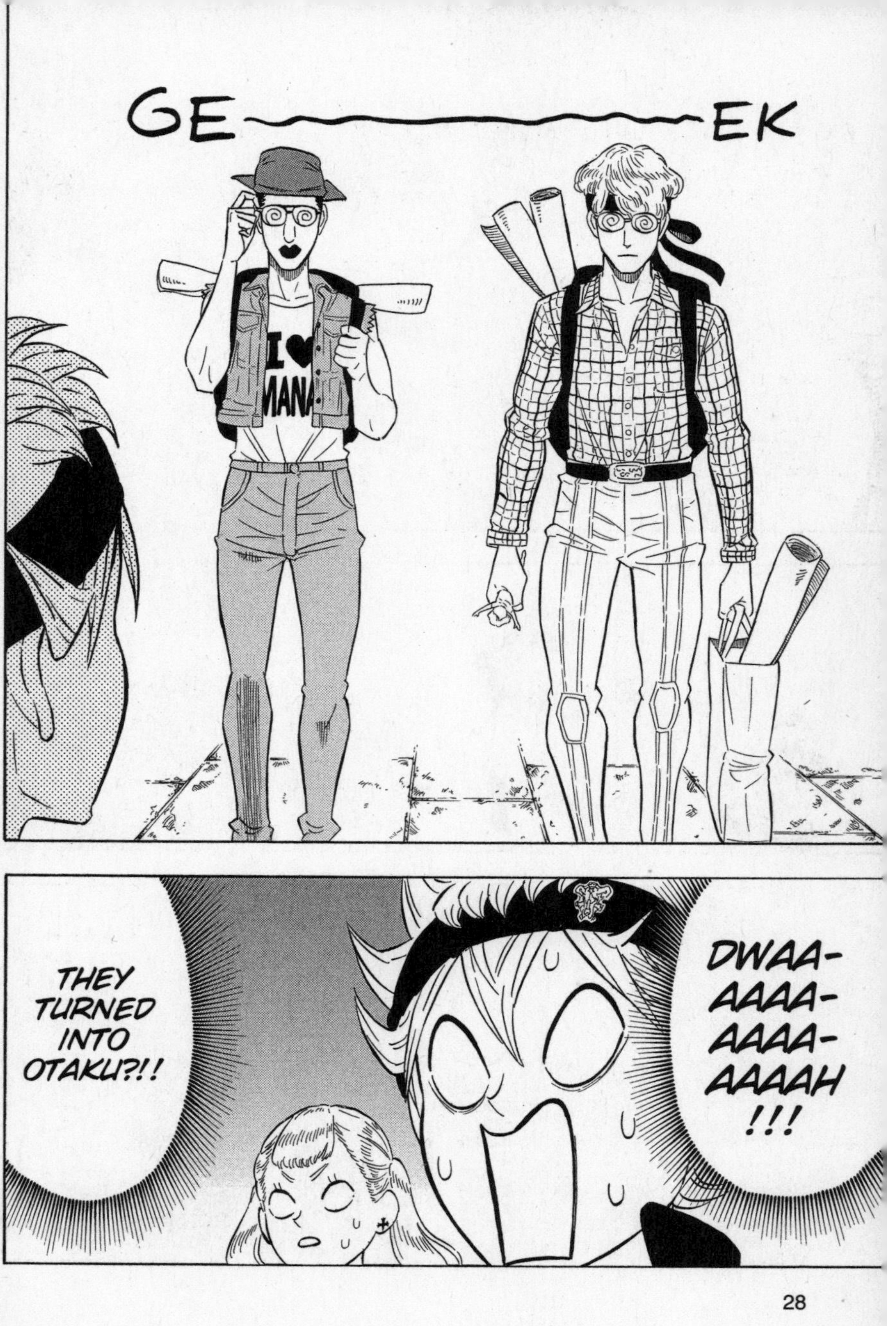
GE———EK
I ♥ MANA
DWAA-AAAA-AAAA-AAAAH!!!
THEY TURNED INTO OTAKU?!!

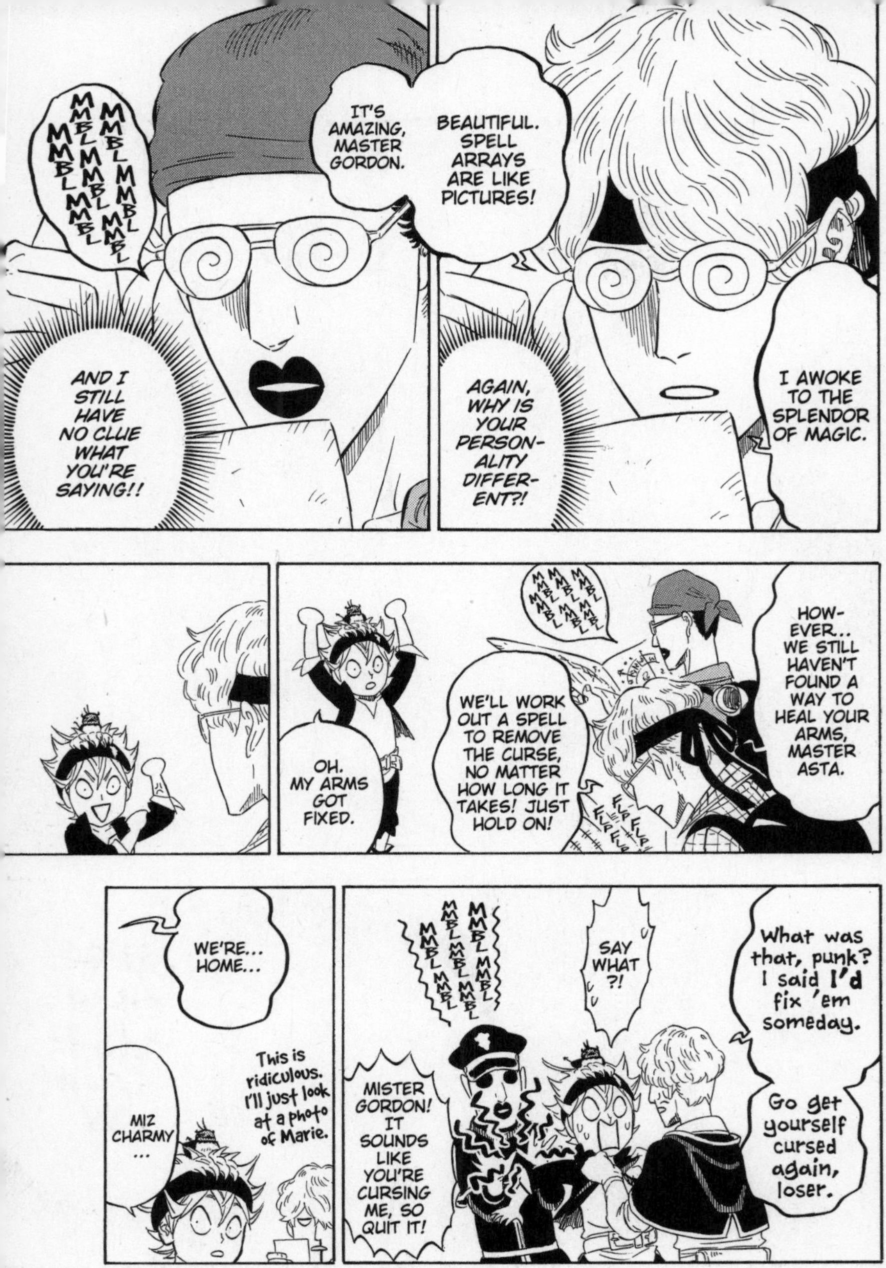
IT'S AMAZING, MASTER GORDON. BEAUTIFUL. SPELL ARRAYS ARE LIKE PICTURES!
I AWOKE TO THE SPLENDOR OF MAGIC.
AGAIN, WHY IS YOUR PERSONALITY DIFFERENT?!
MMBL MMBL MMBL MMBL MMBL MMBL
AND I STILL HAVE NO CLUE WHAT YOU'RE SAYING!!
HOWEVER... WE STILL HAVEN'T FOUND A WAY TO HEAL YOUR ARMS, MASTER ASTA.
MMBL MMBL MMBL MMBL MMBL MMBL
WE'LL WORK OUT A SPELL TO REMOVE THE CURSE, NO MATTER HOW LONG IT TAKES! JUST HOLD ON!
FLP FLP FLP FLP FLP
OH. MY ARMS GOT FIXED.
What was that, punk? I said I'd fix 'em someday.
Go get yourself cursed again, loser.
SAY WHAT?!
MMBL MMBL MMBL MMBL MMBL MMBL
MISTER GORDON! IT SOUNDS LIKE YOU'RE CURSING ME, SO QUIT IT!
WE'RE... HOME...
This is ridiculous. I'll just look at a photo of Marie.
MIZ CHARMY...

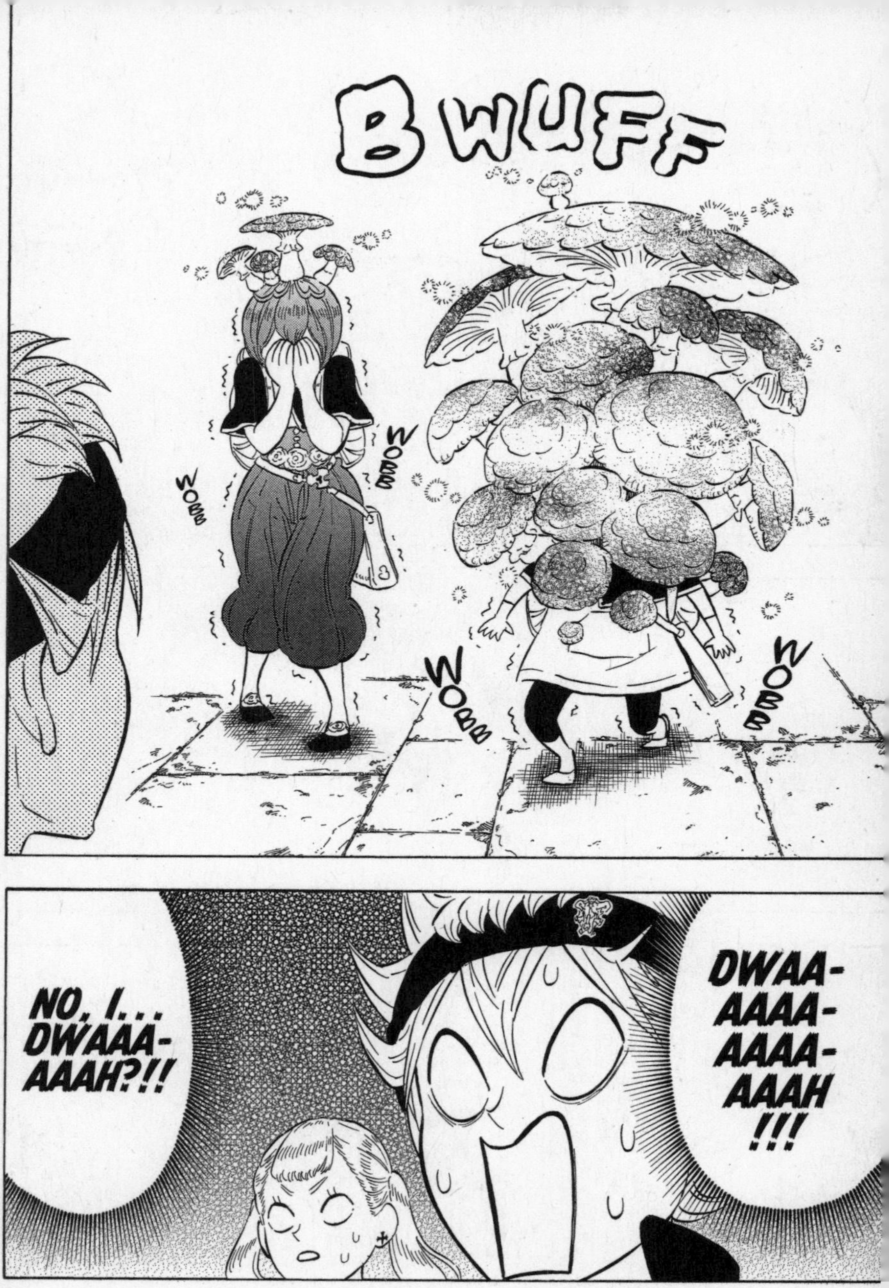
BWUFF
WOBB
WOBB
WOBB
WOBB
DWAA-AAAA-AAAA-AAAH!!!
NO, I... DWAAA-AAAH?!!

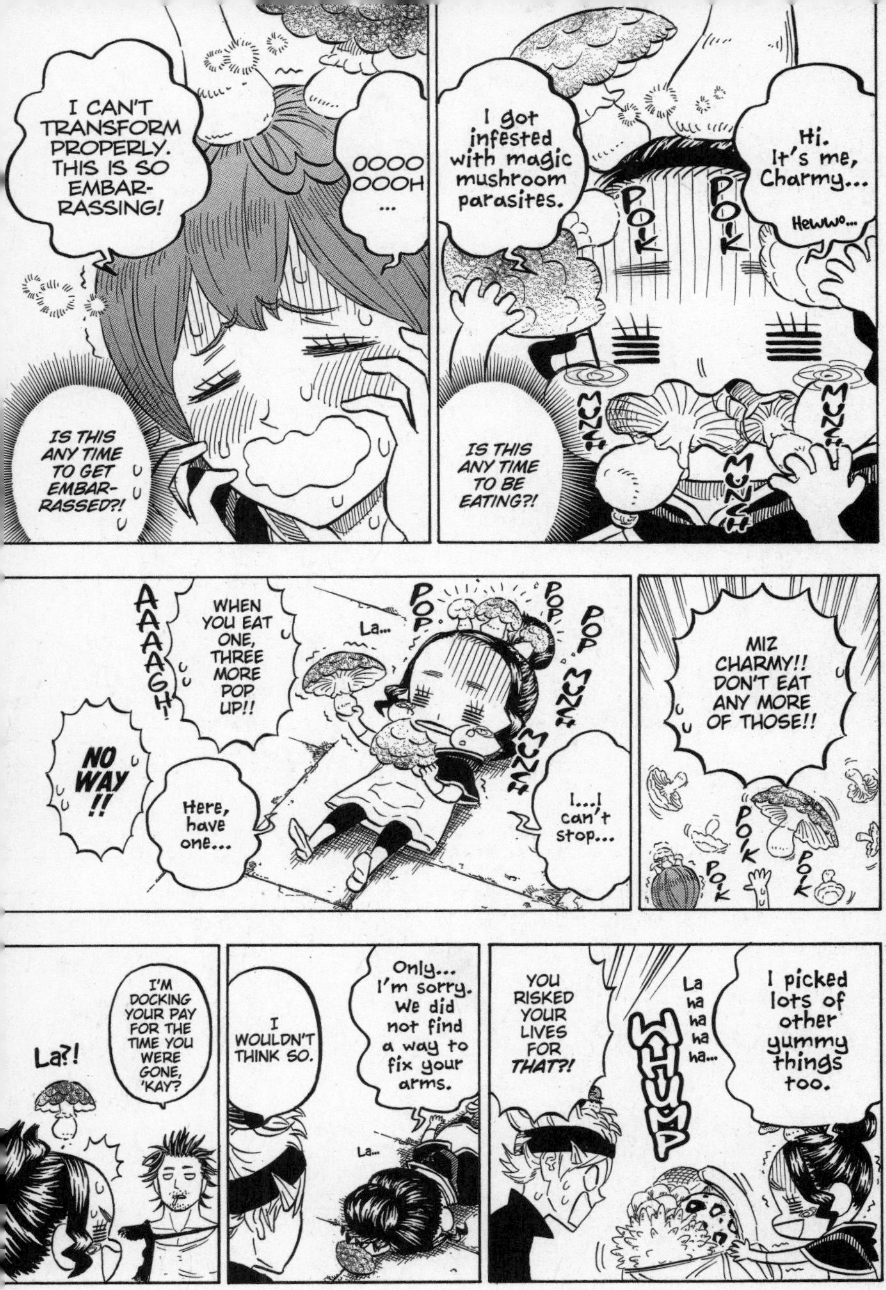
Hi. It's me, Charmy...
Hewwo...
I got infested with magic mushroom parasites.
POIK
POIK
MUNCH
MUNCH
MUNCH
IS THIS ANY TIME TO BE EATING?!
OOOOOOOOH...
I CAN'T TRANSFORM PROPERLY. THIS IS SO EMBARRASSING!
IS THIS ANY TIME TO GET EMBARRASSED?!
MIZ CHARMY!! DON'T EAT ANY MORE OF THOSE!!
POIK
POIK
POIK
POP
POP
POP
MUNCH
MUNCH
I...I can't stop...
La...
WHEN YOU EAT ONE, THREE MORE POP UP!!
AAAAAGH!
Here, have one...
NO WAY!!
I picked lots of other yummy things too.
La ha ha ha ha...
WHUMP
YOU RISKED YOUR LIVES FOR THAT?!
Only... I'm sorry. We did not find a way to fix your arms.
La...
I WOULDN'T THINK SO.
I'M DOCKING YOUR PAY FOR THE TIME YOU WERE GONE, 'KAY?
La?!

MOVING ON. THERE'S A FESTIVAL.

ANYWAY.

YOU KNOW ABOUT IT ALREADY.

SIZZZZ

BOOH

A FESTIVAL...?

La...

A FESTIVAL?

THERE'S A SOCIAL EVENT WHERE THEY ANNOUNCE THE NUMBER OF STARS WON FROM APRIL TO THE END OF THE FOLLOWING MARCH, THEN DETERMINE THE TOP BRIGADE FOR THAT YEAR.

Last Year's Star Numbers		
1	Golden Dawn	96
2	Crimson Lion Kings	93
3	Silver Eagles	88
	Purple Orcas	7
	Blue Rose Knights	7
	Green Praying Mantises	63
	Aqua Deer	53
8	Coral Peacocks	51
9	Black Bulls	-50

MAN... WHAT A PAIN IN THE BUTT.

WE'RE ALWAYS LAST ANYWAY.

BRIGADES COMPETE TO SEE WHO CAN GET THE MOST STARS.

AS YOU ALL KNOW, THE WIZARD KING AWARDS STARS TO THE MAGIC KNIGHT BRIGADES IN RECOGNITION OF THEIR ACHIEVE-MENTS.

32

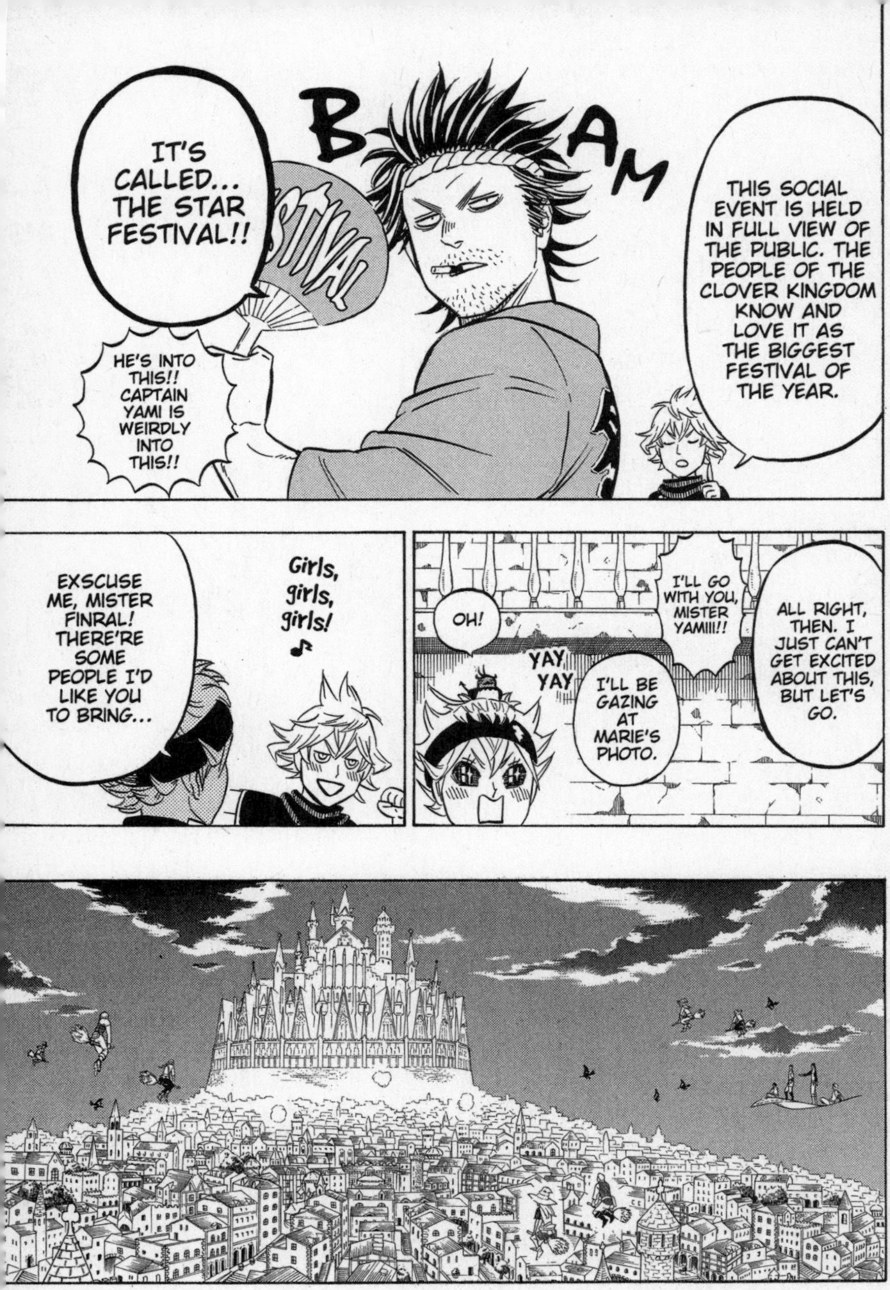
THIS SOCIAL EVENT IS HELD IN FULL VIEW OF THE PUBLIC. THE PEOPLE OF THE CLOVER KINGDOM KNOW AND LOVE IT AS THE BIGGEST FESTIVAL OF THE YEAR.
BAM
IT'S CALLED... THE STAR FESTIVAL!!
FESTIVAL
HE'S INTO THIS!! CAPTAIN YAMI IS WEIRDLY INTO THIS!!
ALL RIGHT, THEN. I JUST CAN'T GET EXCITED ABOUT THIS, BUT LET'S GO.
I'LL GO WITH YOU, MISTER YAMIII!!
OH!
YAY YAY
I'LL BE GAZING AT MARIE'S PHOTO.
Girls, girls, girls! ♪
EXSCUSE ME, MISTER FINRAL! THERE'RE SOME PEOPLE I'D LIKE YOU TO BRING...

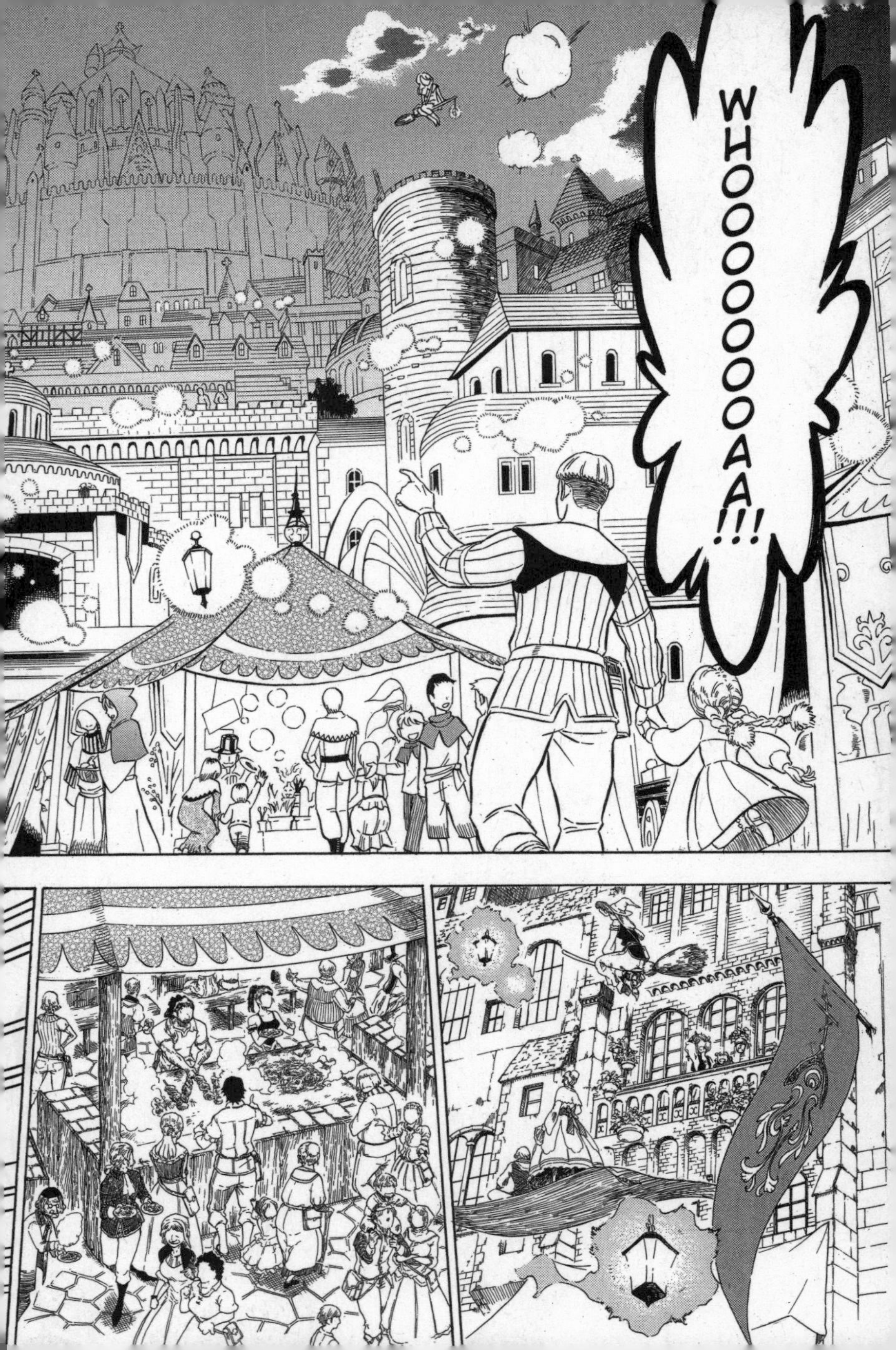
WHOOOOOOOOAA!!!

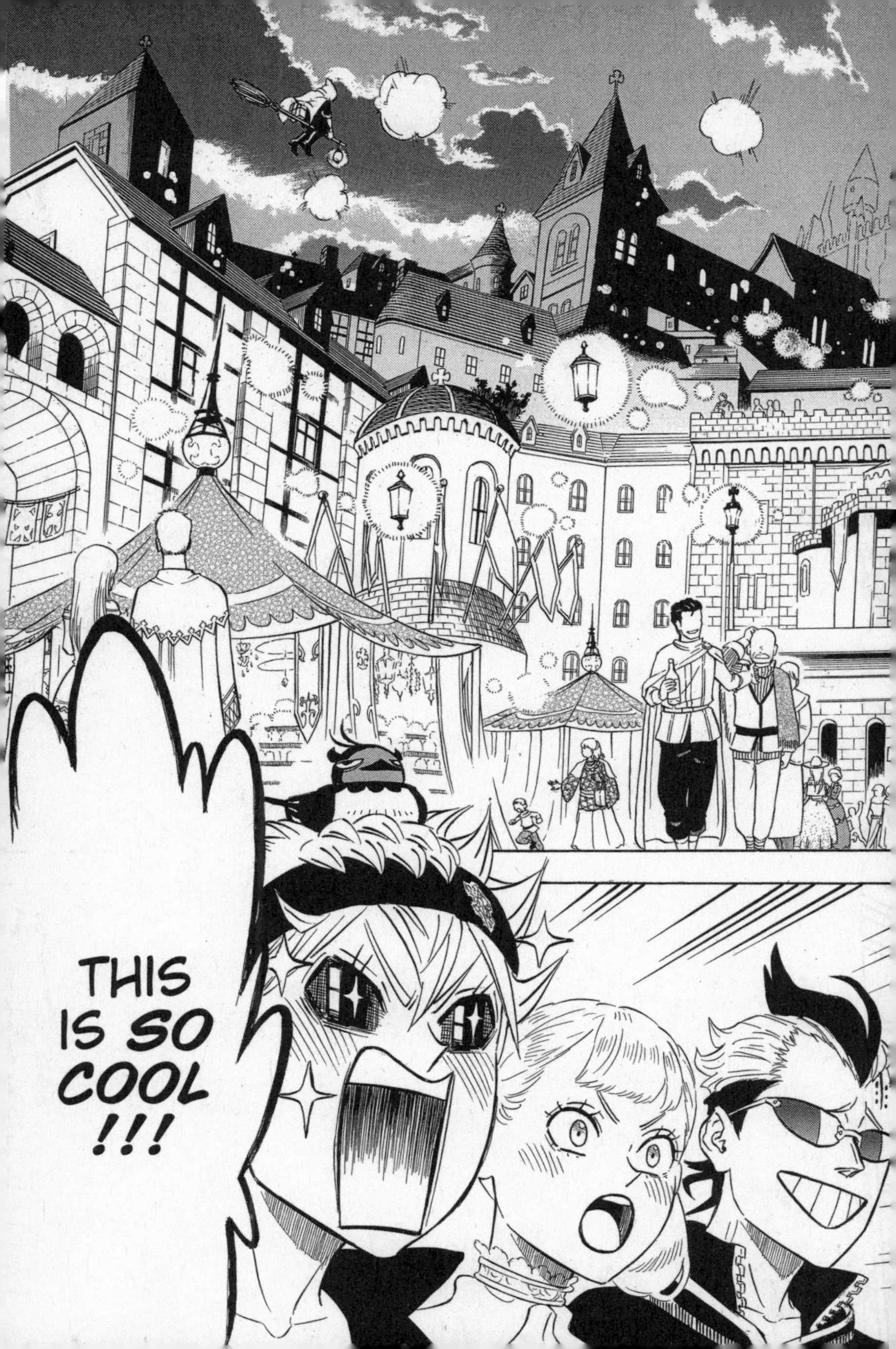
THIS IS SO COOL !!!

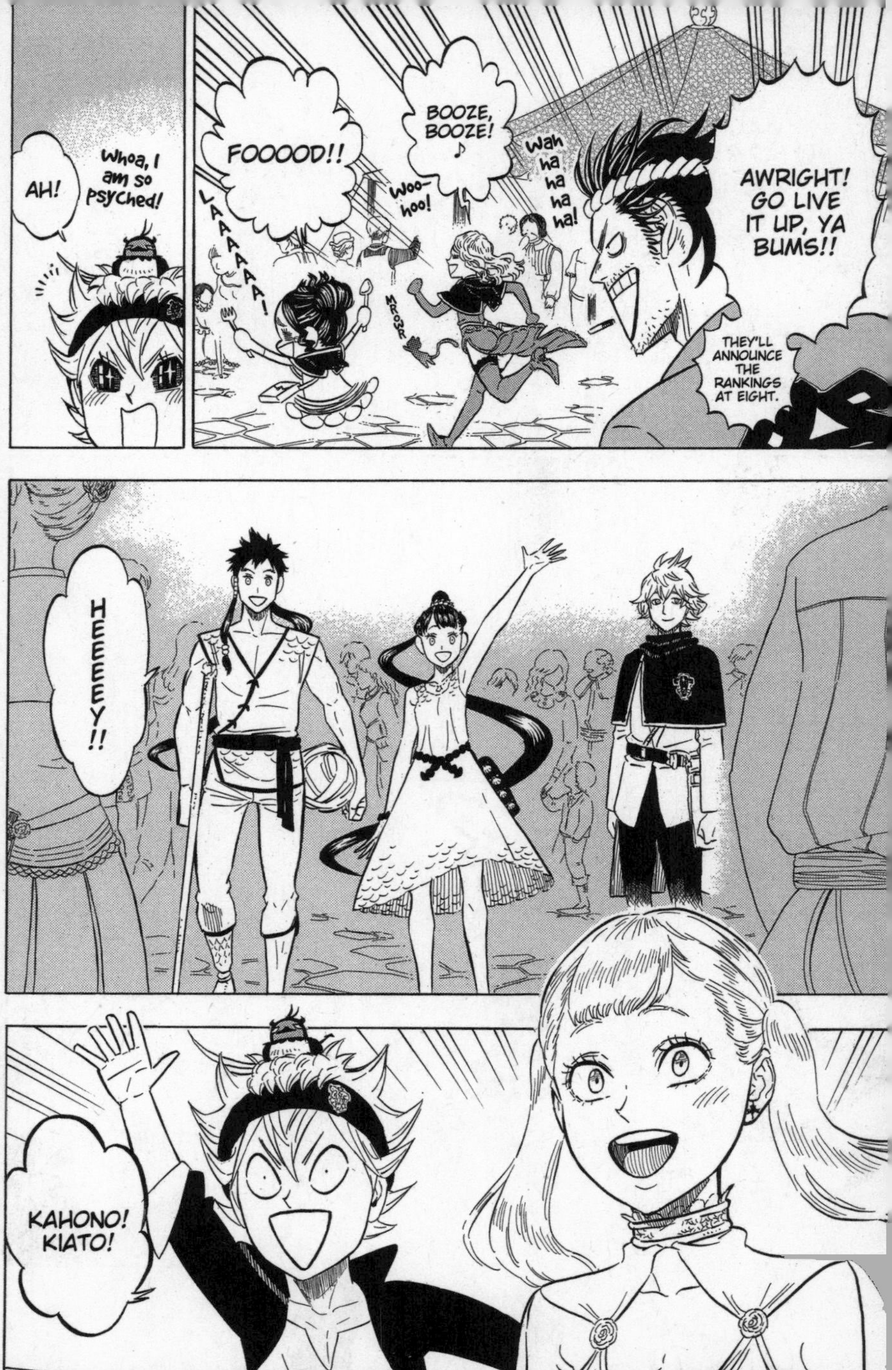
AWRIGHT! GO LIVE IT UP, YA BUMS!!
THEY'LL ANNOUNCE THE RANKINGS AT EIGHT.
Wah ha ha ha ha!
BOOZE, BOOZE! ♪
Woo-hoo!
FOOOOD!!
LAAAAAAA!
MROWR
Whoa, I am so psyched!
AH!
HEEEEY!!
KAHONO! KIATO!

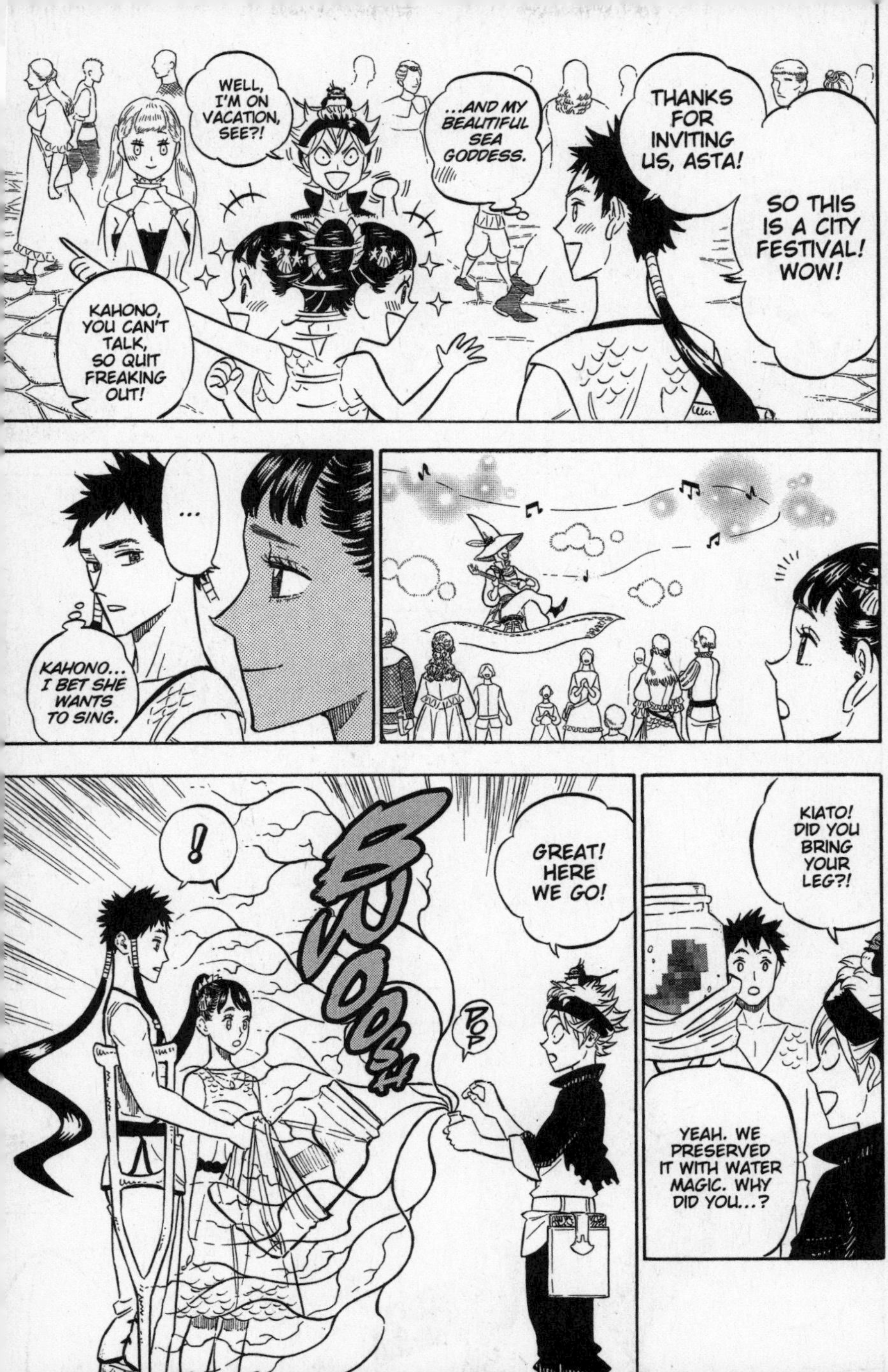
THANKS FOR INVITING US, ASTA!
SO THIS IS A CITY FESTIVAL! WOW!
...AND MY BEAUTIFUL SEA GODDESS.
WELL, I'M ON VACATION, SEE?!
KAHONO, YOU CAN'T TALK, SO QUIT FREAKING OUT!
...
KAHONO... I BET SHE WANTS TO SING.
KIATO! DID YOU BRING YOUR LEG?!
YEAH. WE PRESERVED IT WITH WATER MAGIC. WHY DID YOU...?
GREAT! HERE WE GO!
BOOSH
POP
!

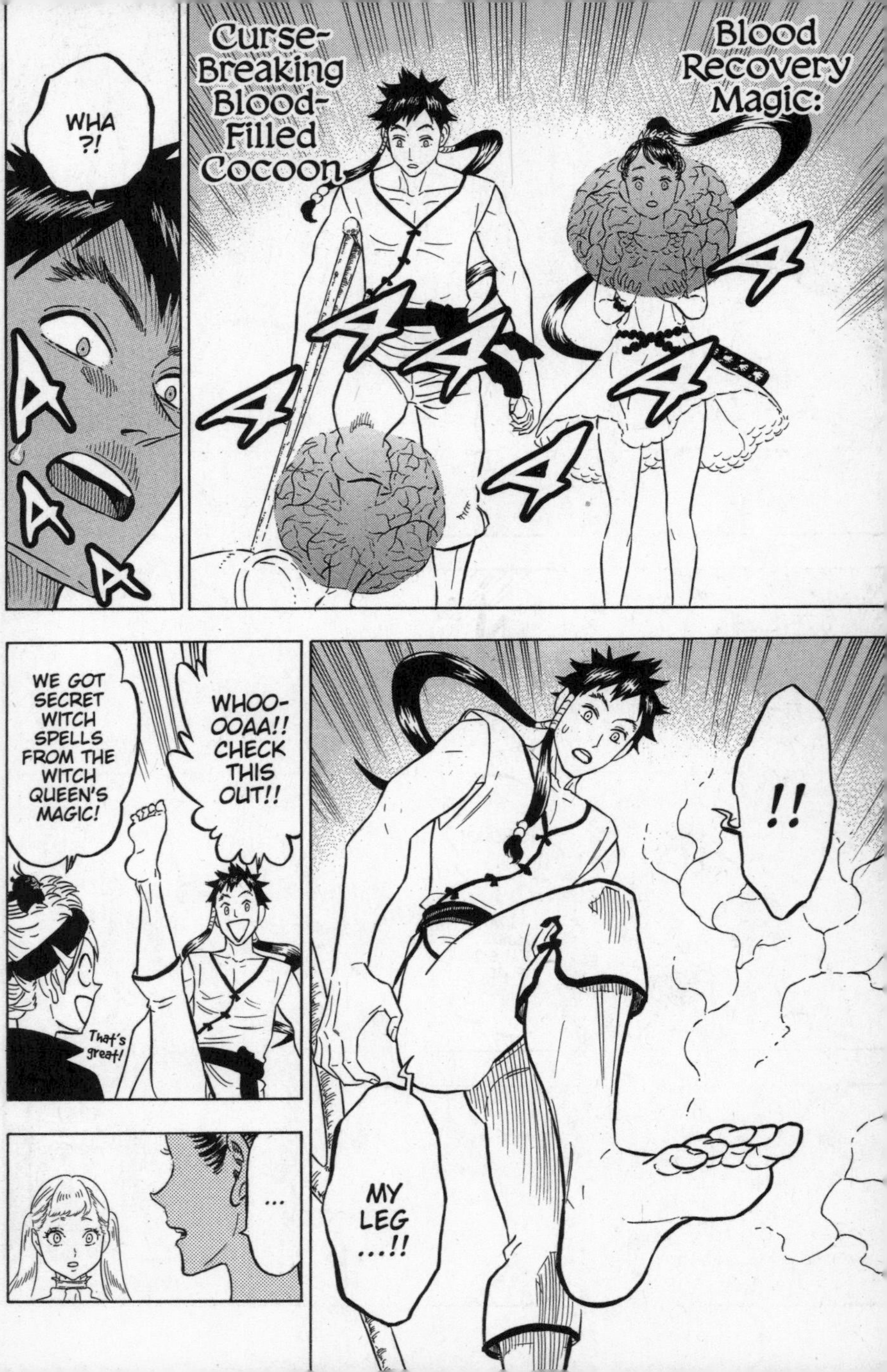
Blood Recovery Magic:
Curse-Breaking Blood-Filled Cocoon
WHA ?!
!!
MY LEG ...!!
WHOO-OOAA!! CHECK THIS OUT!!
WE GOT SECRET WITCH SPELLS FROM THE WITCH QUEEN'S MAGIC!
That's great!
...

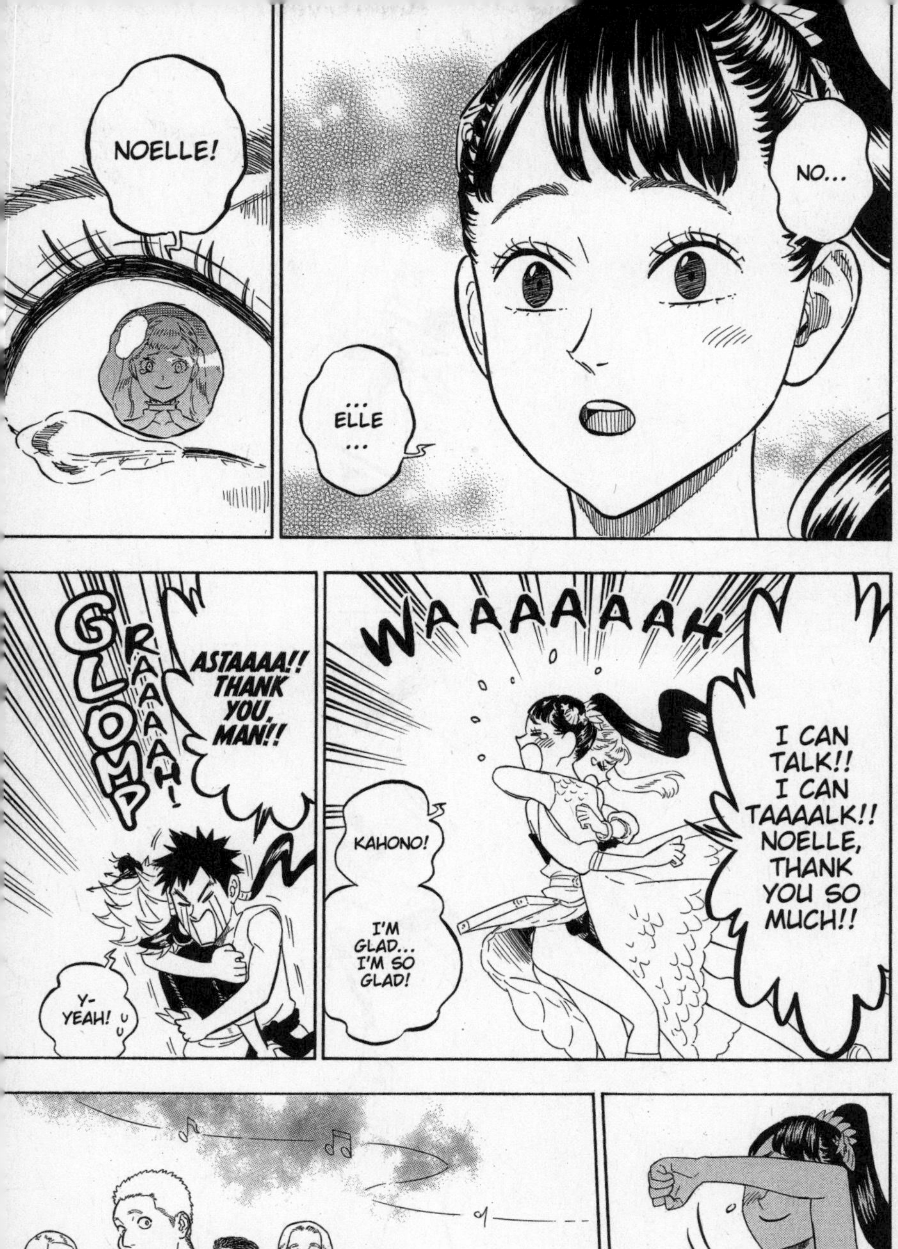
NO...
...
ELLE
...
NOELLE!
WAAAAAAH
I CAN TALK!! I CAN TAAAALK!! NOELLE, THANK YOU SO MUCH!!
KAHONO!
I'M GLAD... I'M SO GLAD!
GRAAAAAH!
ASTAAAA!! THANK YOU, MAN!!
GLOMP
Y-YEAH!

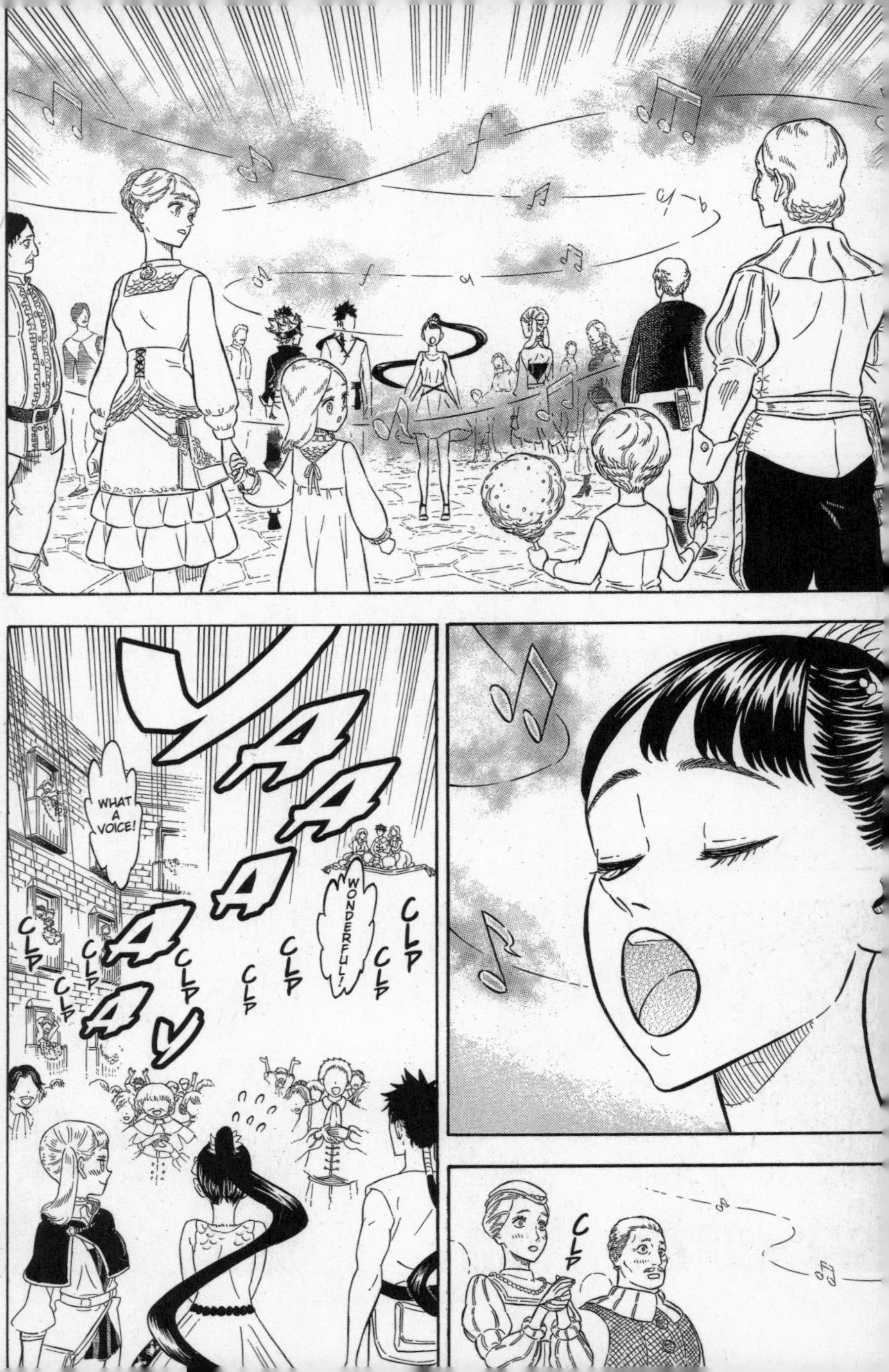
CLP
YAAAAAAY
WHAT A VOICE!
WONDERFUL!
CLP
CLP
CLP
CLP
CLP
CLP
CLP
CLP

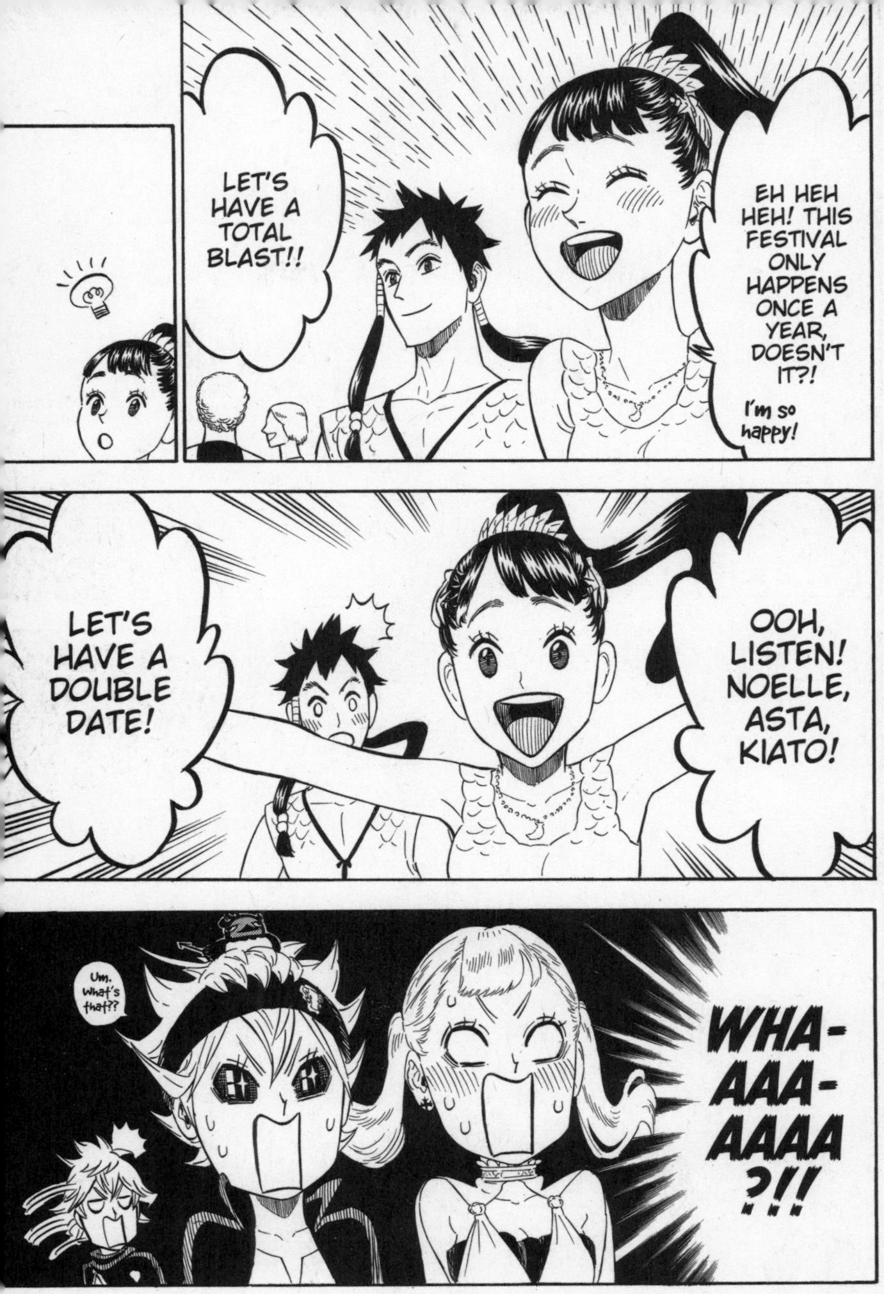
EH HEH HEH! THIS FESTIVAL ONLY HAPPENS ONCE A YEAR, DOESN'T IT?!
I'm so happy!
LET'S HAVE A TOTAL BLAST!!
OOH, LISTEN! NOELLE, ASTA, KIATO!
LET'S HAVE A DOUBLE DATE!
WHA-AAA-AAAA ?!!
Um. what's that??

Queen of Witches
(Real name unknown)

Age: Unknown   Height: 170 cm
Birthday: November 3   Sign: Scorpio   Blood Type: O
Likes: Red wine, misty mornings in the Forest of Witches

Character Profile

❀

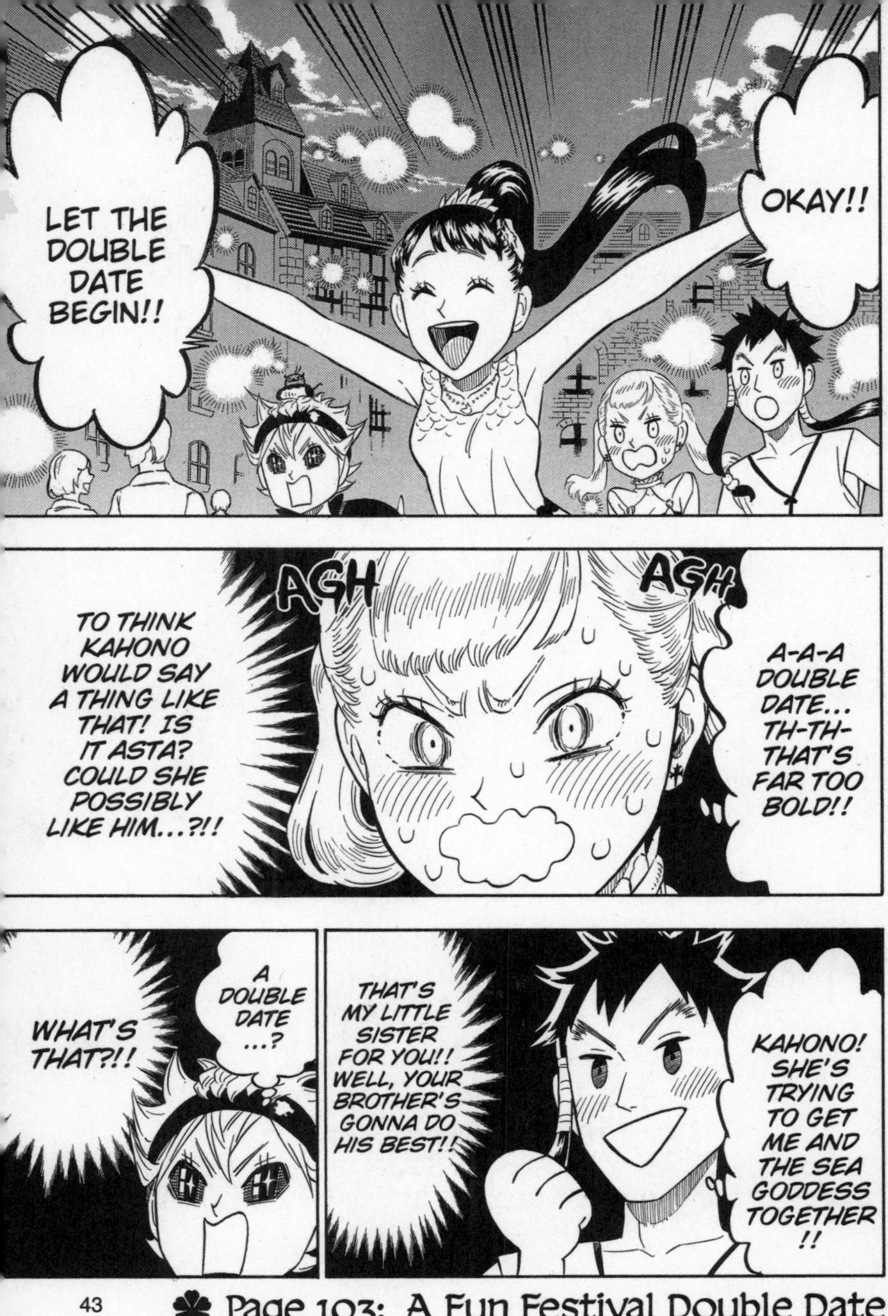
OKAY!!
LET THE DOUBLE DATE BEGIN!!
AGH
A-A-A DOUBLE DATE... TH-TH-THAT'S FAR TOO BOLD!!
AGH
TO THINK KAHONO WOULD SAY A THING LIKE THAT! IS IT ASTA? COULD SHE POSSIBLY LIKE HIM...?!!
KAHONO! SHE'S TRYING TO GET ME AND THE SEA GODDESS TOGETHER!!
THAT'S MY LITTLE SISTER FOR YOU!! WELL, YOUR BROTHER'S GONNA DO HIS BEST!!
A DOUBLE DATE...?
WHAT'S THAT?!!

Page 103: A Fun Festival Double Date

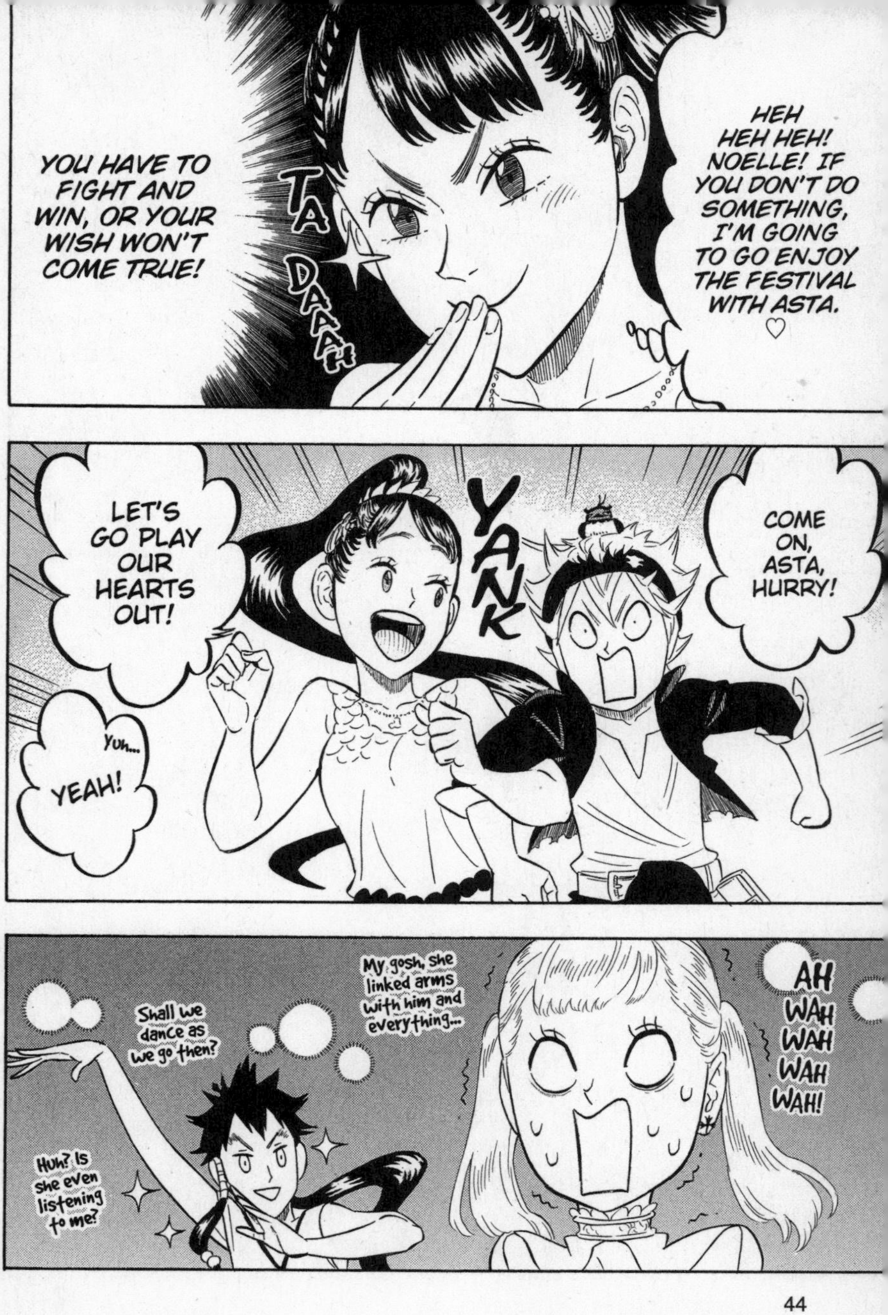
HEH HEH HEH! NOELLE! IF YOU DON'T DO SOMETHING, I'M GOING TO GO ENJOY THE FESTIVAL WITH ASTA. ♡
TA DAAAH
YOU HAVE TO FIGHT AND WIN, OR YOUR WISH WON'T COME TRUE!
COME ON, ASTA, HURRY!
YANK
LET'S GO PLAY OUR HEARTS OUT!
Yuh... YEAH!
AH WAH WAH WAH WAH!
My gosh, she linked arms with him and everything...
Shall we dance as we go then?
Huh? Is she even listening to me?

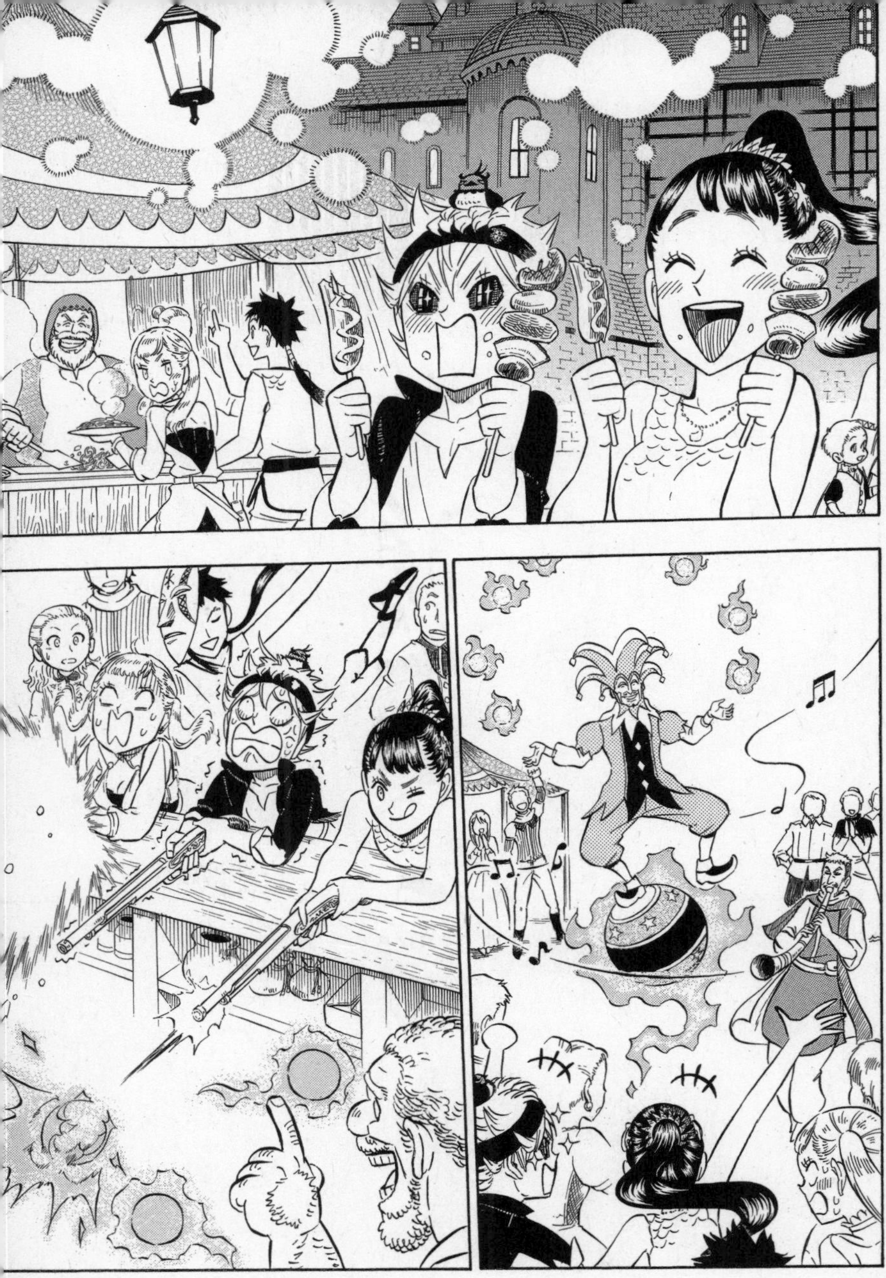

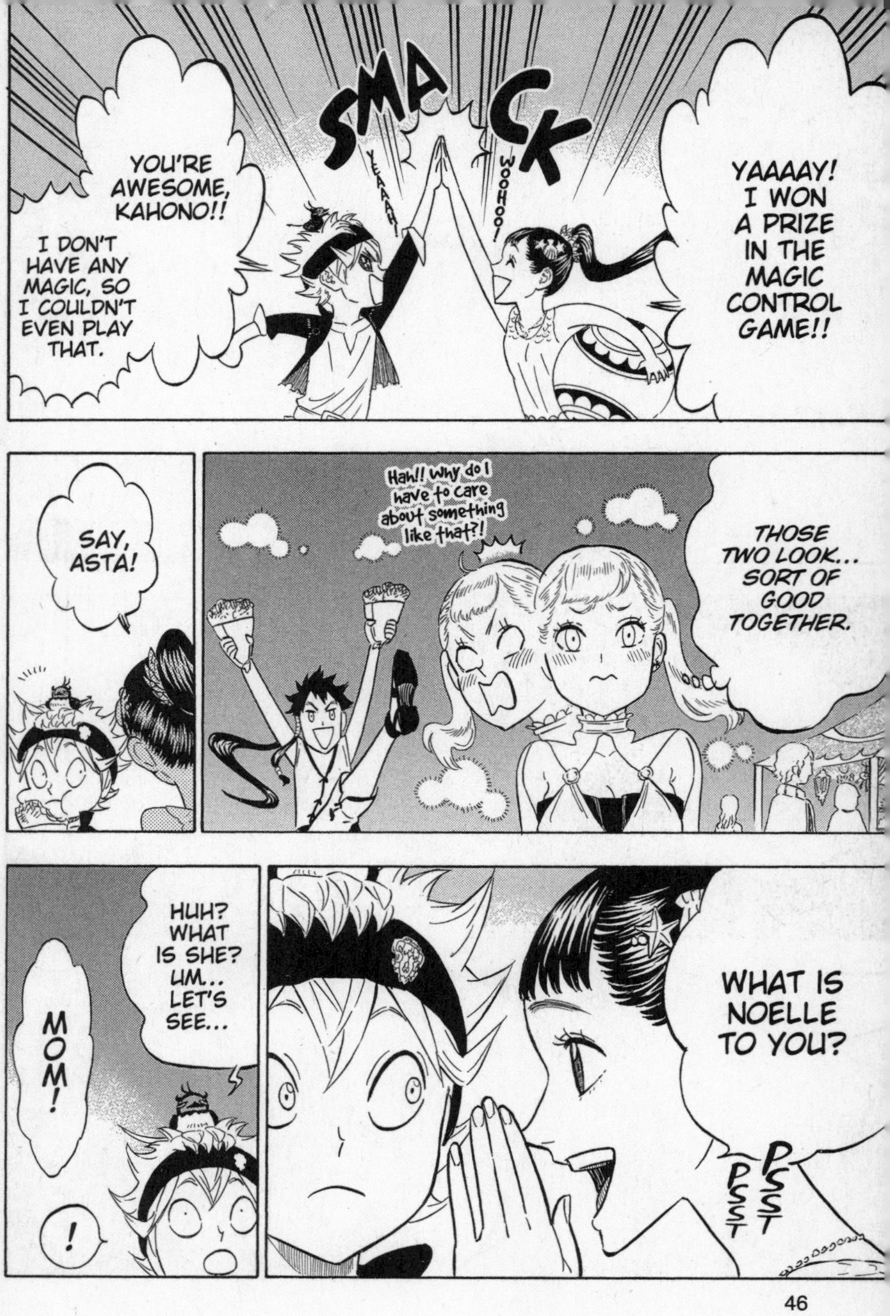
YAAAAY! I WON A PRIZE IN THE MAGIC CONTROL GAME!!
WOOHOO!
SMACK
YEAAAAH!
YOU'RE AWESOME, KAHONO!!
I DON'T HAVE ANY MAGIC, SO I COULDN'T EVEN PLAY THAT.
THOSE TWO LOOK... SORT OF GOOD TOGETHER.
Hah!! Why do I have to care about something like that?!
SAY, ASTA!
WHAT IS NOELLE TO YOU?
PSST PSST
HUH? WHAT IS SHE? UM... LET'S SEE...
MOM!
!

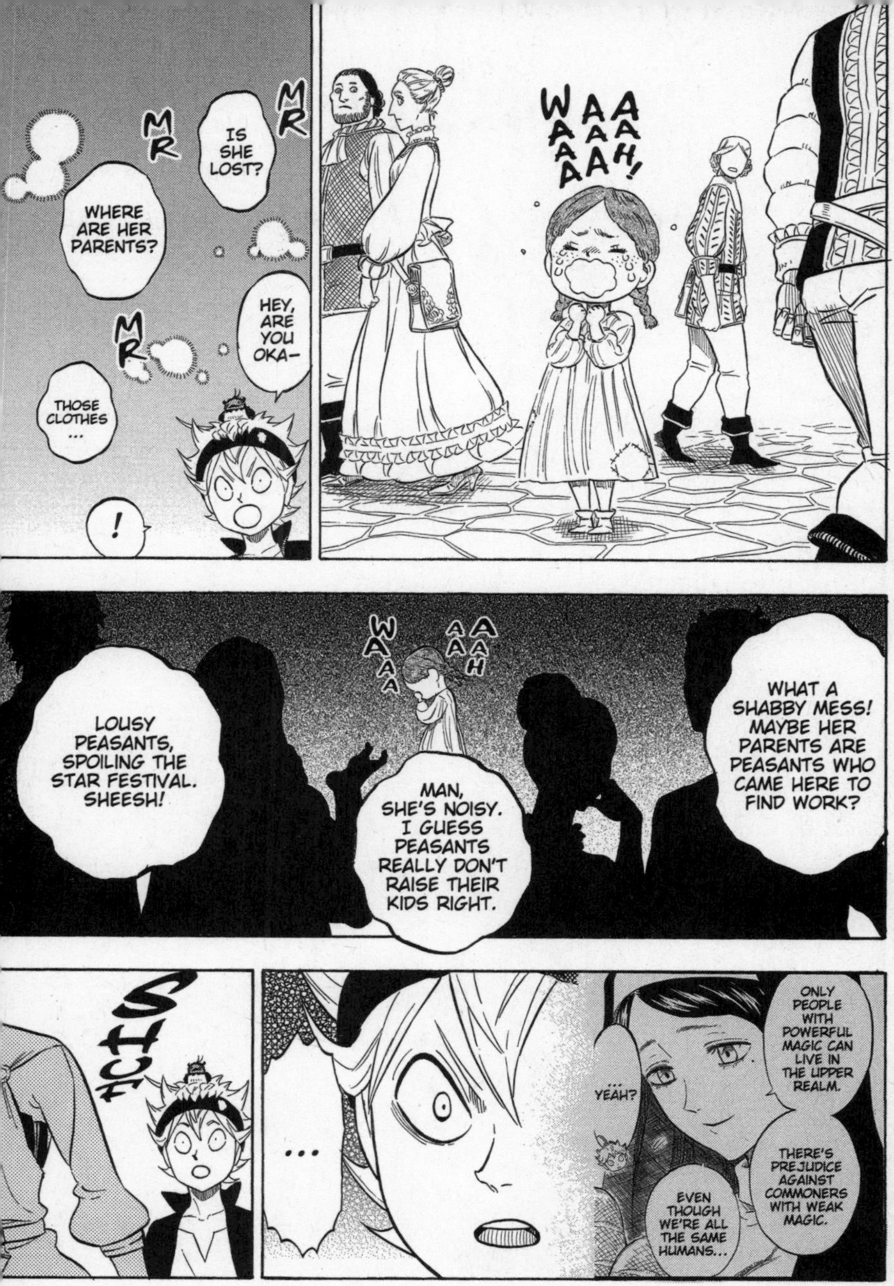

WAAAAAAAAH!
MR
IS SHE LOST?
MR
WHERE ARE HER PARENTS?
HEY, ARE YOU OKA–
THOSE CLOTHES...
!
WHAT A SHABBY MESS! MAYBE HER PARENTS ARE PEASANTS WHO CAME HERE TO FIND WORK?
WAAAAAAH
MAN, SHE'S NOISY. I GUESS PEASANTS REALLY DON'T RAISE THEIR KIDS RIGHT.
LOUSY PEASANTS, SPOILING THE STAR FESTIVAL. SHEESH!
ONLY PEOPLE WITH POWERFUL MAGIC CAN LIVE IN THE UPPER REALM.
...YEAH?
THERE'S PREJUDICE AGAINST COMMONERS WITH WEAK MAGIC.
EVEN THOUGH WE'RE ALL THE SAME HUMANS...
...
SHUF

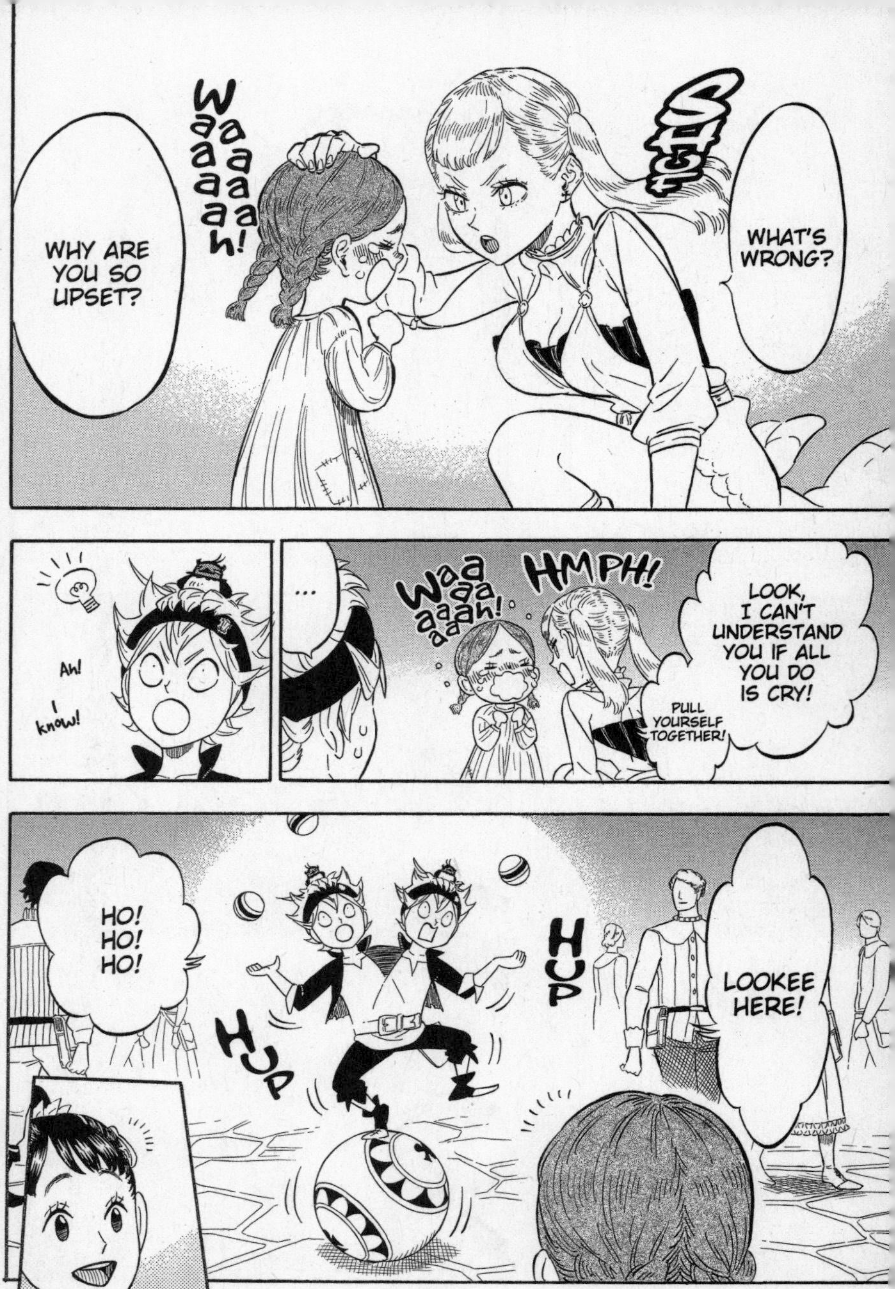
WHAT'S WRONG?
Waaaaaaah!
WHY ARE YOU SO UPSET?
LOOK, I CAN'T UNDERSTAND YOU IF ALL YOU DO IS CRY!
PULL YOURSELF TOGETHER!
HMPH!
Waaaaaaah!
...
Ah!
I know!
LOOKEE HERE!
HUP
HUP
HO! HO! HO!

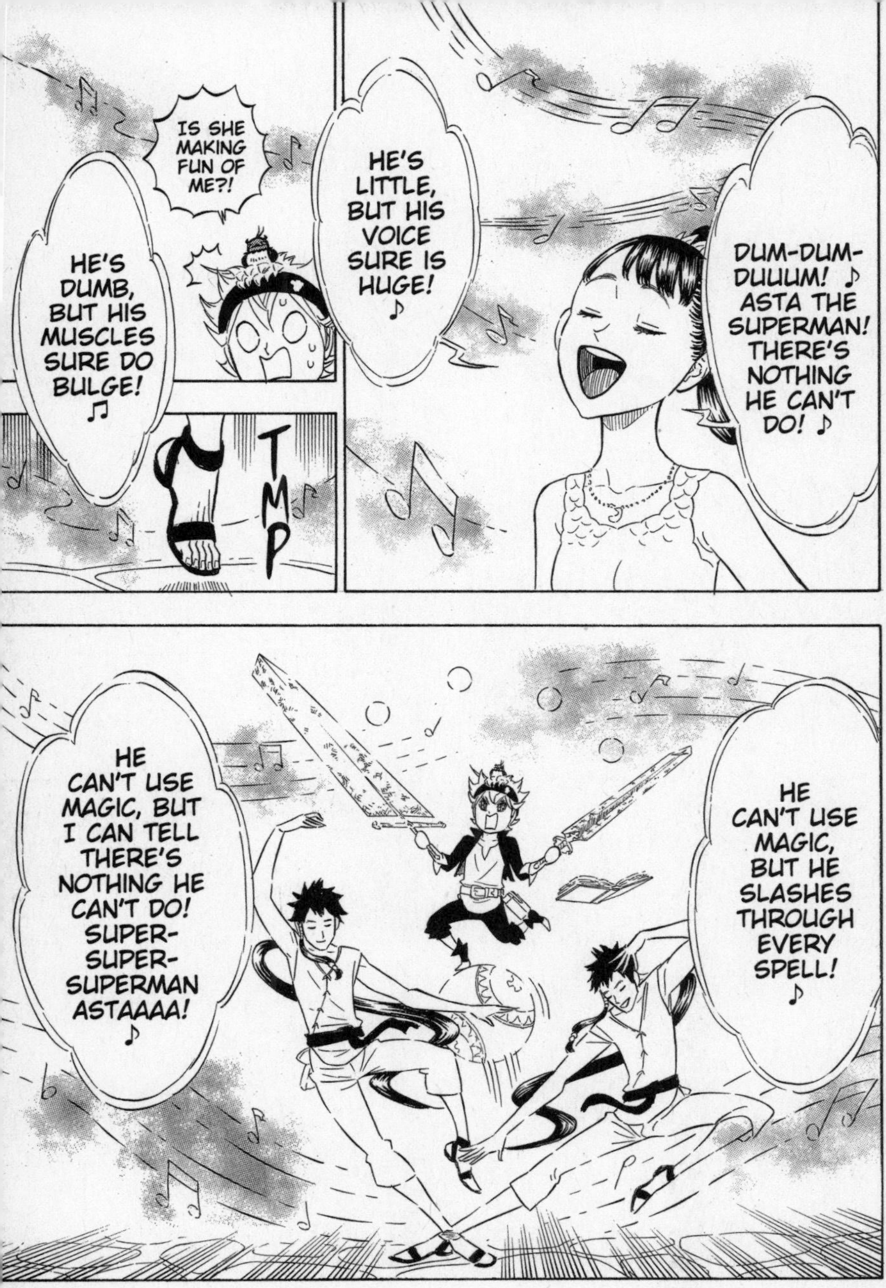
DUM-DUM-DUUUM! ♪ ASTA THE SUPERMAN! THERE'S NOTHING HE CAN'T DO! ♪
HE'S LITTLE, BUT HIS VOICE SURE IS HUGE! ♪
IS SHE MAKING FUN OF ME?!
HE'S DUMB, BUT HIS MUSCLES SURE DO BULGE! ♫
TMP
HE CAN'T USE MAGIC, BUT HE SLASHES THROUGH EVERY SPELL! ♪
HE CAN'T USE MAGIC, BUT I CAN TELL THERE'S NOTHING HE CAN'T DO! SUPER-SUPER-SUPERMAN ASTAAAA! ♪

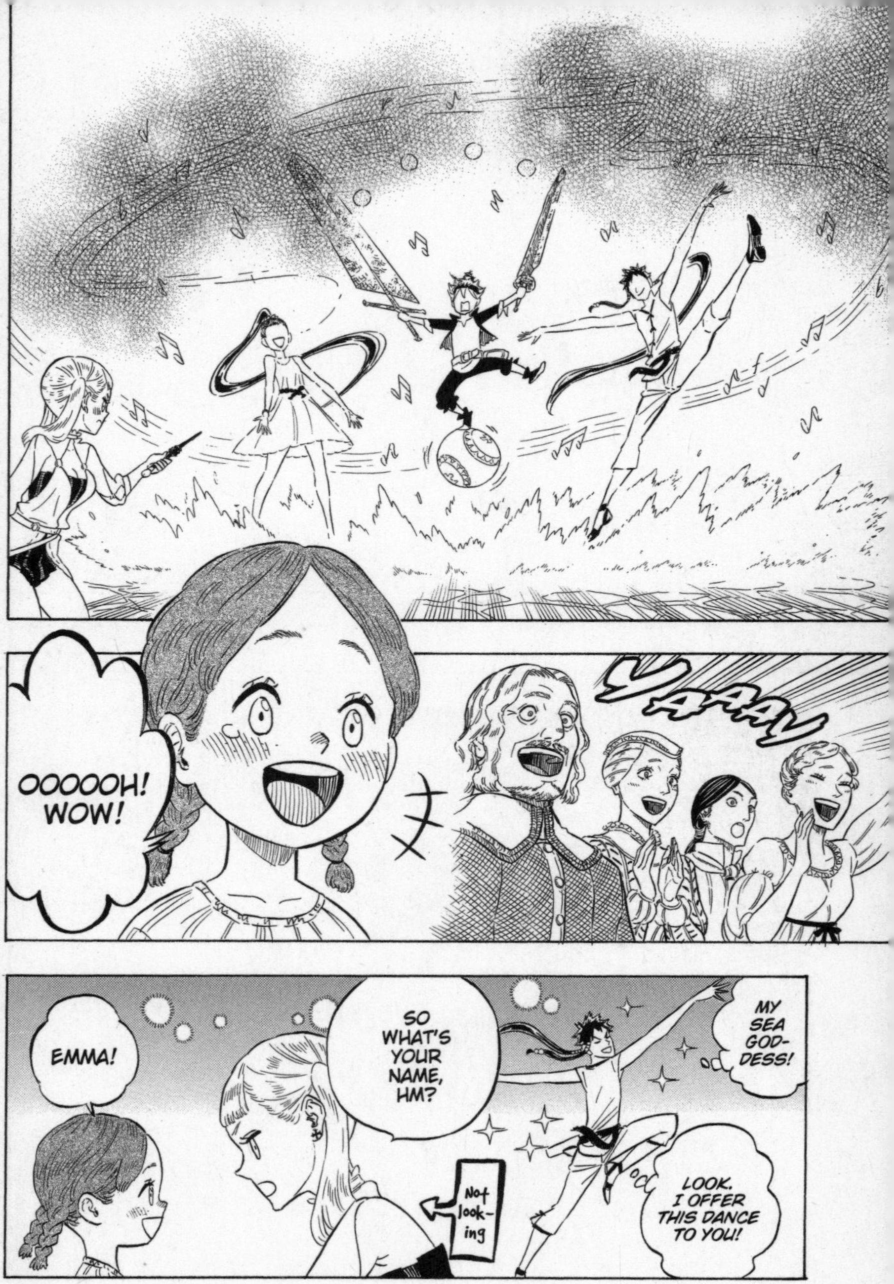
YAAAY
OOOOOH! WOW!
MY SEA GOD-DESS!
LOOK. I OFFER THIS DANCE TO YOU!
Not look-ing
SO WHAT'S YOUR NAME, HM?
EMMA!

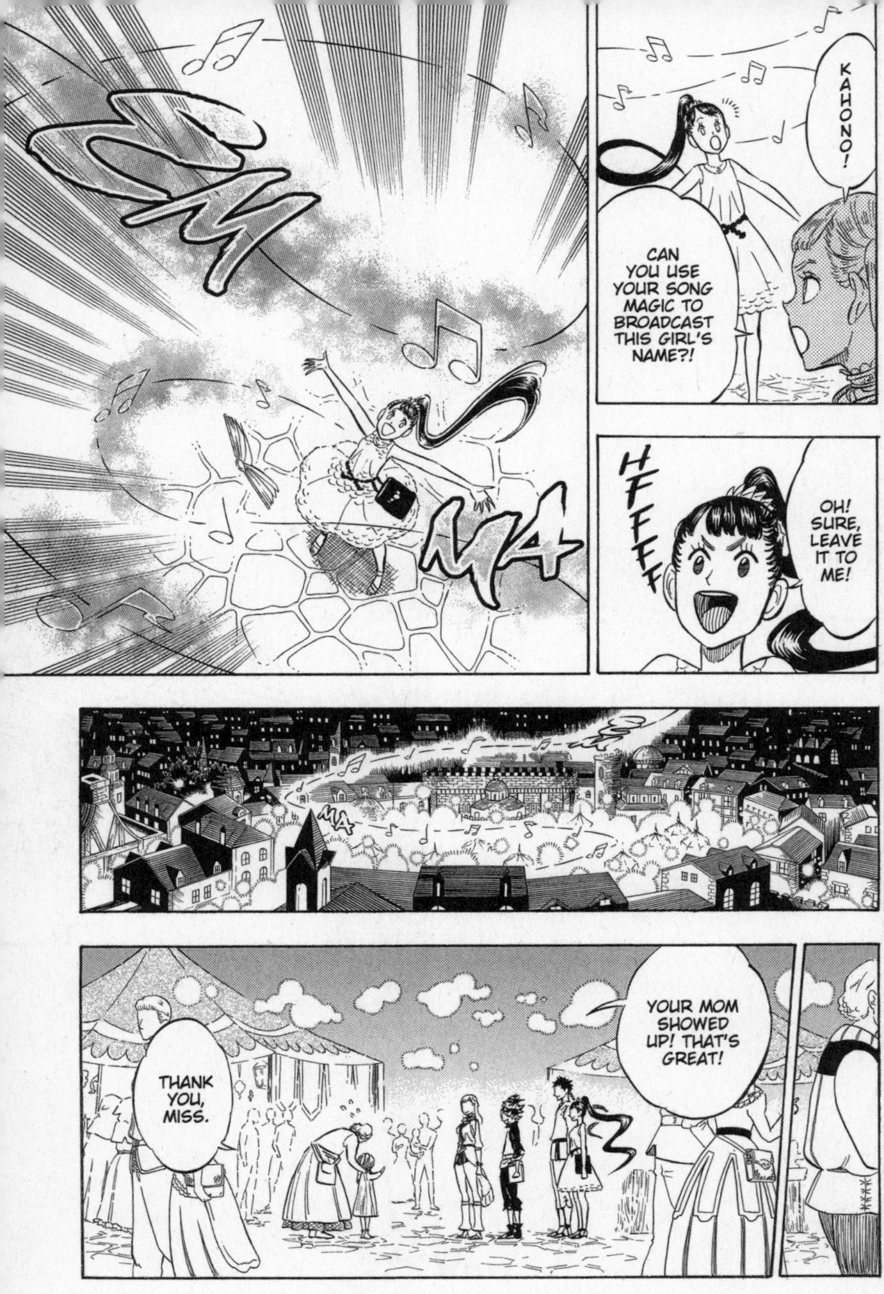

KAHONO!
CAN YOU USE YOUR SONG MAGIC TO BROADCAST THIS GIRL'S NAME?!
HFFFFF
OH! SURE, LEAVE IT TO ME!
MA
MA
YOUR MOM SHOWED UP! THAT'S GREAT!
THANK YOU, MISS.

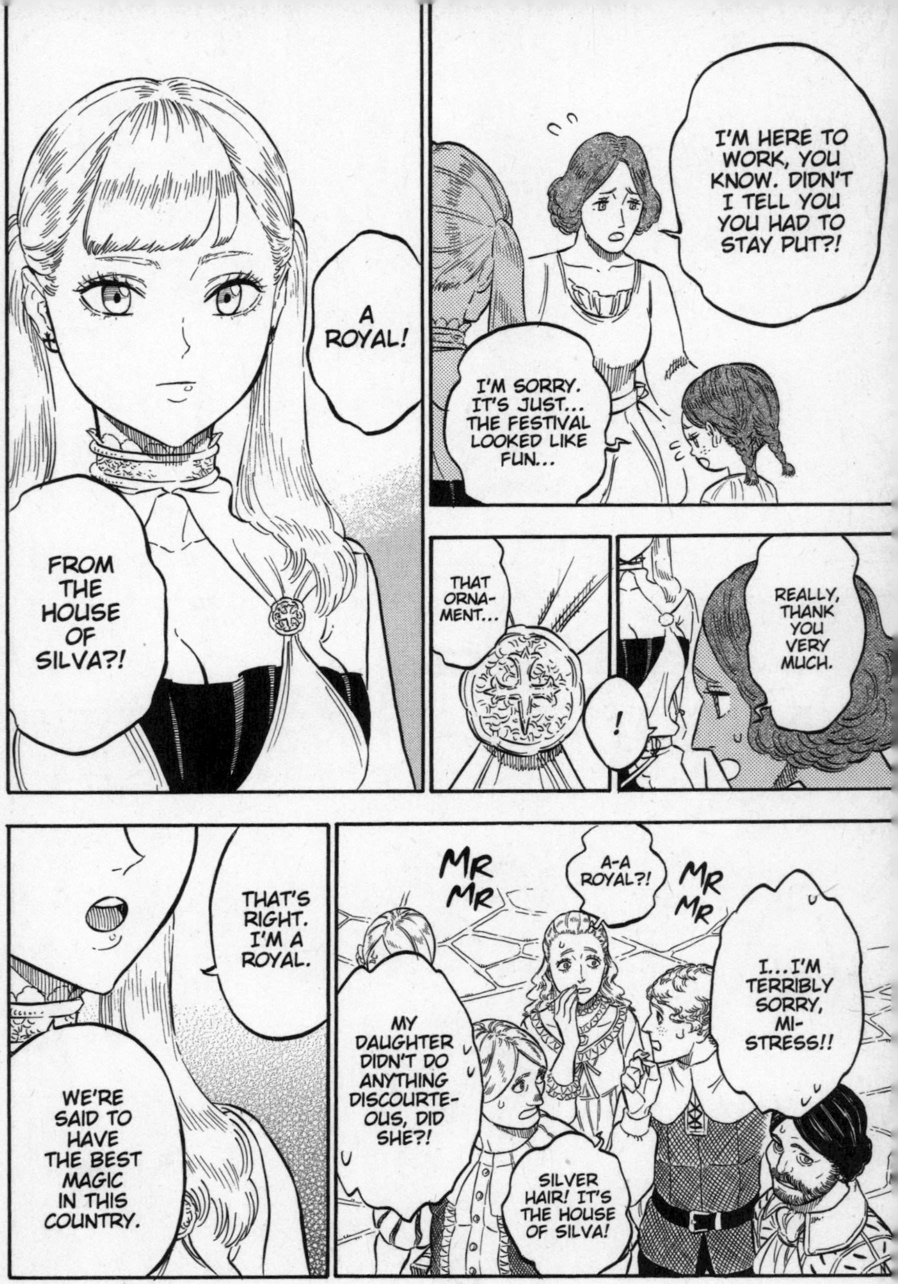
I'M HERE TO WORK, YOU KNOW. DIDN'T I TELL YOU YOU HAD TO STAY PUT?!
I'M SORRY. IT'S JUST... THE FESTIVAL LOOKED LIKE FUN...
REALLY, THANK YOU VERY MUCH.
THAT ORNAMENT...
!
A ROYAL!
FROM THE HOUSE OF SILVA?!
MR MR
I...I'M TERRIBLY SORRY, MISTRESS!!
A-A ROYAL?!
MR MR
MY DAUGHTER DIDN'T DO ANYTHING DISCOURTEOUS, DID SHE?!
SILVER HAIR! IT'S THE HOUSE OF SILVA!
THAT'S RIGHT. I'M A ROYAL.
WE'RE SAID TO HAVE THE BEST MAGIC IN THIS COUNTRY.

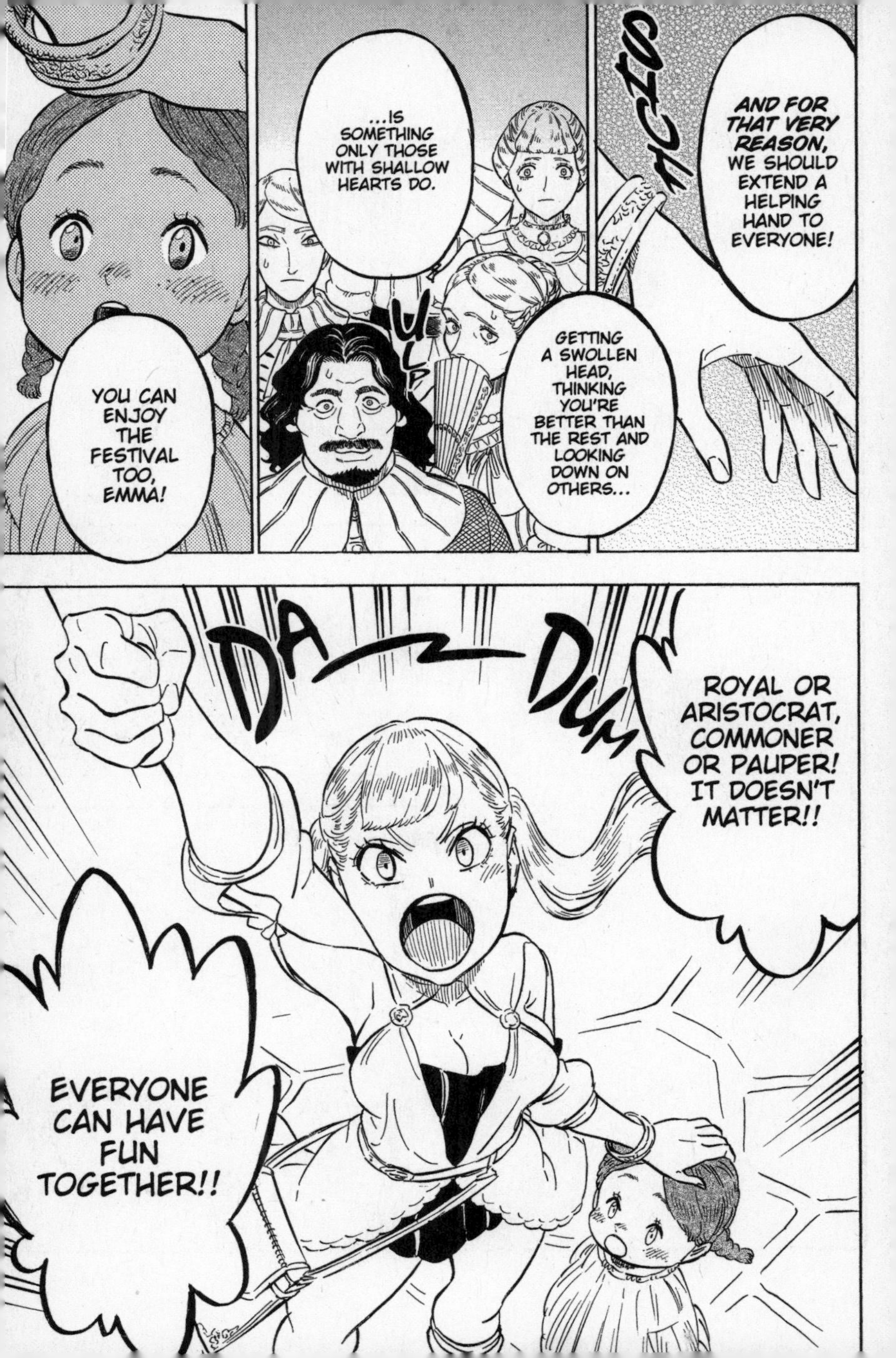
SHICK
AND FOR THAT VERY REASON, WE SHOULD EXTEND A HELPING HAND TO EVERYONE!
GETTING A SWOLLEN HEAD, THINKING YOU'RE BETTER THAN THE REST AND LOOKING DOWN ON OTHERS...
...IS SOMETHING ONLY THOSE WITH SHALLOW HEARTS DO.
ULP
YOU CAN ENJOY THE FESTIVAL TOO, EMMA!
DA-DUM
ROYAL OR ARISTOCRAT, COMMONER OR PAUPER! IT DOESN'T MATTER!!
EVERYONE CAN HAVE FUN TOGETHER!!

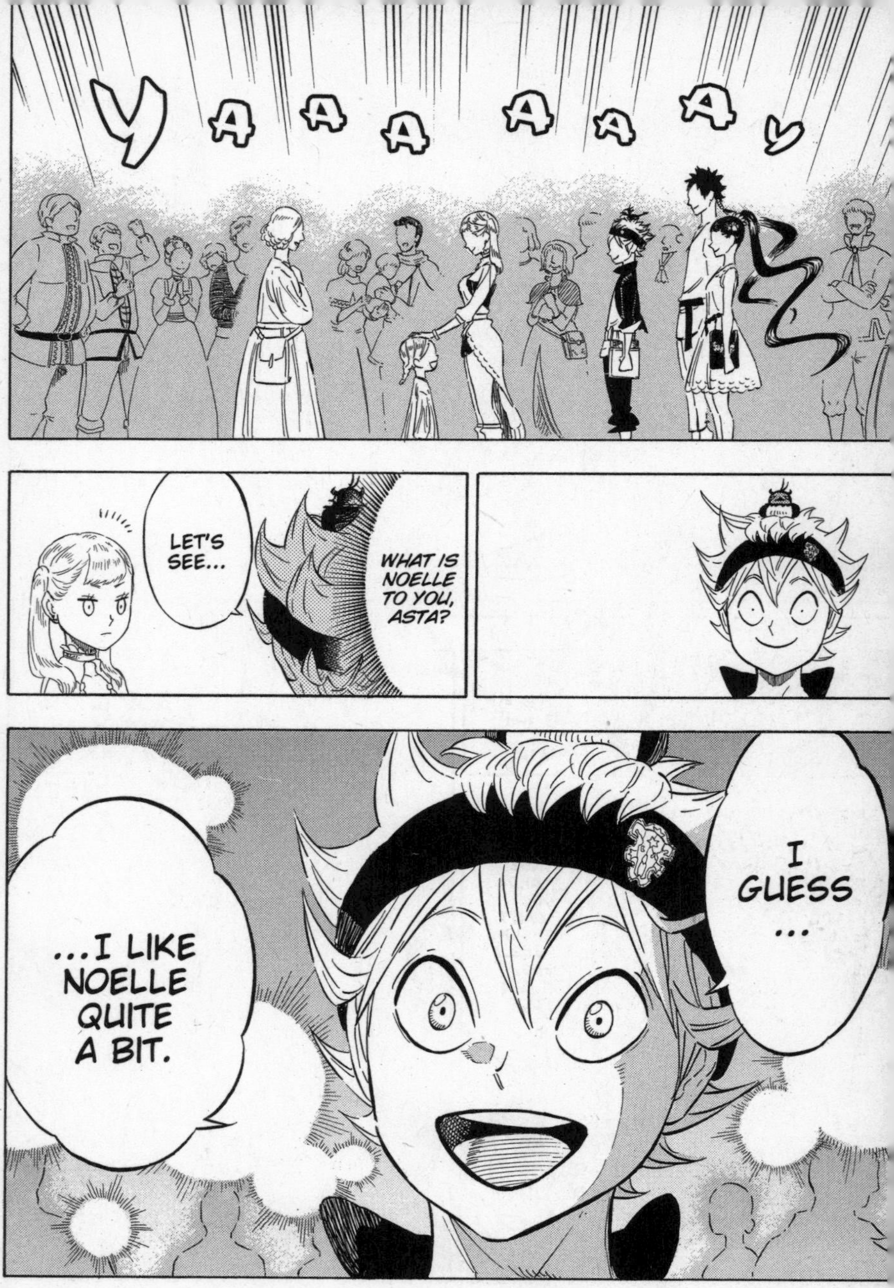
YAAAAAAY
WHAT IS NOELLE TO YOU, ASTA?
LET'S SEE...
I GUESS...
...I LIKE NOELLE QUITE A BIT.

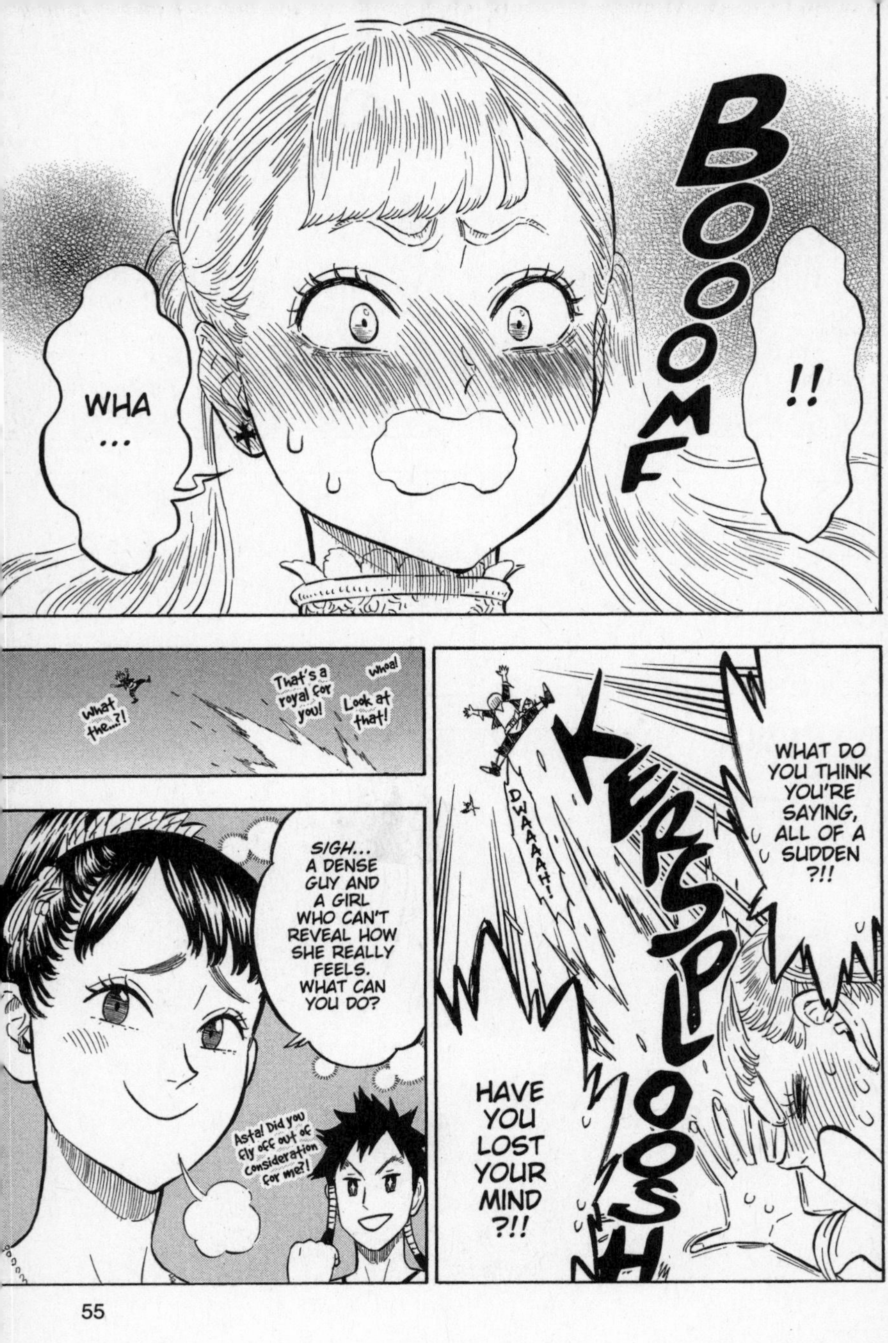
!!
BOOOOMF
WHA ...
WHAT DO YOU THINK YOU'RE SAYING, ALL OF A SUDDEN ?!!
KERSPLOOOSH
DWAAAAAH!
HAVE YOU LOST YOUR MIND ?!!
Whoa!
Look at that!
That's a royal for you!
What the...?!
SIGH... A DENSE GUY AND A GIRL WHO CAN'T REVEAL HOW SHE REALLY FEELS. WHAT CAN YOU DO?
Asta! Did you fly off out of consideration for me?!

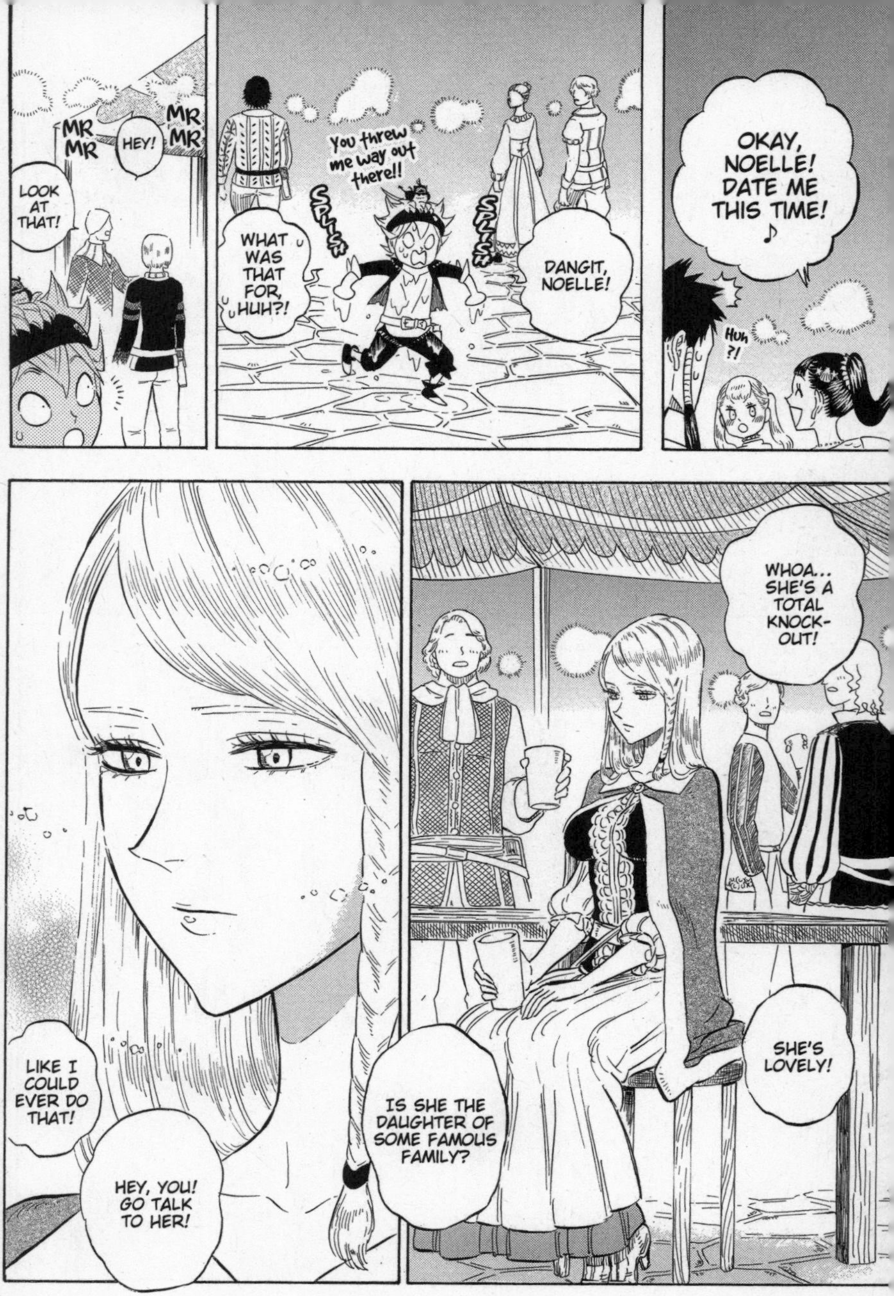
OKAY, NOELLE! DATE ME THIS TIME! ♪
Huh?!
DANGIT, NOELLE!
SPLISH
You threw me way out there!!
SPLISH
WHAT WAS THAT FOR, HUH?!
MR MR
HEY!
MR MR
LOOK AT THAT!
WHOA... SHE'S A TOTAL KNOCK-OUT!
SHE'S LOVELY!
IS SHE THE DAUGHTER OF SOME FAMOUS FAMILY?
HEY, YOU! GO TALK TO HER!
LIKE I COULD EVER DO THAT!

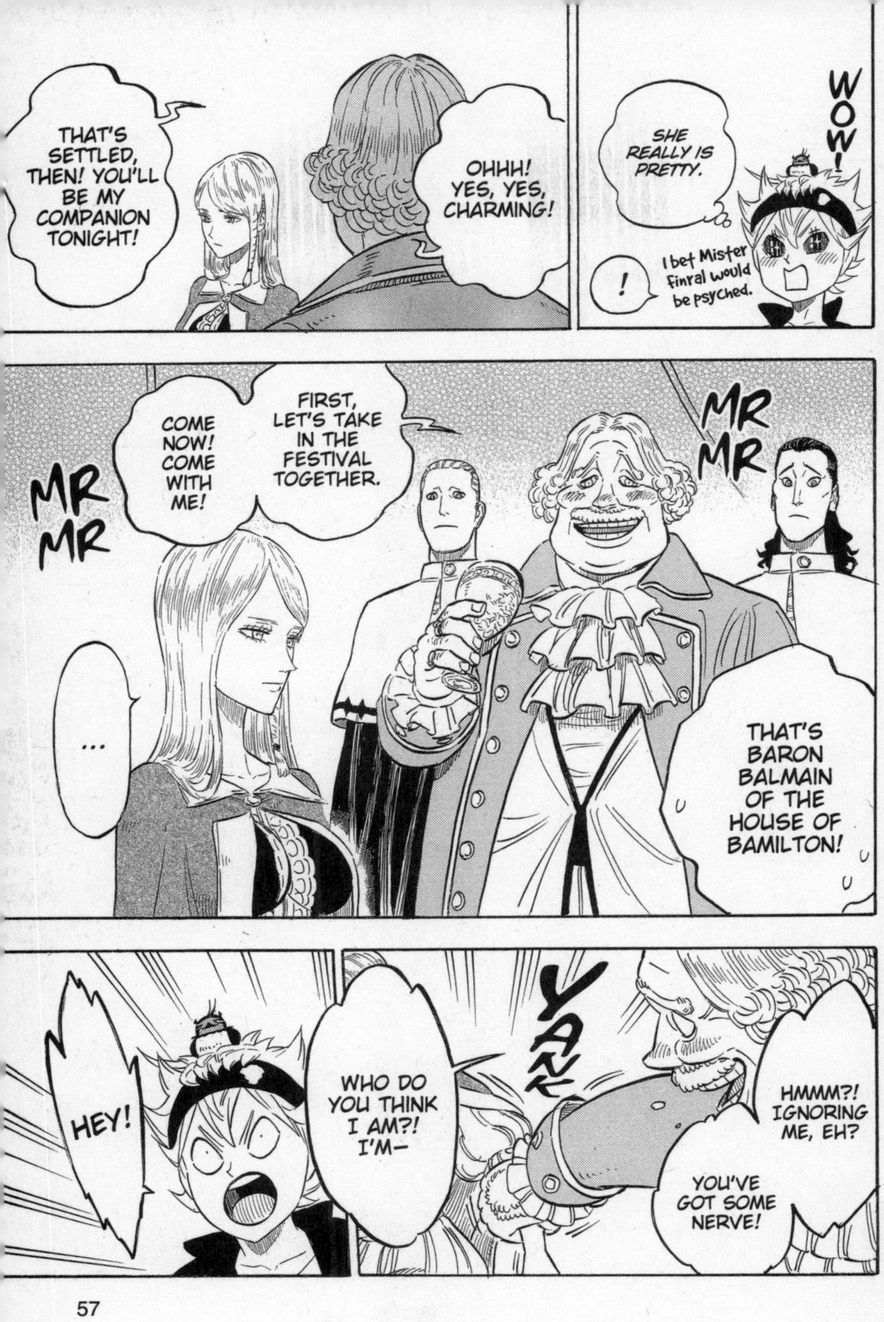
WOW!
SHE REALLY IS PRETTY.
I bet Mister Finral would be psyched.
!
OHHH! YES, YES, CHARMING!
THAT'S SETTLED, THEN! YOU'LL BE MY COMPANION TONIGHT!
MR MR
THAT'S BARON BALMAIN OF THE HOUSE OF BAMILTON!
FIRST, LET'S TAKE IN THE FESTIVAL TOGETHER.
COME NOW! COME WITH ME!
MR MR
...
HMMM?! IGNORING ME, EH?
YOU'VE GOT SOME NERVE!
YANK
WHO DO YOU THINK I AM?! I'M—
HEY!

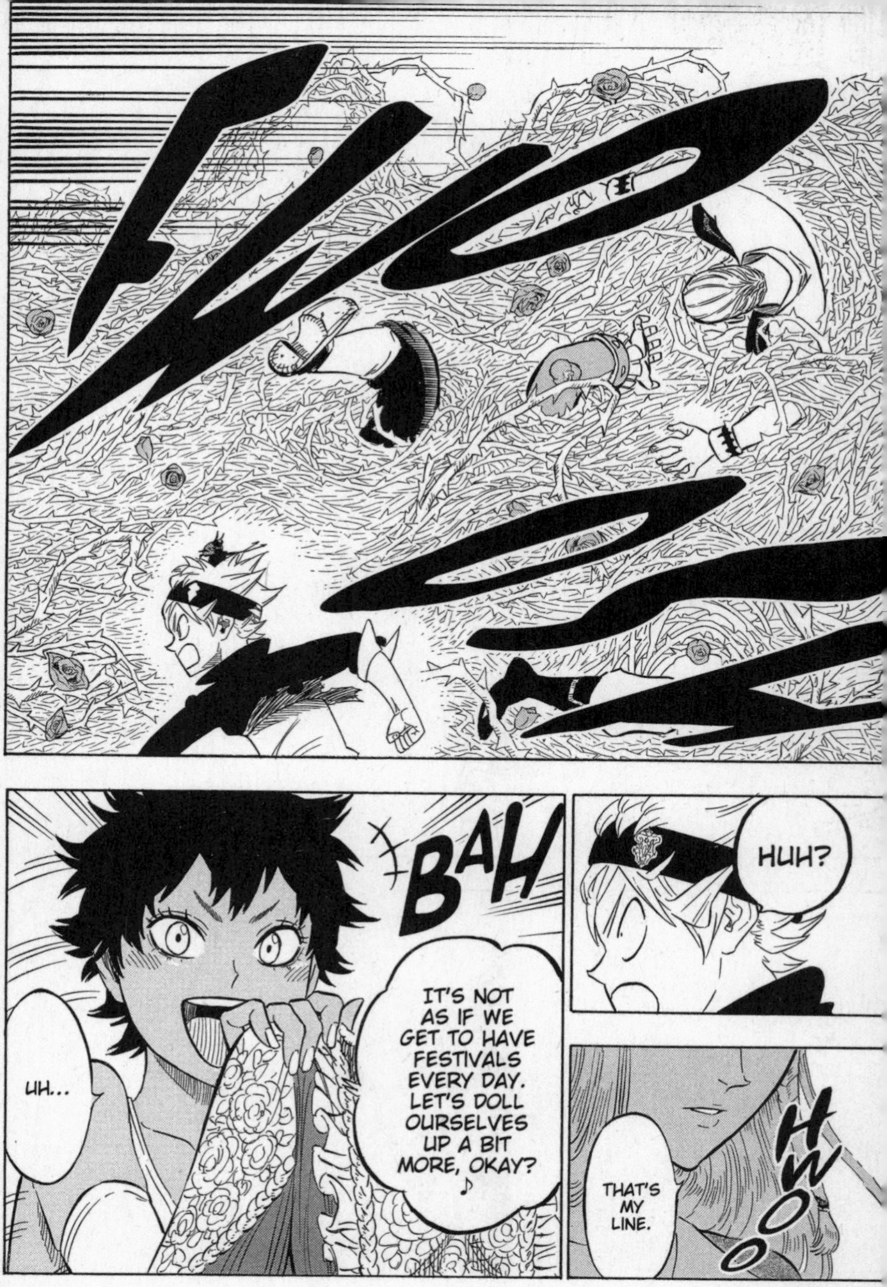
HUH?
HWOOO
THAT'S MY LINE.
BAH
IT'S NOT AS IF WE GET TO HAVE FESTIVALS EVERY DAY. LET'S DOLL OURSELVES UP A BIT MORE, OKAY? ♪
UH...

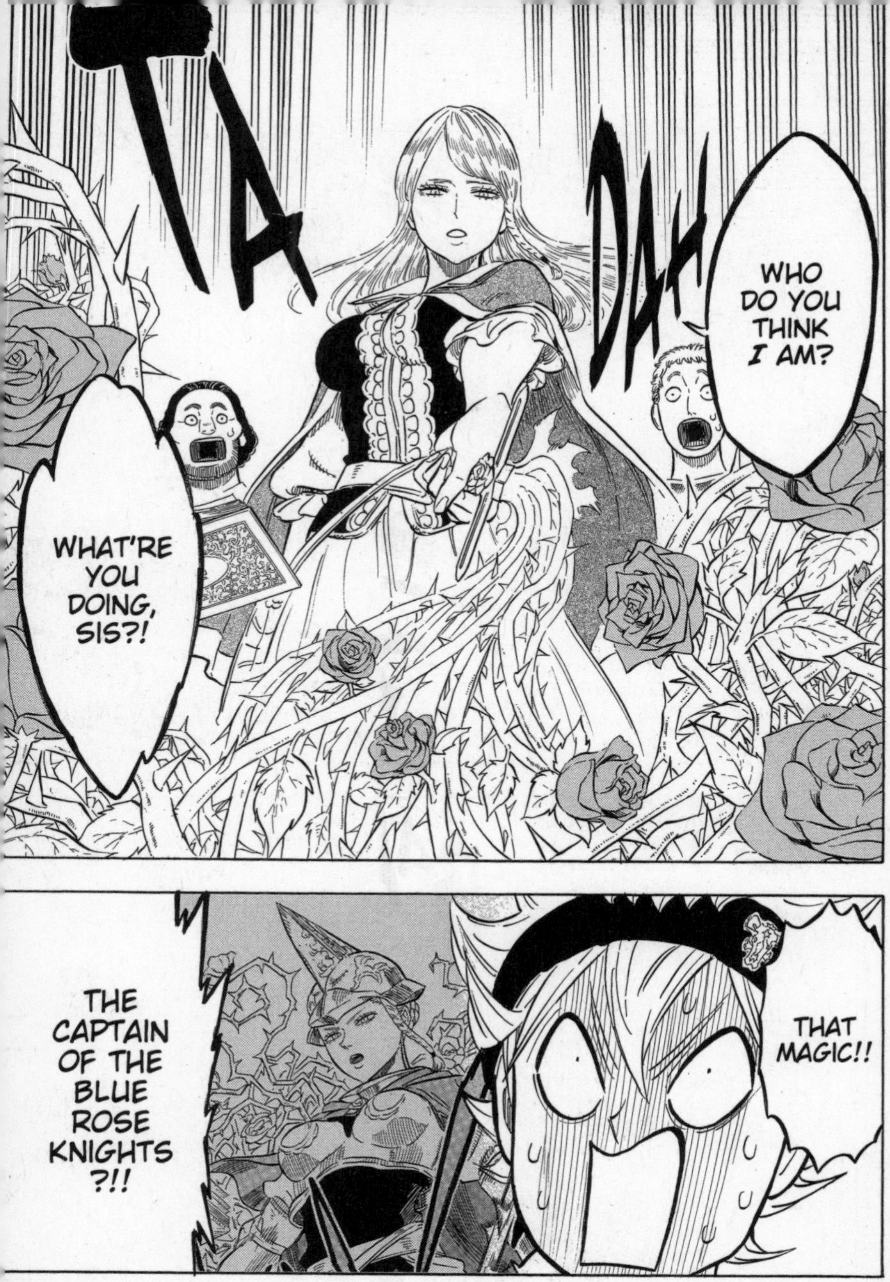
TA DAH
WHO DO YOU THINK I AM?
WHAT'RE YOU DOING, SIS?!
THAT MAGIC!!
THE CAPTAIN OF THE BLUE ROSE KNIGHTS?!!

The Assorted Questions Brigade No. 1

Good day! Good evening! Good morning!

It's time for the letters corner. We got lots of letters this time! Thank you very much!!!

Q: I have a question for the members of the Black Bulls!! Please tell me what type of person you like. (Natsumi, Niigata Prefecture)

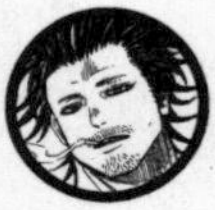

"A woman who can drink with me. Somebody who can fight alongside me."

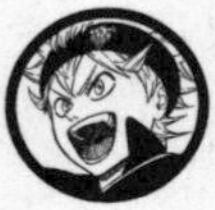

"The nun!!!"

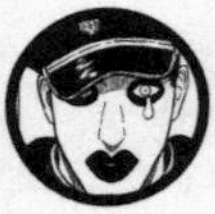

"Mmbl-mmbl-mmbl-mmbl... (Somebody who isn't afraid of me.)"

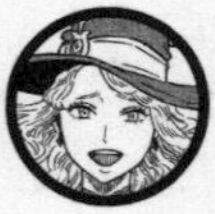

"Wild men with muscles ♥."

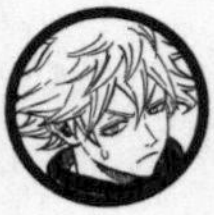

"Every girl out there!! ...Especially the ones who are pure and fleeting."

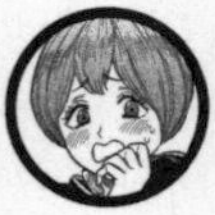

"Somebody who will lead me and... be gentle..."

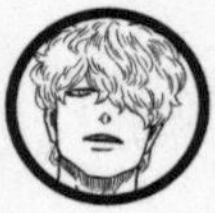

"Marie."

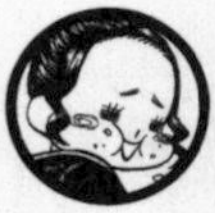

"Heh heh heh. Meal-saving prince... I think I'll just leave it at that."

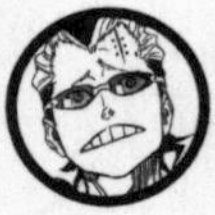

"A lively woman who can keep up with me!"

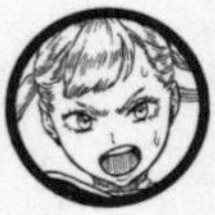

"Hmph. I have no such thing. ...M-maybe guys who are dumb and straightforward..."

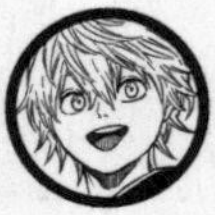

"? ...! Somebody strong who can go at it again and again!"

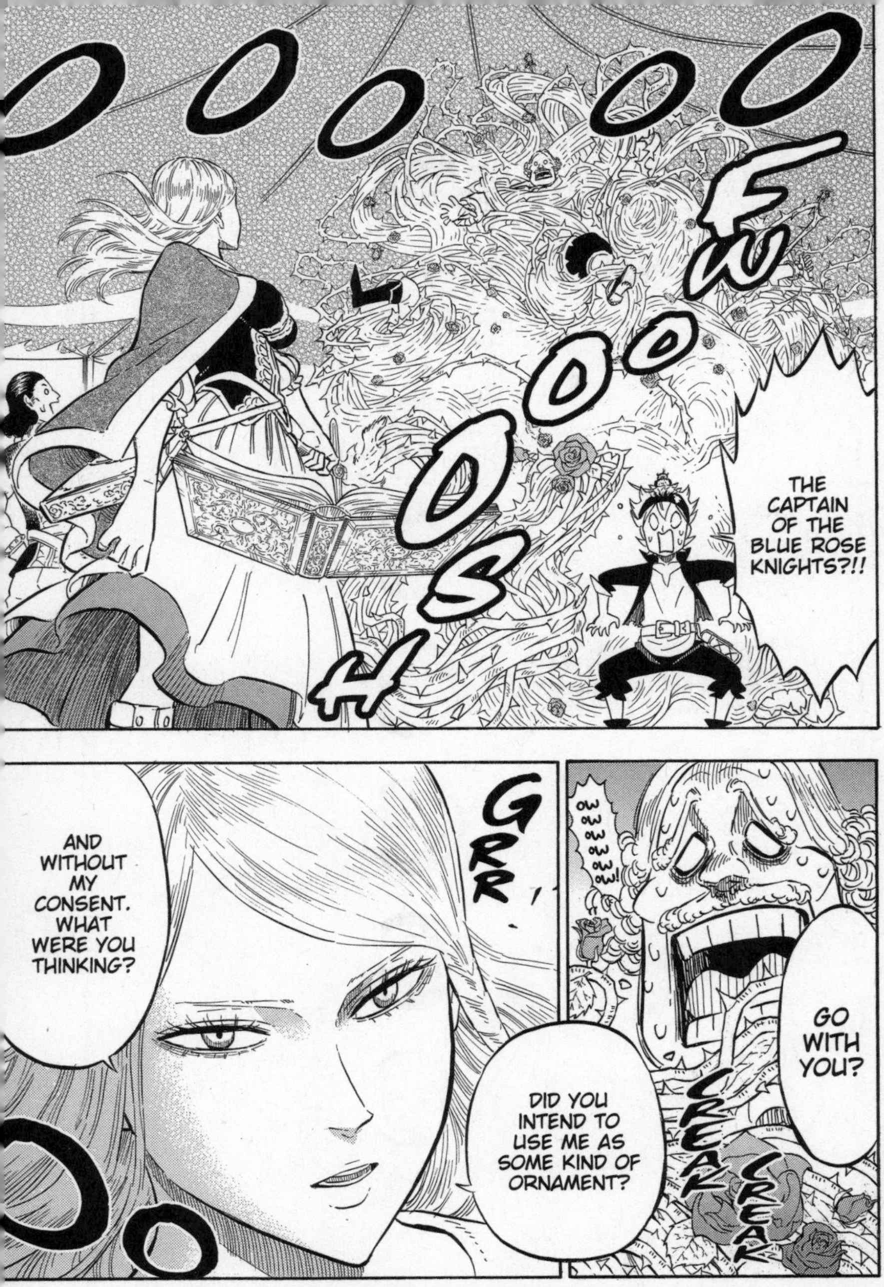
OOOOOO
FWOOOOSH
THE CAPTAIN OF THE BLUE ROSE KNIGHTS?!!
OW OW OW OW OW OW!
GO WITH YOU?
CREAK CREAK
GRR
AND WITHOUT MY CONSENT. WHAT WERE YOU THINKING?
DID YOU INTEND TO USE ME AS SOME KIND OF ORNAMENT?
OO

✤ Page 104: The Briar Maiden's Melancholy

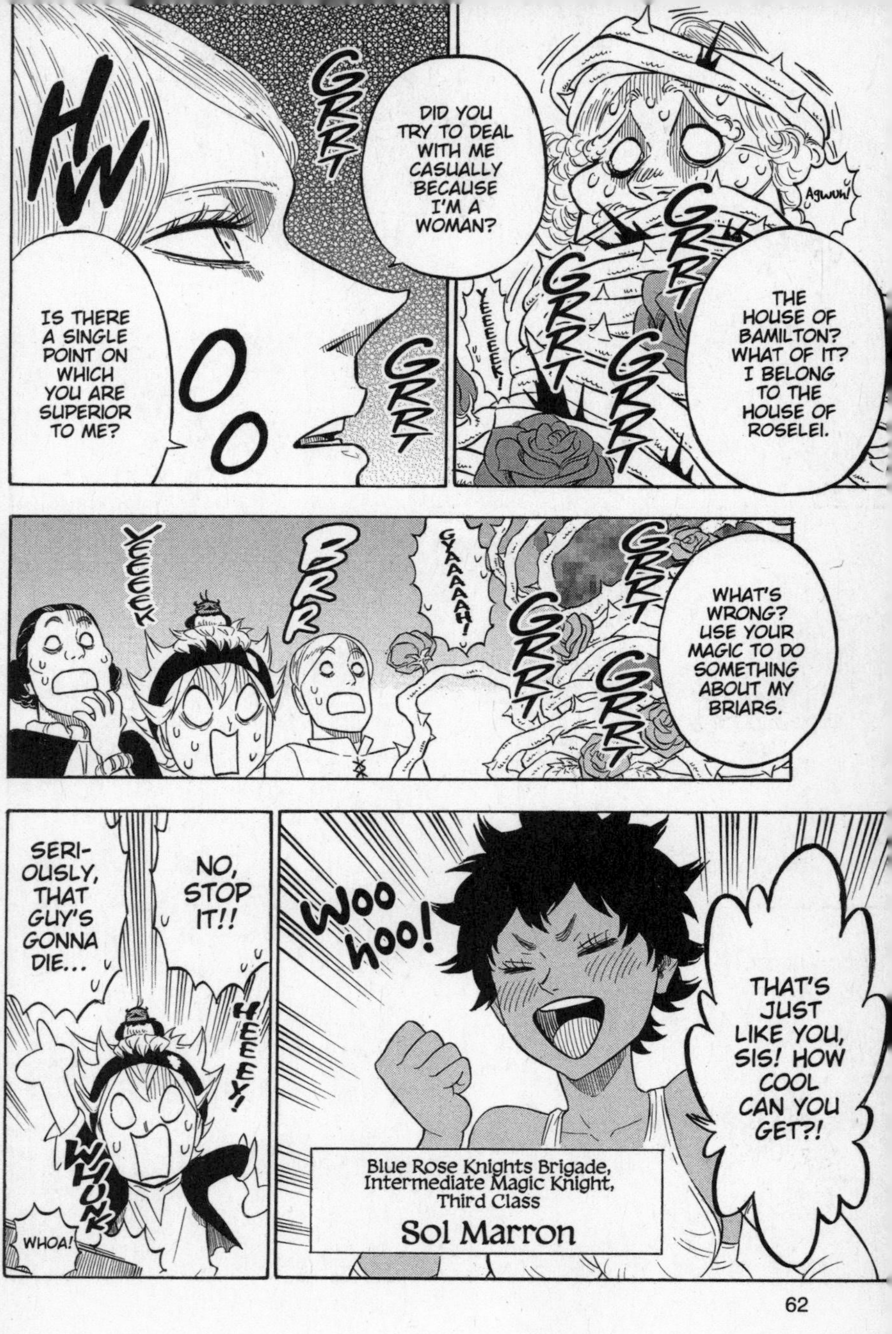
Agwuh!
GRRT
GRRT
YEEEEEK!
GRRT
THE HOUSE OF BAMILTON? WHAT OF IT? I BELONG TO THE HOUSE OF ROSELEI.
GRRT
DID YOU TRY TO DEAL WITH ME CASUALLY BECAUSE I'M A WOMAN?
HWOO
IS THERE A SINGLE POINT ON WHICH YOU ARE SUPERIOR TO ME?
GRRT
GRRT
WHAT'S WRONG? USE YOUR MAGIC TO DO SOMETHING ABOUT MY BRIARS.
GRRT
GRRT
GRRT
GYAAAAAH!
BRRR
YEEEEK
THAT'S JUST LIKE YOU, SIS! HOW COOL CAN YOU GET?!
Woo hoo!
Blue Rose Knights Brigade, Intermediate Magic Knight, Third Class
Sol Marron
NO, STOP IT!!
SERIOUSLY, THAT GUY'S GONNA DIE...
HEEEEY!
WHUNK
WHOA!

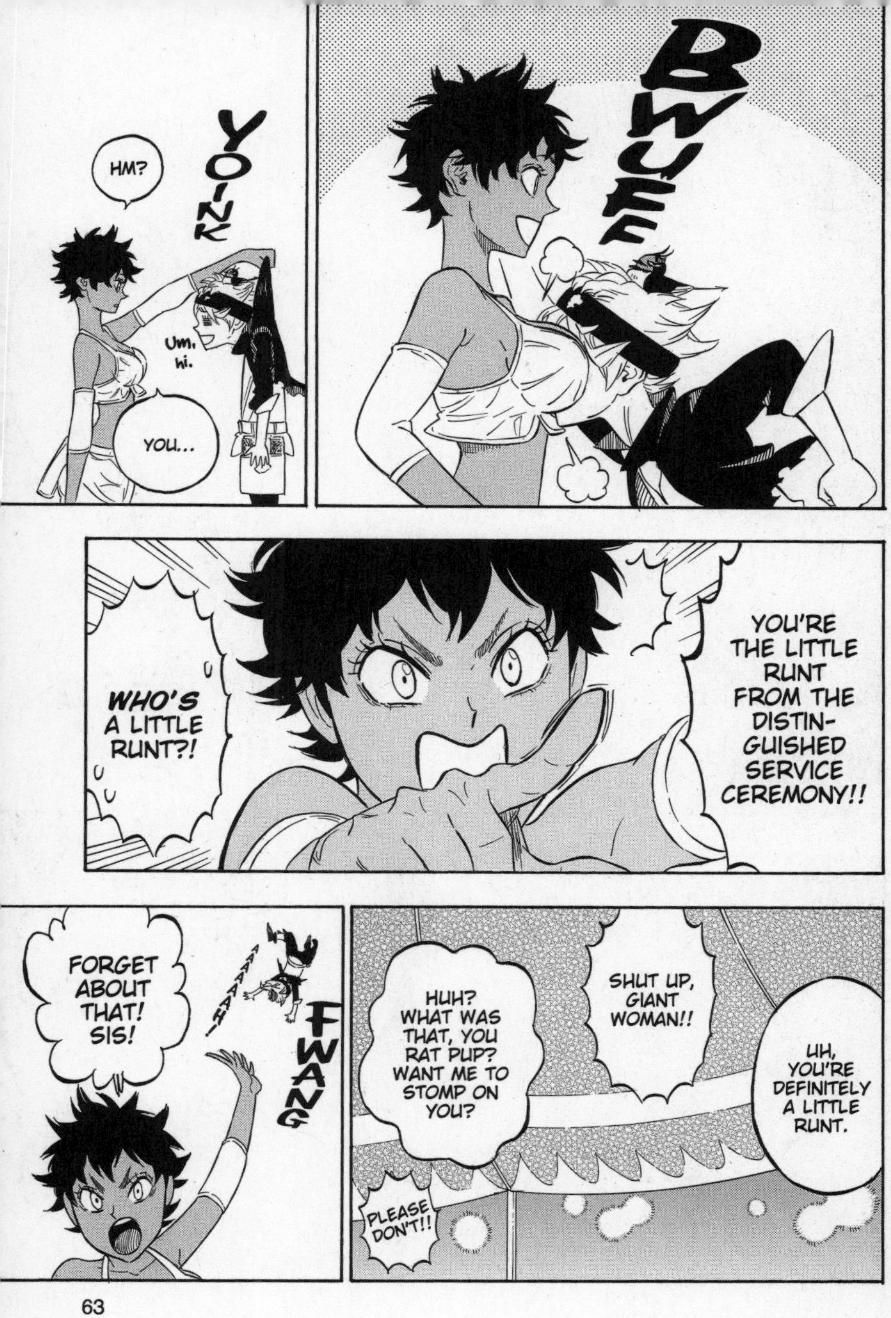
BWUFF
YOINK
HM?
Um, hi.
YOU...
YOU'RE THE LITTLE RUNT FROM THE DISTIN-GUISHED SERVICE CEREMONY!!
WHO'S A LITTLE RUNT?!
UH, YOU'RE DEFINITELY A LITTLE RUNT.
SHUT UP, GIANT WOMAN!!
HUH? WHAT WAS THAT, YOU RAT PUP? WANT ME TO STOMP ON YOU?
PLEASE DON'T!!
FWANG
AAAAAAH!
FORGET ABOUT THAT! SIS!

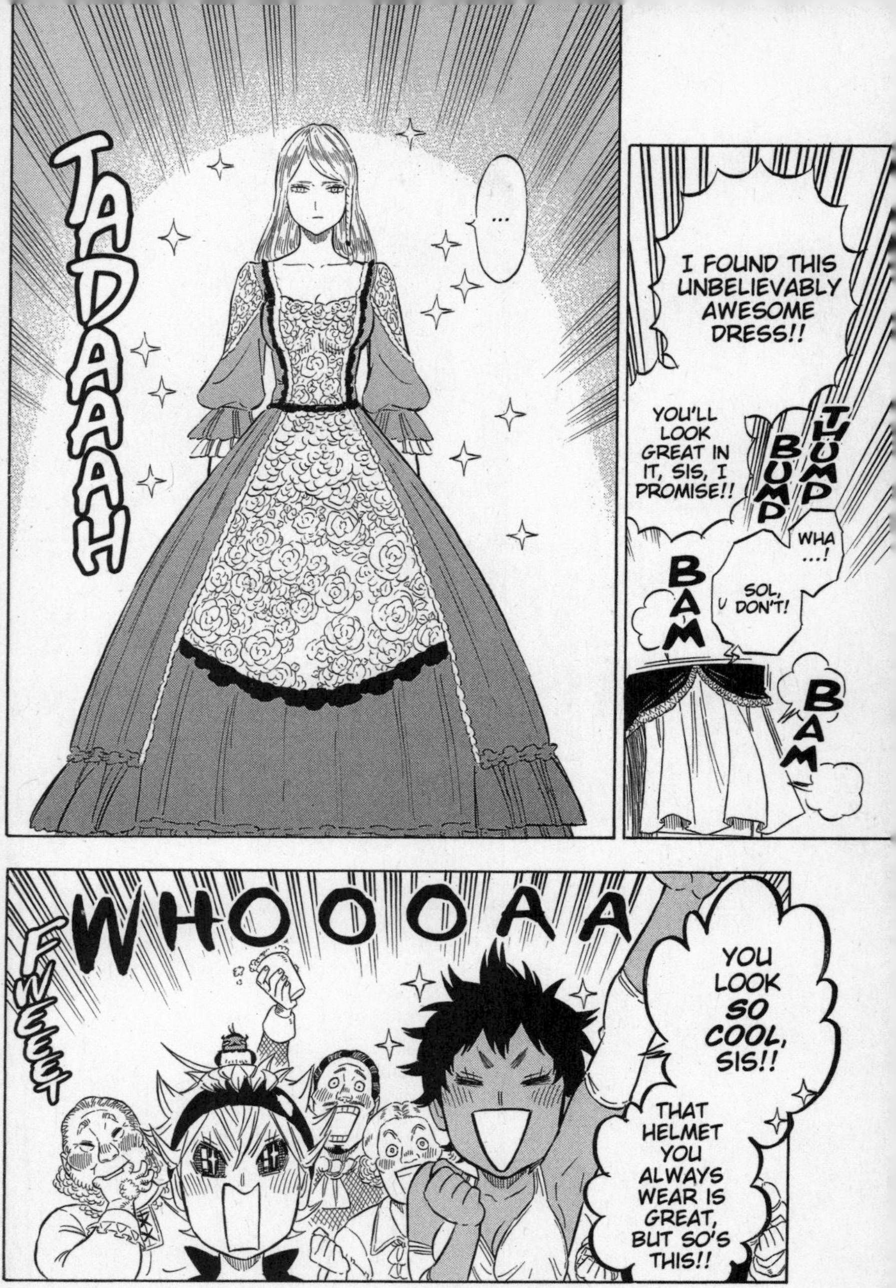
I FOUND THIS UNBELIEVABLY AWESOME DRESS!!
THUMP
BUMP
YOU'LL LOOK GREAT IN IT, SIS, I PROMISE!!
WHA...!
SOL, DON'T!
BAM
BAM
TADAAAAH
...
WHOOOAA
YOU LOOK SO COOL, SIS!!
THAT HELMET YOU ALWAYS WEAR IS GREAT, BUT SO'S THIS!!

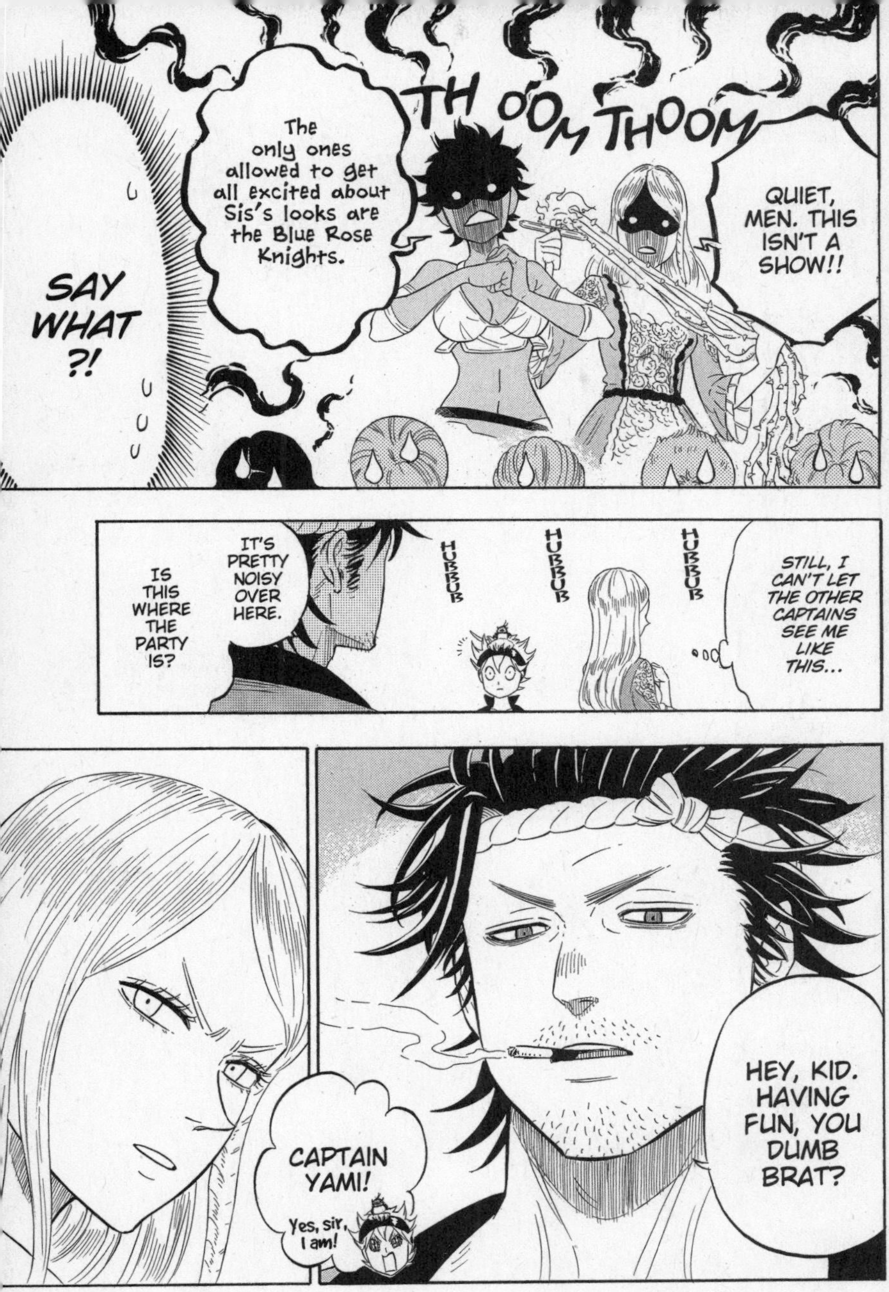
QUIET, MEN. THIS ISN'T A SHOW!!
THOOM THOOM
The only ones allowed to get all excited about Sis's looks are the Blue Rose Knights.
SAY WHAT?!
STILL, I CAN'T LET THE OTHER CAPTAINS SEE ME LIKE THIS...
HUBBUB
HUBBUB
HUBBUB
IT'S PRETTY NOISY OVER HERE.
IS THIS WHERE THE PARTY IS?
HEY, KID. HAVING FUN, YOU DUMB BRAT?
CAPTAIN YAMI!
Yes, sir, I am!

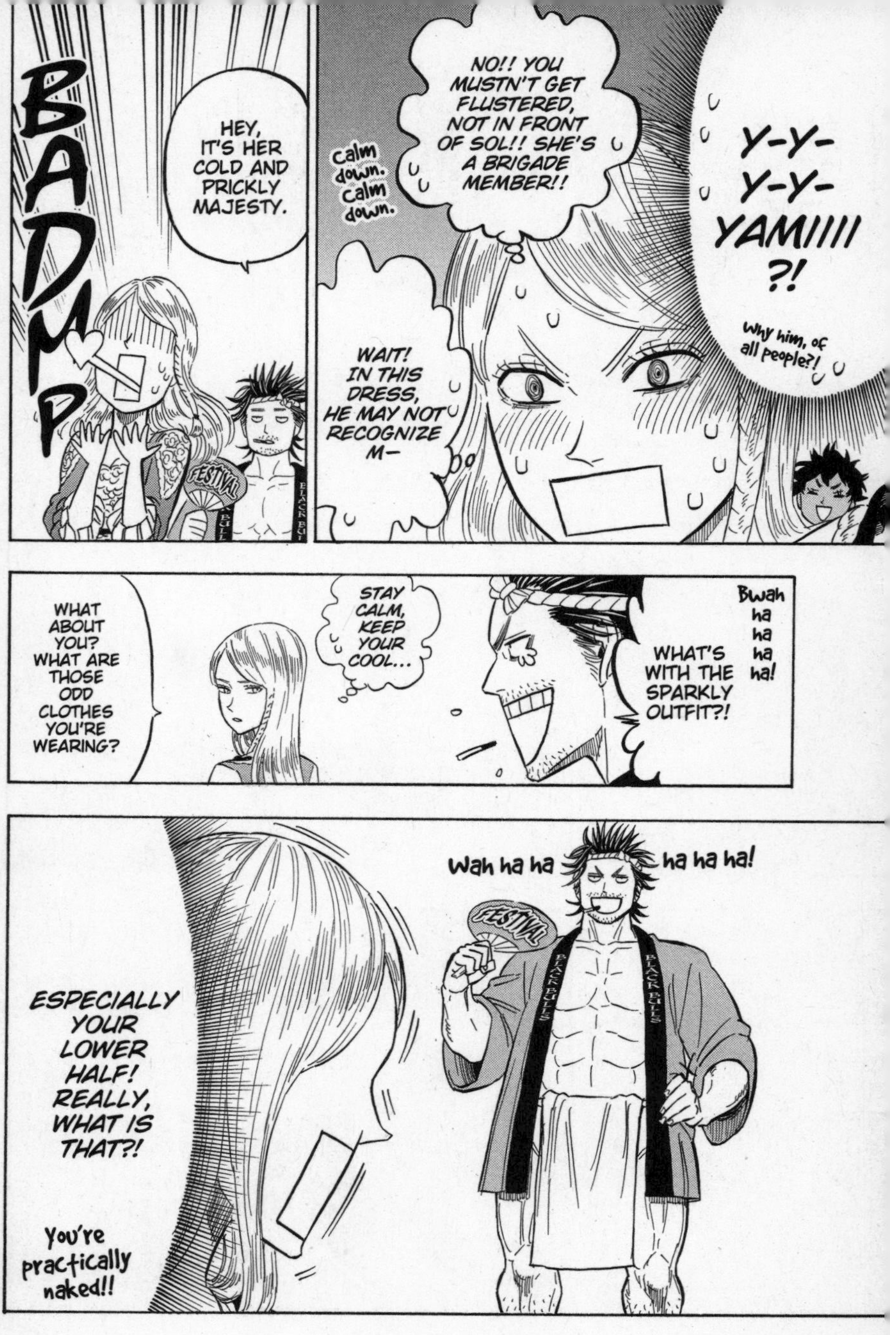
Y-Y-Y-Y-YAM!!!!?!
Why him, of all people?!
NO!! YOU MUSTN'T GET FLUSTERED, NOT IN FRONT OF SOL!! SHE'S A BRIGADE MEMBER!!
Calm down. Calm down.
WAIT! IN THIS DRESS, HE MAY NOT RECOGNIZE M–
HEY, IT'S HER COLD AND PRICKLY MAJESTY.
BADMP
FESTIVAL
Bwah ha ha ha ha!
WHAT'S WITH THE SPARKLY OUTFIT?!
STAY CALM, KEEP YOUR COOL...
WHAT ABOUT YOU? WHAT ARE THOSE ODD CLOTHES YOU'RE WEARING?
Wah ha ha ha ha ha!
FESTIVAL
BLACK BULLS
ESPECIALLY YOUR LOWER HALF! REALLY, WHAT IS THAT?!
You're practically naked!!

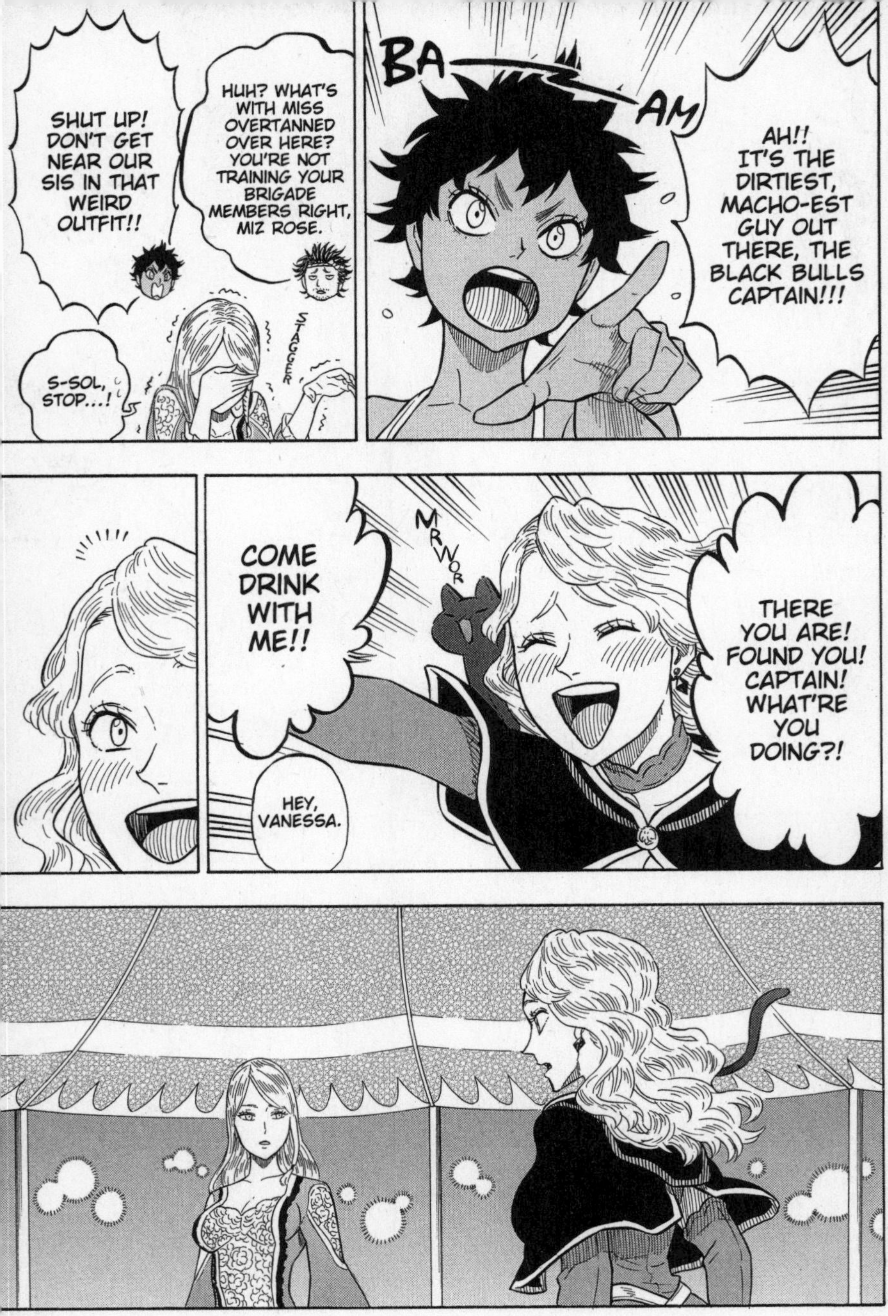
BA—AM
AH!! IT'S THE DIRTIEST, MACHO-EST GUY OUT THERE, THE BLACK BULLS CAPTAIN!!!
HUH? WHAT'S WITH MISS OVERTANNED OVER HERE? YOU'RE NOT TRAINING YOUR BRIGADE MEMBERS RIGHT, MIZ ROSE.
SHUT UP! DON'T GET NEAR OUR SIS IN THAT WEIRD OUTFIT!!
STAGGER
S-SOL, STOP...!
THERE YOU ARE! FOUND YOU! CAPTAIN! WHAT'RE YOU DOING?!
MRNOR
COME DRINK WITH ME!!
HEY, VANESSA.

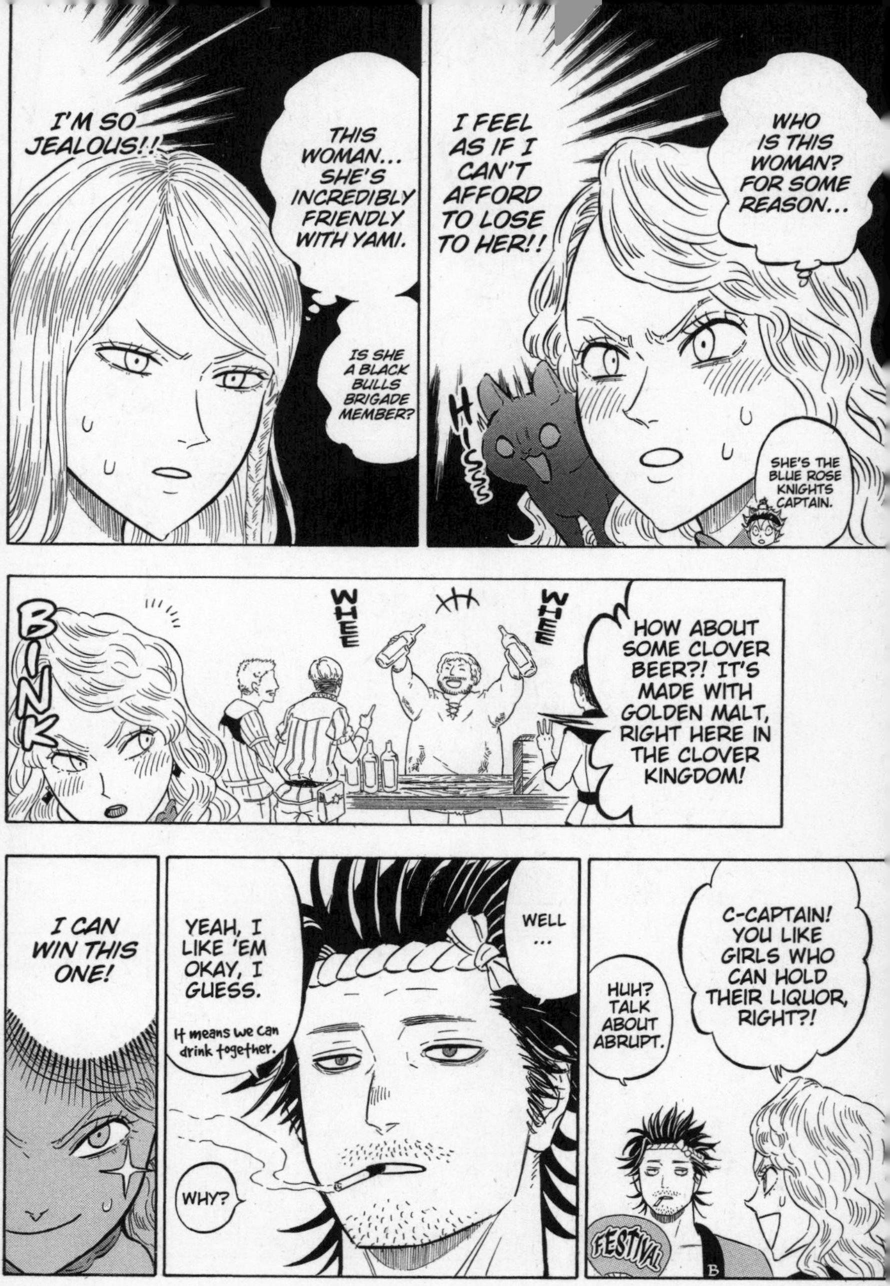
WHO IS THIS WOMAN? FOR SOME REASON...
I FEEL AS IF I CAN'T AFFORD TO LOSE TO HER!!
HISSS
SHE'S THE BLUE ROSE KNIGHTS CAPTAIN.
THIS WOMAN... SHE'S INCREDIBLY FRIENDLY WITH YAMI.
I'M SO JEALOUS!!
IS SHE A BLACK BULLS BRIGADE MEMBER?
HOW ABOUT SOME CLOVER BEER?! IT'S MADE WITH GOLDEN MALT, RIGHT HERE IN THE CLOVER KINGDOM!
WHEE
WHEE
BINK
C-CAPTAIN! YOU LIKE GIRLS WHO CAN HOLD THEIR LIQUOR, RIGHT?!
HUH? TALK ABOUT ABRUPT.
FESTIVAL
WELL...
YEAH, I LIKE 'EM OKAY, I GUESS.
It means we can drink together.
WHY?
I CAN WIN THIS ONE!

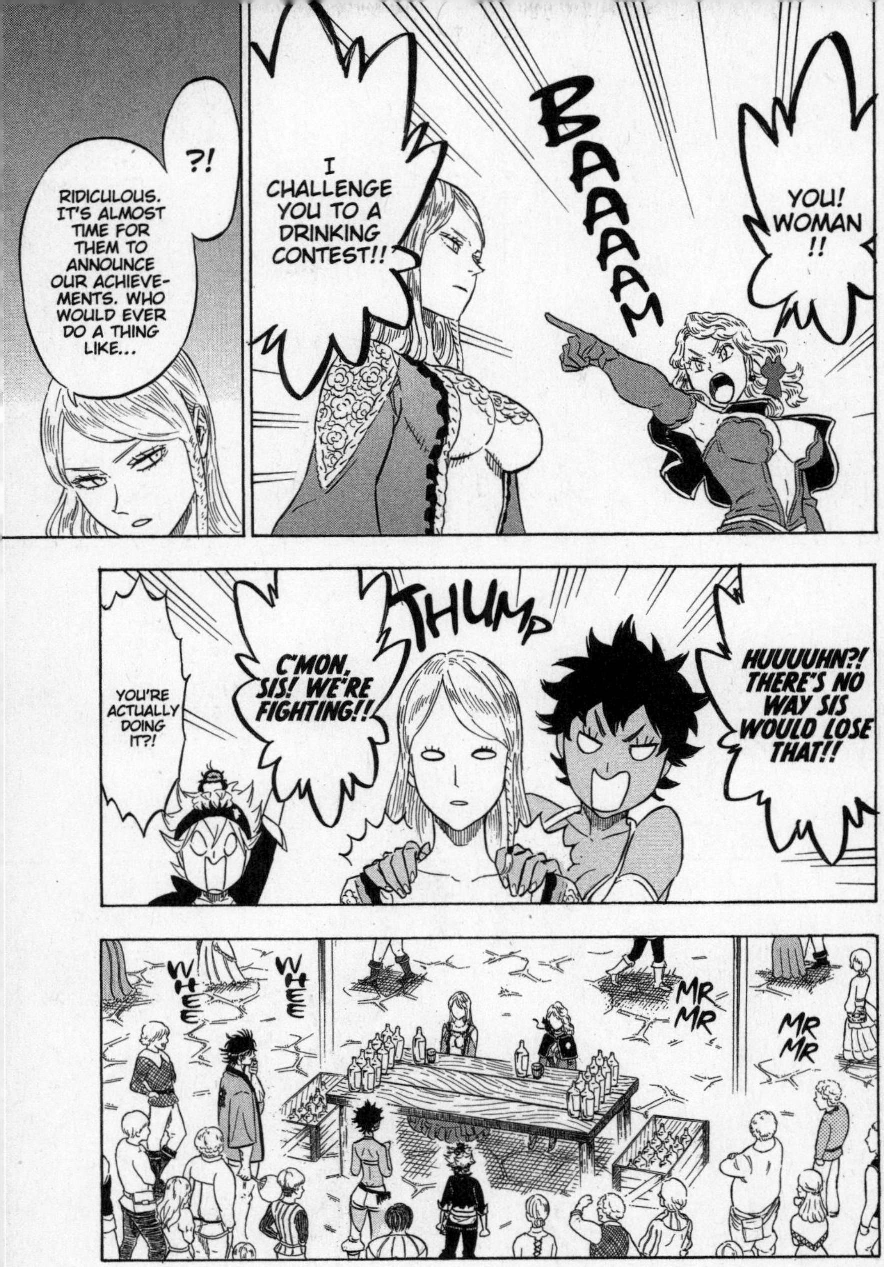

YOU! WOMAN !!
BAAAAM
I CHALLENGE YOU TO A DRINKING CONTEST!!
?!
RIDICULOUS. IT'S ALMOST TIME FOR THEM TO ANNOUNCE OUR ACHIEVEMENTS. WHO WOULD EVER DO A THING LIKE...
HUUUUHN?! THERE'S NO WAY SIS WOULD LOSE THAT!!
THUMP
C'MON, SIS! WE'RE FIGHTING!!
YOU'RE ACTUALLY DOING IT?!
MR MR
MR MR
WHEE
WHEE

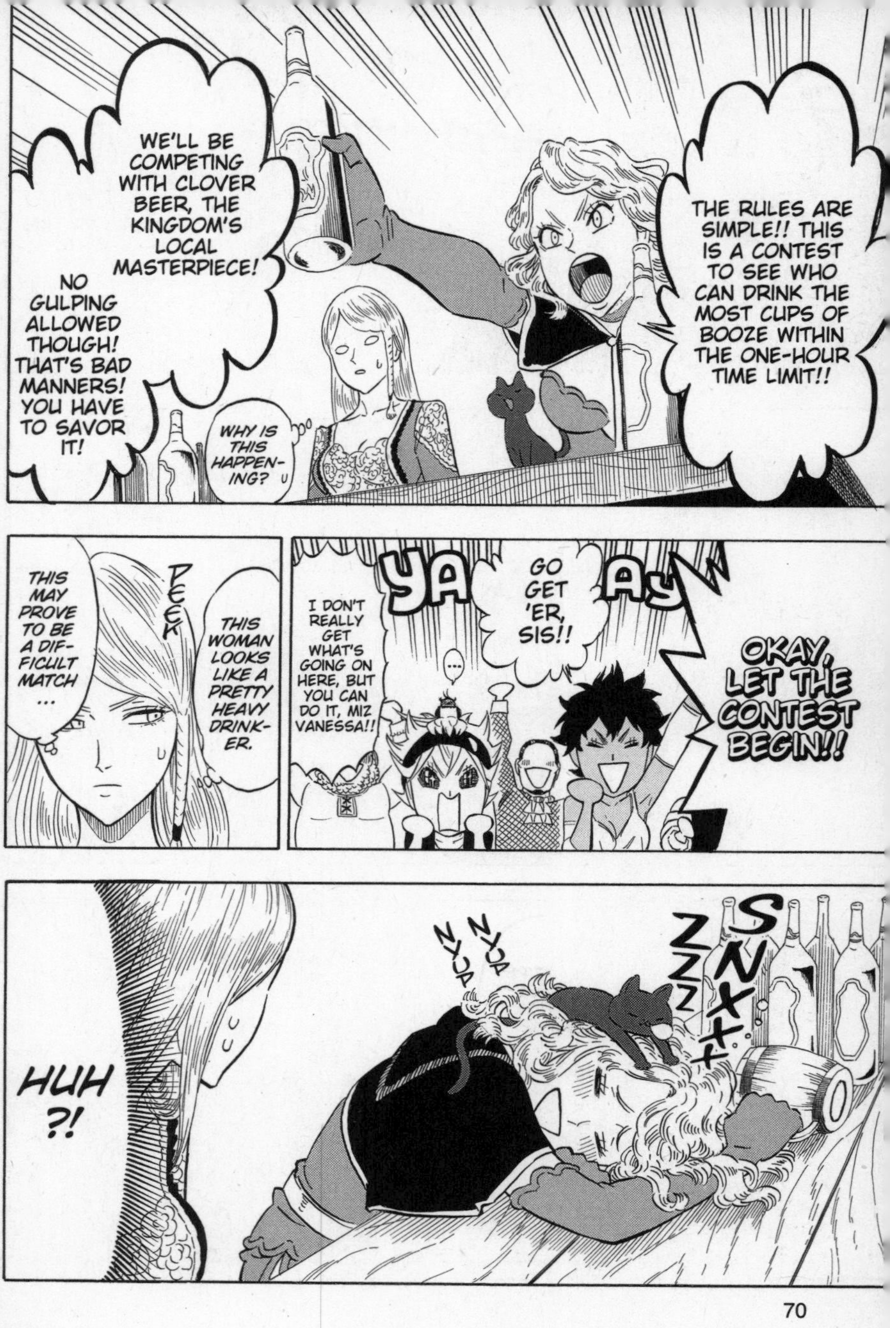

THE RULES ARE SIMPLE!! THIS IS A CONTEST TO SEE WHO CAN DRINK THE MOST CUPS OF BOOZE WITHIN THE ONE-HOUR TIME LIMIT!!
WE'LL BE COMPETING WITH CLOVER BEER, THE KINGDOM'S LOCAL MASTERPIECE!
NO GULPING ALLOWED THOUGH! THAT'S BAD MANNERS! YOU HAVE TO SAVOR IT!
WHY IS THIS HAPPEN-ING?
OKAY, LET THE CONTEST BEGIN!!
YA AY
GO GET 'ER, SIS!!
I DON'T REALLY GET WHAT'S GOING ON HERE, BUT YOU CAN DO IT, MIZ VANESSA!!
...
PEEK
THIS WOMAN LOOKS LIKE A PRETTY HEAVY DRINK-ER.
THIS MAY PROVE TO BE A DIF-FICULT MATCH ...
SNXXX
ZZZ
NYUA NYUA
HUH ?!

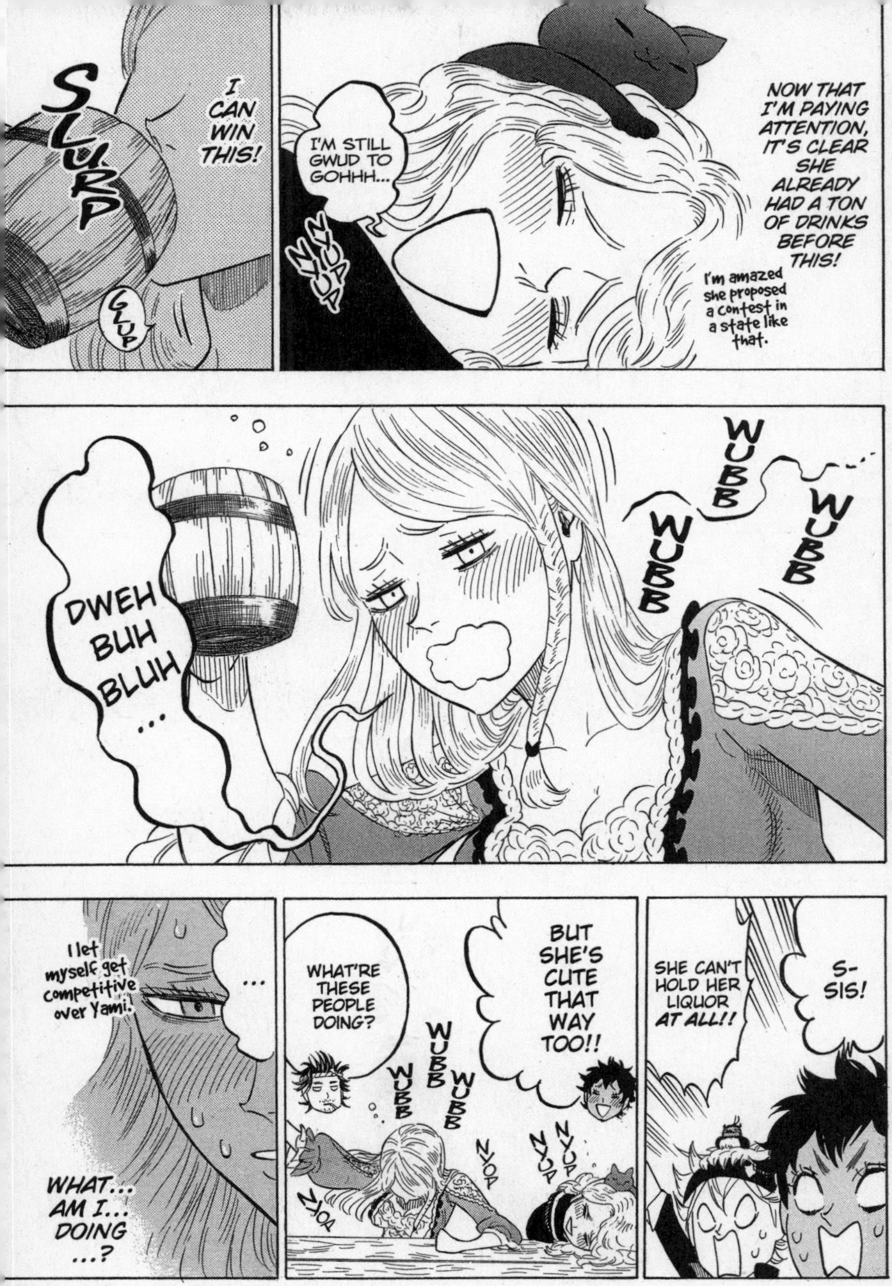
NOW THAT I'M PAYING ATTENTION, IT'S CLEAR SHE ALREADY HAD A TON OF DRINKS BEFORE THIS!
I'm amazed she proposed a contest in a state like that.
I'M STILL GWUD TO GOHHH...
NYUP NYUP
I CAN WIN THIS!
SLURP
GLUP
WUBB
WUBB
WUBB
DWEH BUH BLUH ...
S-SIS!
SHE CAN'T HOLD HER LIQUOR AT ALL!!
BUT SHE'S CUTE THAT WAY TOO!!
WHAT'RE THESE PEOPLE DOING?
WUBB WUBB WUBB
NYUP NYUP
NYOP
...
I let myself get competitive over Yami.
WHAT... AM I... DOING ...?

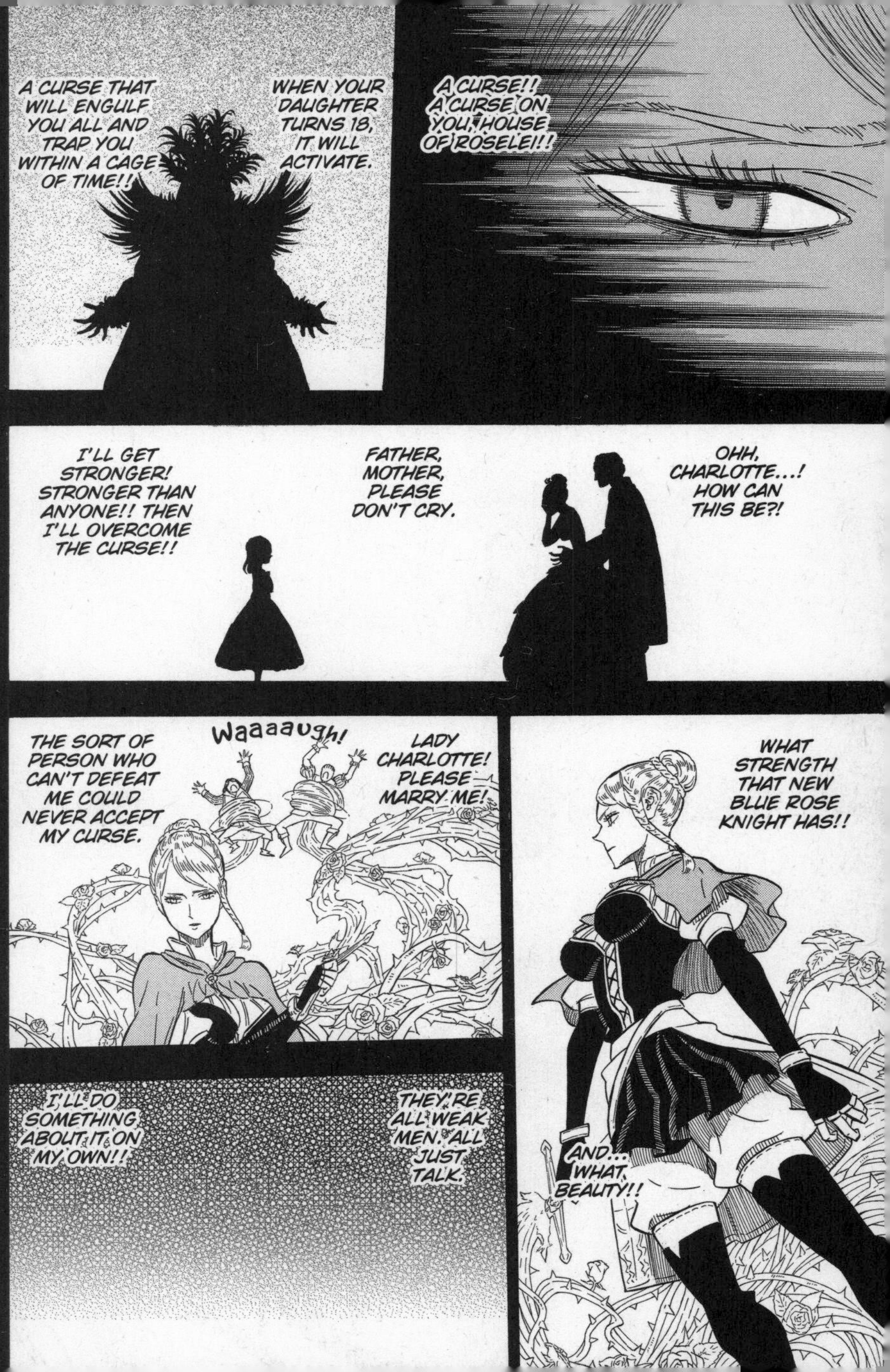
A CURSE!! A CURSE ON YOU, HOUSE OF ROSELEI!!
WHEN YOUR DAUGHTER TURNS 18, IT WILL ACTIVATE.
A CURSE THAT WILL ENGULF YOU ALL AND TRAP YOU WITHIN A CAGE OF TIME!!
OHH, CHARLOTTE...! HOW CAN THIS BE?!
FATHER, MOTHER, PLEASE DON'T CRY.
I'LL GET STRONGER! STRONGER THAN ANYONE!! THEN I'LL OVERCOME THE CURSE!!
WHAT STRENGTH THAT NEW BLUE ROSE KNIGHT HAS!!
AND... WHAT BEAUTY!!
LADY CHARLOTTE! PLEASE MARRY ME!
Waaaaugh!
THE SORT OF PERSON WHO CAN'T DEFEAT ME COULD NEVER ACCEPT MY CURSE.
THEY'RE ALL WEAK MEN. ALL JUST TALK.
I'LL DO SOMETHING ABOUT IT ON MY OWN!!

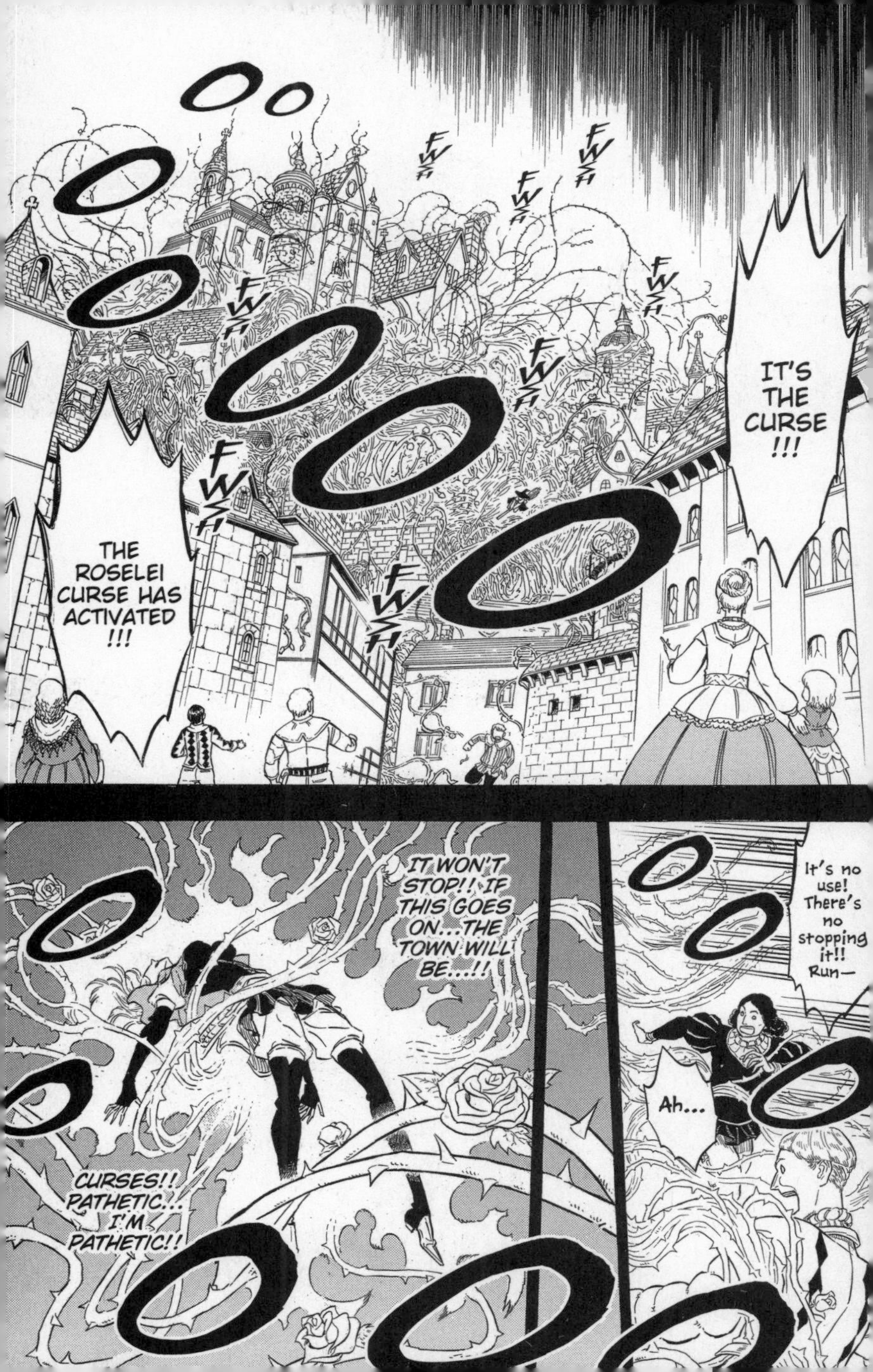

IT'S THE CURSE!!!
FWSH
FWSH
FWSH
FWSH
FWSH
FWSH
FWSH
THE ROSELEI CURSE HAS ACTIVATED!!!
It's no use! There's no stopping it!! Run—
Ah...
IT WON'T STOP!! IF THIS GOES ON...THE TOWN WILL BE...!!
CURSES!! PATHETIC... I'M PATHETIC!!

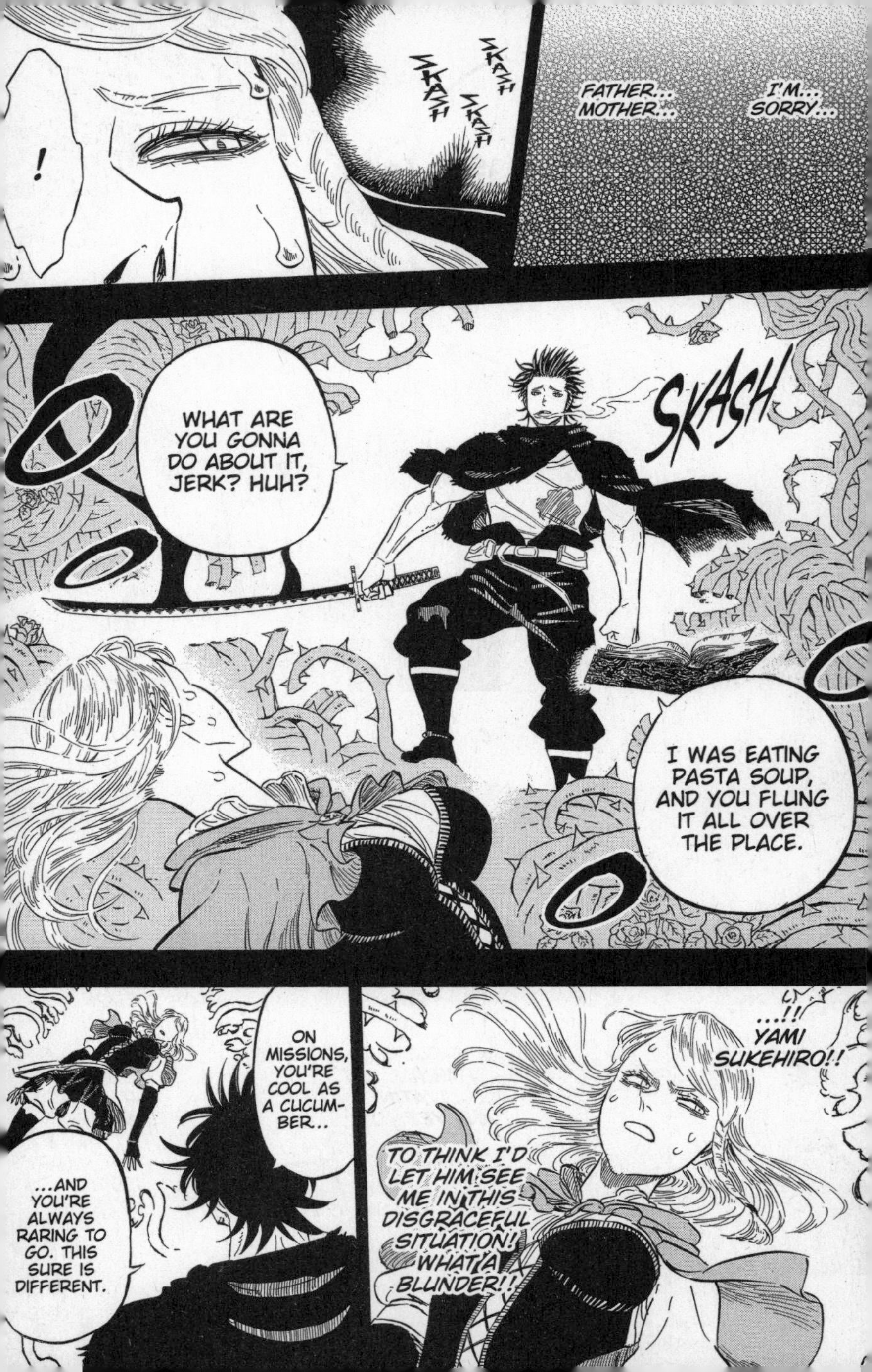
FATHER... MOTHER...
I'M... SORRY...
SKASH
SKASH
SKASH
!
SKASH
I WAS EATING PASTA SOUP, AND YOU FLUNG IT ALL OVER THE PLACE.
WHAT ARE YOU GONNA DO ABOUT IT, JERK? HUH?
...!! YAMI SUKEHIRO!!
TO THINK I'D LET HIM SEE ME IN THIS DISGRACEFUL SITUATION! WHAT A BLUNDER!!
ON MISSIONS, YOU'RE COOL AS A CUCUMBER...
...AND YOU'RE ALWAYS RARING TO GO. THIS SURE IS DIFFERENT.

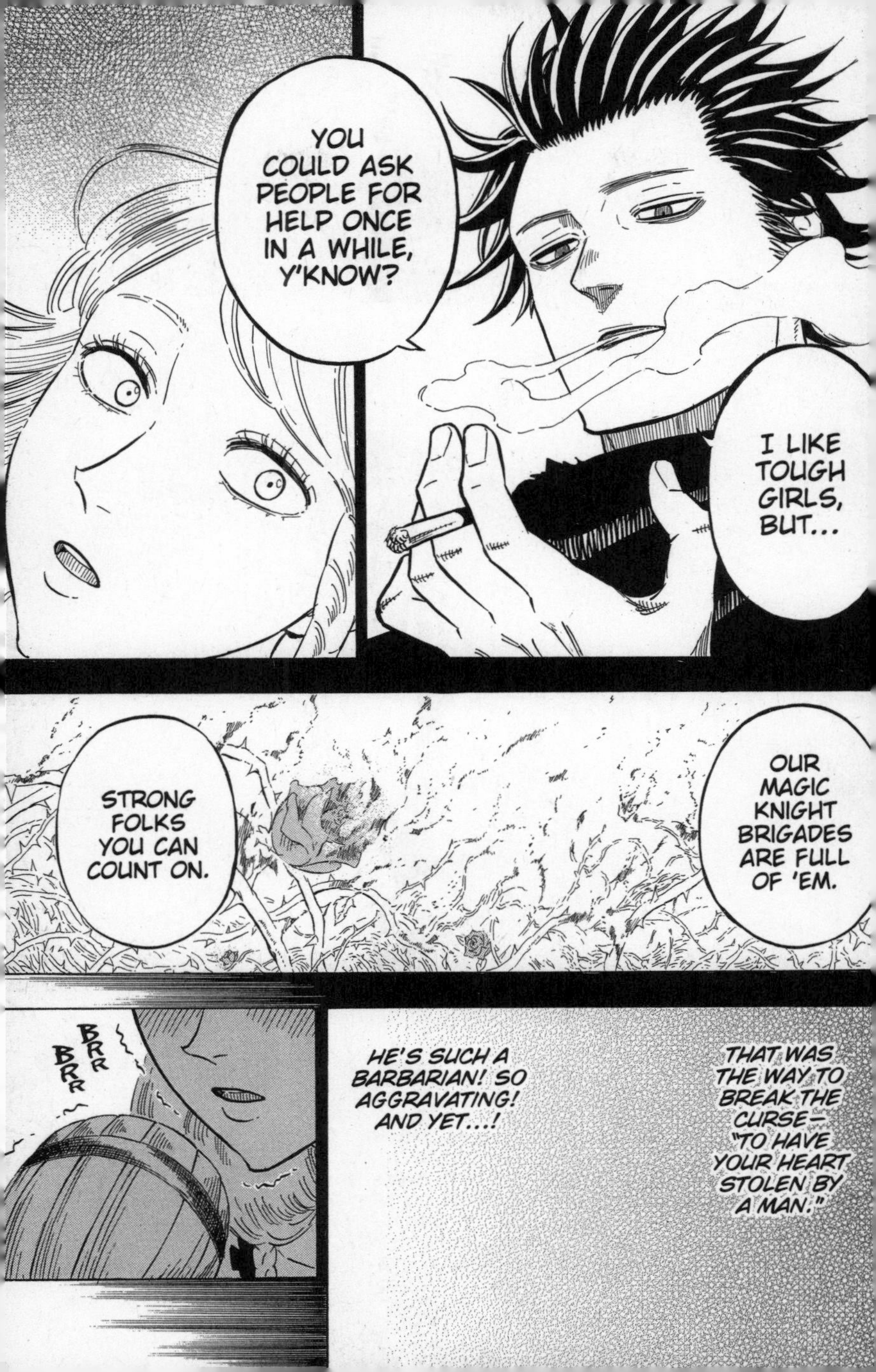
I LIKE TOUGH GIRLS, BUT...
YOU COULD ASK PEOPLE FOR HELP ONCE IN A WHILE, Y'KNOW?
OUR MAGIC KNIGHT BRIGADES ARE FULL OF 'EM.
STRONG FOLKS YOU CAN COUNT ON.
THAT WAS THE WAY TO BREAK THE CURSE— "TO HAVE YOUR HEART STOLEN BY A MAN."
HE'S SUCH A BARBARIAN! SO AGGRAVATING! AND YET...!
BRR BRR

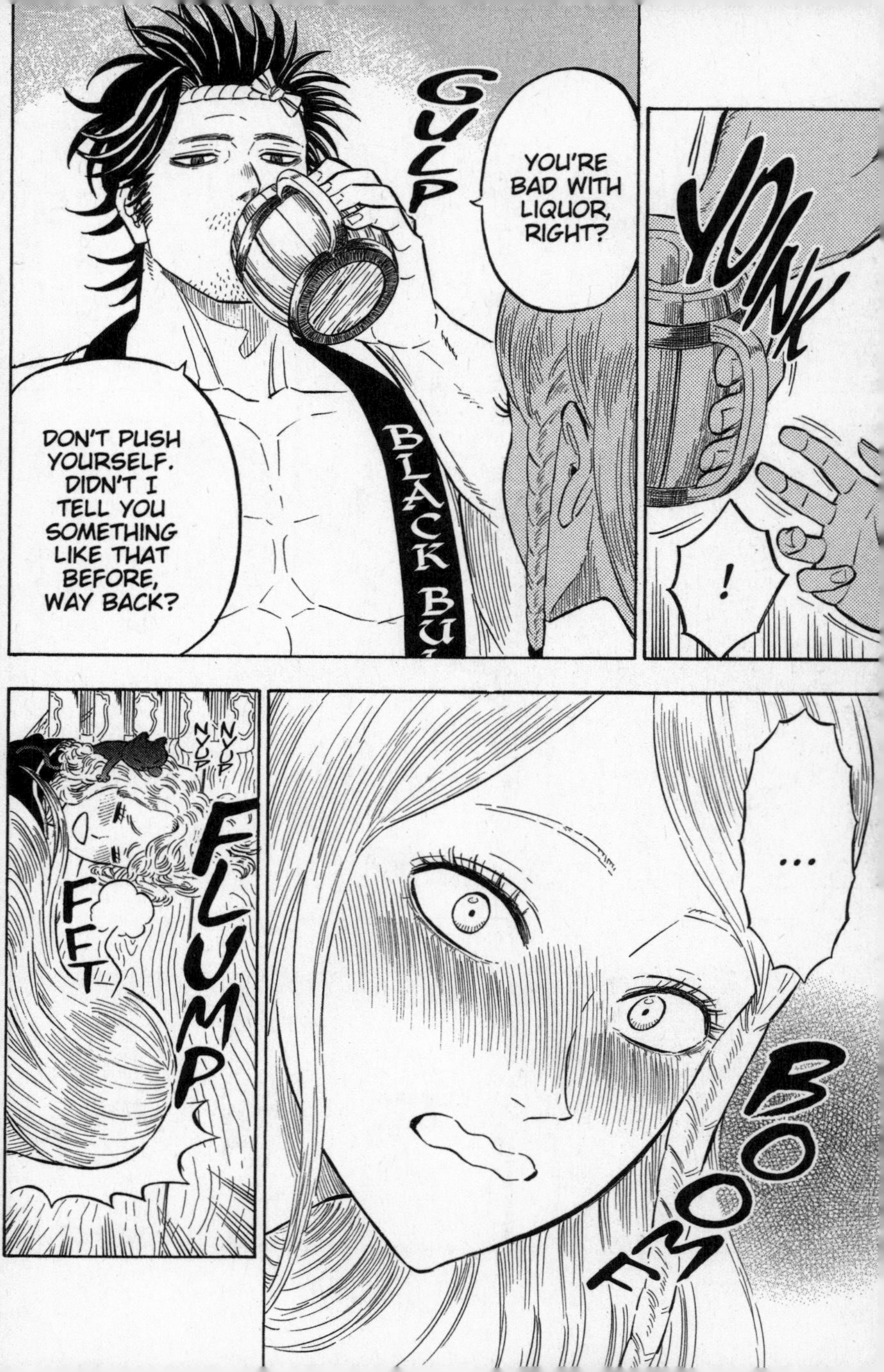
YOINK
!
GULP
YOU'RE BAD WITH LIQUOR, RIGHT?
DON'T PUSH YOURSELF. DIDN'T I TELL YOU SOMETHING LIKE THAT BEFORE, WAY BACK?
BLACK BU
...
BOOM
NYUP NYUP
FLUMP
FFFT

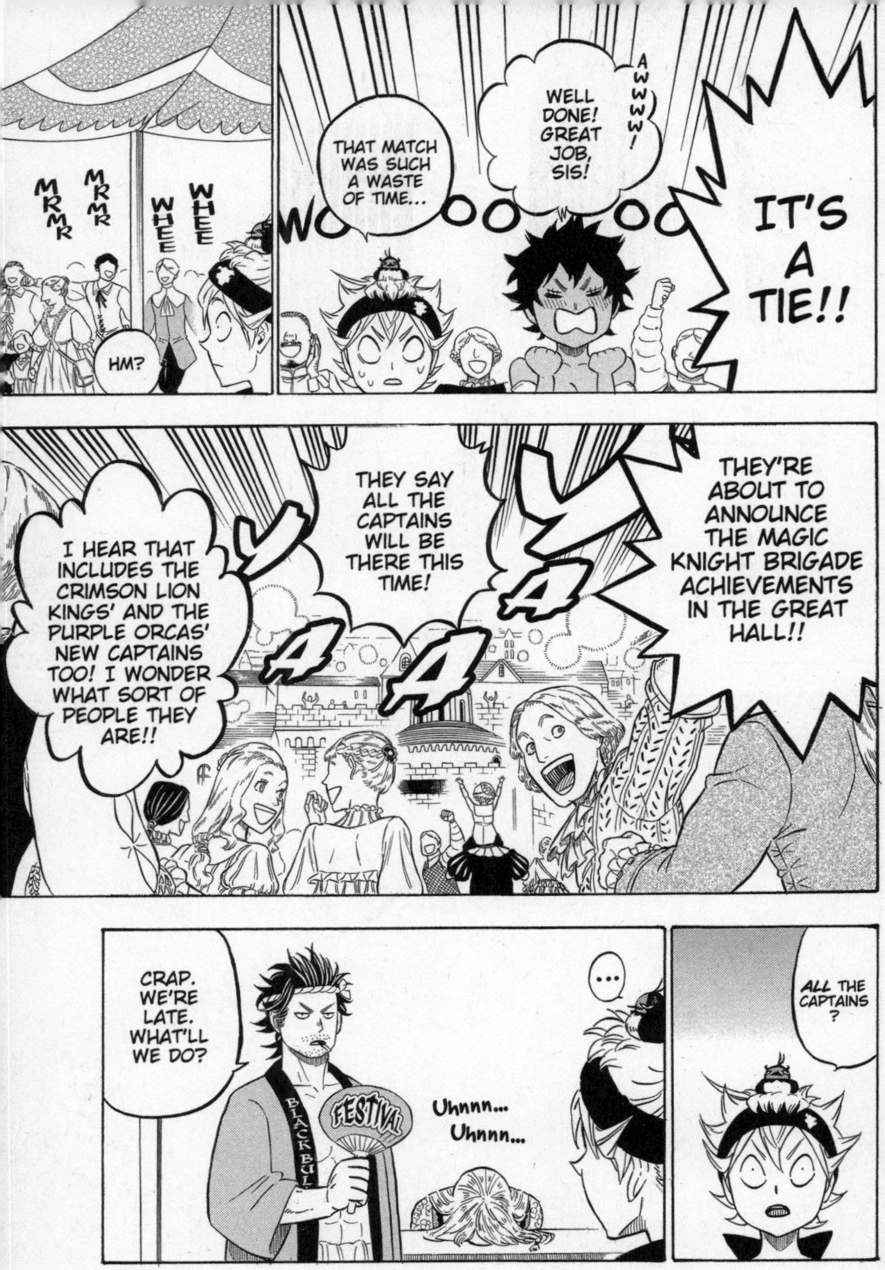
IT'S A TIE!!
AWWWW!
WELL DONE! GREAT JOB, SIS!
WOOOOOO
THAT MATCH WAS SUCH A WASTE OF TIME...
WHEE
WHEE
MRMR
MRMR
HM?
THEY'RE ABOUT TO ANNOUNCE THE MAGIC KNIGHT BRIGADE ACHIEVEMENTS IN THE GREAT HALL!!
YAAA
THEY SAY ALL THE CAPTAINS WILL BE THERE THIS TIME!
I HEAR THAT INCLUDES THE CRIMSON LION KINGS' AND THE PURPLE ORCAS' NEW CAPTAINS TOO! I WONDER WHAT SORT OF PEOPLE THEY ARE!!
ALL THE CAPTAINS?
...
Uhnnn...
Uhnnn...
CRAP. WE'RE LATE. WHAT'LL WE DO?
FESTIVAL
BLACK BUL

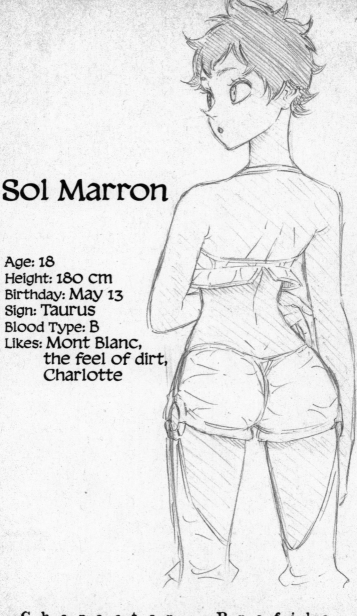

Sol Marron

Age: 18
Height: 180 cm
Birthday: May 13
Sign: Taurus
Blood Type: B
Likes: Mont Blanc,
     the feel of dirt,
     Charlotte

Character Profile

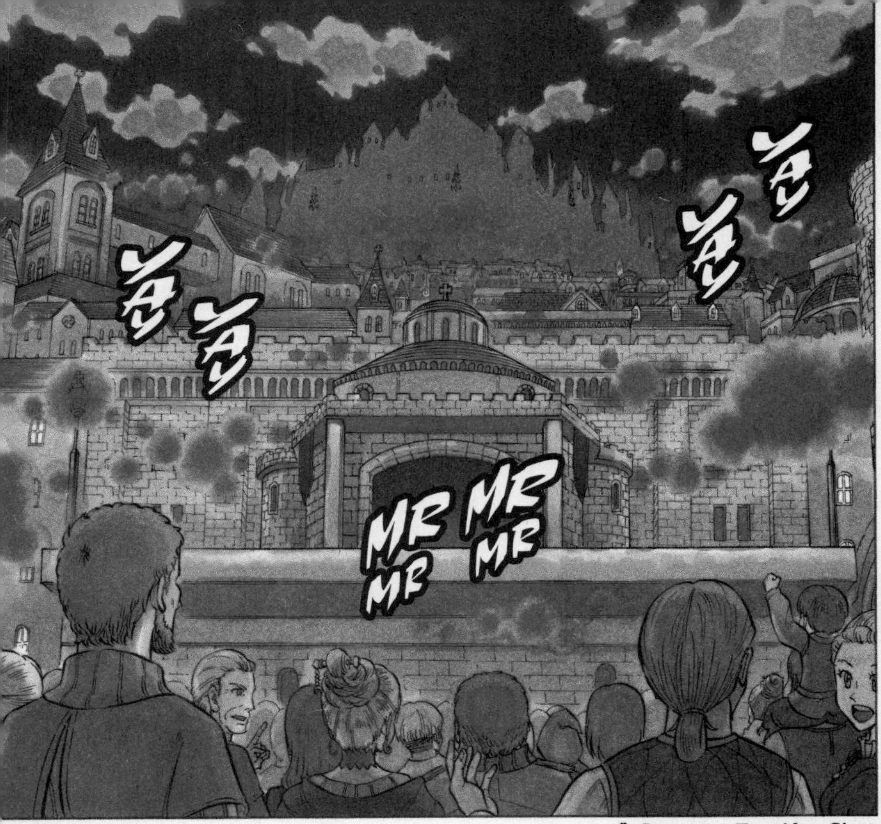
YAY
YAY
MR MR
MR MR
YAY
YAY

Page 105: Two New Stars

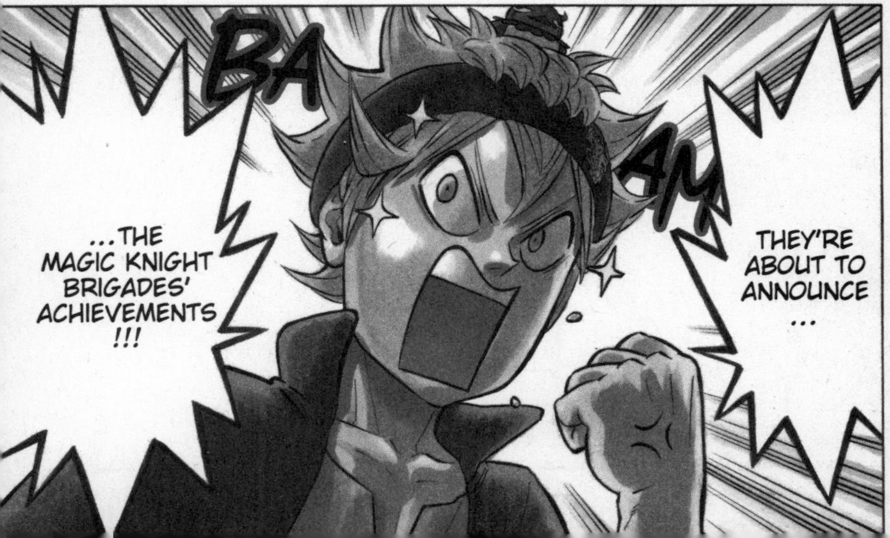
BA
AM
THEY'RE ABOUT TO ANNOUNCE ...
...THE MAGIC KNIGHT BRIGADES' ACHIEVEMENTS !!!

Page 105: Two New Stars

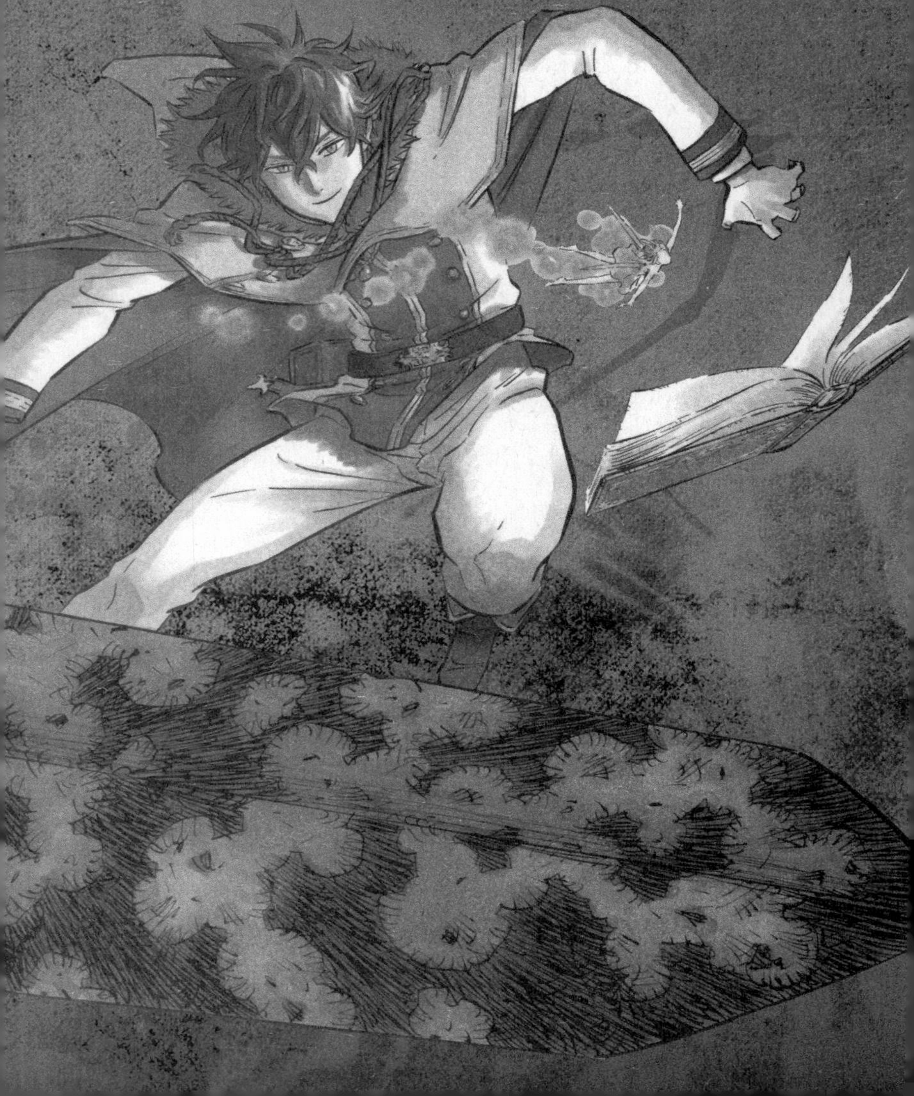

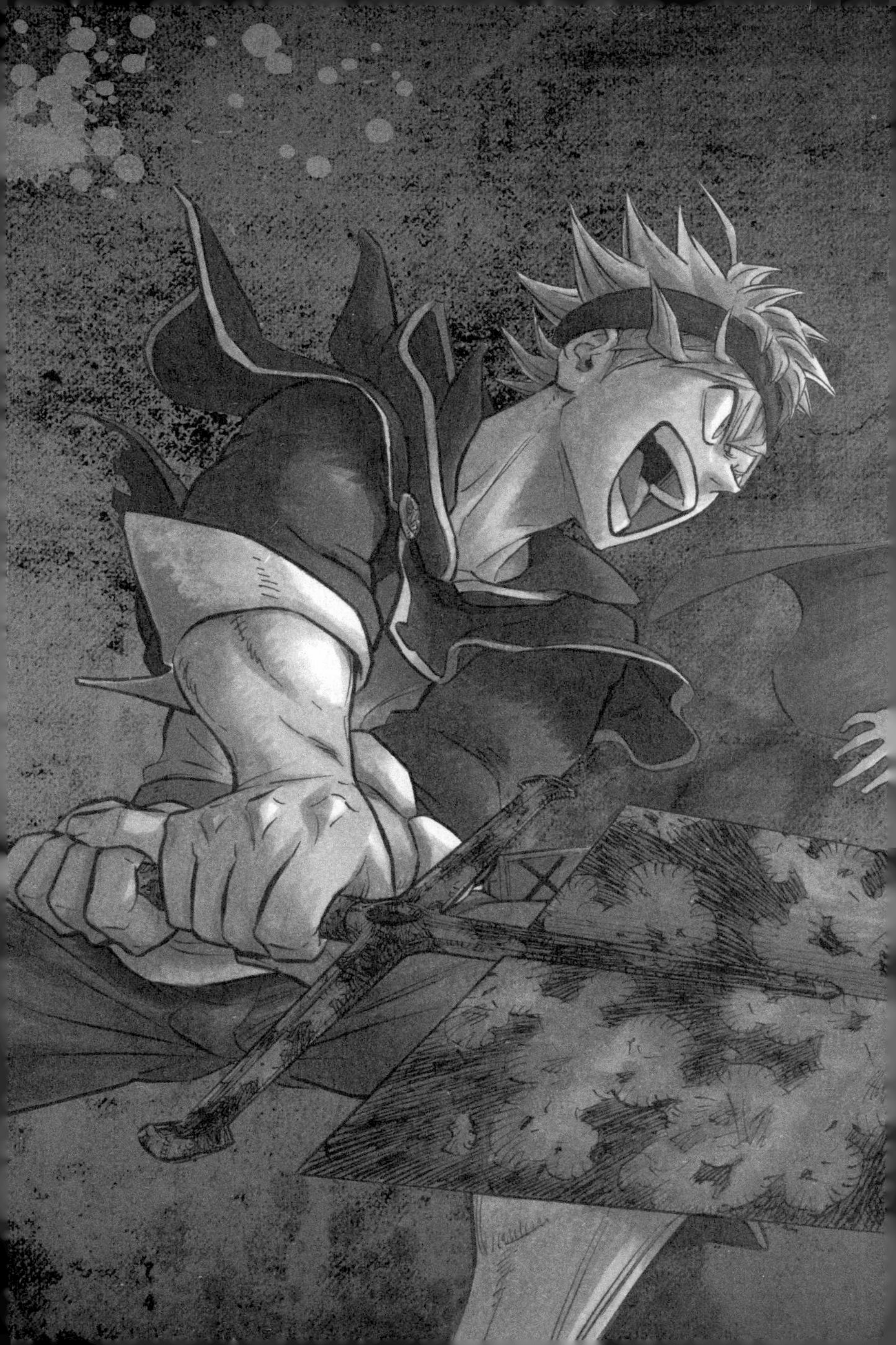

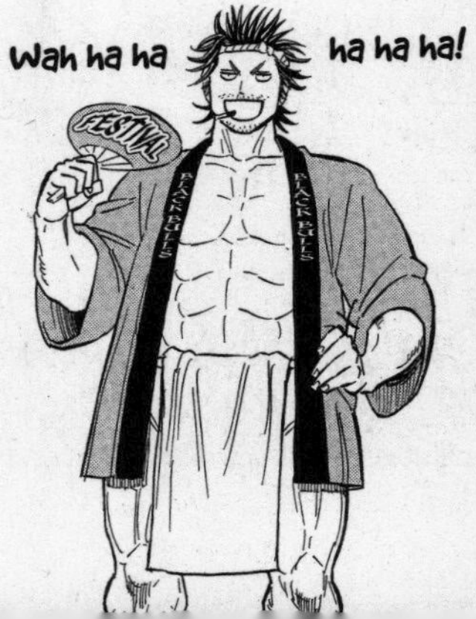
Wah ha ha
ha ha ha!
FESTIVAL
BLACK BULLS
BLACK BULLS

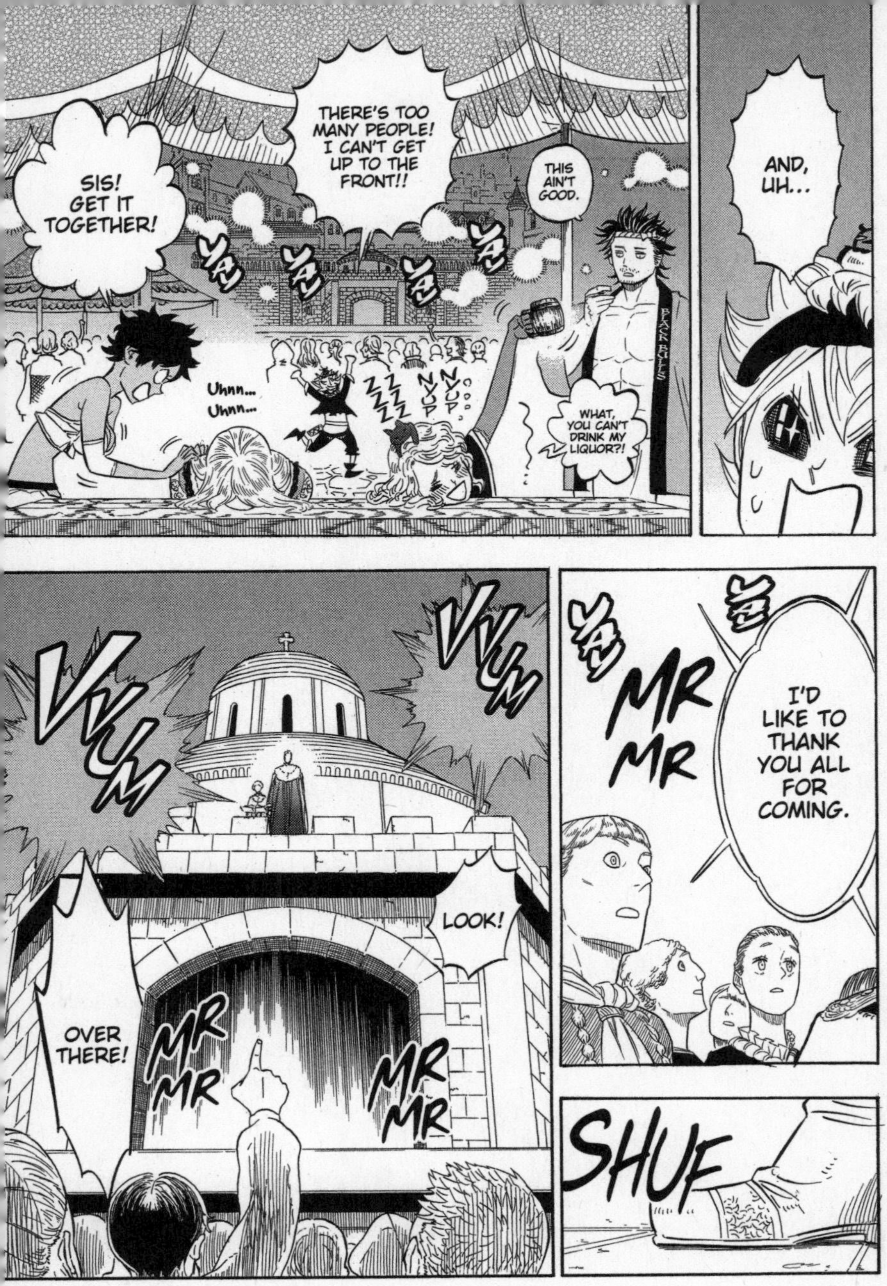
AND, UH...
THIS AIN'T GOOD.
THERE'S TOO MANY PEOPLE! I CAN'T GET UP TO THE FRONT!!
SIS! GET IT TOGETHER!
YAY YAY YAY YAY YAY
WHAT, YOU CAN'T DRINK MY LIQUOR?!
NYUP NYUP
ZZZZ ZZZZ
Uhnn... Uhnn...
YAY YAY
MR MR
I'D LIKE TO THANK YOU ALL FOR COMING.
SHUF
VVUM
VVUM
LOOK!
MR MR
MR MR
OVER THERE!

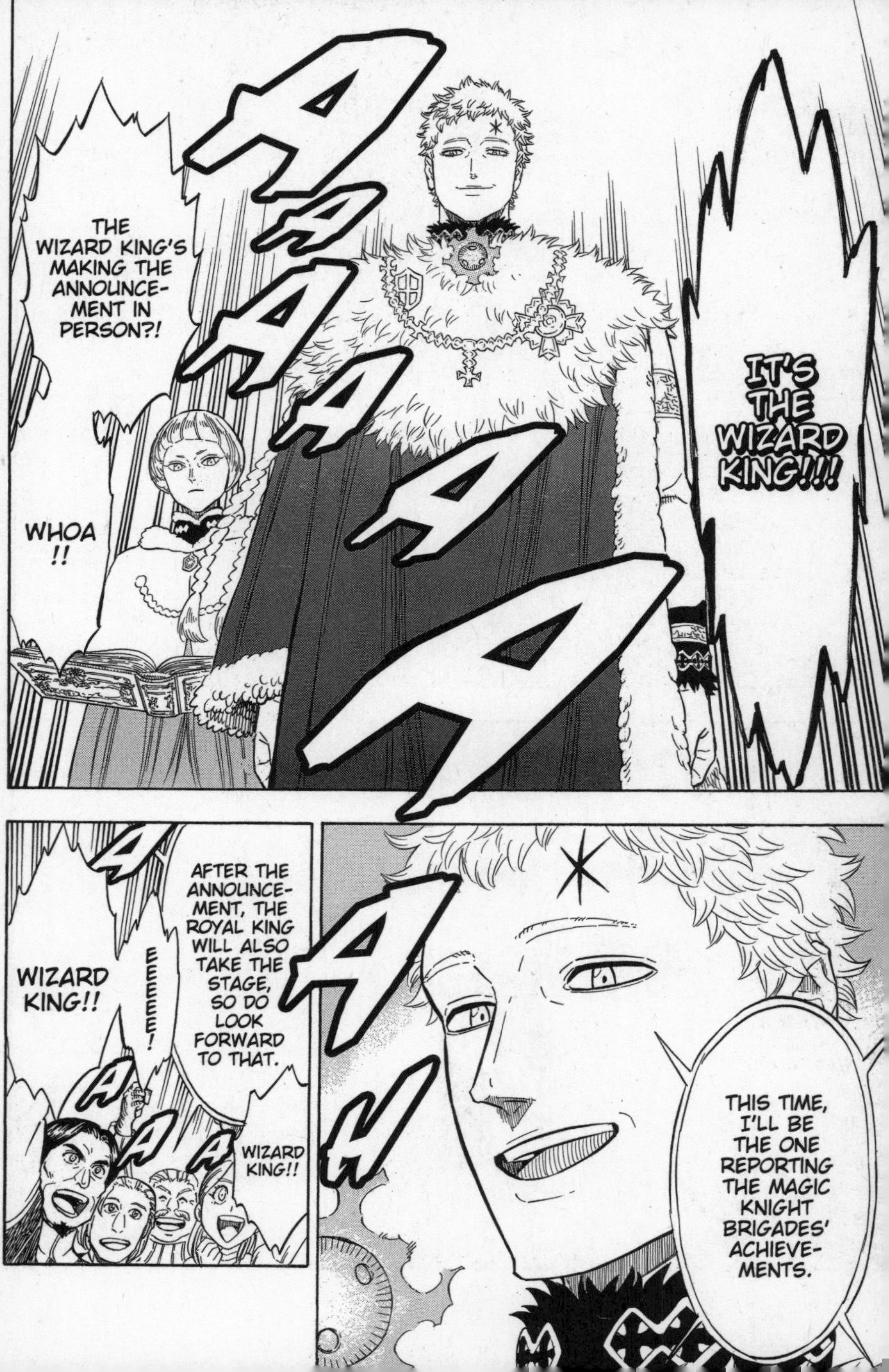
IT'S THE WIZARD KING!!!
AAAAAA
THE WIZARD KING'S MAKING THE ANNOUNCE-MENT IN PERSON?!
WHOA!!
AAH
THIS TIME, I'LL BE THE ONE REPORTING THE MAGIC KNIGHT BRIGADES' ACHIEVE-MENTS.
AFTER THE ANNOUNCE-MENT, THE ROYAL KING WILL ALSO TAKE THE STAGE, SO DO LOOK FORWARD TO THAT.
EEEEEE!
WIZARD KING!!
AAA
WIZARD KING!!

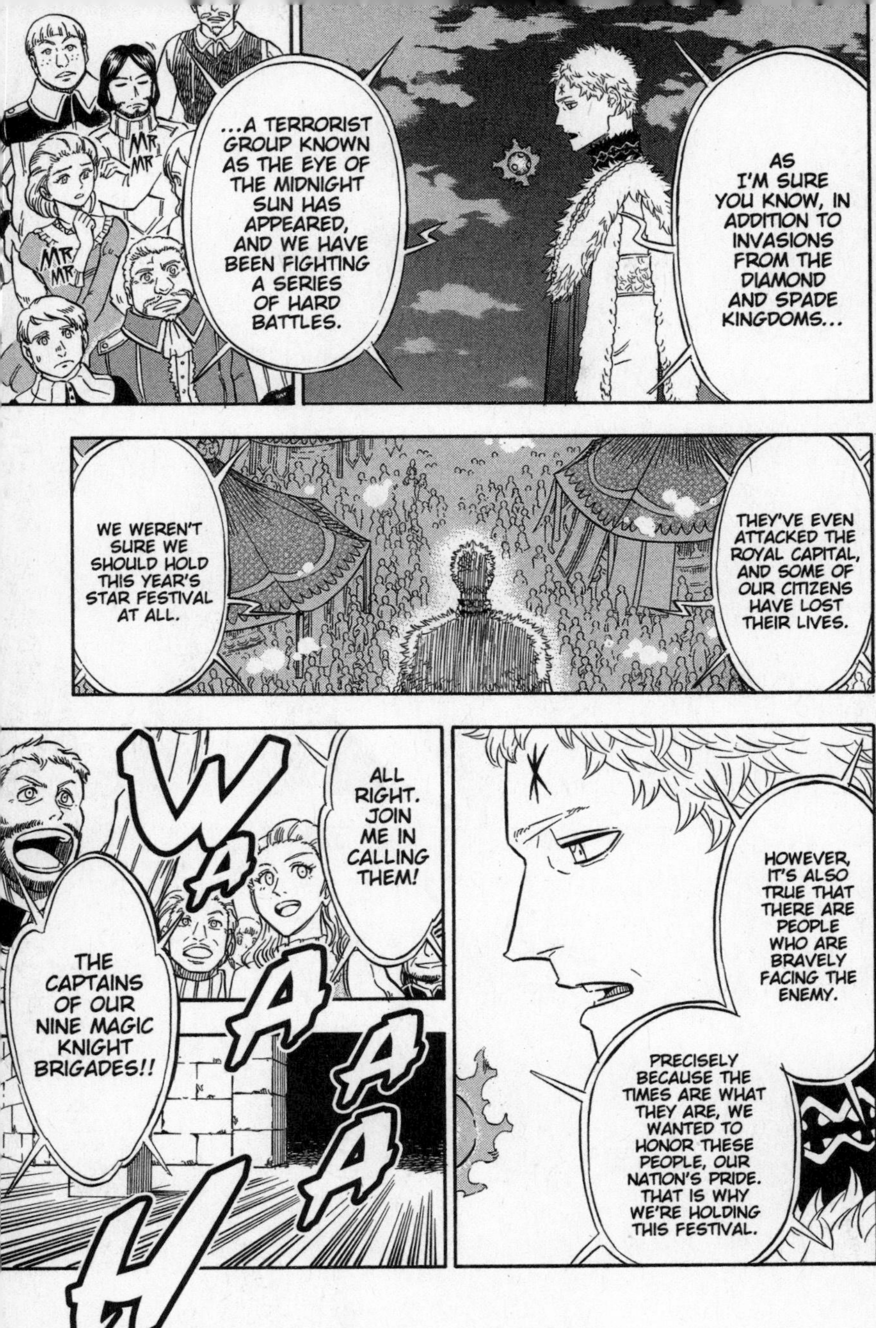
AS I'M SURE YOU KNOW, IN ADDITION TO INVASIONS FROM THE DIAMOND AND SPADE KINGDOMS...
...A TERRORIST GROUP KNOWN AS THE EYE OF THE MIDNIGHT SUN HAS APPEARED, AND WE HAVE BEEN FIGHTING A SERIES OF HARD BATTLES.
MR MR
MR MR
THEY'VE EVEN ATTACKED THE ROYAL CAPITAL, AND SOME OF OUR CITIZENS HAVE LOST THEIR LIVES.
WE WEREN'T SURE WE SHOULD HOLD THIS YEAR'S STAR FESTIVAL AT ALL.
HOWEVER, IT'S ALSO TRUE THAT THERE ARE PEOPLE WHO ARE BRAVELY FACING THE ENEMY.
PRECISELY BECAUSE THE TIMES ARE WHAT THEY ARE, WE WANTED TO HONOR THESE PEOPLE, OUR NATION'S PRIDE. THAT IS WHY WE'RE HOLDING THIS FESTIVAL.
ALL RIGHT. JOIN ME IN CALLING THEM!
THE CAPTAINS OF OUR NINE MAGIC KNIGHT BRIGADES!!
WAAAAH

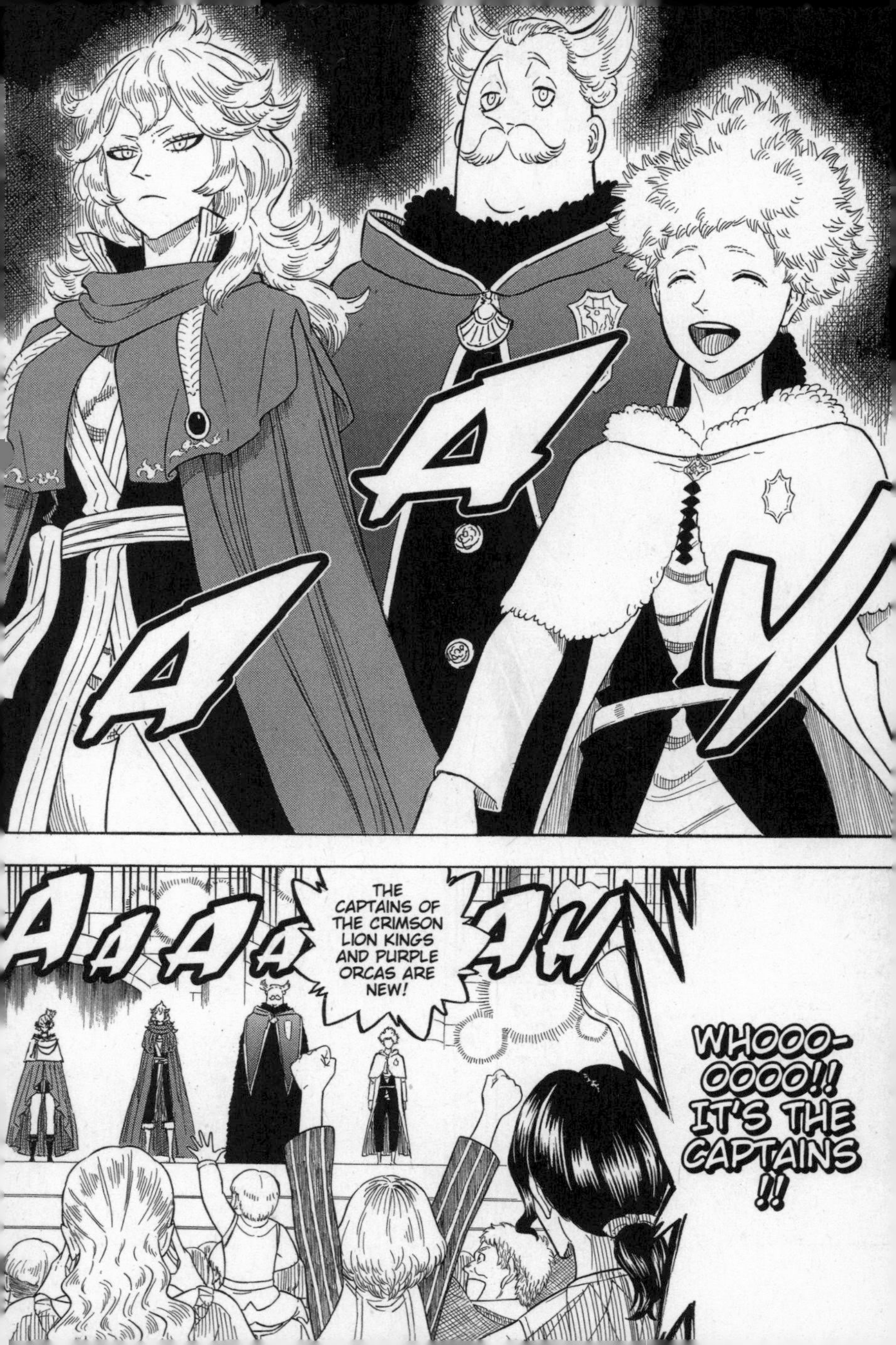
AAY
AAAAAH
THE CAPTAINS OF THE CRIMSON LION KINGS AND PURPLE ORCAS ARE NEW!
WHOOOO-OOOOO!! IT'S THE CAPTAINS!!

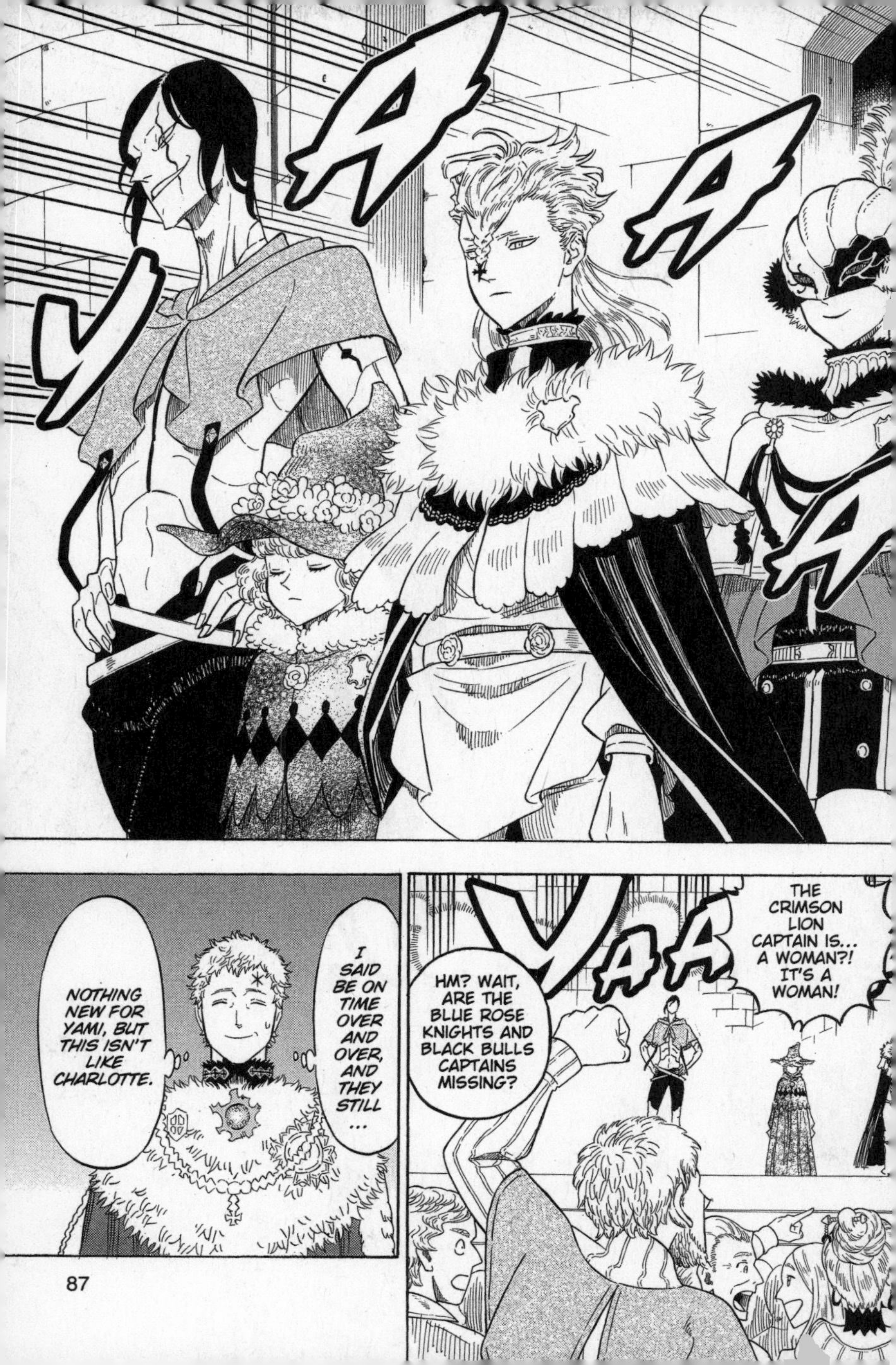
YAAA
YAA
THE CRIMSON LION CAPTAIN IS... A WOMAN?! IT'S A WOMAN!
HM? WAIT, ARE THE BLUE ROSE KNIGHTS AND BLACK BULLS CAPTAINS MISSING?
I SAID BE ON TIME OVER AND OVER, AND THEY STILL ...
NOTHING NEW FOR YAMI, BUT THIS ISN'T LIKE CHARLOTTE.

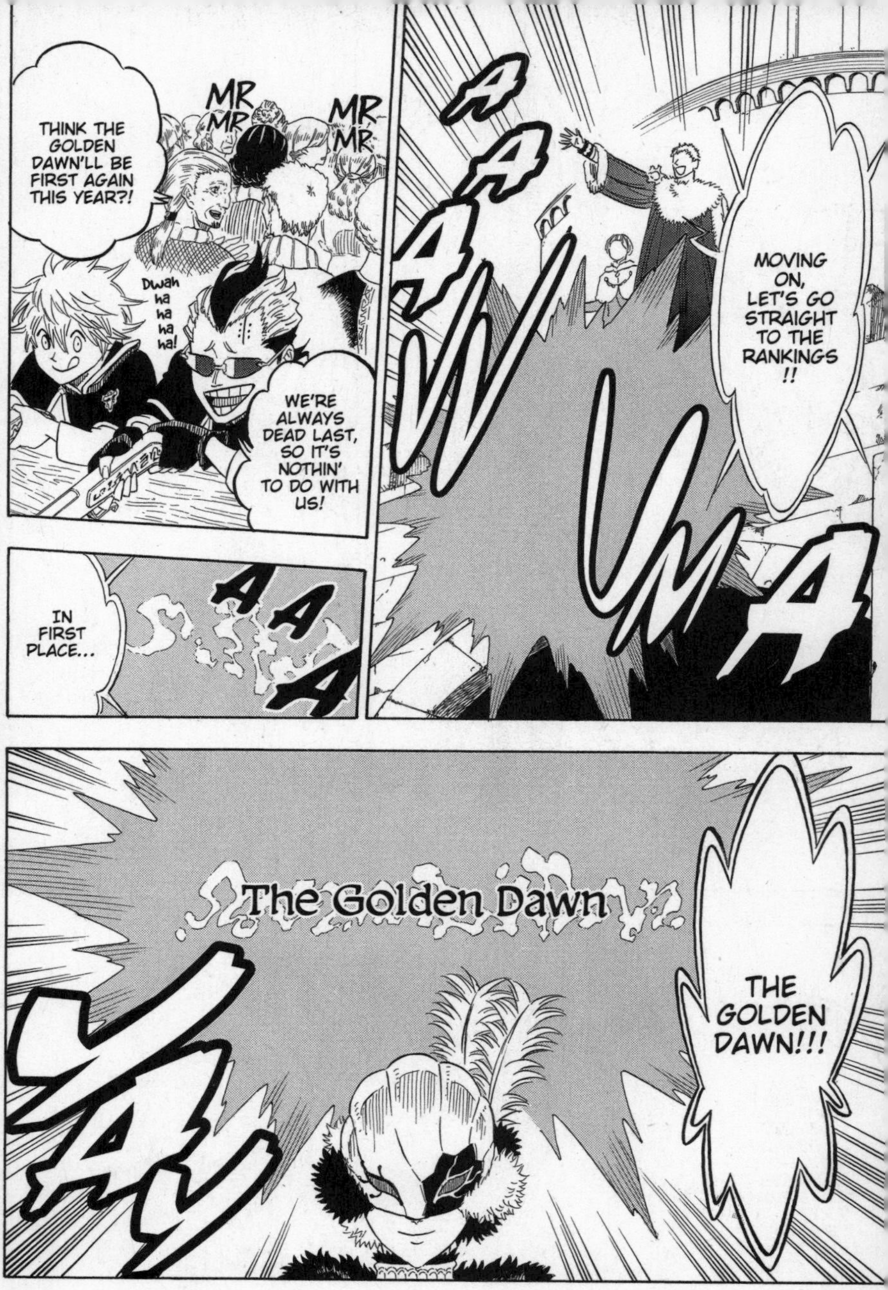
MOVING ON, LET'S GO STRAIGHT TO THE RANKINGS!!
AAAAWWAAA
MR MR
MR MR
THINK THE GOLDEN DAWN'LL BE FIRST AGAIN THIS YEAR?!
Dwah ha ha ha ha!
WE'RE ALWAYS DEAD LAST, SO IT'S NOTHIN' TO DO WITH US!
IN FIRST PLACE...
AAAA
THE GOLDEN DAWN!!!
The Golden Dawn
YAY

...

THAT'S A BIG JUMP OVER THEIR RECORD OF 96 FROM LAST YEAR!!

THE GOLDEN DAWN IS UNSTOPPABLE!!

Spade Kingdom invaders defeated	3
Diamond Kingdom invaders defeated	3
Spade Kingdom officer defeated	5
Magic bandits group defeated	1
Spade Kingdom spy unit defeated	3
Dungeon explored and rare items discovered	
Dungeon fully explored	
Royal capital defended	
Eye of the Midnight Sun executive defeated	
Eye of the Midnight Sun combat personnel defeated	
Forbidden magic user captured	
Magical substances broker arrested	
Illegal magic items importer arrested	
Kiten defended	

WITH AN INCREDIBLE 125 STARS!!!

NOW LET'S HAVE THE MEMBER WHO MADE THE BIGGEST CONTRIBUTION TO THAT STAR RECORD TAKE THE STAGE.

THE GOLDEN DAWN ONCE AGAIN SHOWED US SOME FANTASTIC FEATS THIS TERM!

THAT'S AMAZING!!

THE GOLDEN DAWN'S ON A WHOLE OTHER LEVEL!

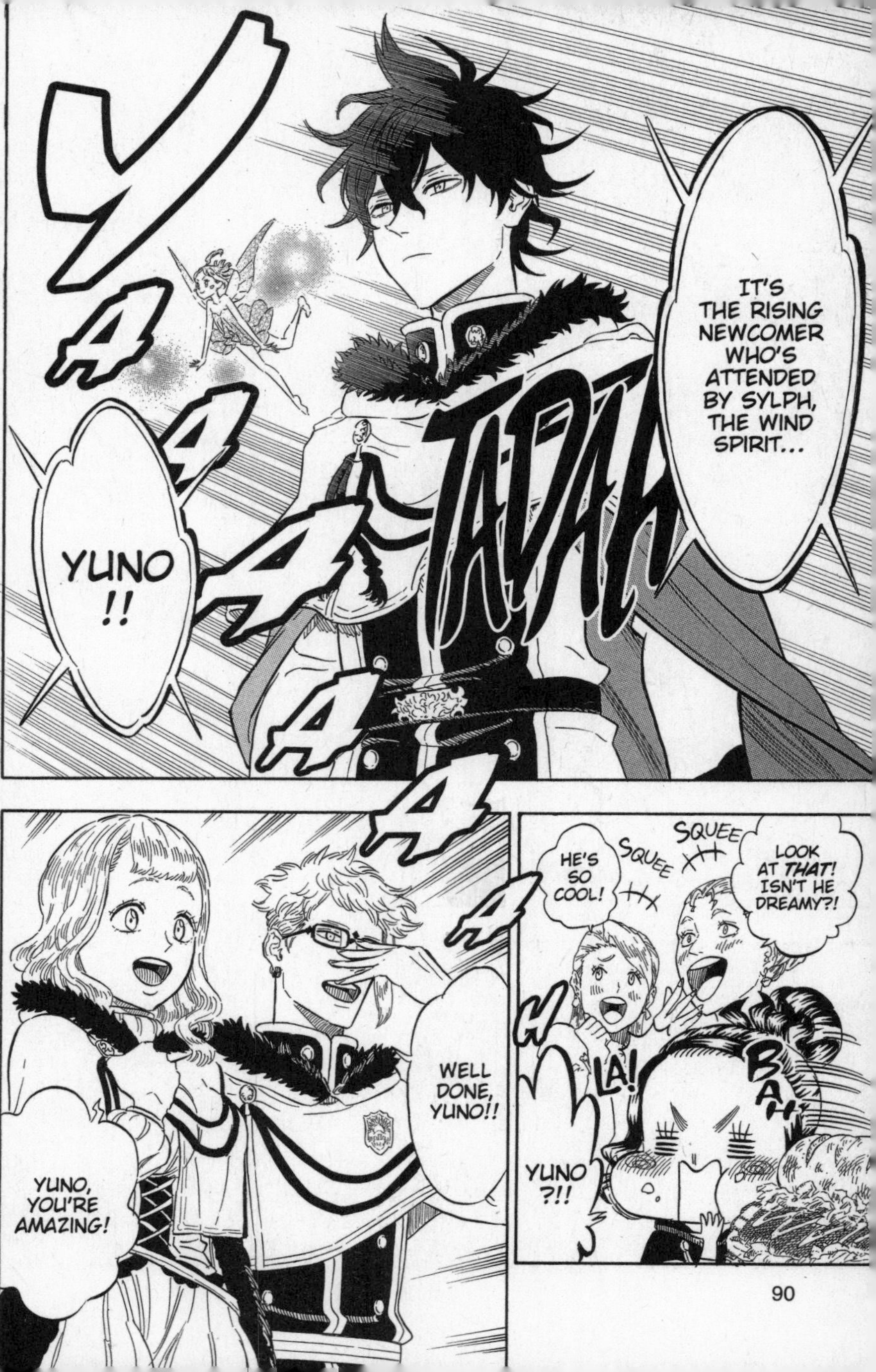

IT'S THE RISING NEWCOMER WHO'S ATTENDED BY SYLPH, THE WIND SPIRIT...
TA-DAH
YUNO !!
LOOK AT *THAT*! ISN'T HE DREAMY?!
SQUEE
SQUEE
HE'S SO COOL!
BAH
LA!
YUNO ?!!
WELL DONE, YUNO!!
YUNO, YOU'RE AMAZING!

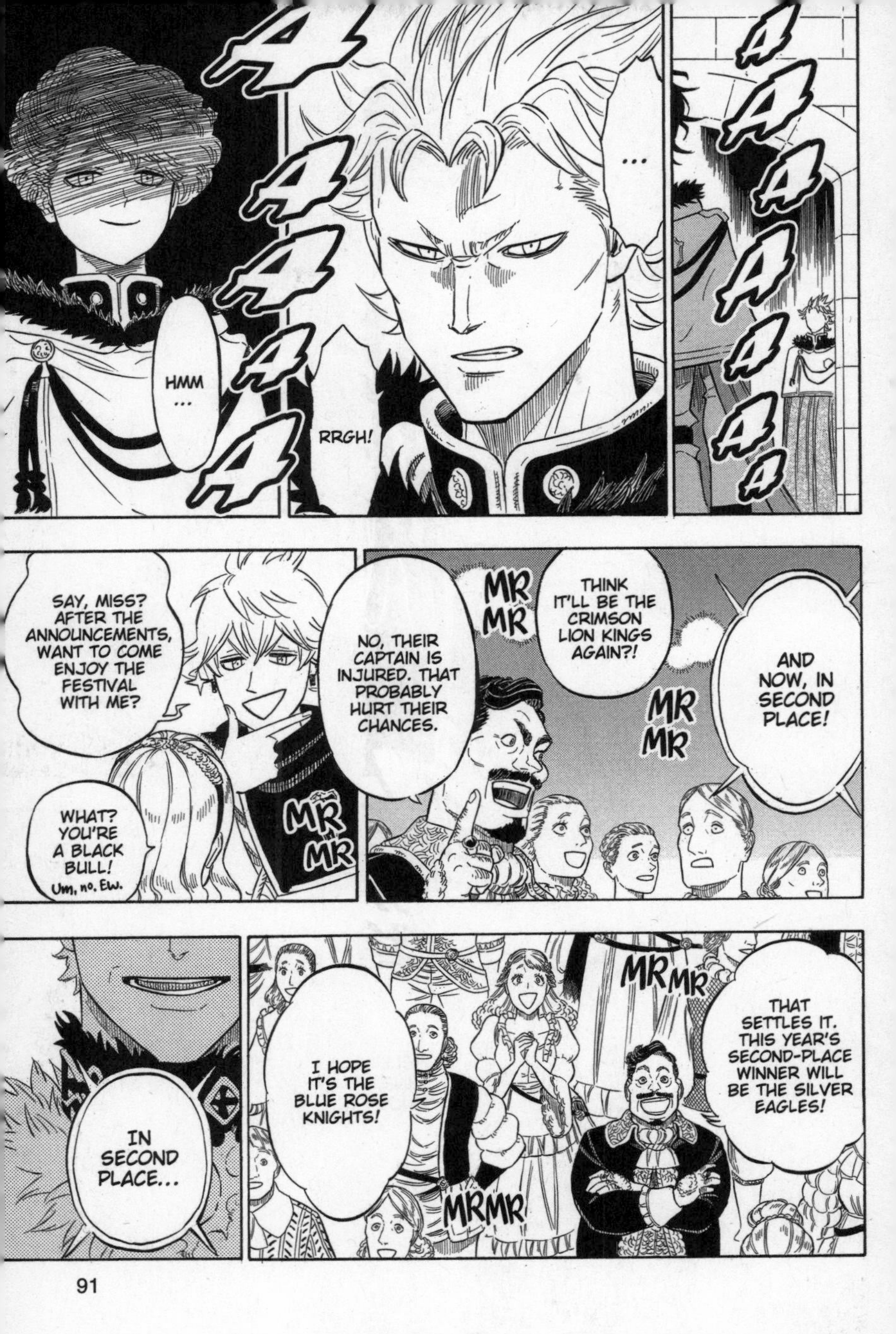
...
RRGH!
HMM ...
AND NOW, IN SECOND PLACE!
THINK IT'LL BE THE CRIMSON LION KINGS AGAIN?!
MR MR
MR MR
NO, THEIR CAPTAIN IS INJURED. THAT PROBABLY HURT THEIR CHANCES.
SAY, MISS? AFTER THE ANNOUNCEMENTS, WANT TO COME ENJOY THE FESTIVAL WITH ME?
MR MR
WHAT? YOU'RE A BLACK BULL!
Um, no. Ew.
THAT SETTLES IT. THIS YEAR'S SECOND-PLACE WINNER WILL BE THE SILVER EAGLES!
MR MR
I HOPE IT'S THE BLUE ROSE KNIGHTS!
MRMR
IN SECOND PLACE...

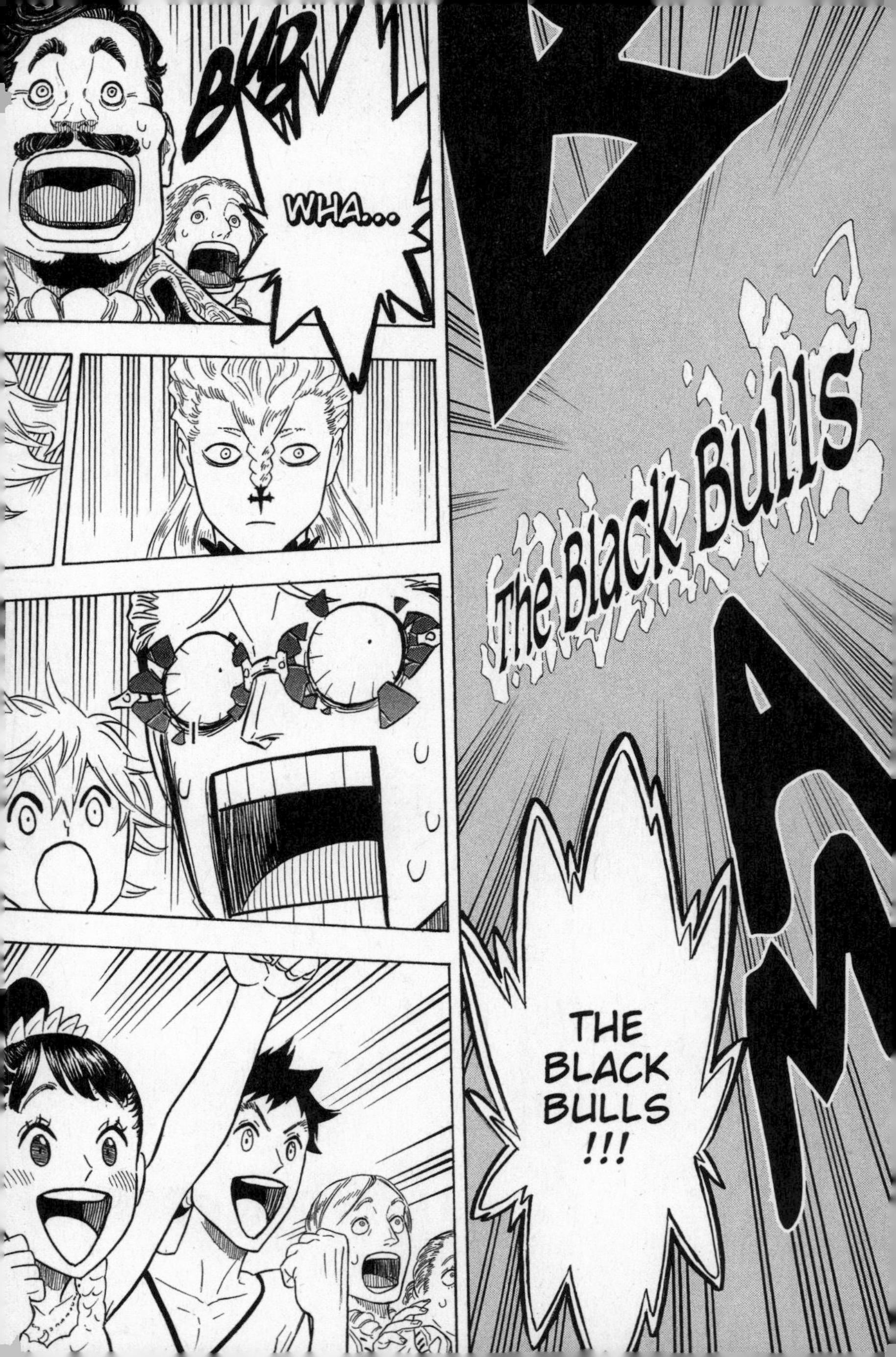
The Black Bulls
THE BLACK BULLS!!!
WHA...

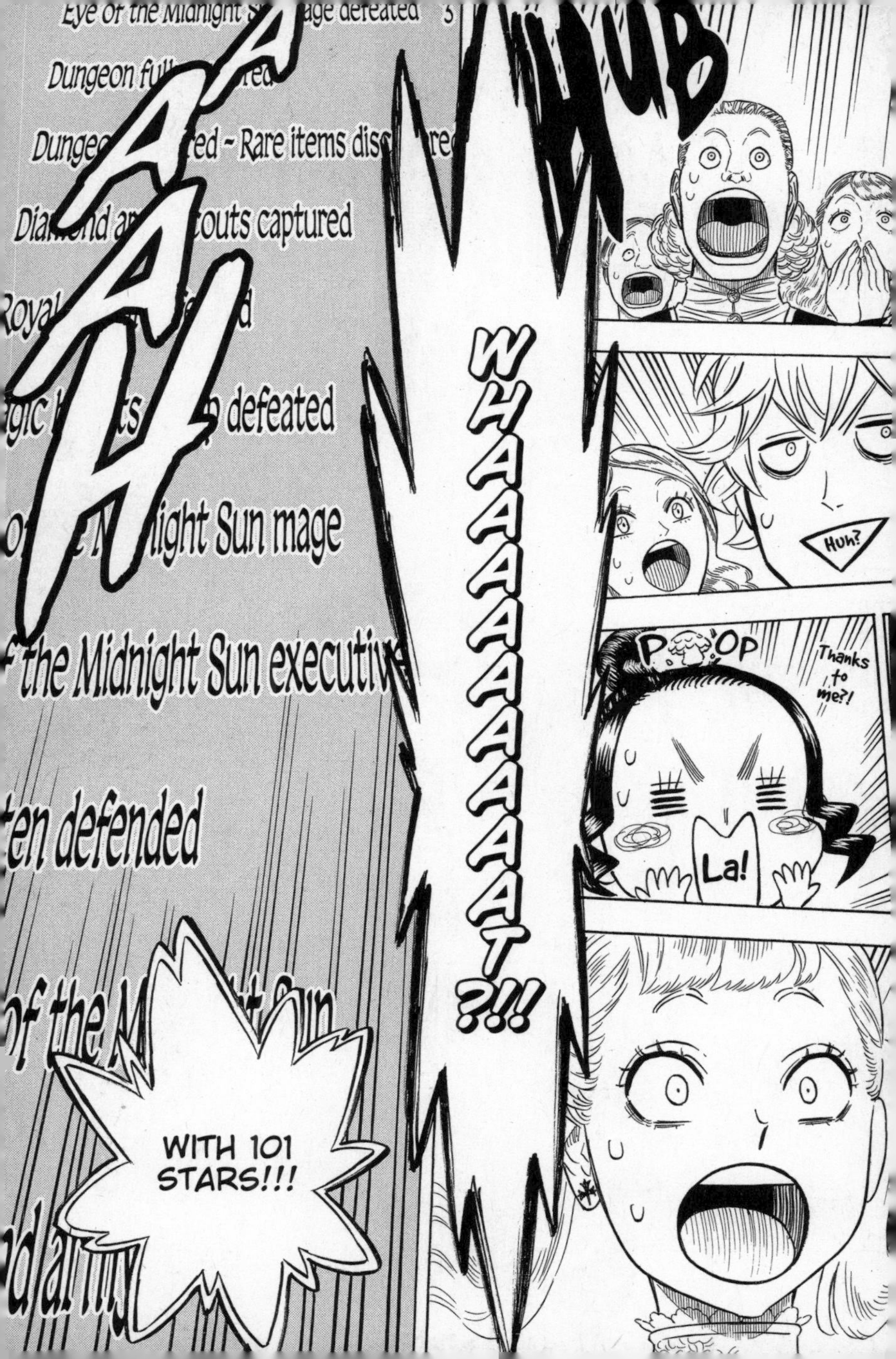
WHAAAAAAAAAT?!!
Huh?
P OP
Thanks to me?!
La!
WITH 101 STARS!!!

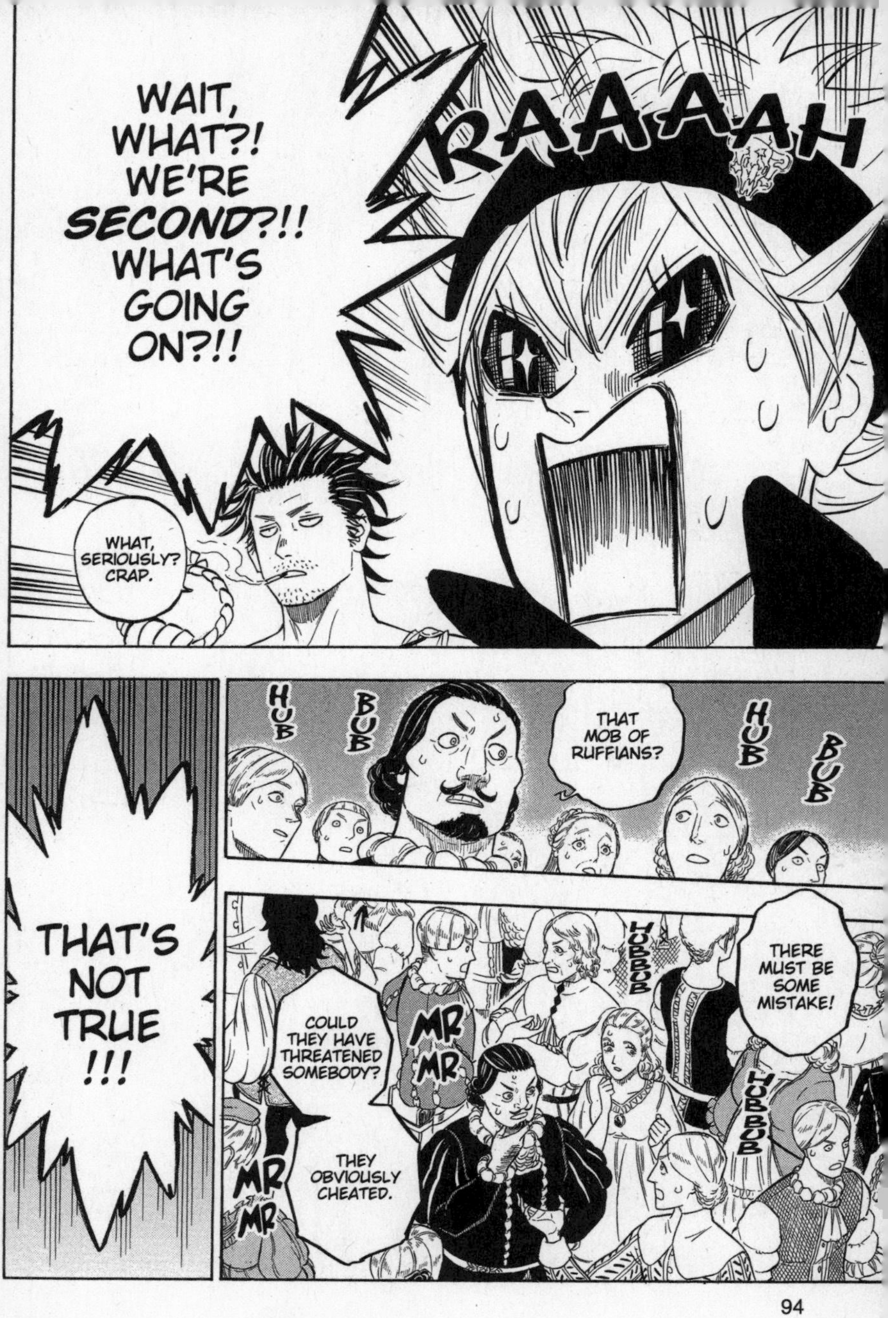
RAAAAH
WAIT, WHAT?! WE'RE SECOND?!! WHAT'S GOING ON?!!
WHAT, SERIOUSLY? CRAP.
HUB BUB
THAT MOB OF RUFFIANS?
HUB BUB
THERE MUST BE SOME MISTAKE!
HUBBUB
HUBBUB
COULD THEY HAVE THREATENED SOMEBODY?
MR MR
THEY OBVIOUSLY CHEATED.
MR MR
THAT'S NOT TRUE!!!

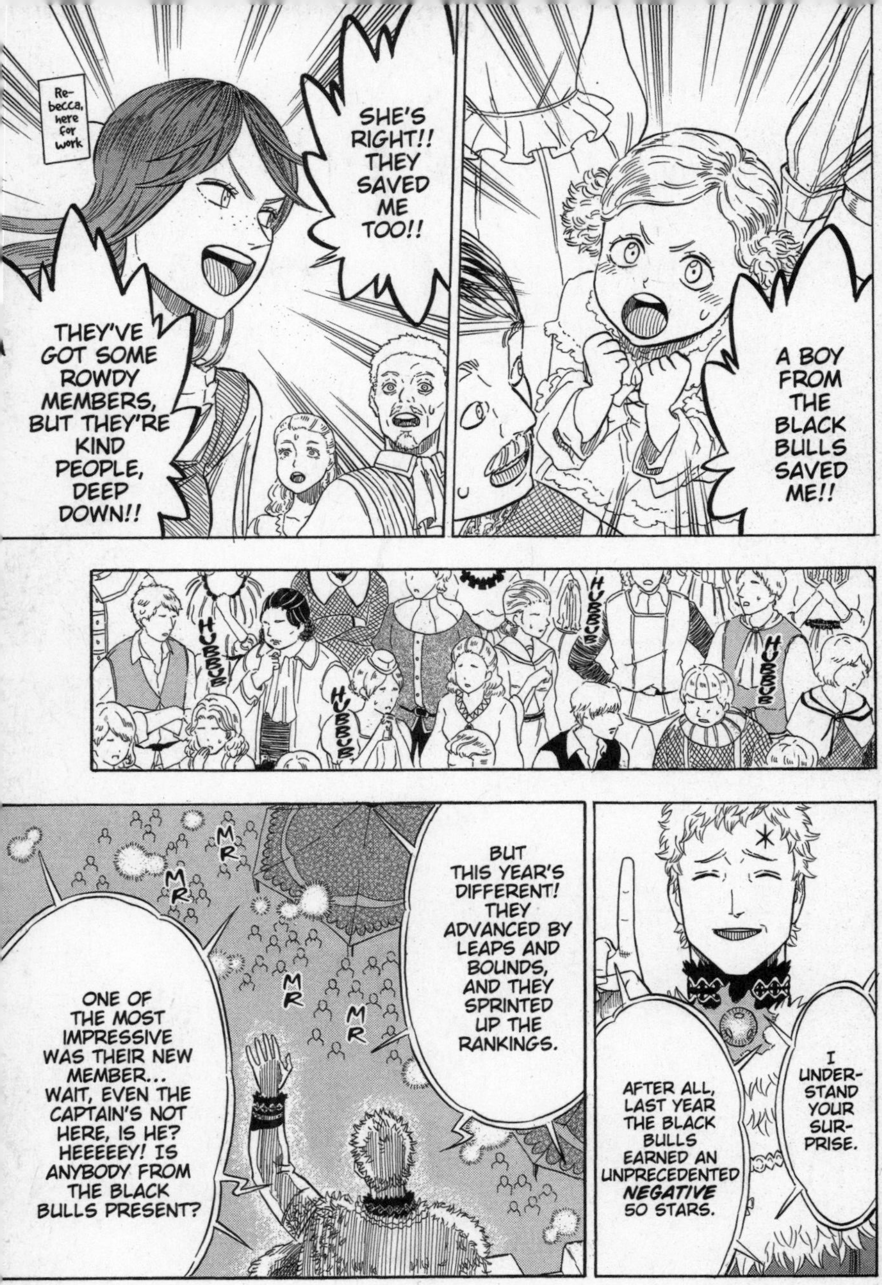
A BOY FROM THE BLACK BULLS SAVED ME!!
SHE'S RIGHT!! THEY SAVED ME TOO!!
Re-becca, here for work
THEY'VE GOT SOME ROWDY MEMBERS, BUT THEY'RE KIND PEOPLE, DEEP DOWN!!
HUBBUB
HUBBUB
HUBBUB
HUBBUB
I UNDER-STAND YOUR SUR-PRISE.
AFTER ALL, LAST YEAR THE BLACK BULLS EARNED AN UNPRECEDENTED *NEGATIVE* 50 STARS.
BUT THIS YEAR'S DIFFERENT! THEY ADVANCED BY LEAPS AND BOUNDS, AND THEY SPRINTED UP THE RANKINGS.
MR
MR
MR
MR
ONE OF THE MOST IMPRESSIVE WAS THEIR NEW MEMBER... WAIT, EVEN THE CAPTAIN'S NOT HERE, IS HE? HEEEEEY! IS ANYBODY FROM THE BLACK BULLS PRESENT?

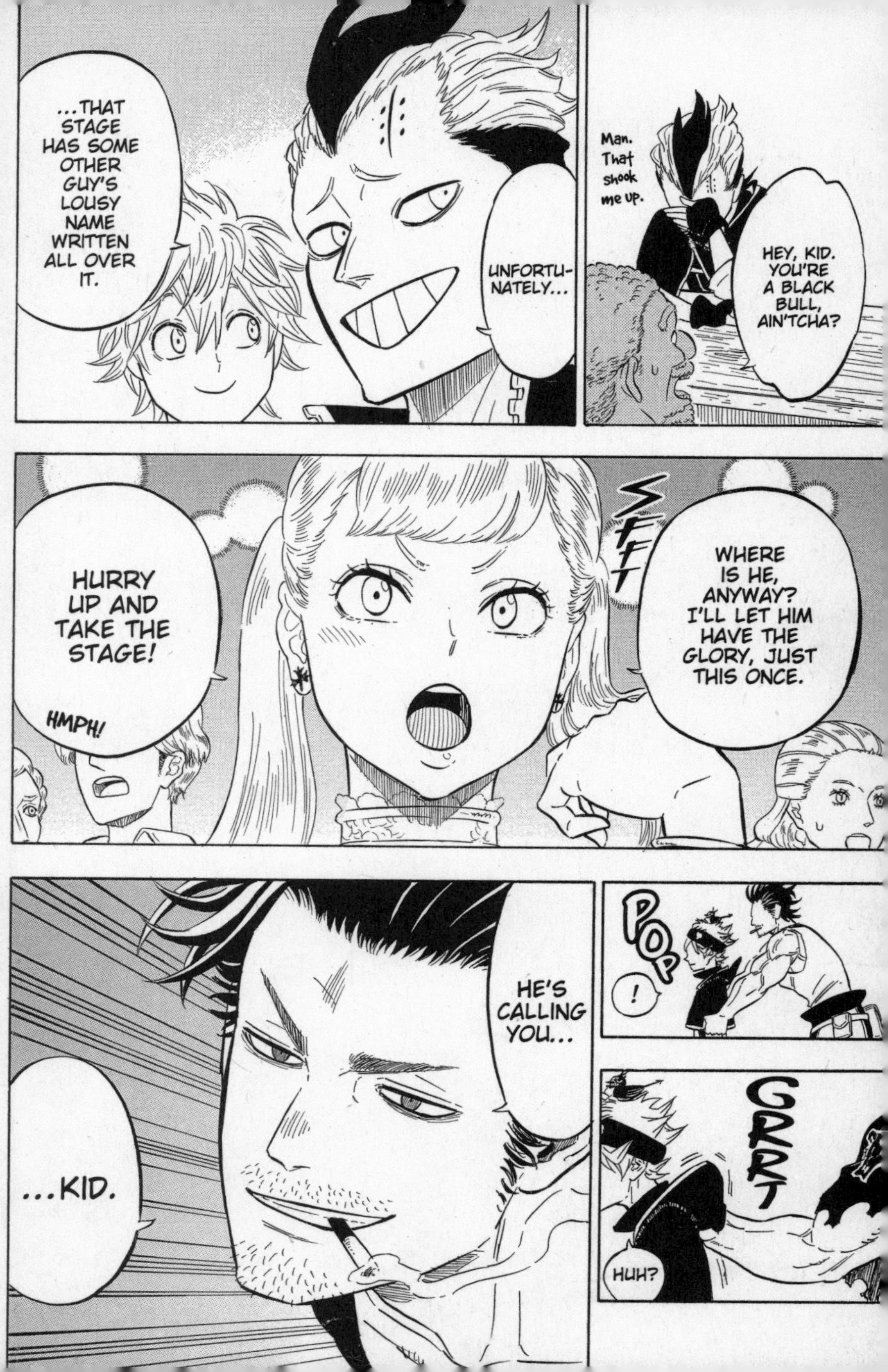
HEY, KID. YOU'RE A BLACK BULL, AIN'TCHA?
Man. That shook me up.
UNFORTU-NATELY...
...THAT STAGE HAS SOME OTHER GUY'S LOUSY NAME WRITTEN ALL OVER IT.
WHERE IS HE, ANYWAY? I'LL LET HIM HAVE THE GLORY, JUST THIS ONCE.
SFFT
HURRY UP AND TAKE THE STAGE!
HMPH!
POP
!
GRRRT
HUH?
HE'S CALLING YOU...
...KID.

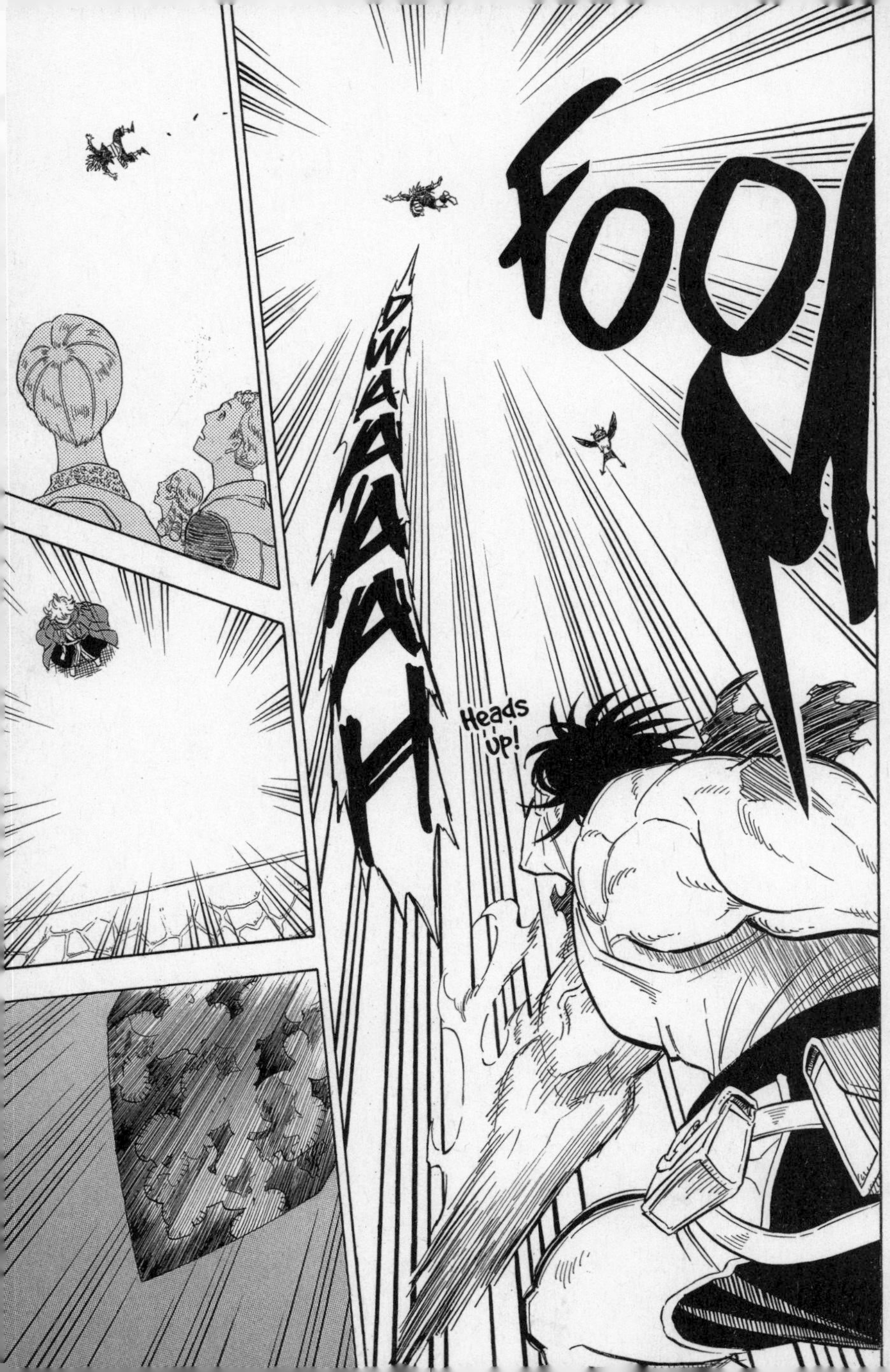
FOOM
DWAAAAAAH
Heads up!

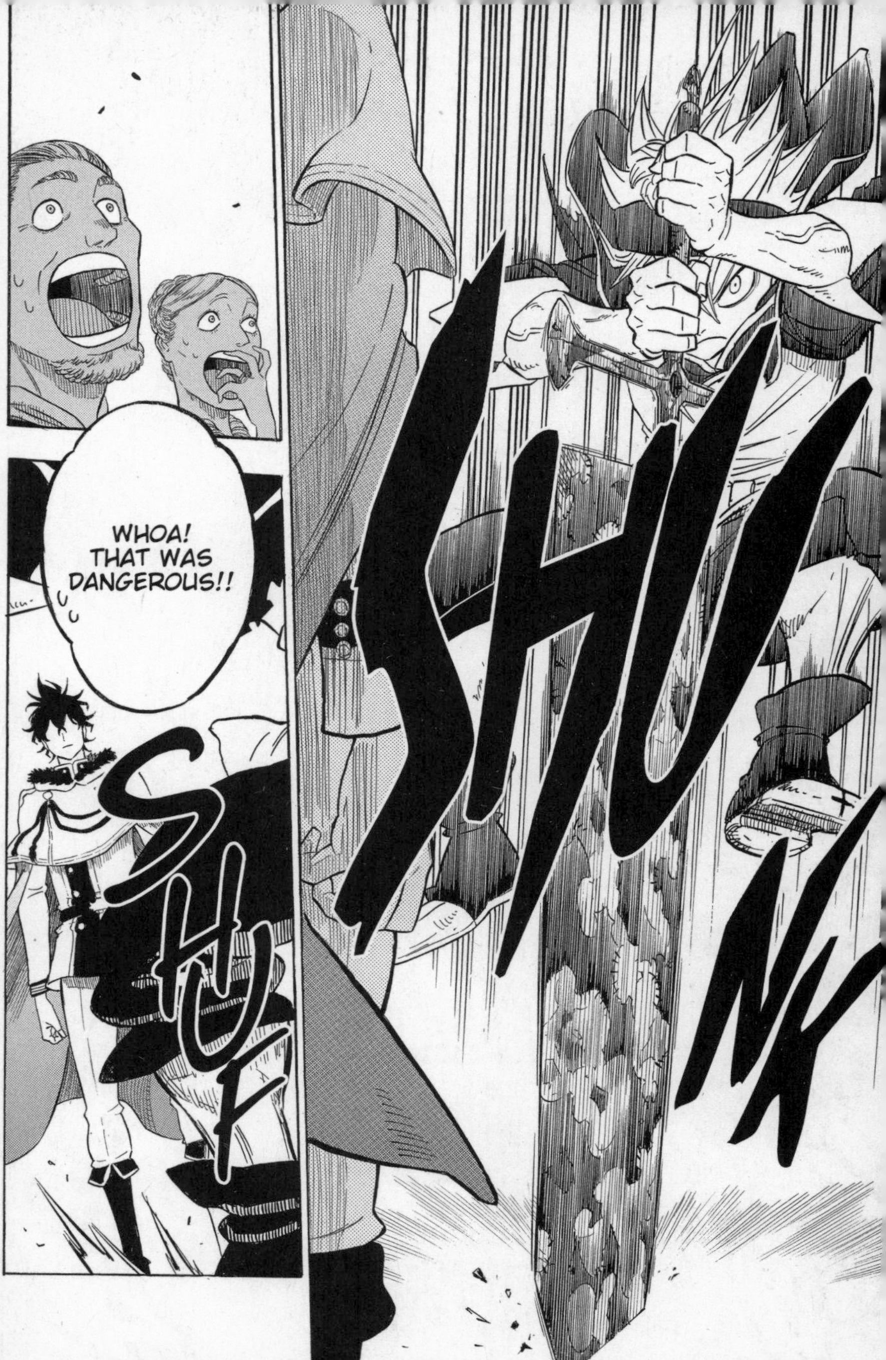
SHUNK
WHOA! THAT WAS DANGEROUS!!
SHUF

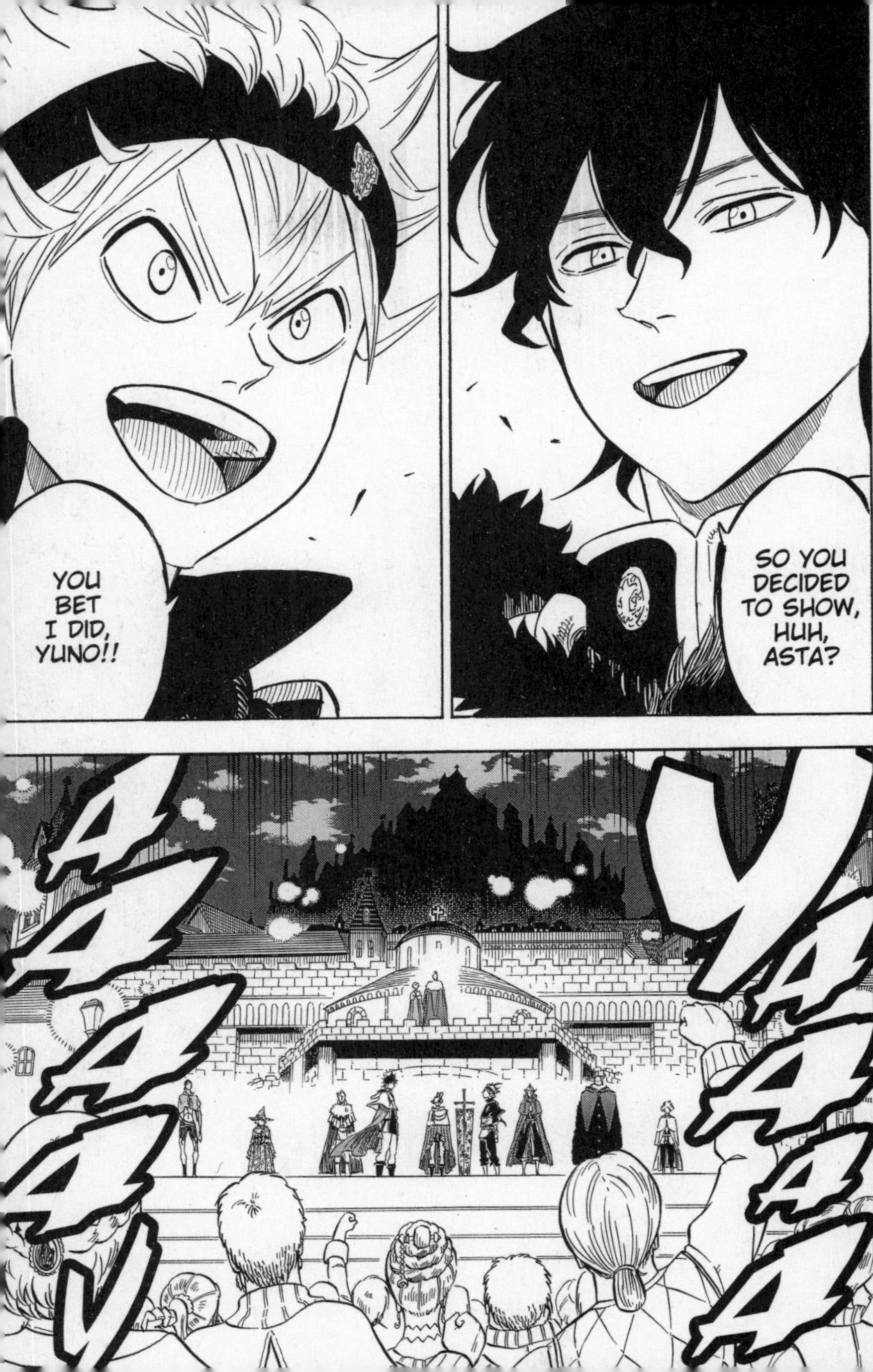
SO YOU DECIDED TO SHOW, HUH, ASTA?
YOU BET I DID, YUNO!!
YAAAAA

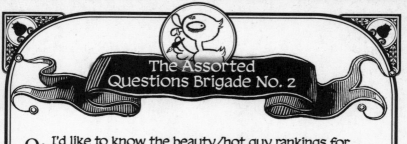

The Assorted Questions Brigade No. 2

Q: I'd like to know the beauty/hot guy rankings for *Black Clover*. (Yoshiko Sugisaki and others, Tokyo)

A: Here are the rankings according to the people of the Clover Kingdom and my personal preferences!!!

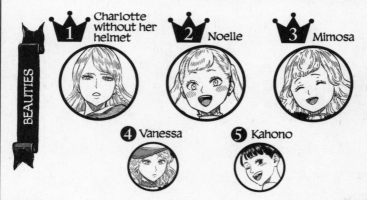

BEAUTIES

1 Charlotte without her helmet

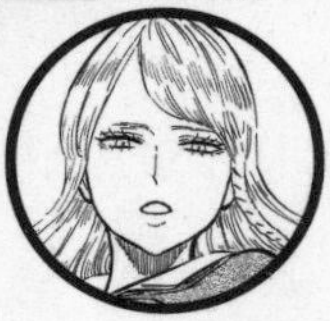

2 Noelle

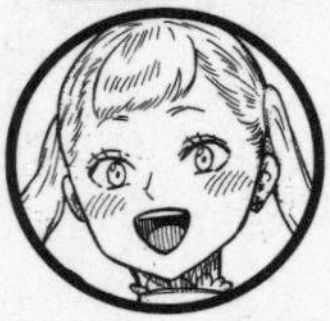

3 Mimosa

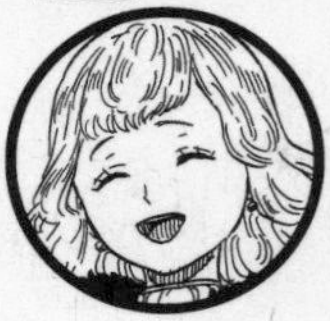

4 Vanessa

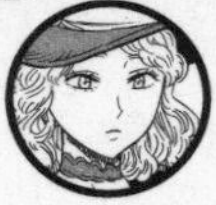

5 Kahono

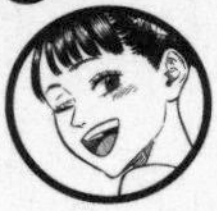

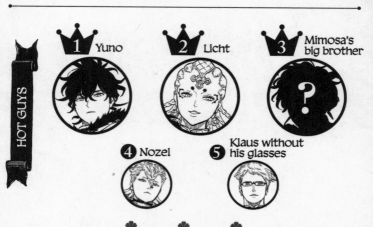

HOT GUYS

1 Yuno

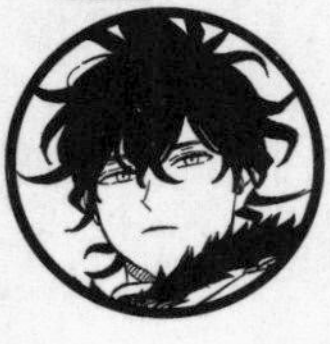

2 Licht

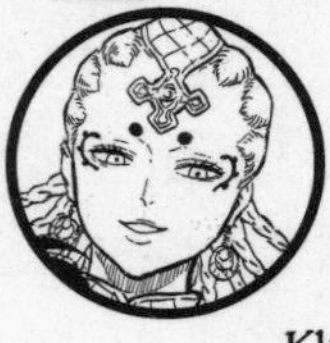

3 Mimosa's big brother

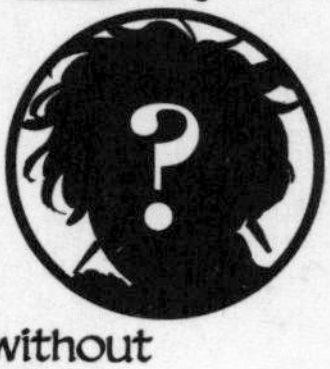
?

4 Nozel

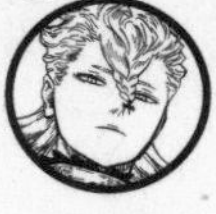

5 Klaus without his glasses

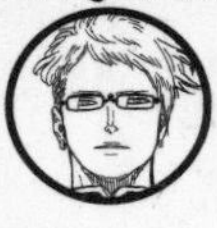

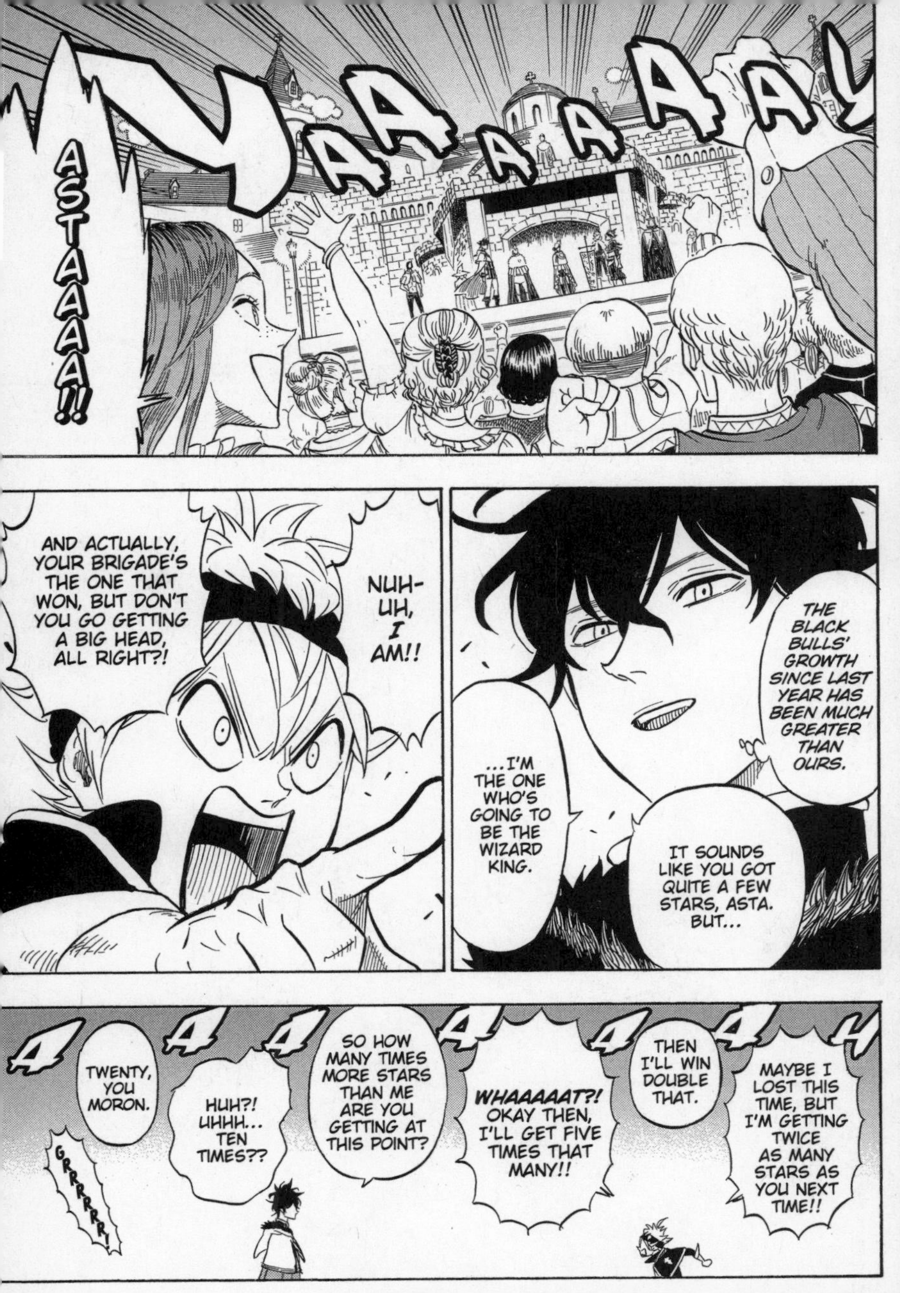
YAAAAAAY
ASTAAAAAA!!
THE BLACK BULLS' GROWTH SINCE LAST YEAR HAS BEEN MUCH GREATER THAN OURS.
IT SOUNDS LIKE YOU GOT QUITE A FEW STARS, ASTA. BUT...
...I'M THE ONE WHO'S GOING TO BE THE WIZARD KING.
NUH-UH, *I* AM!!
AND ACTUALLY, YOUR BRIGADE'S THE ONE THAT WON, BUT DON'T YOU GO GETTING A BIG HEAD, ALL RIGHT?!
AAAAAAH
MAYBE I LOST THIS TIME, BUT I'M GETTING TWICE AS MANY STARS AS YOU NEXT TIME!!
THEN I'LL WIN DOUBLE THAT.
WHAAAAAT?! OKAY THEN, I'LL GET FIVE TIMES THAT MANY!!
SO HOW MANY TIMES MORE STARS THAN ME ARE YOU GETTING AT THIS POINT?
HUH?! UHHH... TEN TIMES??
TWENTY, YOU MORON.
GRRRRRR!

Page 106: We Got This Far

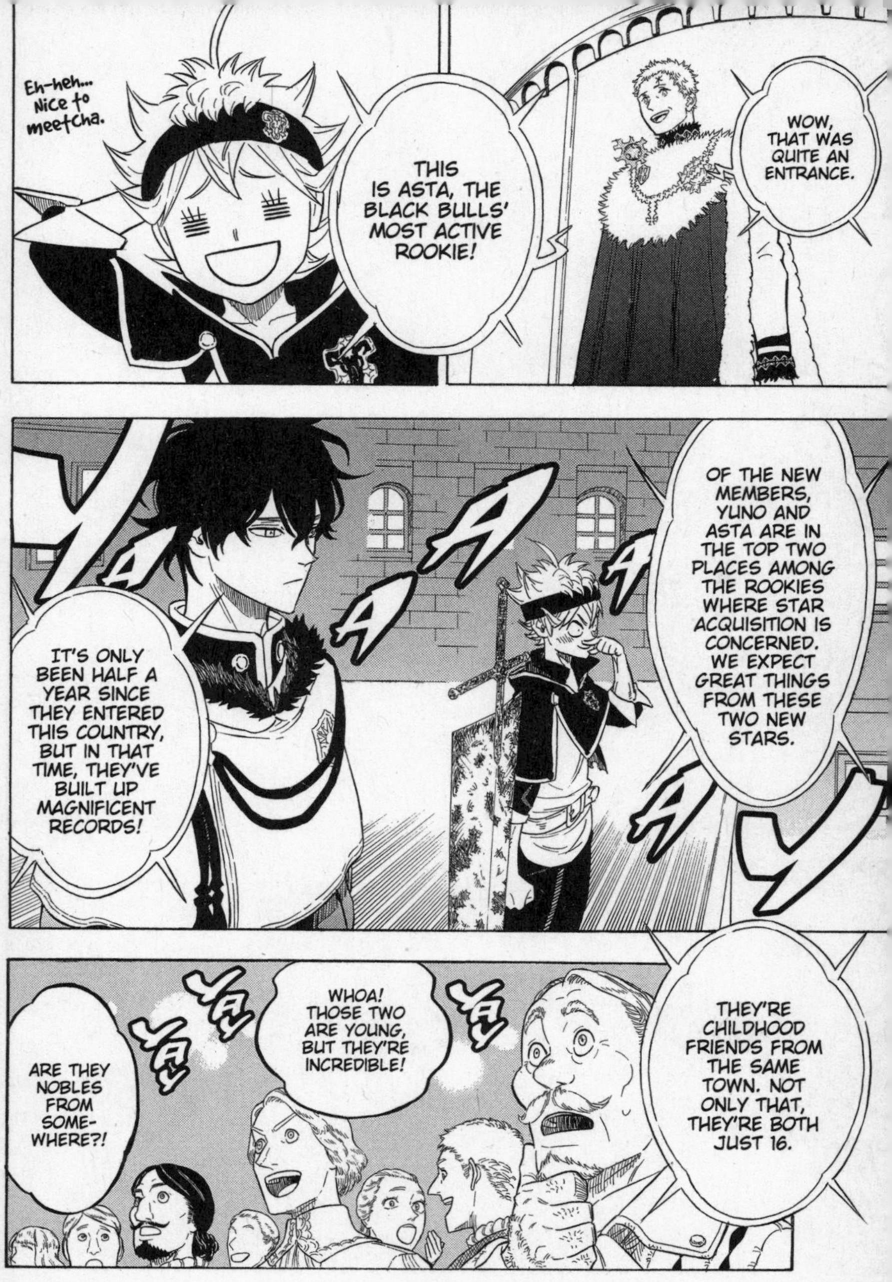
WOW, THAT WAS QUITE AN ENTRANCE.
THIS IS ASTA, THE BLACK BULLS' MOST ACTIVE ROOKIE!
Eh-heh... Nice to meetcha.
OF THE NEW MEMBERS, YUNO AND ASTA ARE IN THE TOP TWO PLACES AMONG THE ROOKIES WHERE STAR ACQUISITION IS CONCERNED. WE EXPECT GREAT THINGS FROM THESE TWO NEW STARS.
IT'S ONLY BEEN HALF A YEAR SINCE THEY ENTERED THIS COUNTRY, BUT IN THAT TIME, THEY'VE BUILT UP MAGNIFICENT RECORDS!
THEY'RE CHILDHOOD FRIENDS FROM THE SAME TOWN. NOT ONLY THAT, THEY'RE BOTH JUST 16.
Yay
WHOA! THOSE TWO ARE YOUNG, BUT THEY'RE INCREDIBLE!
Yay Yay
ARE THEY NOBLES FROM SOME-WHERE?!

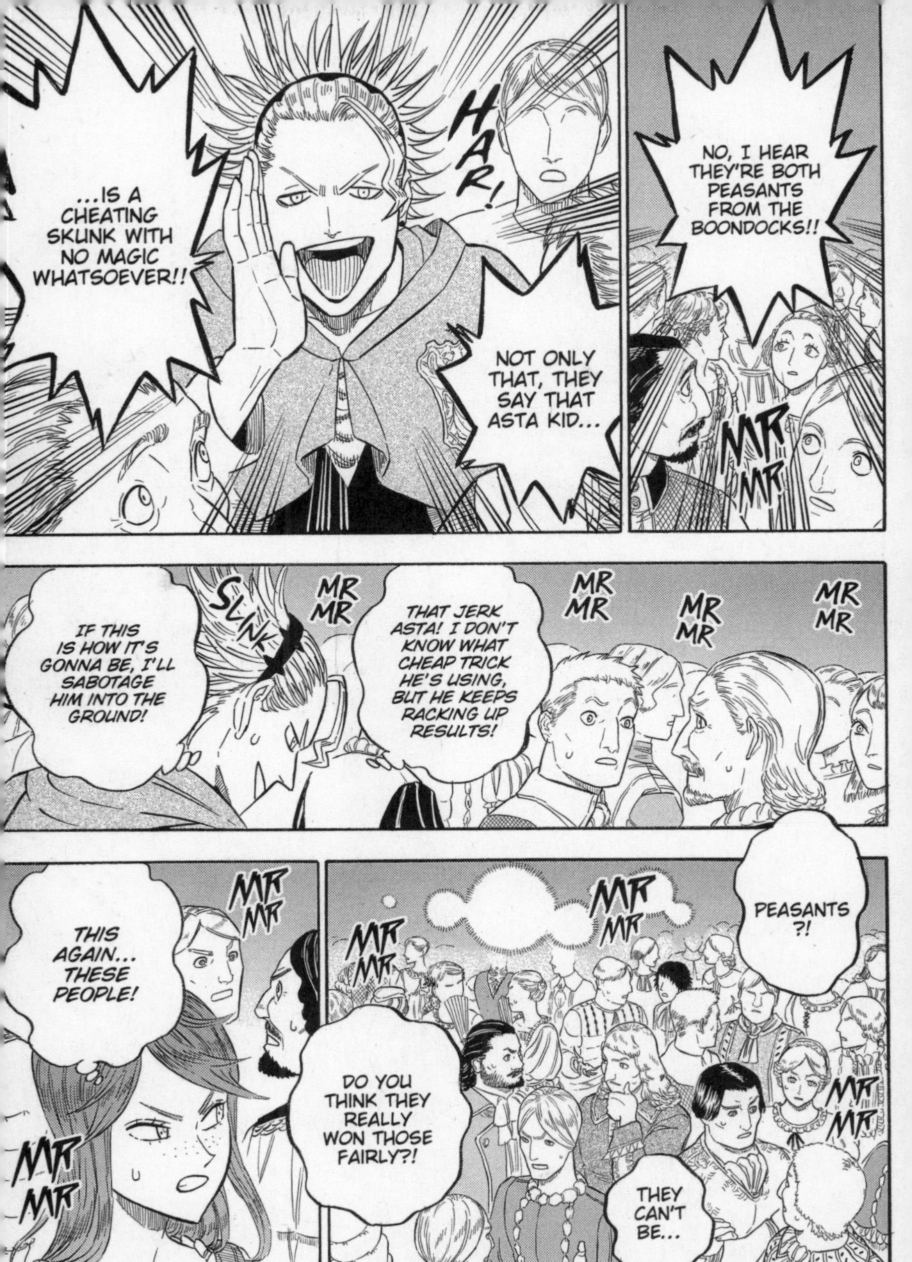
NO, I HEAR THEY'RE BOTH PEASANTS FROM THE BOONDOCKS!!
MR MR
HAR!
NOT ONLY THAT, THEY SAY THAT ASTA KID...
...IS A CHEATING SKUNK WITH NO MAGIC WHATSOEVER!!
MR MR
MR MR
MR MR
THAT JERK ASTA! I DON'T KNOW WHAT CHEAP TRICK HE'S USING, BUT HE KEEPS RACKING UP RESULTS!
MR MR
SLINK
IF THIS IS HOW IT'S GONNA BE, I'LL SABOTAGE HIM INTO THE GROUND!
PEASANTS?!
MR MR
MR MR
MR MR
DO YOU THINK THEY REALLY WON THOSE FAIRLY?!
THEY CAN'T BE...
MR MR
THIS AGAIN... THESE PEOPLE!
MR MR

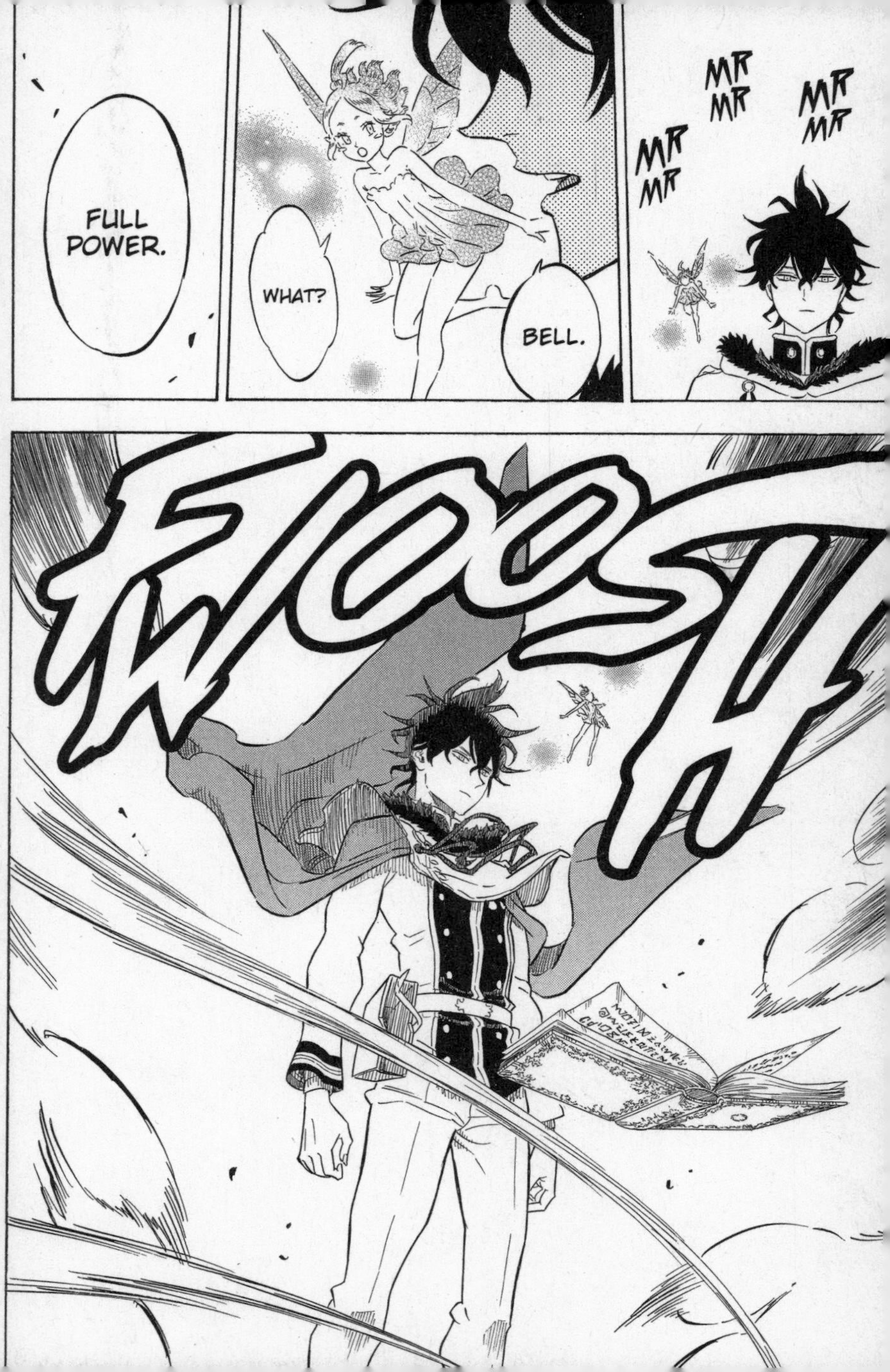
MR MR
MR MR
MR MR
BELL.
WHAT?
FULL POWER.
WHOOSH

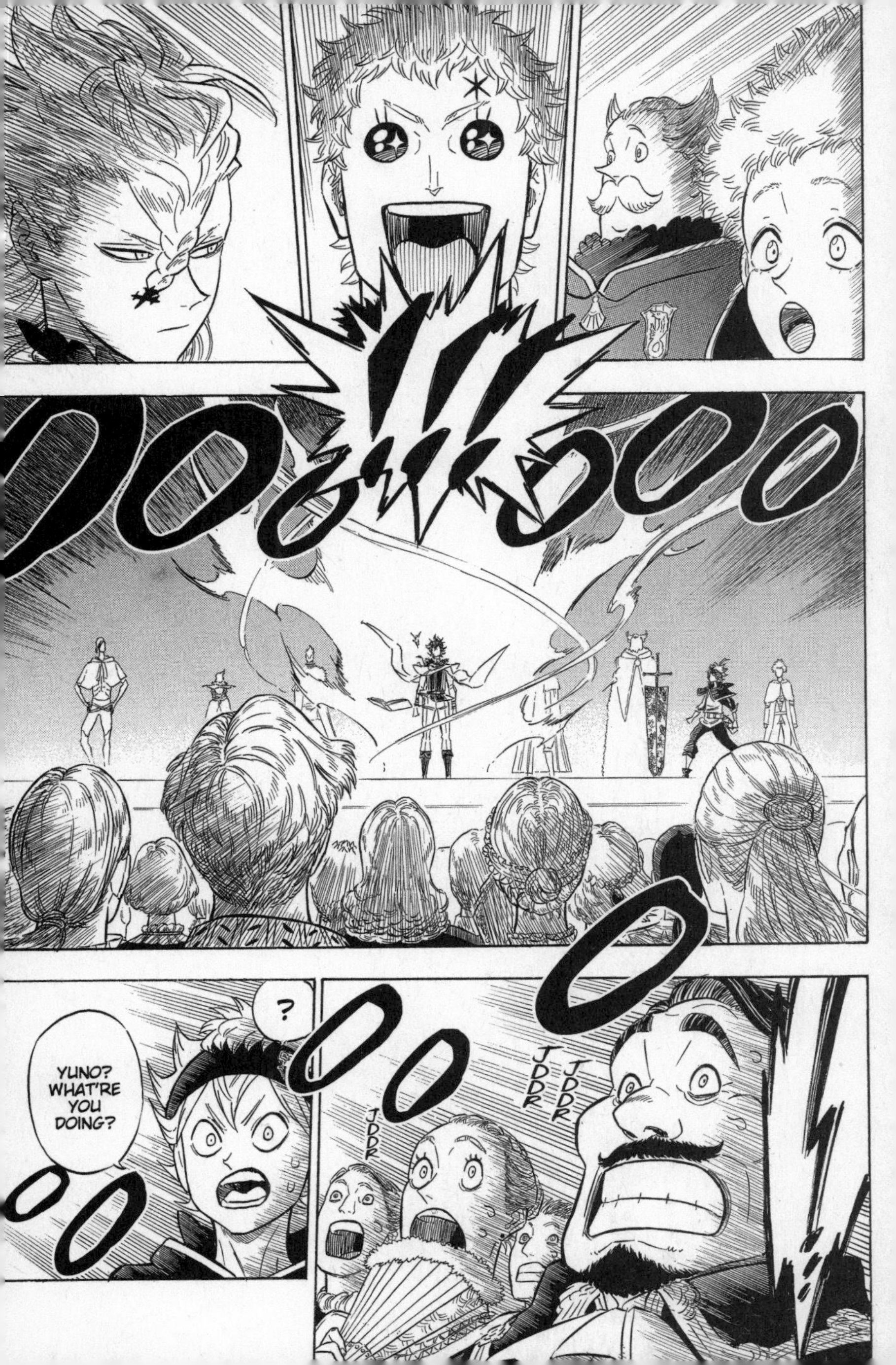
OOOOOO!!OOOOOO
OOOOO
JDDR
JDDR
JDDR
?
YUNO? WHAT'RE YOU DOING?
OOO

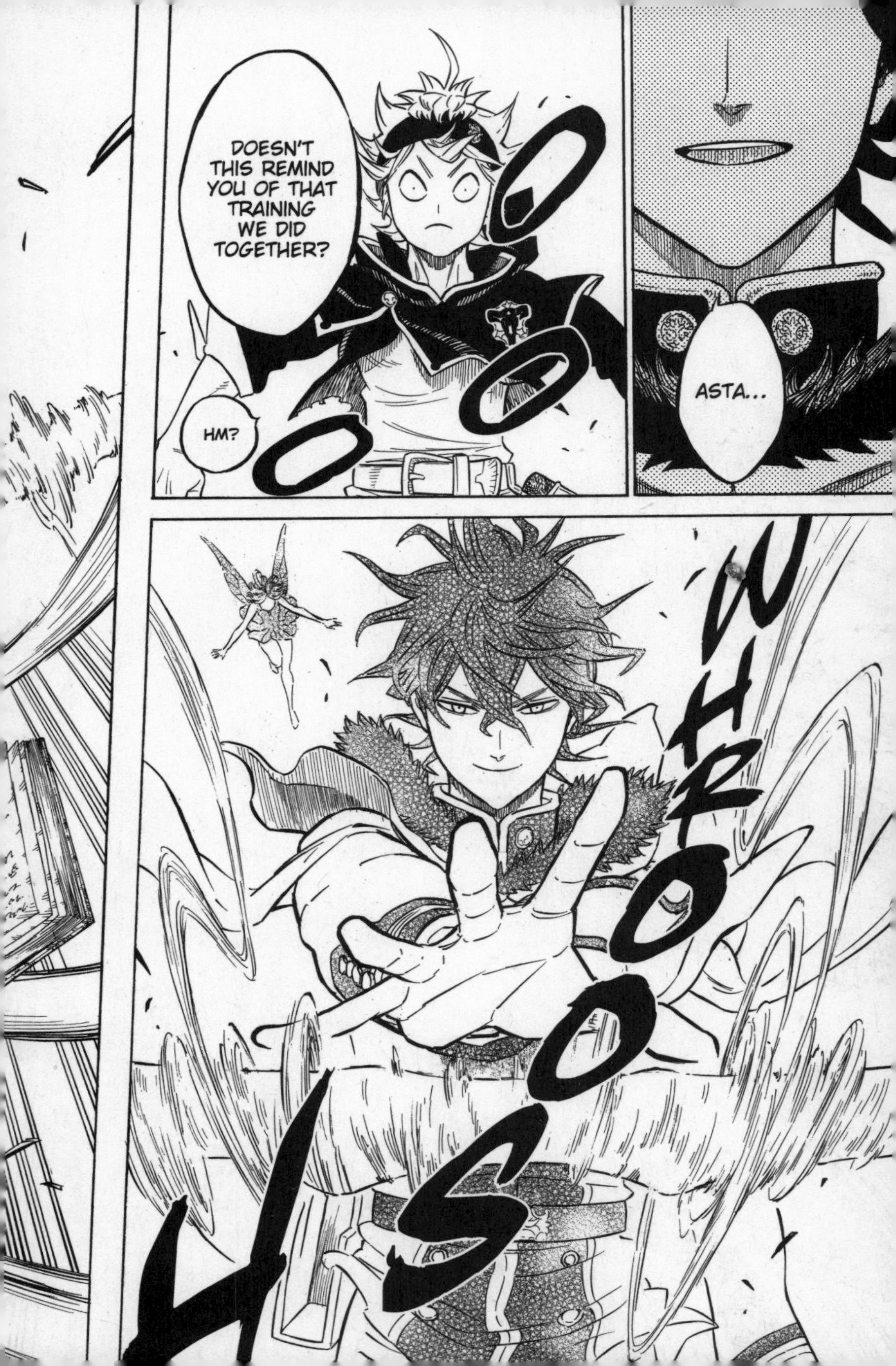
ASTA...
DOESN'T THIS REMIND YOU OF THAT TRAINING WE DID TOGETHER?
HM?
WHROOOSH

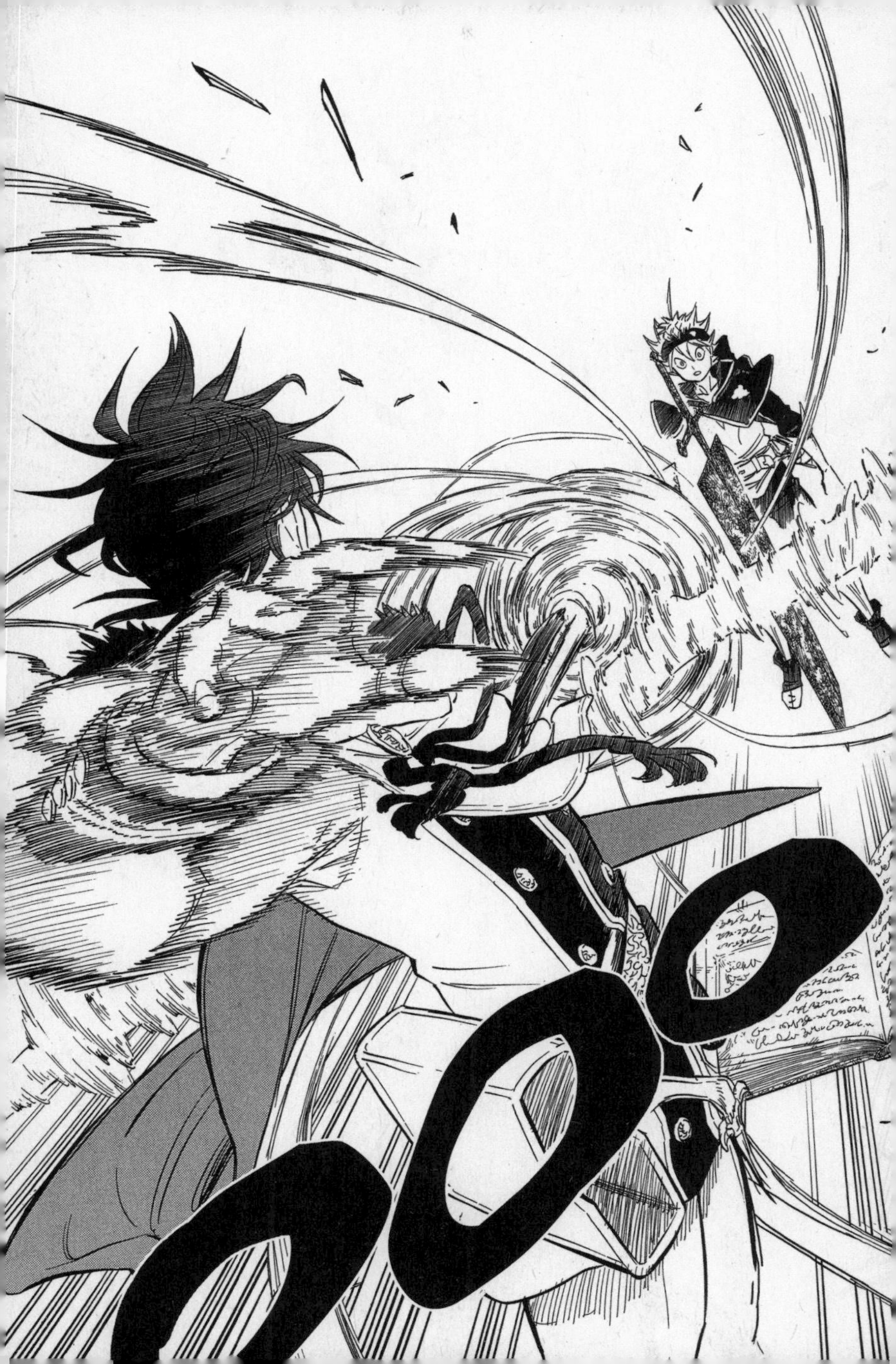

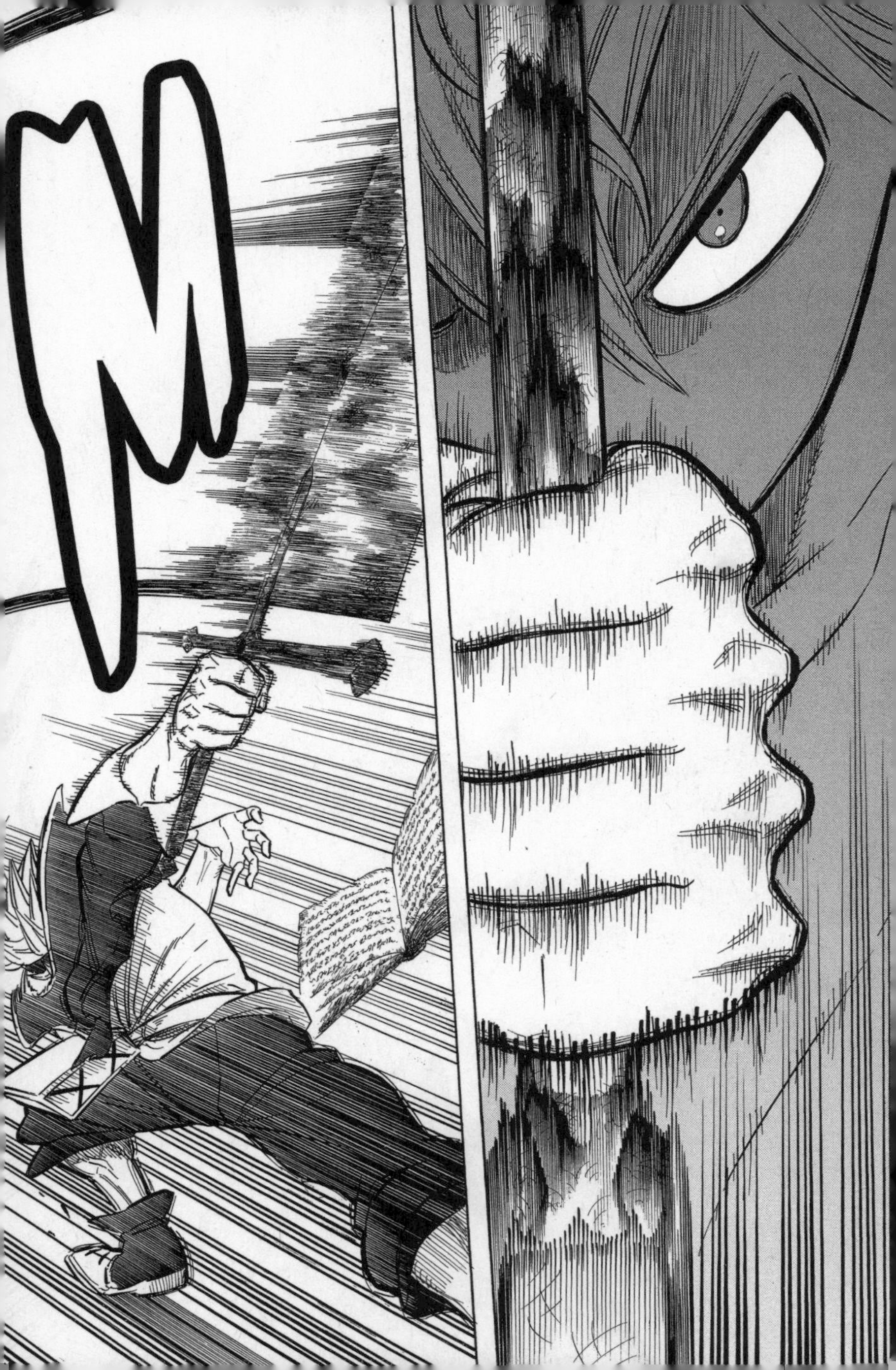
M

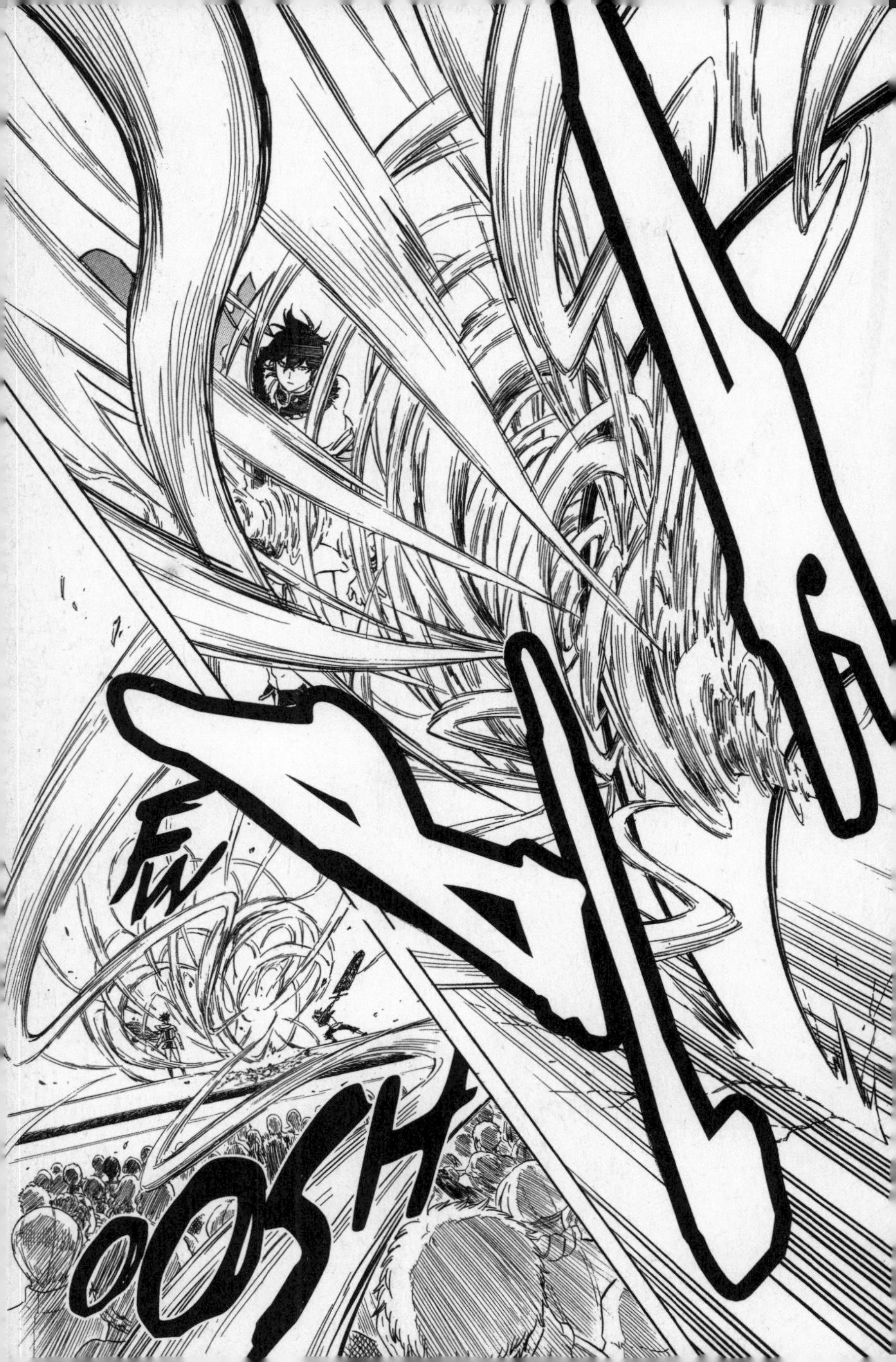

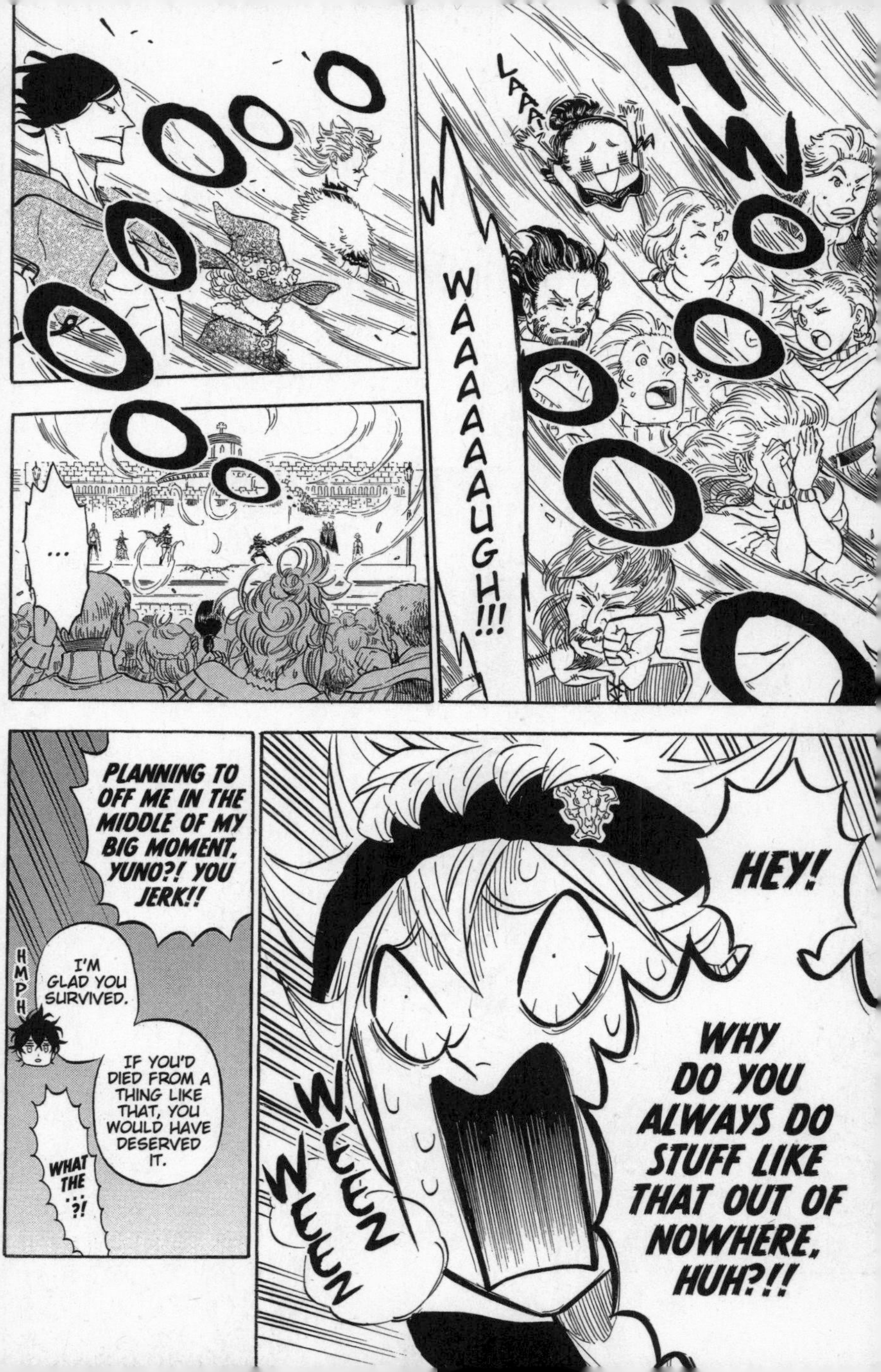
HWOOOOOOOOOOOOOO
LAAAA!
WAAAAAAAAUGH!!!
...
HEY!
WHY DO YOU ALWAYS DO STUFF LIKE THAT OUT OF NOWHERE, HUH?!!
WEEUN WEEUN
PLANNING TO OFF ME IN THE MIDDLE OF MY BIG MOMENT, YUNO?! YOU JERK!!
HMPH
I'M GLAD YOU SURVIVED.
IF YOU'D DIED FROM A THING LIKE THAT, YOU WOULD HAVE DESERVED IT.
WHAT THE...?!

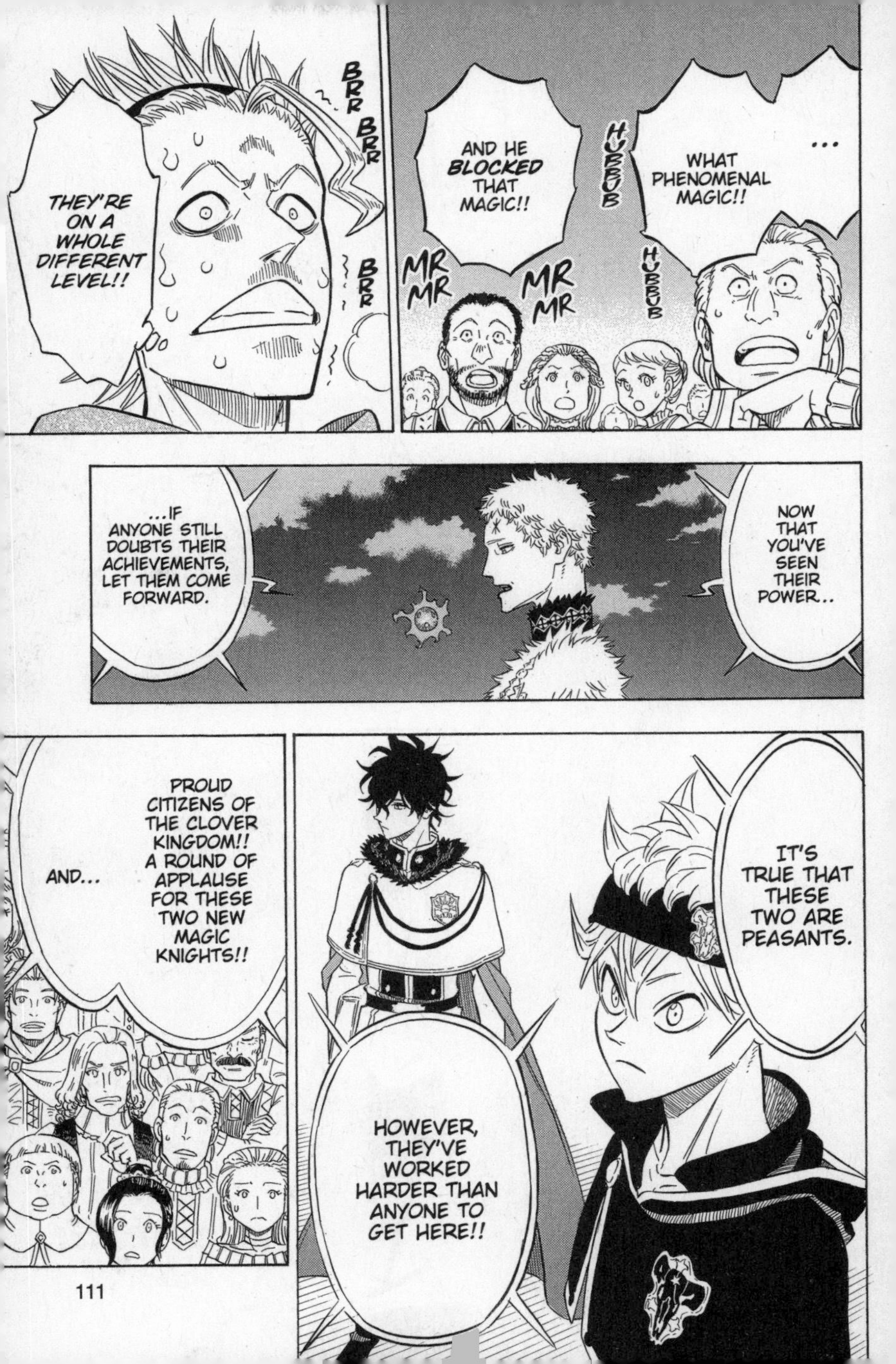
...
WHAT PHENOMENAL MAGIC!!
HUBBUB
HUBBUB
AND HE *BLOCKED* THAT MAGIC!!
MR MR
MR MR
BRR BRR BRR
BRR
THEY'RE ON A WHOLE DIFFERENT LEVEL!!
NOW THAT YOU'VE SEEN THEIR POWER...
...IF ANYONE STILL DOUBTS THEIR ACHIEVEMENTS, LET THEM COME FORWARD.
IT'S TRUE THAT THESE TWO ARE PEASANTS.
HOWEVER, THEY'VE WORKED HARDER THAN ANYONE TO GET HERE!!
AND...
PROUD CITIZENS OF THE CLOVER KINGDOM!! A ROUND OF APPLAUSE FOR THESE TWO NEW MAGIC KNIGHTS!!

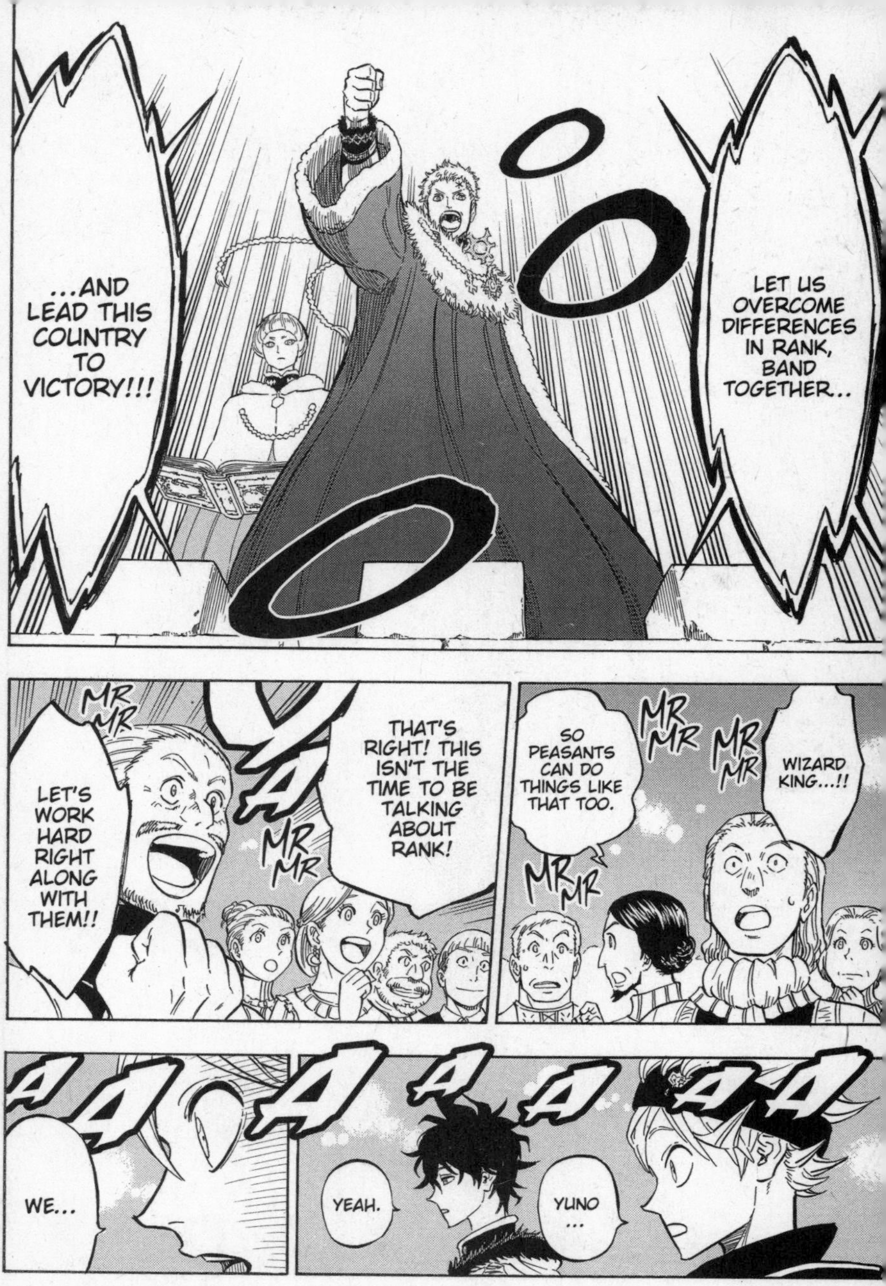

LET US OVERCOME DIFFERENCES IN RANK, BAND TOGETHER...
...AND LEAD THIS COUNTRY TO VICTORY!!!
OOO
WIZARD KING...!!
MR MR
MR MR
SO PEASANTS CAN DO THINGS LIKE THAT TOO.
MR MR
THAT'S RIGHT! THIS ISN'T THE TIME TO BE TALKING ABOUT RANK!
MR MR
A
MR MR
LET'S WORK HARD RIGHT ALONG WITH THEM!!
AAAAAAAA
YUNO ...
YEAH.
WE...

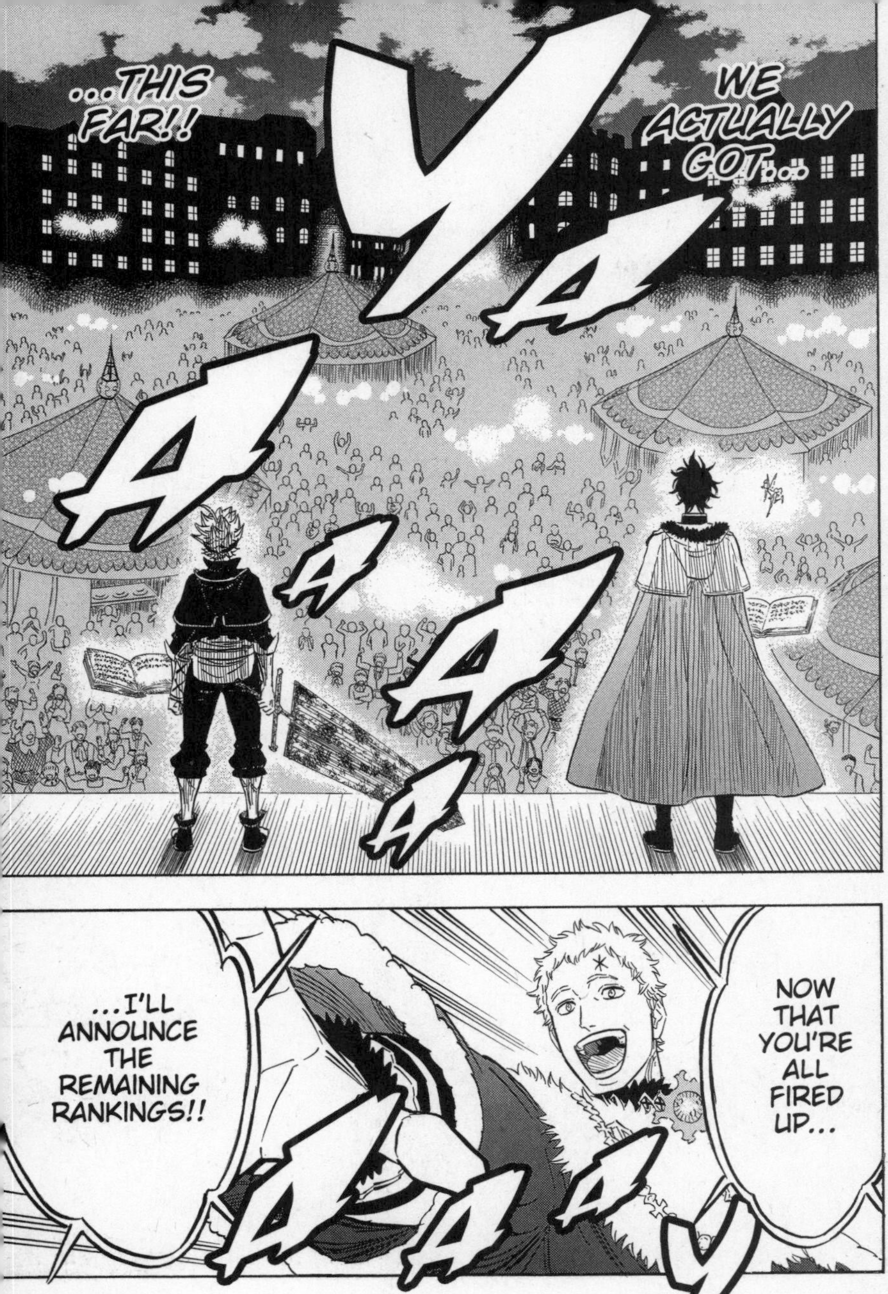
WE ACTUALLY GOT...
...THIS FAR!!
YAAAAA
NOW THAT YOU'RE ALL FIRED UP...
...I'LL ANNOUNCE THE REMAINING RANKINGS!!
AAAAY

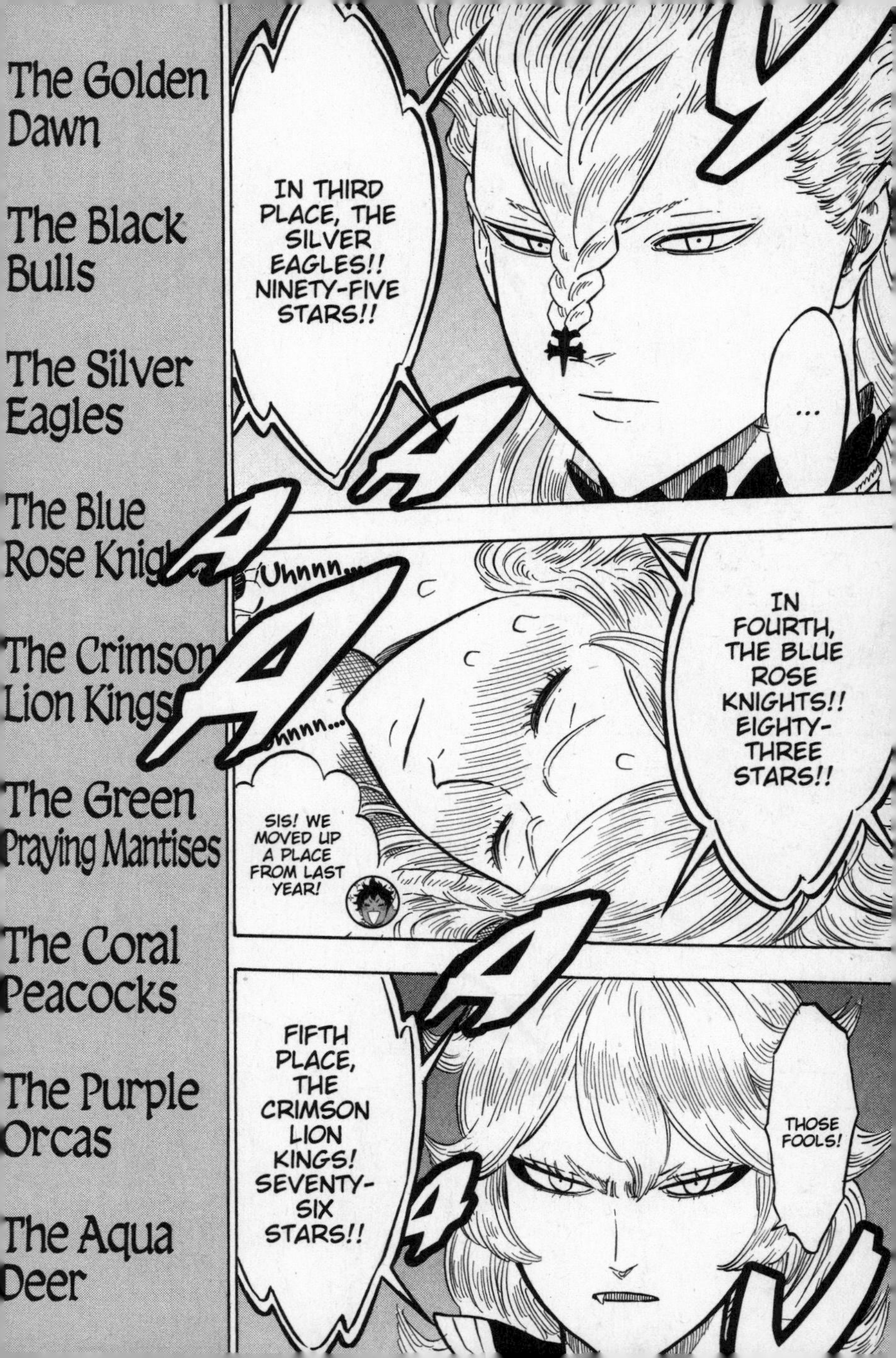
IN THIRD PLACE, THE SILVER EAGLES!! NINETY-FIVE STARS!!
...
IN FOURTH, THE BLUE ROSE KNIGHTS!! EIGHTY-THREE STARS!!
Uhnnn...
hnnn...
SIS! WE MOVED UP A PLACE FROM LAST YEAR!
FIFTH PLACE, THE CRIMSON LION KINGS! SEVENTY-SIX STARS!!
THOSE FOOLS!
The Golden Dawn
The Black Bulls
The Silver Eagles
The Blue Rose Knights
The Crimson Lion Kings
The Green Praying Mantises
The Coral Peacocks
The Purple Orcas
The Aqua Deer

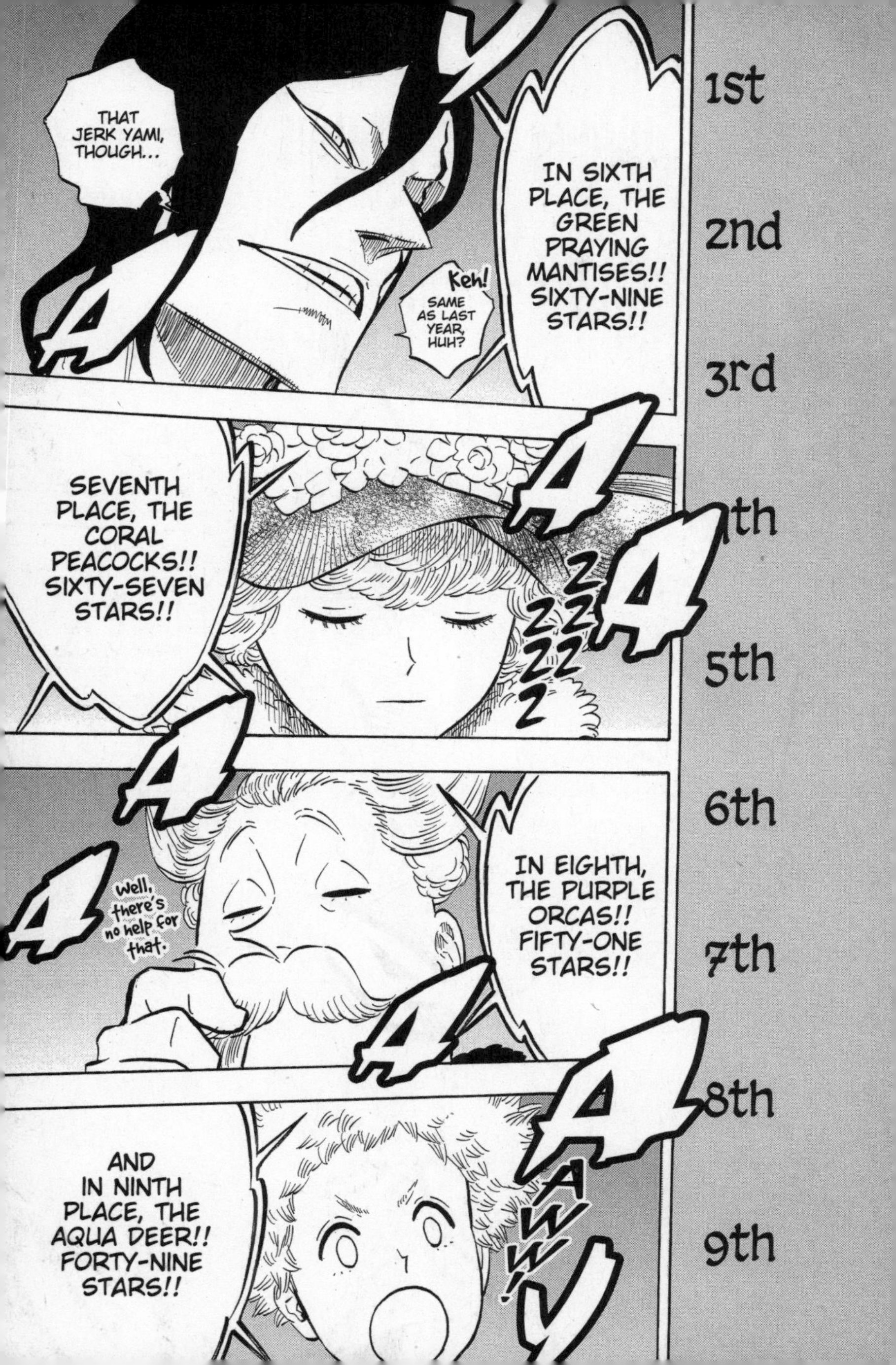

IN SIXTH PLACE, THE GREEN PRAYING MANTISES!! SIXTY-NINE STARS!!
Keh! SAME AS LAST YEAR, HUH?
THAT JERK YAMI, THOUGH...
SEVENTH PLACE, THE CORAL PEACOCKS!! SIXTY-SEVEN STARS!!
ZZZZZZZ
IN EIGHTH, THE PURPLE ORCAS!! FIFTY-ONE STARS!!
Well, there's no help for that.
AND IN NINTH PLACE, THE AQUA DEER!! FORTY-NINE STARS!!
AWW!
1st
2nd
3rd
5th
6th
7th
8th
9th

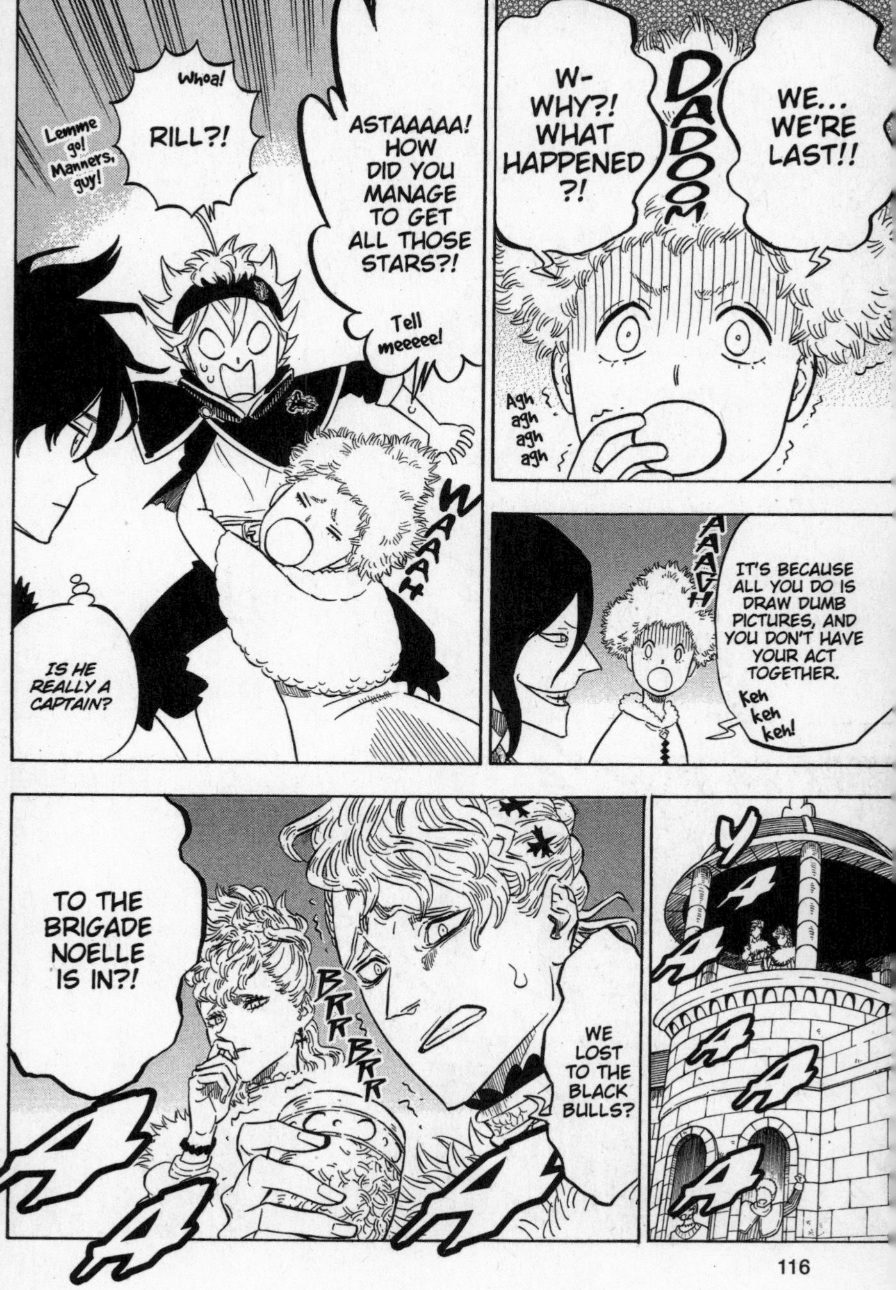
WE... WE'RE LAST!!
DADOOM
W-WHY?! WHAT HAPPENED?!
Agh agh agh agh
AAAAH
IT'S BECAUSE ALL YOU DO IS DRAW DUMB PICTURES, AND YOU DON'T HAVE YOUR ACT TOGETHER.
Keh keh keh!
ASTAAAAA! HOW DID YOU MANAGE TO GET ALL THOSE STARS?!
Tell meeeee!
Whoa!
RILL?!
Lemme go! Manners, guy!
WAAAAH
IS HE REALLY A CAPTAIN?
YAAAAA
WE LOST TO THE BLACK BULLS?
BRRR BRRR
TO THE BRIGADE NOELLE IS IN?!
AAAA

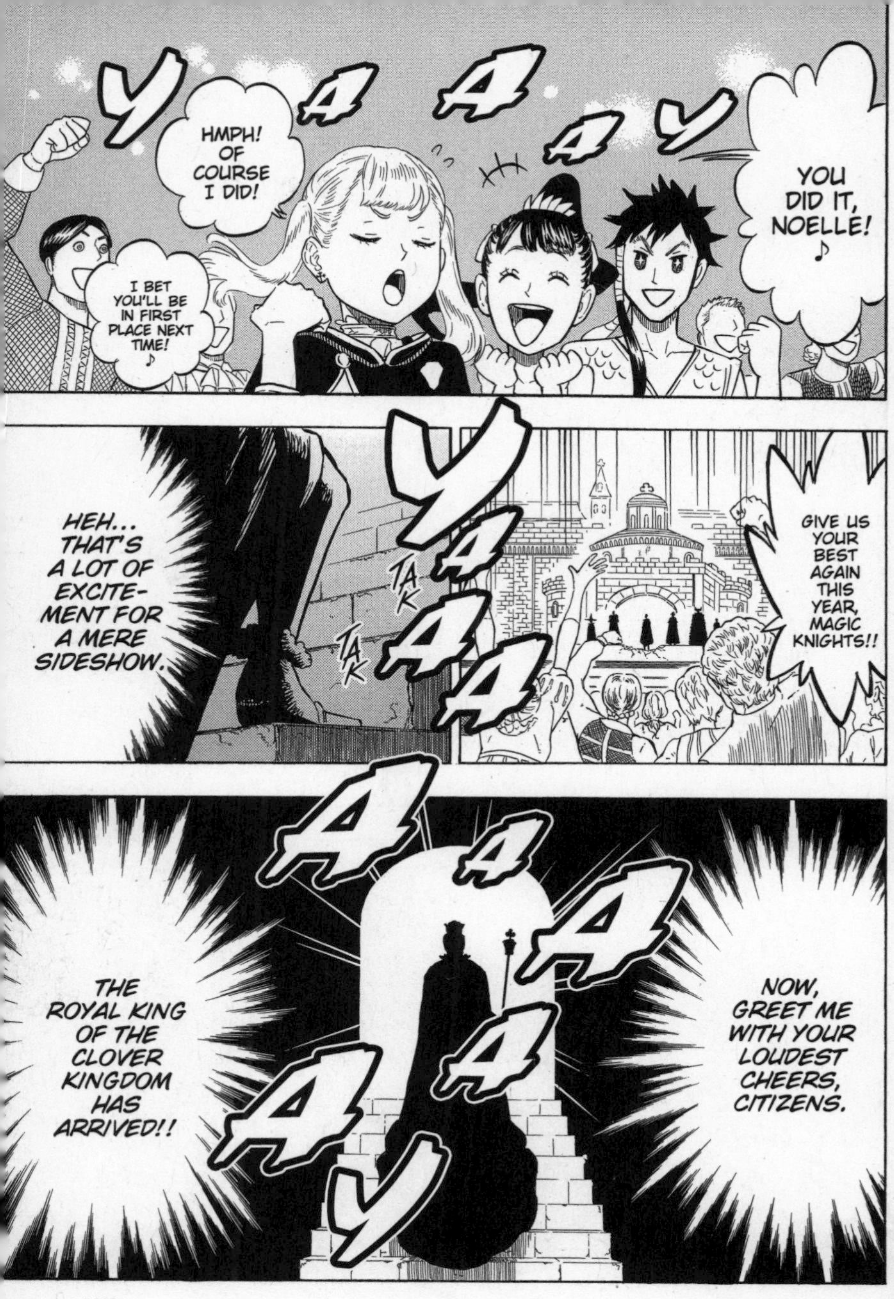

YAAAAY
YOU DID IT, NOELLE! ♪
HMPH! OF COURSE I DID!
I BET YOU'LL BE IN FIRST PLACE NEXT TIME! ♪
YAAAA
GIVE US YOUR BEST AGAIN THIS YEAR, MAGIC KNIGHTS!!
TAK
TAK
HEH... THAT'S A LOT OF EXCITEMENT FOR A MERE SIDESHOW.
AAAAAY
NOW, GREET ME WITH YOUR LOUDEST CHEERS, CITIZENS.
THE ROYAL KING OF THE CLOVER KINGDOM HAS ARRIVED!!

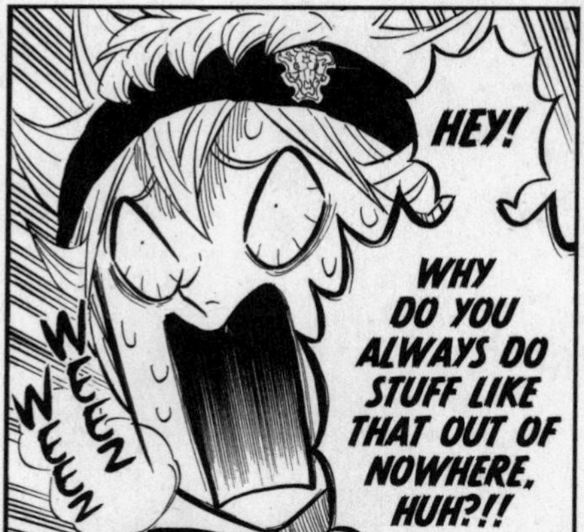
HEY!
WHY DO YOU ALWAYS DO STUFF LIKE THAT OUT OF NOWHERE, HUH?!!
WEEN WEEN

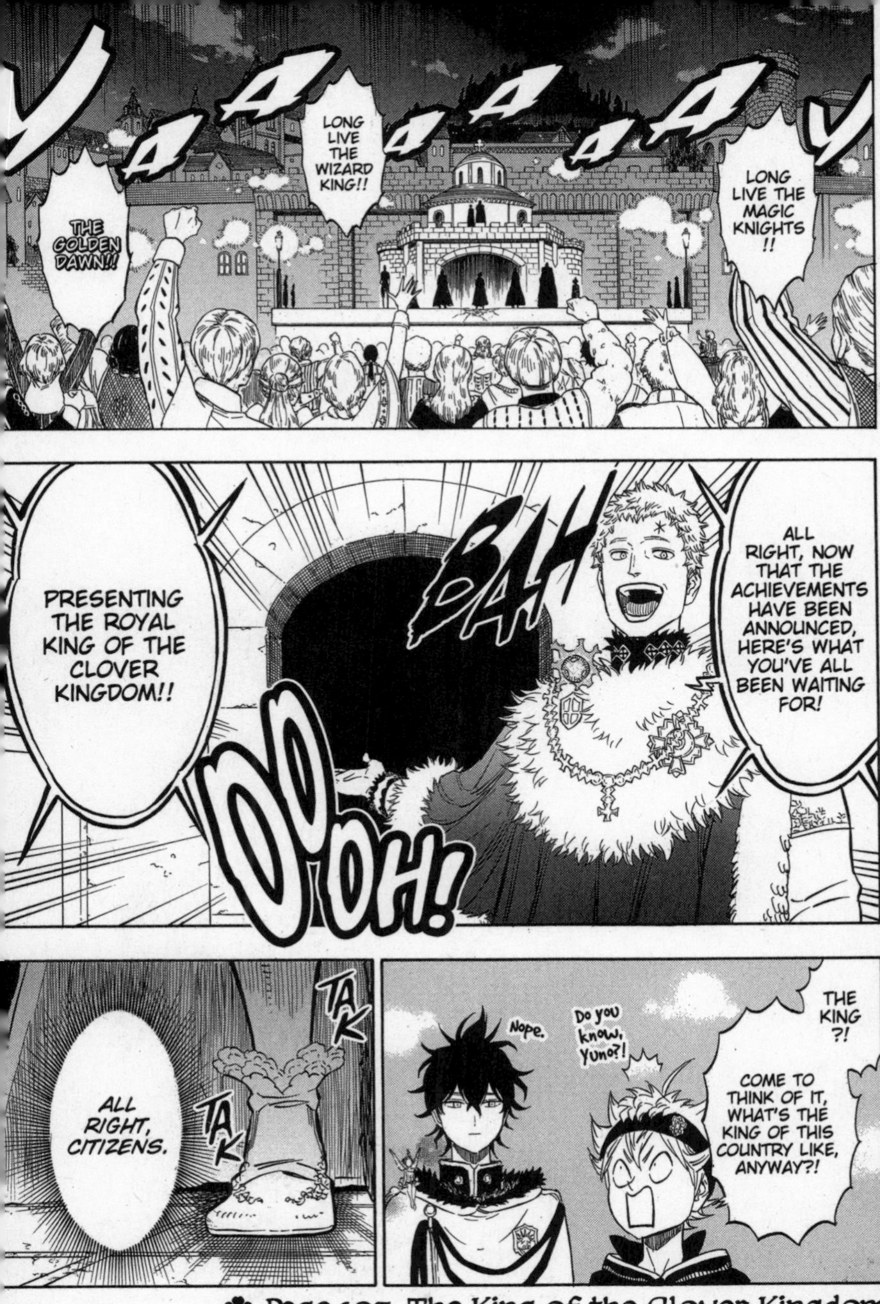
LONG LIVE THE MAGIC KNIGHTS!!
LONG LIVE THE WIZARD KING!!
THE GOLDEN DAWN!!
YAAAAAAY
ALL RIGHT, NOW THAT THE ACHIEVEMENTS HAVE BEEN ANNOUNCED, HERE'S WHAT YOU'VE ALL BEEN WAITING FOR!
BAH
PRESENTING THE ROYAL KING OF THE CLOVER KINGDOM!!
OOOOH!
THE KING?!
COME TO THINK OF IT, WHAT'S THE KING OF THIS COUNTRY LIKE, ANYWAY?!
Do you know, Yuno?!
Nope.
TAK
TAK
ALL RIGHT, CITIZENS.

Page 107: The King of the Clover Kingdom

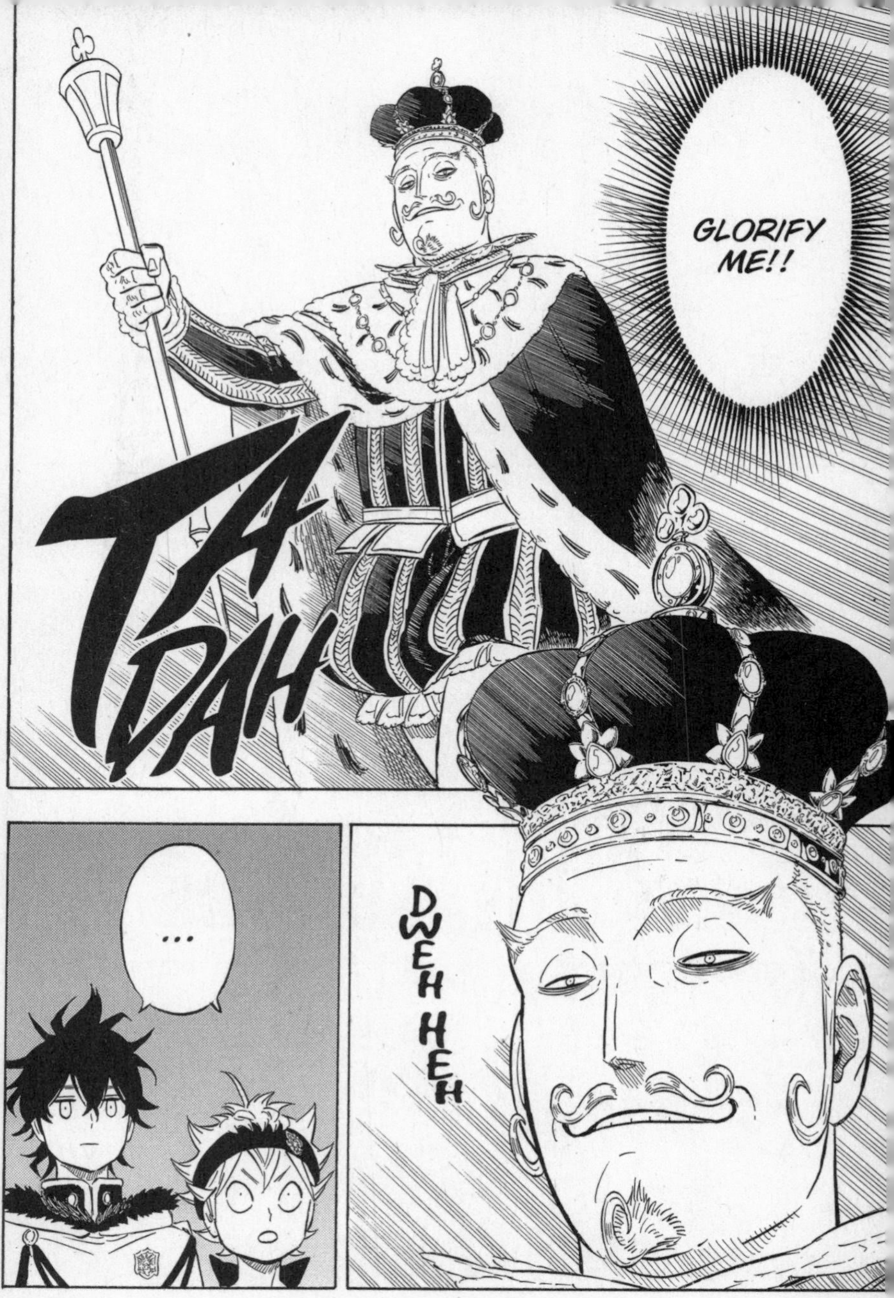
GLORIFY ME!!
TA DAH
DWEH HEH
...

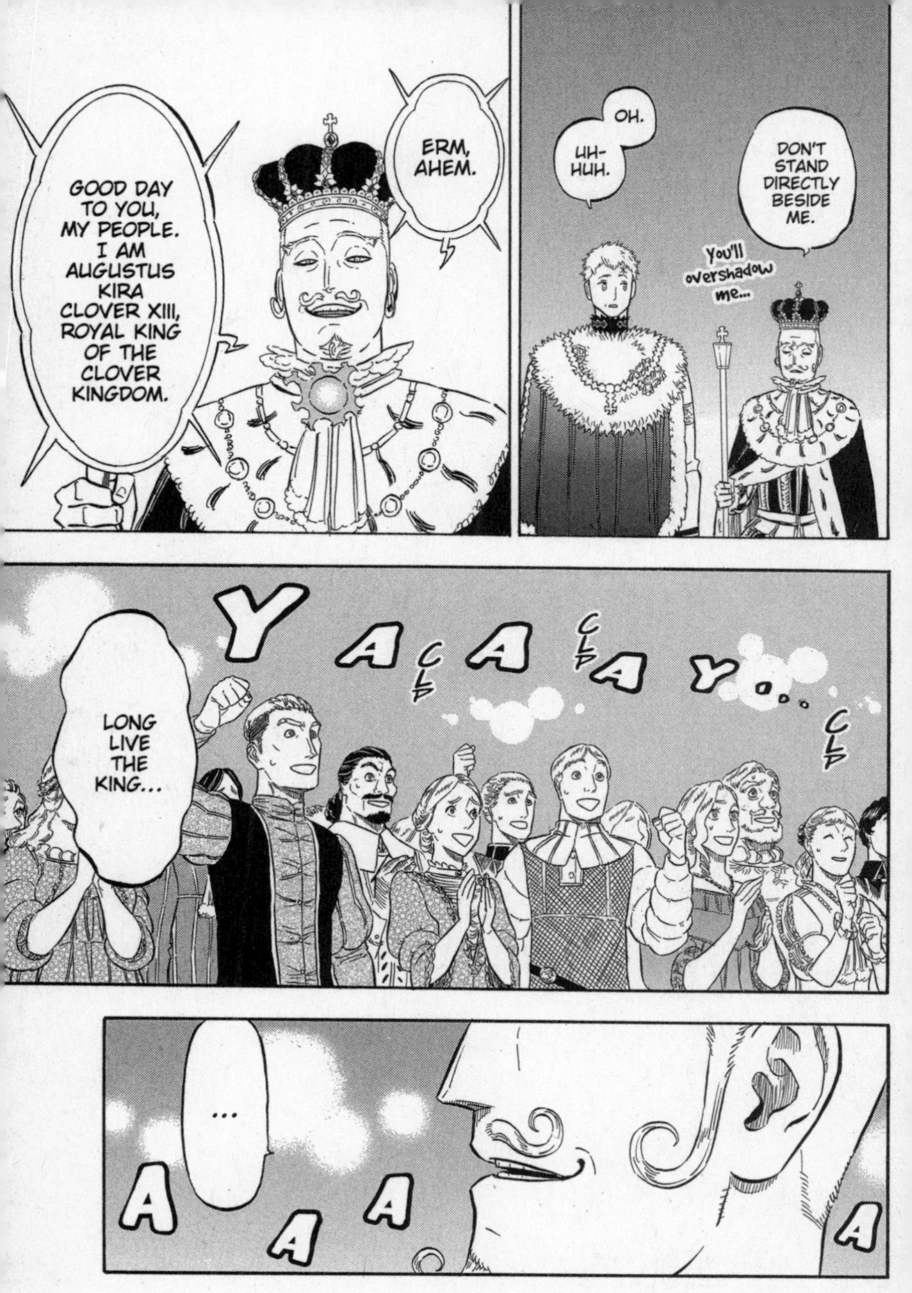

DON'T STAND DIRECTLY BESIDE ME.
You'll overshadow me...
OH.
UH-HUH.
ERM, AHEM.
GOOD DAY TO YOU, MY PEOPLE. I AM AUGUSTUS KIRA CLOVER XIII, ROYAL KING OF THE CLOVER KINGDOM.
YAAAAY...
CLP CLP CLP
LONG LIVE THE KING...
...
AAAAA

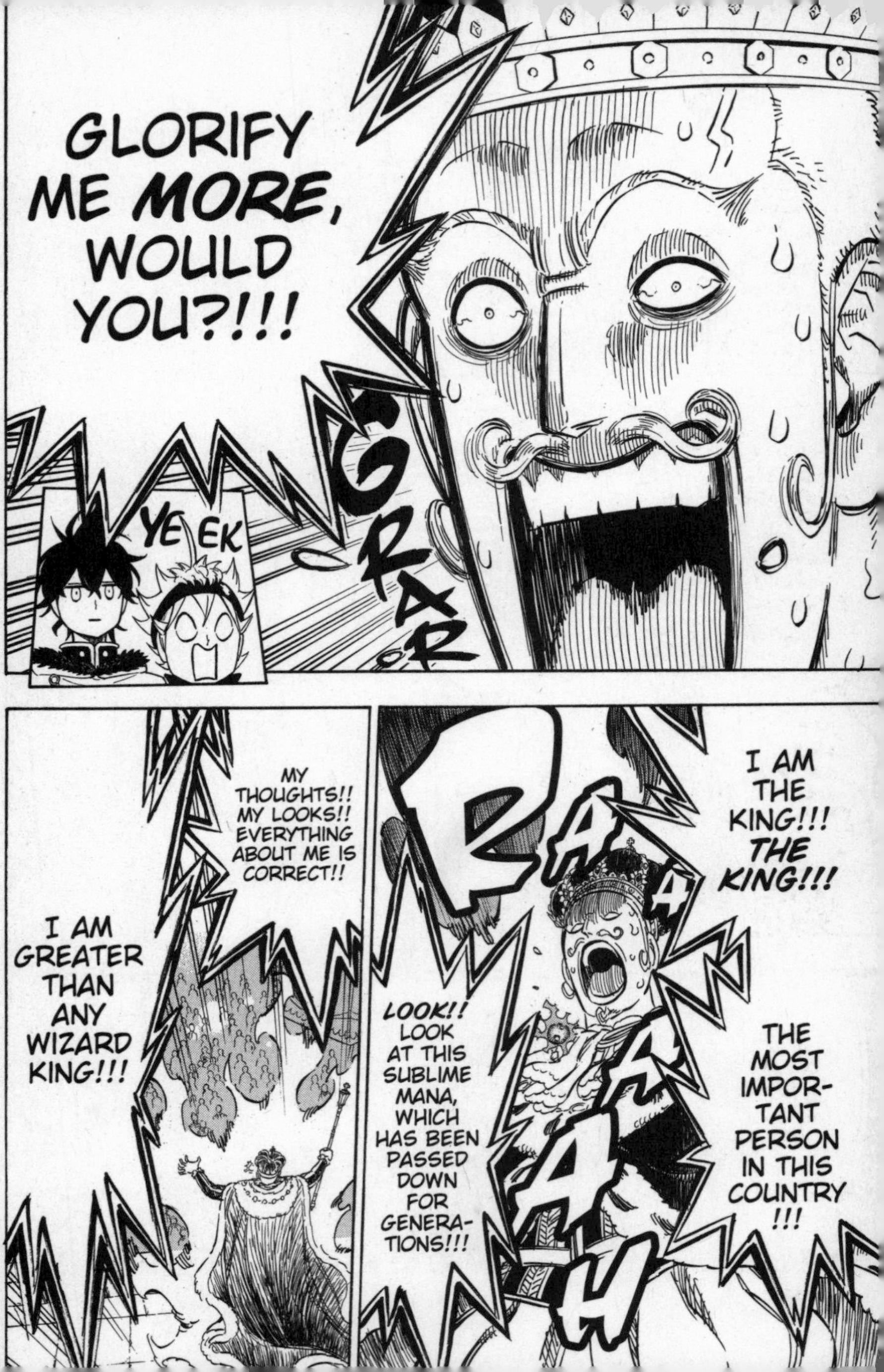
GRAR
GLORIFY ME MORE, WOULD YOU?!!!
YEEK
I AM THE KING!!! THE KING!!!
RAAAAH
THE MOST IMPORTANT PERSON IN THIS COUNTRY!!!
LOOK!! LOOK AT THIS SUBLIME MANA, WHICH HAS BEEN PASSED DOWN FOR GENERATIONS!!!
MY THOUGHTS!! MY LOOKS!! EVERYTHING ABOUT ME IS CORRECT!!
I AM GREATER THAN ANY WIZARD KING!!!

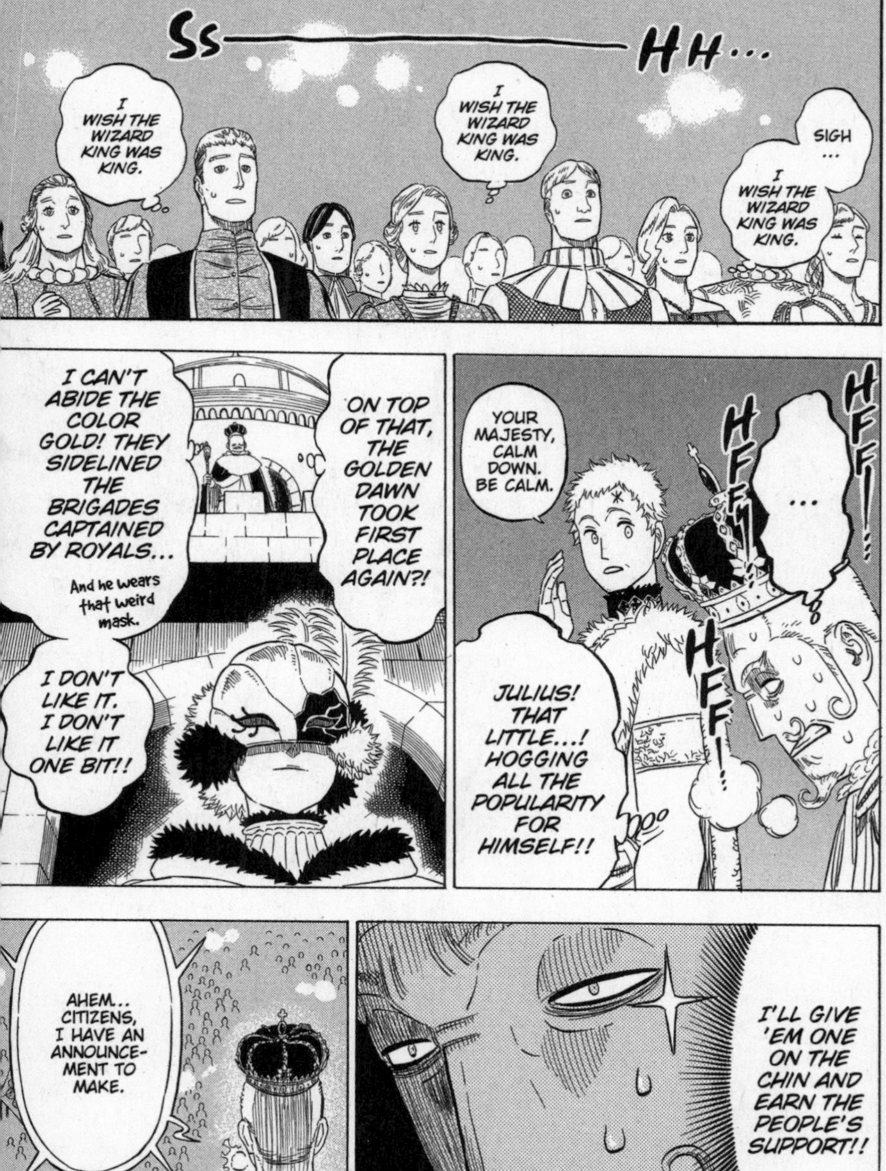
Ss————HH...
SIGH... I WISH THE WIZARD KING WAS KING.
I WISH THE WIZARD KING WAS KING.
I WISH THE WIZARD KING WAS KING.
HFF!!
HFF
...
YOUR MAJESTY, CALM DOWN. BE CALM.
JULIUS! THAT LITTLE...! HOGGING ALL THE POPULARITY FOR HIMSELF!!
HFF!!
ON TOP OF THAT, THE GOLDEN DAWN TOOK FIRST PLACE AGAIN?!
I CAN'T ABIDE THE COLOR GOLD! THEY SIDELINED THE BRIGADES CAPTAINED BY ROYALS...
And he wears that weird mask.
I DON'T LIKE IT. I DON'T LIKE IT ONE BIT!!
I'LL GIVE 'EM ONE ON THE CHIN AND EARN THE PEOPLE'S SUPPORT!!
AHEM.. CITIZENS, I HAVE AN ANNOUNCE-MENT TO MAKE.

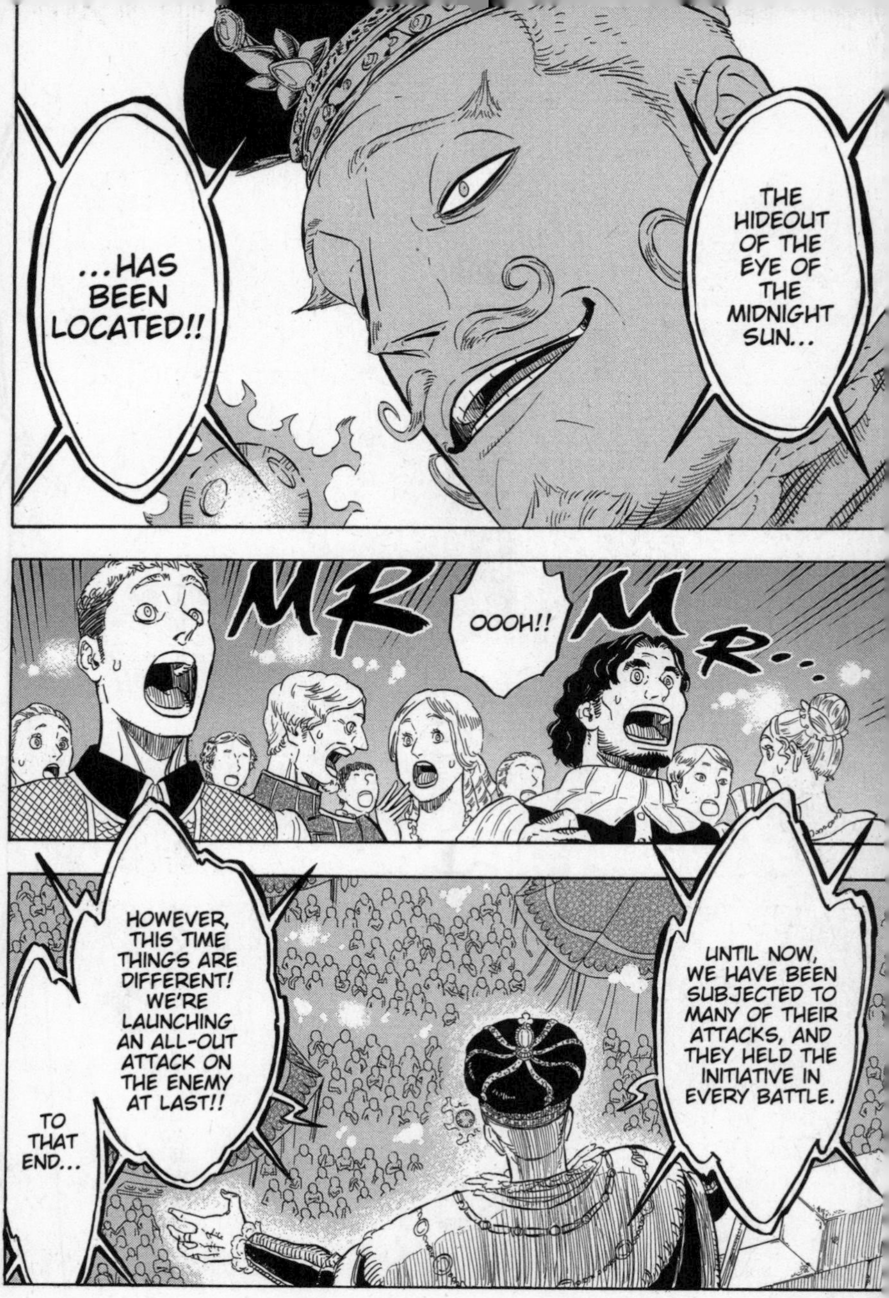
THE HIDEOUT OF THE EYE OF THE MIDNIGHT SUN...
...HAS BEEN LOCATED!!
MRMR...
OOOH!!
UNTIL NOW, WE HAVE BEEN SUBJECTED TO MANY OF THEIR ATTACKS, AND THEY HELD THE INITIATIVE IN EVERY BATTLE.
HOWEVER, THIS TIME THINGS ARE DIFFERENT! WE'RE LAUNCHING AN ALL-OUT ATTACK ON THE ENEMY AT LAST!!
TO THAT END...

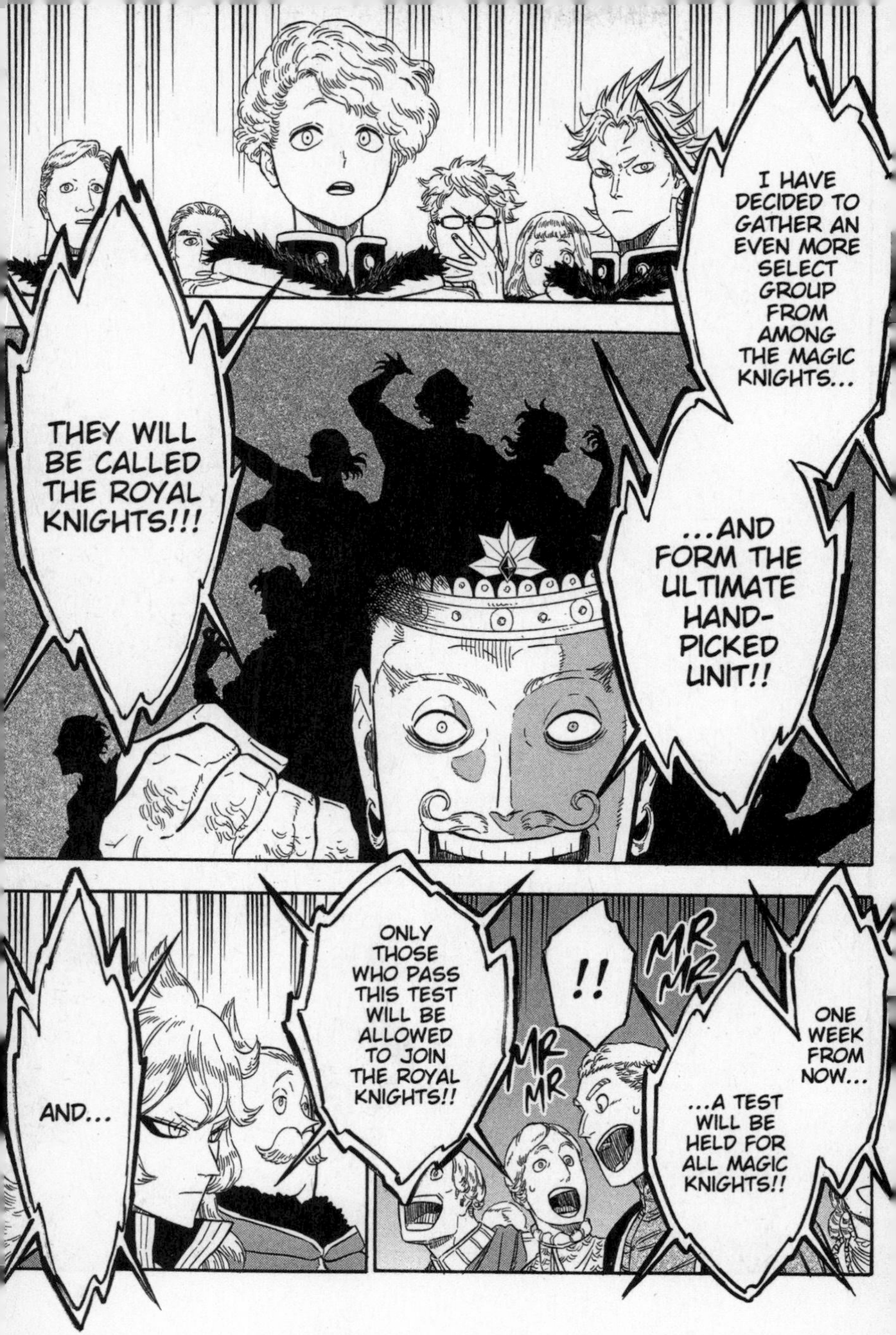
I HAVE DECIDED TO GATHER AN EVEN MORE SELECT GROUP FROM AMONG THE MAGIC KNIGHTS...
...AND FORM THE ULTIMATE HAND-PICKED UNIT!!
THEY WILL BE CALLED THE ROYAL KNIGHTS!!!
ONE WEEK FROM NOW...
...A TEST WILL BE HELD FOR ALL MAGIC KNIGHTS!!
!!
MR MR
MR MR
ONLY THOSE WHO PASS THIS TEST WILL BE ALLOWED TO JOIN THE ROYAL KNIGHTS!!
AND...

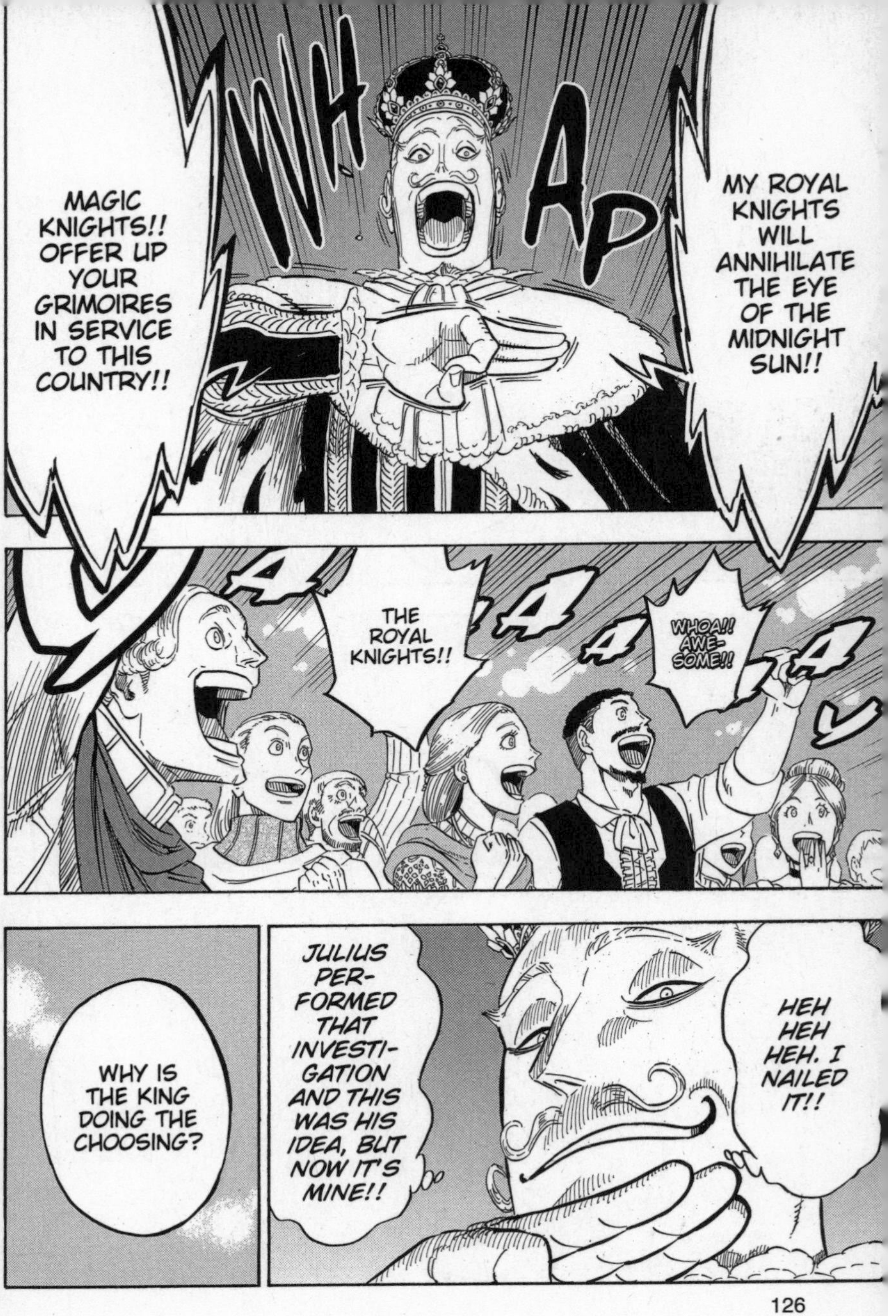
MY ROYAL KNIGHTS WILL ANNIHILATE THE EYE OF THE MIDNIGHT SUN!!
MAGIC KNIGHTS!! OFFER UP YOUR GRIMOIRES IN SERVICE TO THIS COUNTRY!!
WHOA!! AWE-SOME!!
THE ROYAL KNIGHTS!!
HEH HEH HEH. I NAILED IT!!
JULIUS PER-FORMED THAT INVESTI-GATION AND THIS WAS HIS IDEA, BUT NOW IT'S MINE!!
WHY IS THE KING DOING THE CHOOSING?

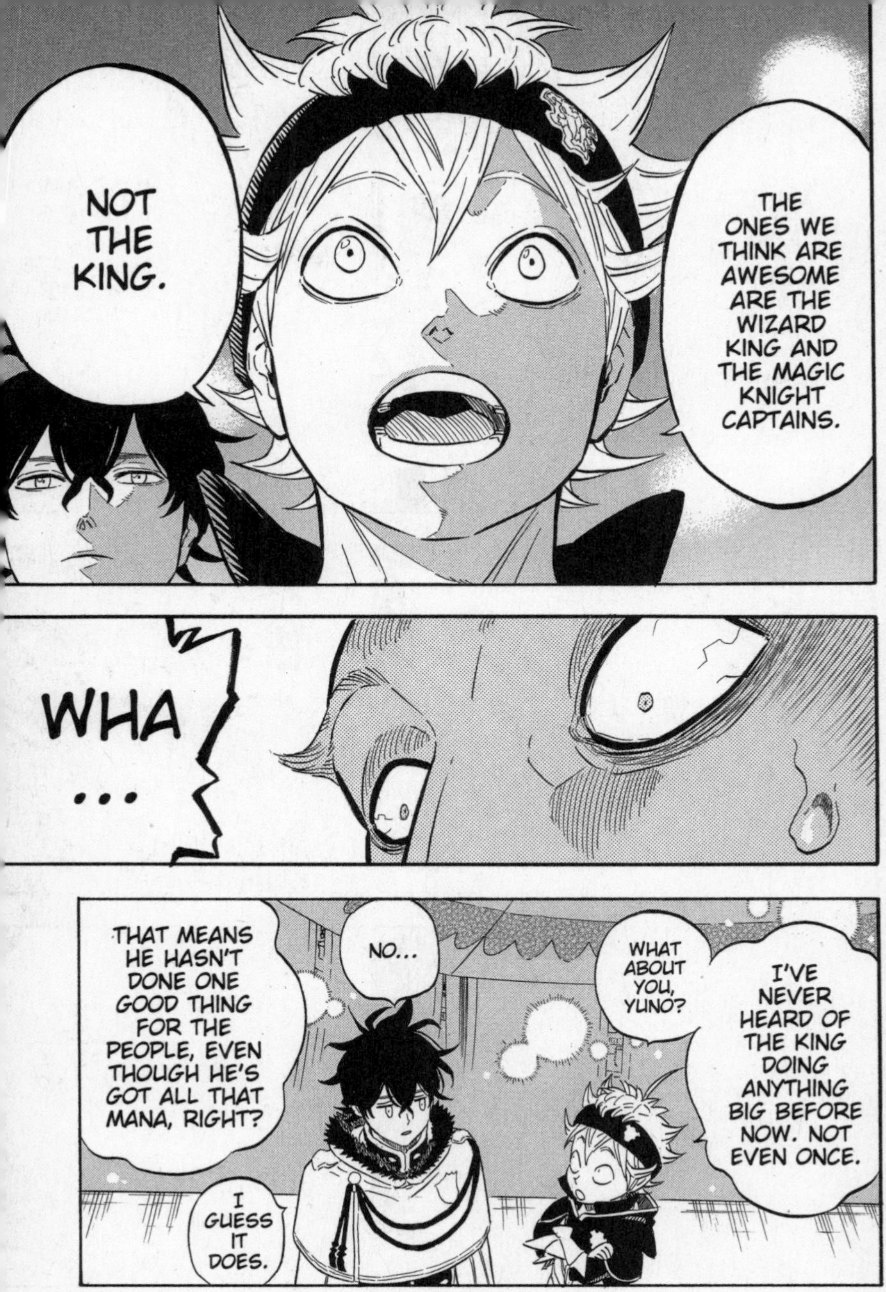
THE ONES WE THINK ARE AWESOME ARE THE WIZARD KING AND THE MAGIC KNIGHT CAPTAINS.
NOT THE KING.
WHA...
WHAT ABOUT YOU, YUNO?
I'VE NEVER HEARD OF THE KING DOING ANYTHING BIG BEFORE NOW. NOT EVEN ONCE.
NO...
THAT MEANS HE HASN'T DONE ONE GOOD THING FOR THE PEOPLE, EVEN THOUGH HE'S GOT ALL THAT MANA, RIGHT?
I GUESS IT DOES.

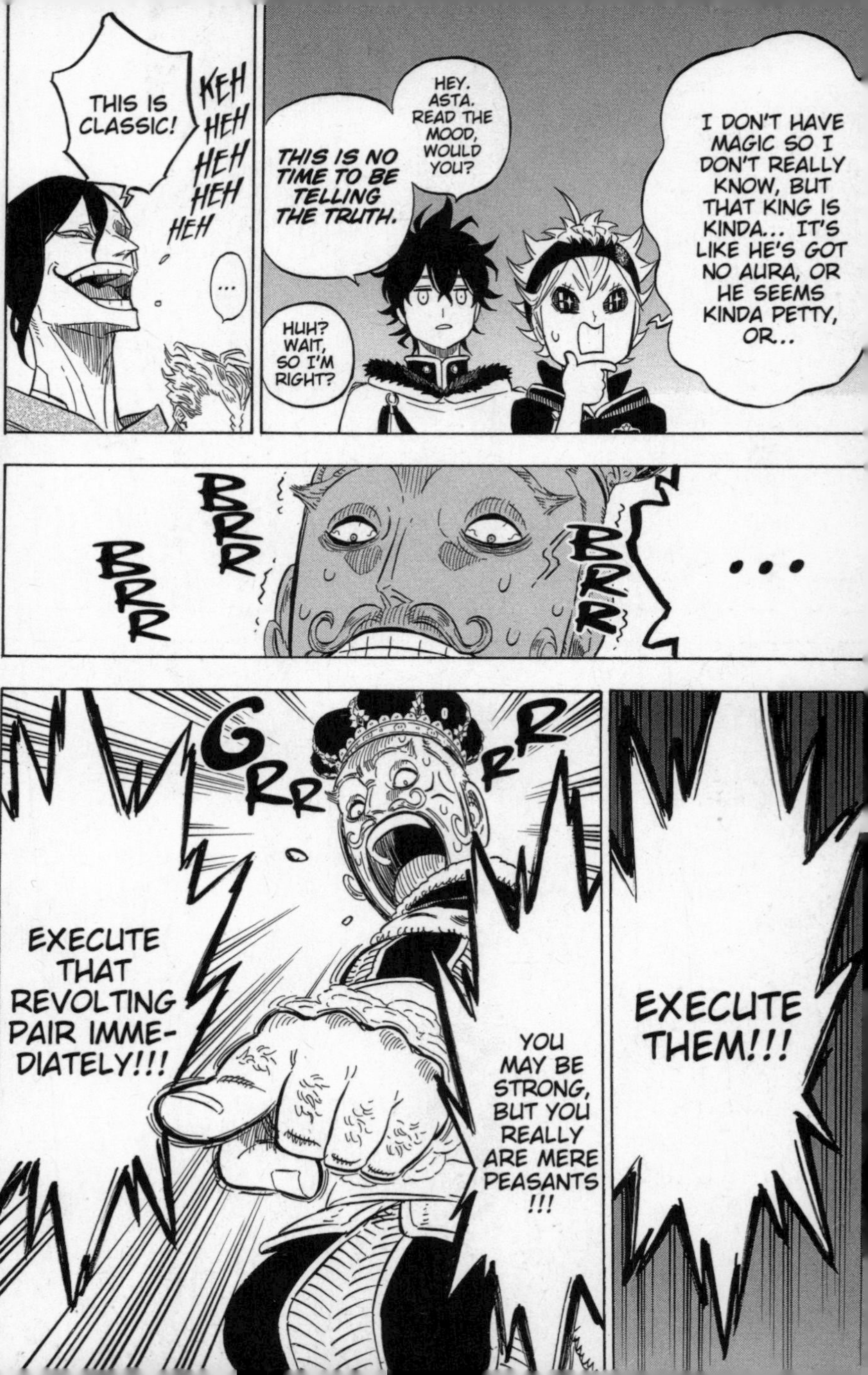
I DON'T HAVE MAGIC SO I DON'T REALLY KNOW, BUT THAT KING IS KINDA... IT'S LIKE HE'S GOT NO AURA, OR HE SEEMS KINDA PETTY, OR...
HEY. ASTA. READ THE MOOD, WOULD YOU?
THIS IS NO TIME TO BE TELLING THE TRUTH.
HUH? WAIT, SO I'M RIGHT?
THIS IS CLASSIC!
KEH HEH HEH HEH HEH
...
...
BRRR
BRRR
BRRR
EXECUTE THEM!!!
GRRRR
YOU MAY BE STRONG, BUT YOU REALLY ARE MERE PEASANTS!!!
EXECUTE THAT REVOLTING PAIR IMME-DIATELY!!!

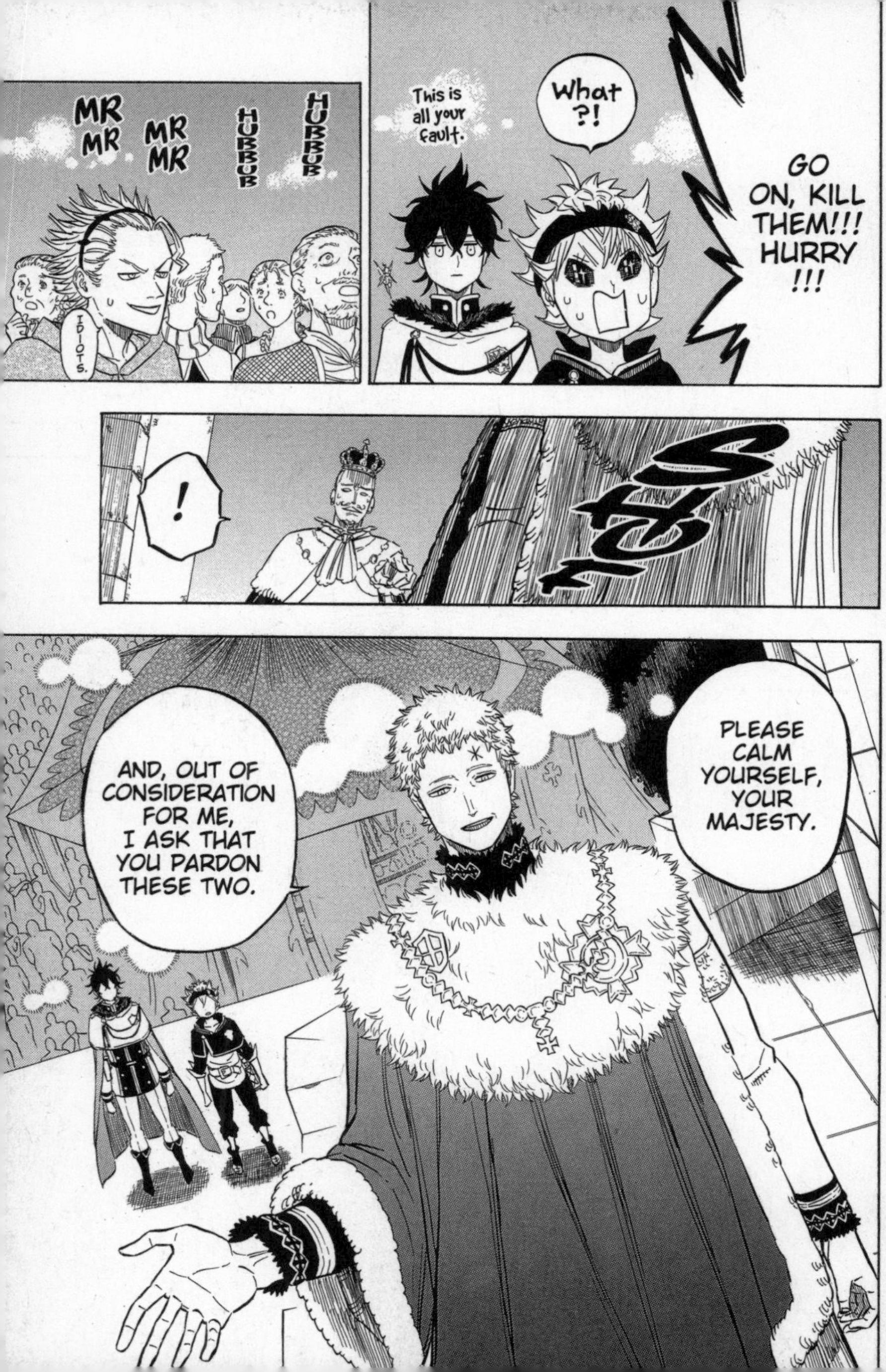
GO ON, KILL THEM!!! HURRY!!!
What ?!
This is all your fault.
HUBBUB
HUBBUB
MR MR
MR MR
IDIOTS.
SHF
!
PLEASE CALM YOURSELF, YOUR MAJESTY.
AND, OUT OF CONSIDERATION FOR ME, I ASK THAT YOU PARDON THESE TWO.

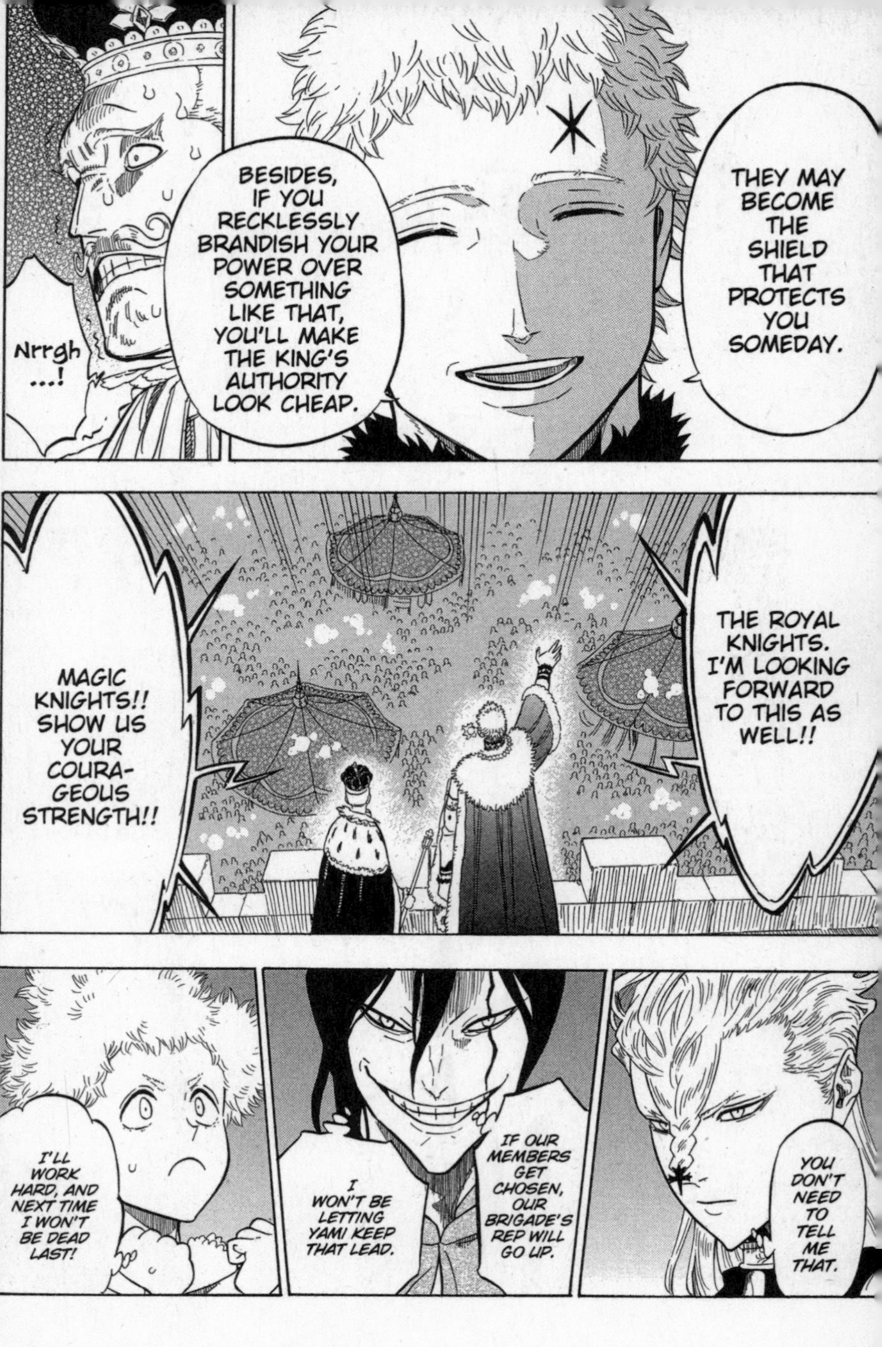
THEY MAY BECOME THE SHIELD THAT PROTECTS YOU SOMEDAY.
BESIDES, IF YOU RECKLESSLY BRANDISH YOUR POWER OVER SOMETHING LIKE THAT, YOU'LL MAKE THE KING'S AUTHORITY LOOK CHEAP.
Nrrgh ...!
THE ROYAL KNIGHTS. I'M LOOKING FORWARD TO THIS AS WELL!!
MAGIC KNIGHTS!! SHOW US YOUR COURAGEOUS STRENGTH!!
YOU DON'T NEED TO TELL ME THAT.
IF OUR MEMBERS GET CHOSEN, OUR BRIGADE'S REP WILL GO UP.
I WON'T BE LETTING YAMI KEEP THAT LEAD.
I'LL WORK HARD, AND NEXT TIME I WON'T BE DEAD LAST!

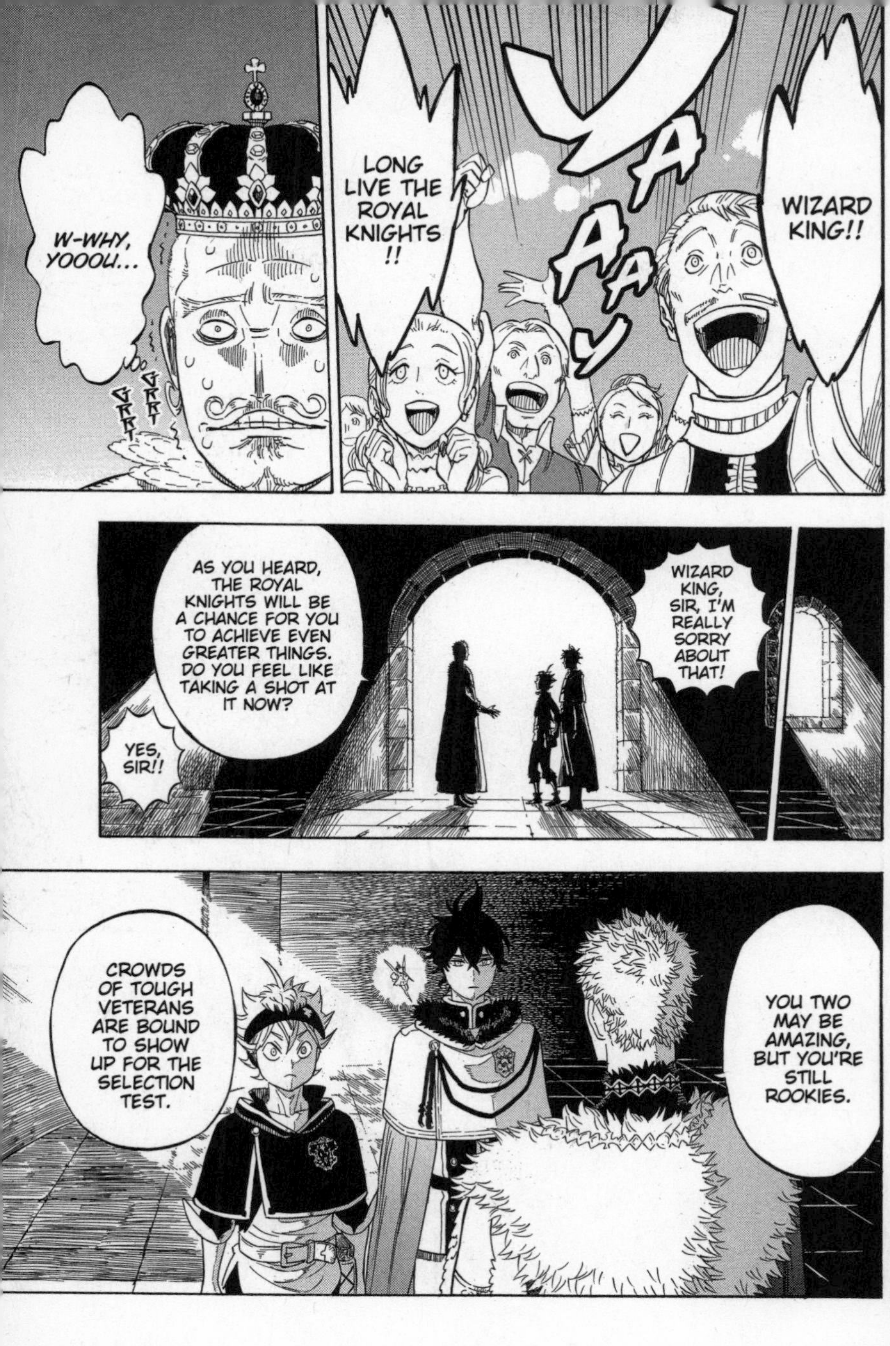
WIZARD KING!!
YAAAY
LONG LIVE THE ROYAL KNIGHTS!!
W-WHY, YOOOU...
GRRT GRRT
WIZARD KING, SIR, I'M REALLY SORRY ABOUT THAT!
AS YOU HEARD, THE ROYAL KNIGHTS WILL BE A CHANCE FOR YOU TO ACHIEVE EVEN GREATER THINGS. DO YOU FEEL LIKE TAKING A SHOT AT IT NOW?
YES, SIR!!
YOU TWO MAY BE AMAZING, BUT YOU'RE STILL ROOKIES.
CROWDS OF TOUGH VETERANS ARE BOUND TO SHOW UP FOR THE SELECTION TEST.

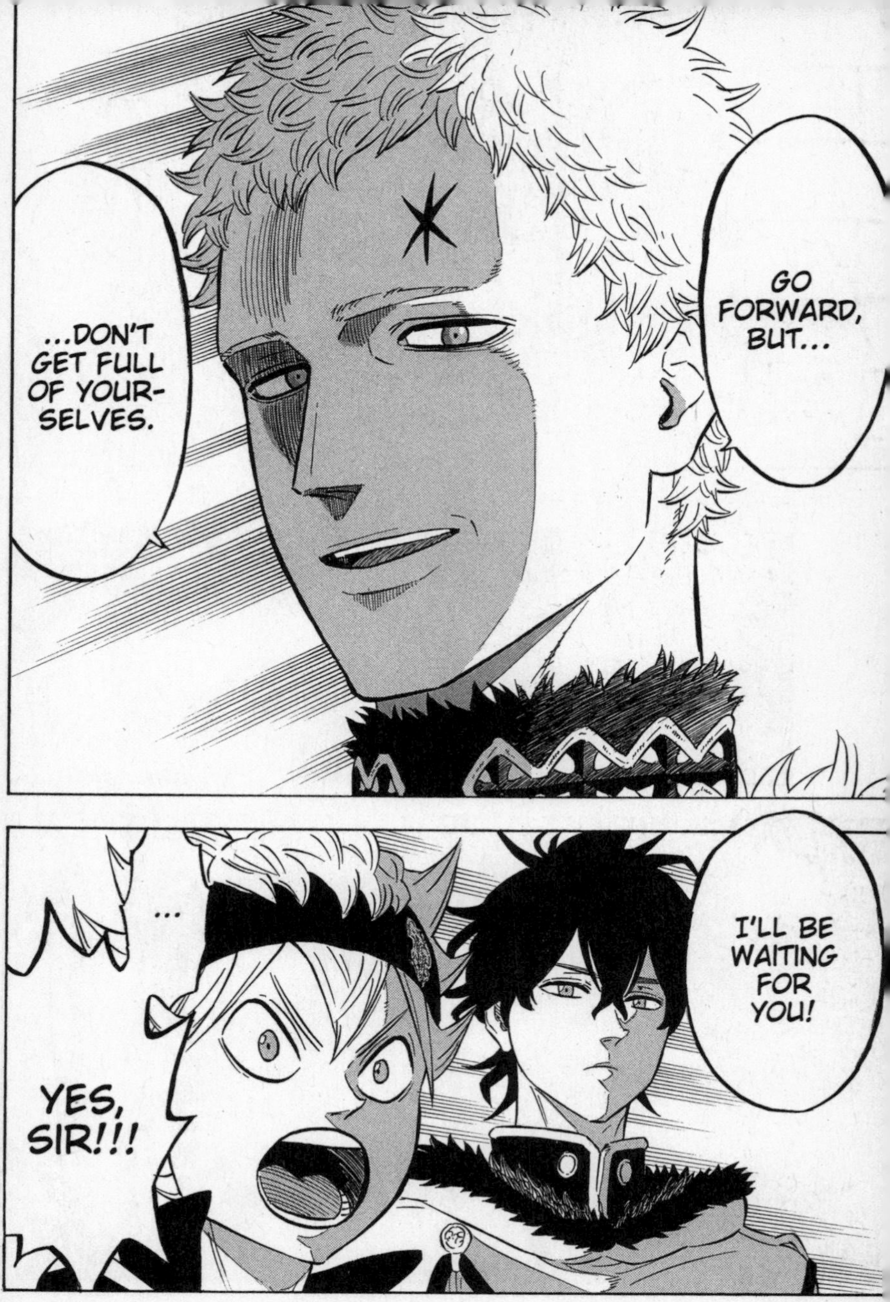
GO FORWARD, BUT...
...DON'T GET FULL OF YOUR-SELVES.
I'LL BE WAITING FOR YOU!
...
YES, SIR!!!

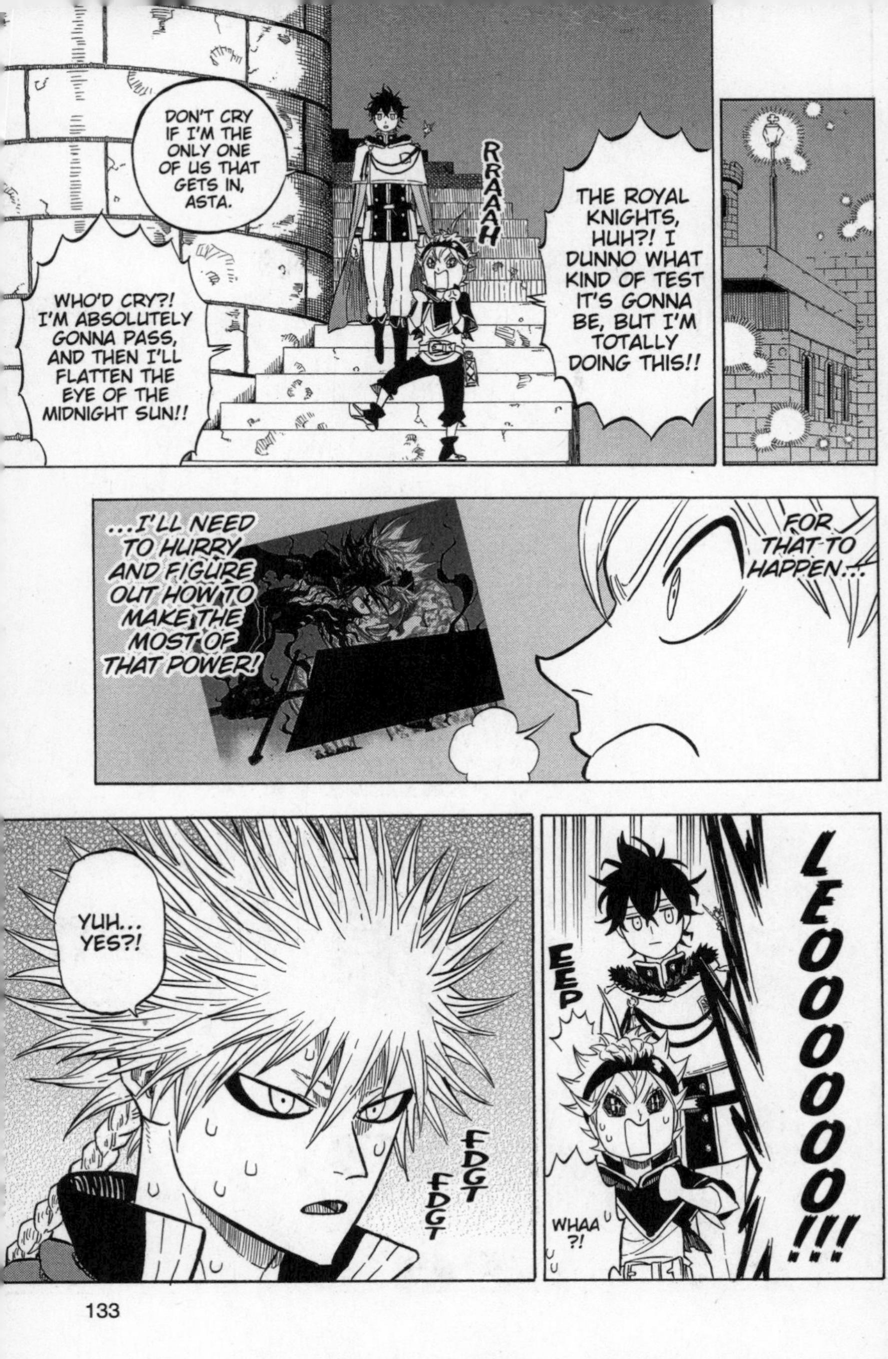
DON'T CRY IF I'M THE ONLY ONE OF US THAT GETS IN, ASTA.
WHO'D CRY?! I'M ABSOLUTELY GONNA PASS, AND THEN I'LL FLATTEN THE EYE OF THE MIDNIGHT SUN!!
RRAAAH
THE ROYAL KNIGHTS, HUH?! I DUNNO WHAT KIND OF TEST IT'S GONNA BE, BUT I'M TOTALLY DOING THIS!!
FOR THAT TO HAPPEN...
...I'LL NEED TO HURRY AND FIGURE OUT HOW TO MAKE THE MOST OF THAT POWER!
LEOOOOOOO!!!
EEP
WHAA ?!
YUH... YES?!
FDGT
FDGT

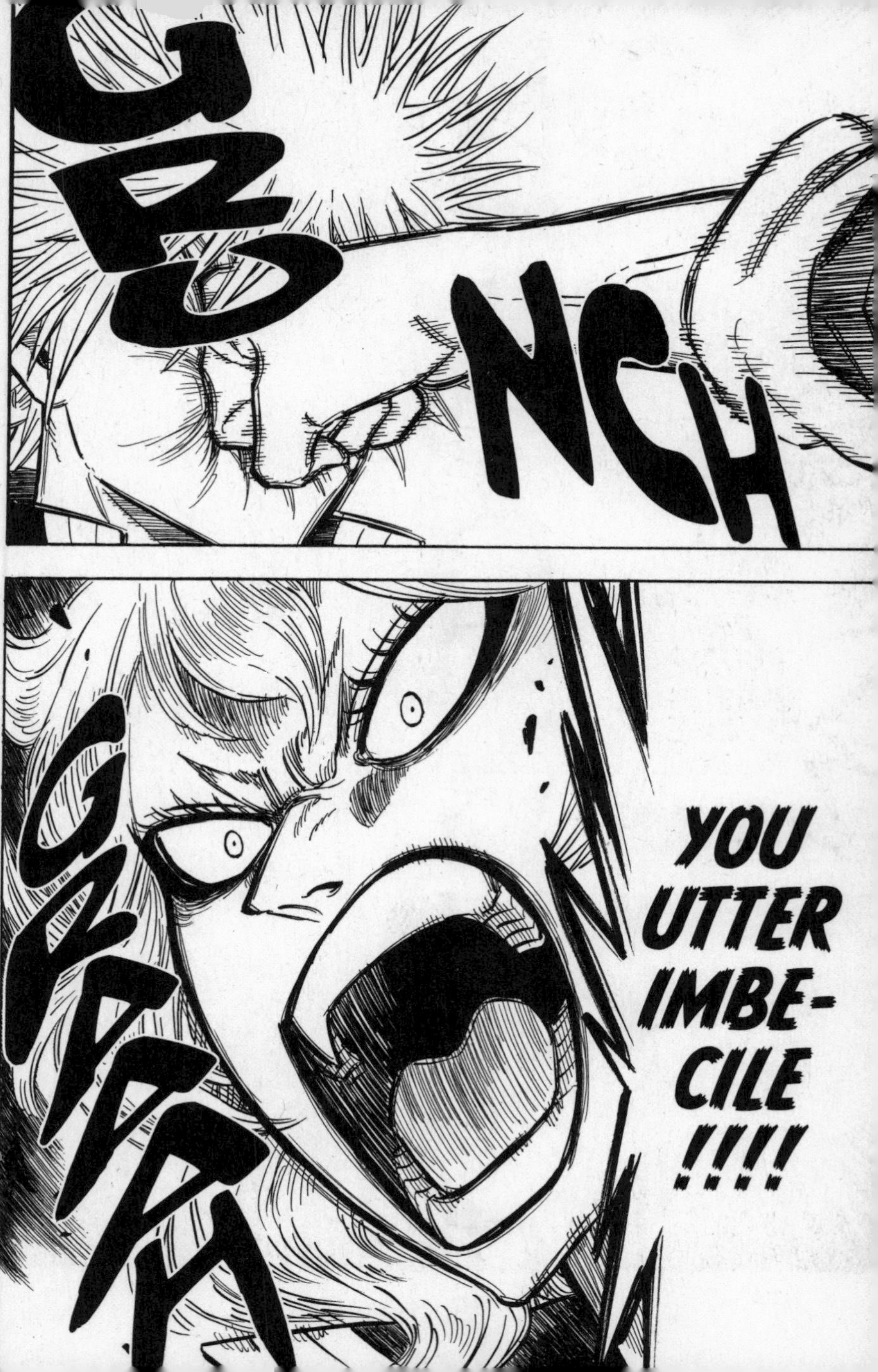
CRUNCH
YOU UTTER IMBE-CILE!!!!
GWAAAA

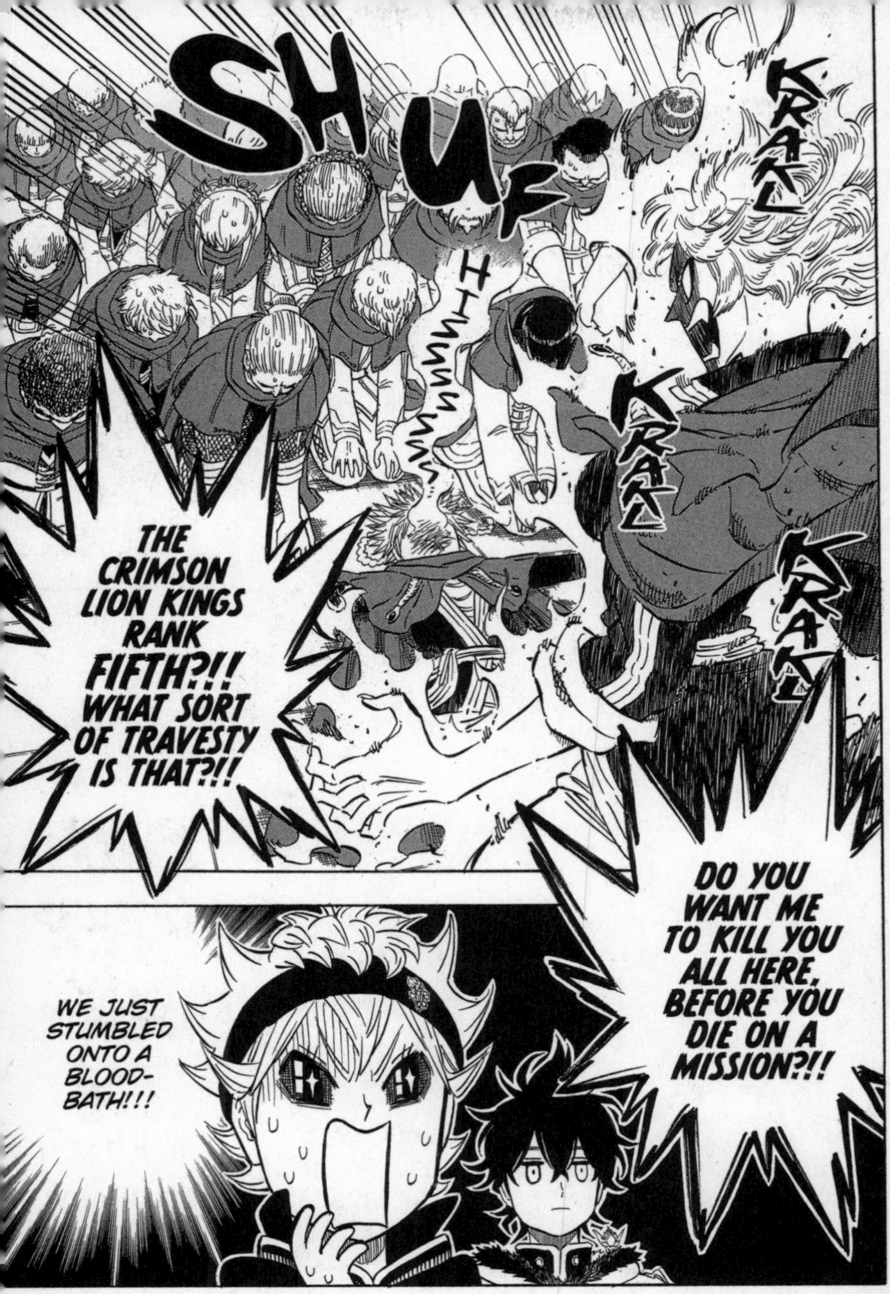
KRAL
KRAL
KRAL
SHUF
HISSSSSSSS
THE CRIMSON LION KINGS RANK FIFTH?!! WHAT SORT OF TRAVESTY IS THAT?!!
DO YOU WANT ME TO KILL YOU ALL HERE, BEFORE YOU DIE ON A MISSION?!!
WE JUST STUMBLED ONTO A BLOOD-BATH!!!

Augustus Kira Clover

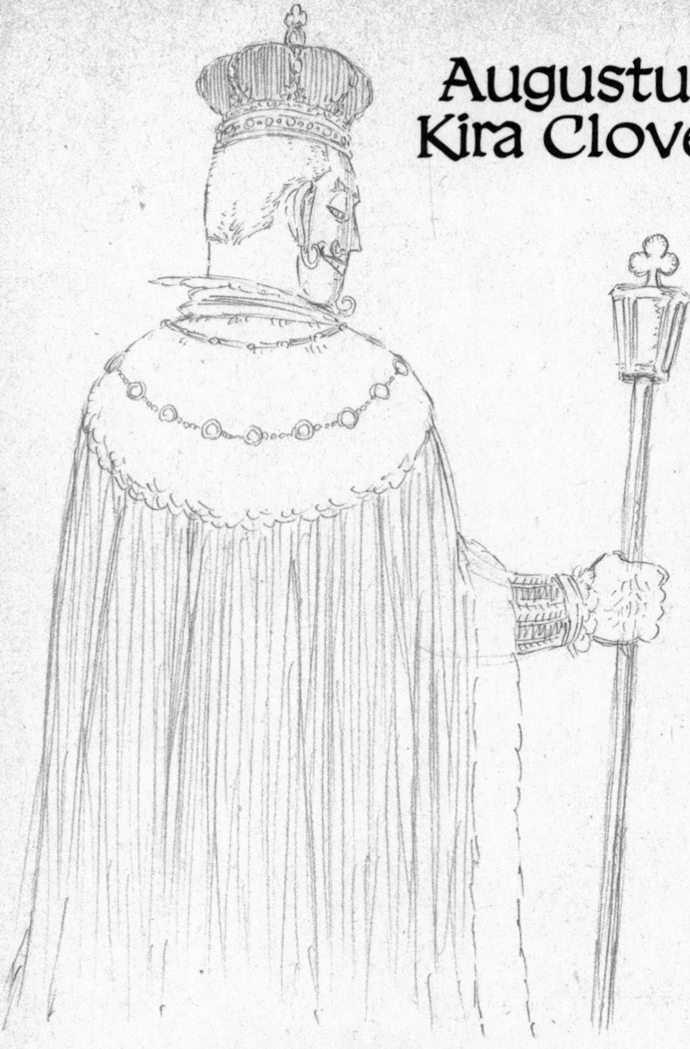

Age: 35 Height: 160 cm
Birthday: October 22 Sign: Libra Blood Type: AB
Likes: Being praised extravagantly,
looking down over the country from the castle

Character Profile

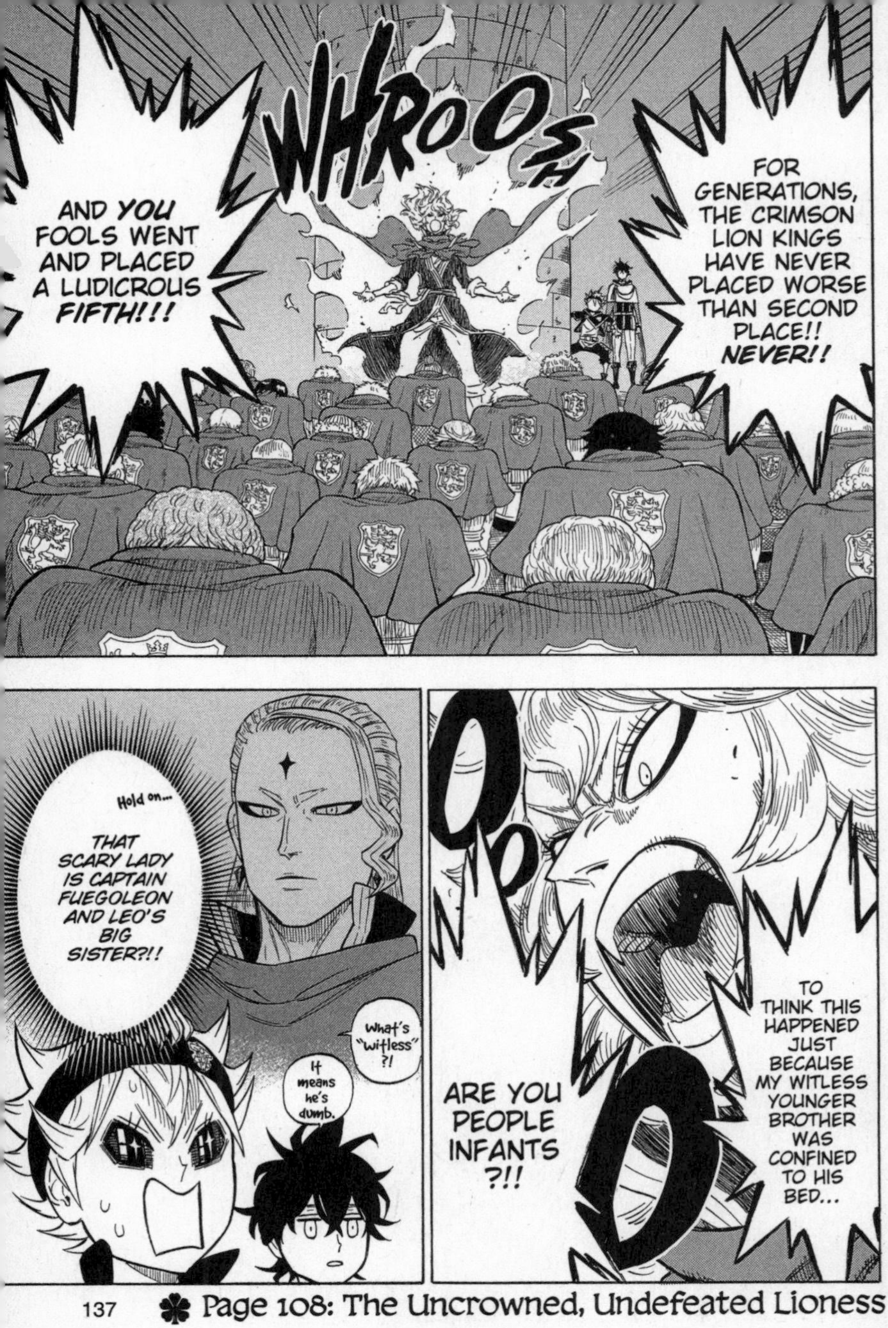
WHROOSH
FOR GENERATIONS, THE CRIMSON LION KINGS HAVE NEVER PLACED WORSE THAN SECOND PLACE!! *NEVER!!*
AND *YOU* FOOLS WENT AND PLACED A LUDICROUS *FIFTH!!!*
TO THINK THIS HAPPENED JUST BECAUSE MY WITLESS YOUNGER BROTHER WAS CONFINED TO HIS BED...
ARE YOU PEOPLE INFANTS?!!
Hold on...
THAT SCARY LADY IS CAPTAIN FUEGOLEON AND LEO'S BIG SISTER?!!
What's "witless"?!
It means he's dumb.

Page 108: The Uncrowned, Undefeated Lioness

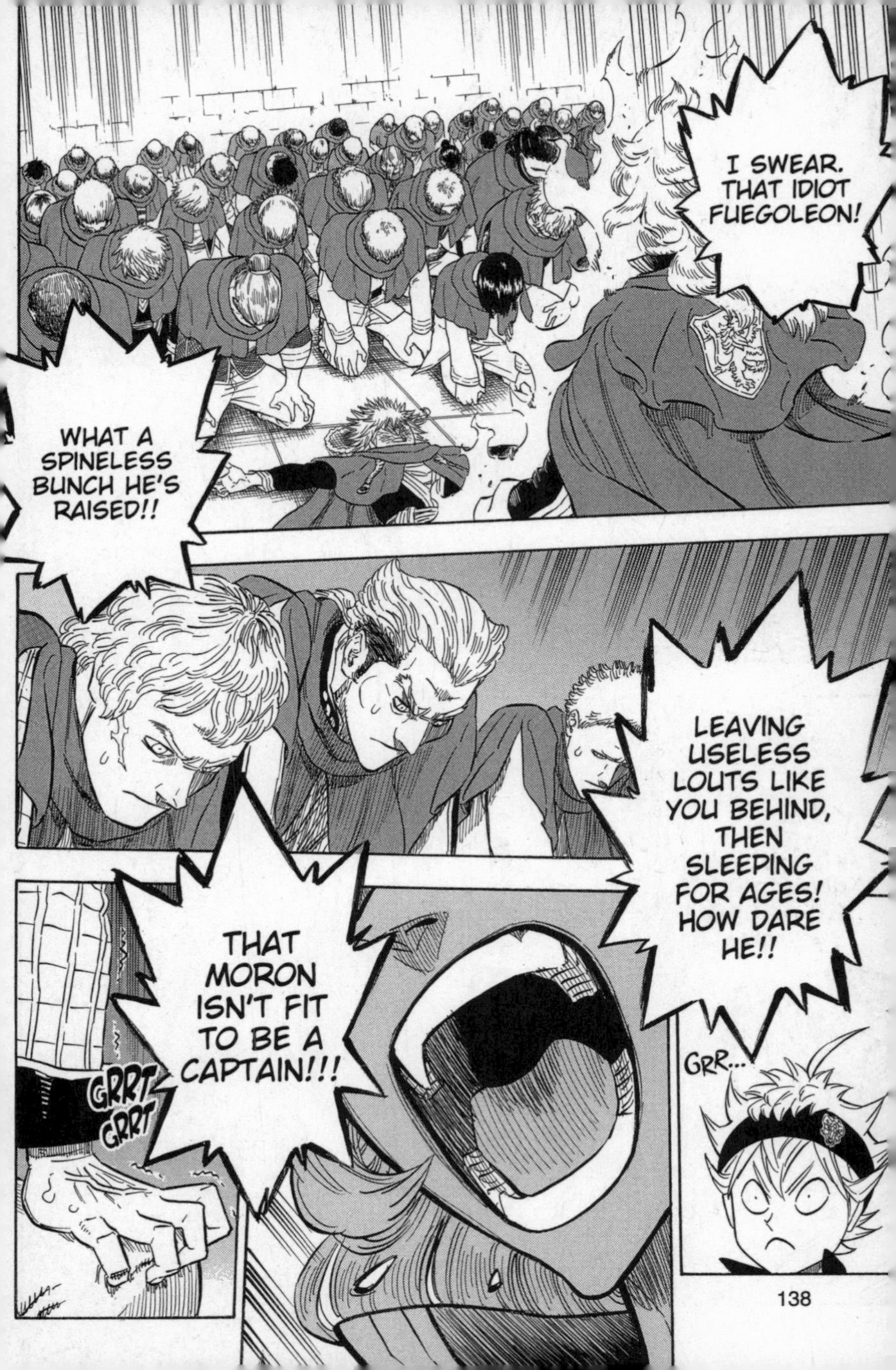
I SWEAR. THAT IDIOT FUEGOLEON!
WHAT A SPINELESS BUNCH HE'S RAISED!!
LEAVING USELESS LOUTS LIKE YOU BEHIND, THEN SLEEPING FOR AGES! HOW DARE HE!!
GRR...
THAT MORON ISN'T FIT TO BE A CAPTAIN!!!
GRRT GRRT

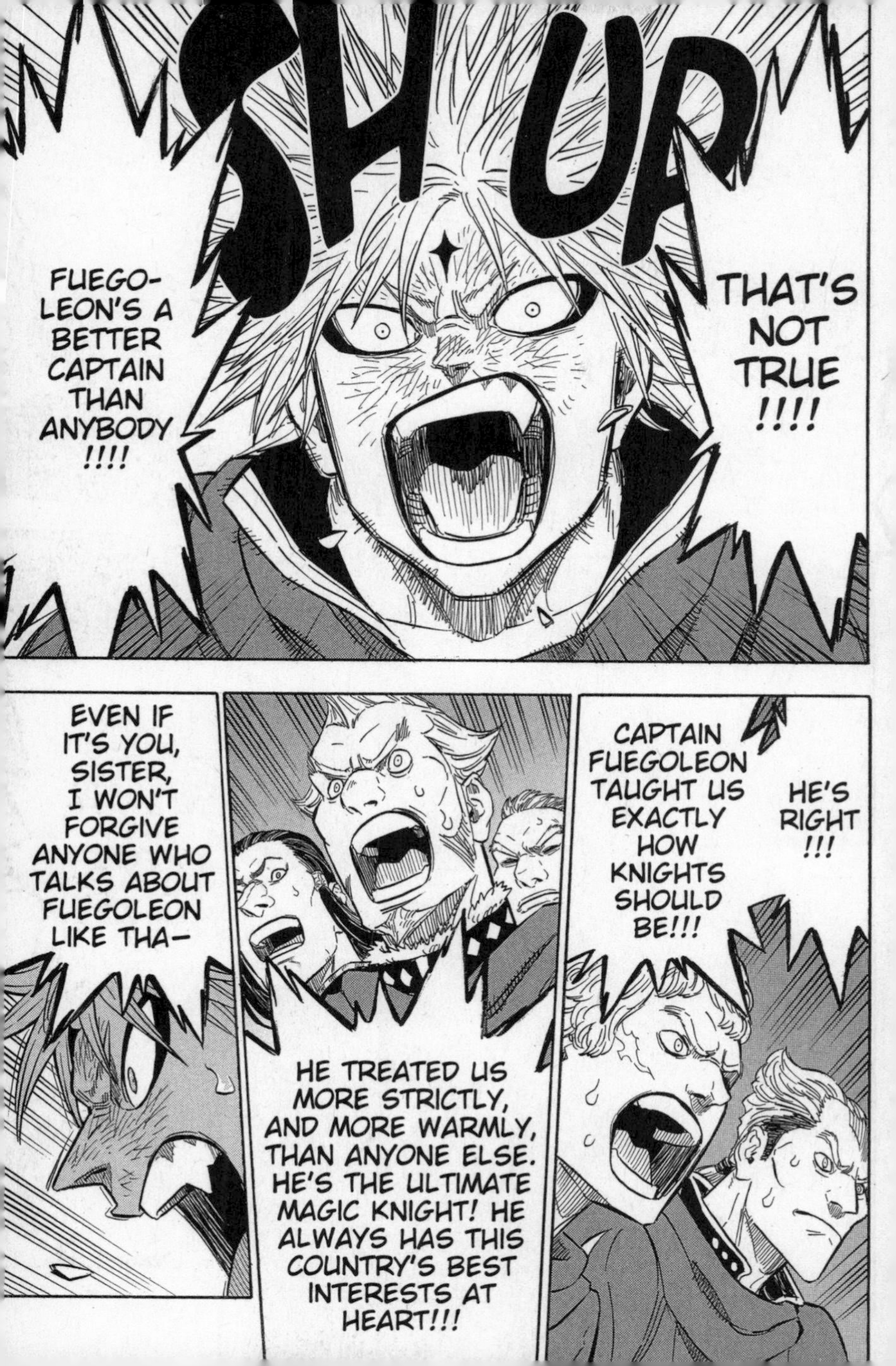
SHUP
THAT'S NOT TRUE!!!!
FUEGO-LEON'S A BETTER CAPTAIN THAN ANYBODY!!!!
HE'S RIGHT!!!
CAPTAIN FUEGOLEON TAUGHT US EXACTLY HOW KNIGHTS SHOULD BE!!!
HE TREATED US MORE STRICTLY, AND MORE WARMLY, THAN ANYONE ELSE. HE'S THE ULTIMATE MAGIC KNIGHT! HE ALWAYS HAS THIS COUNTRY'S BEST INTERESTS AT HEART!!!
EVEN IF IT'S YOU, SISTER, I WON'T FORGIVE ANYONE WHO TALKS ABOUT FUEGOLEON LIKE THA-

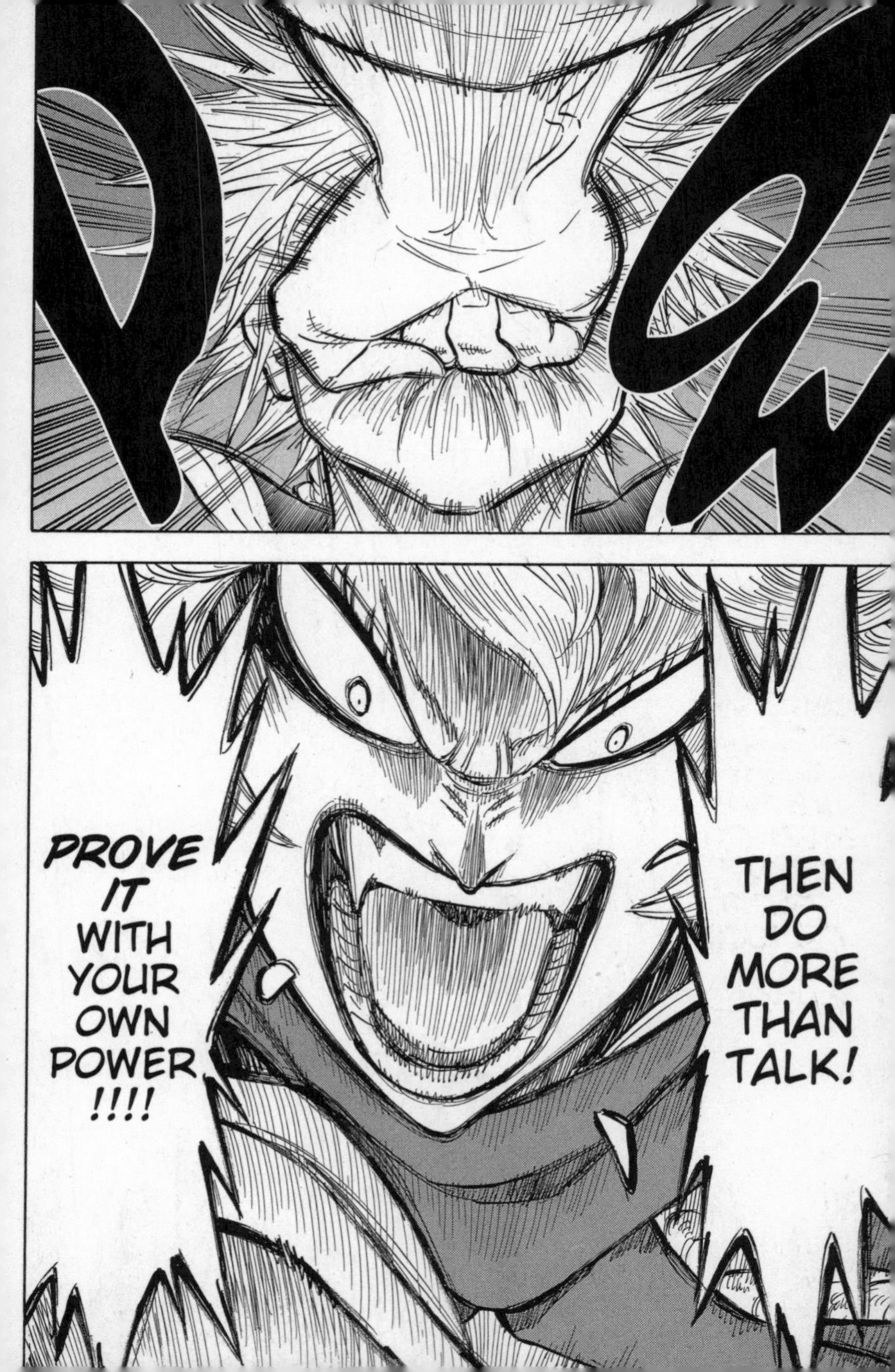
THEN DO MORE THAN TALK!
PROVE IT WITH YOUR OWN POWER!!!!

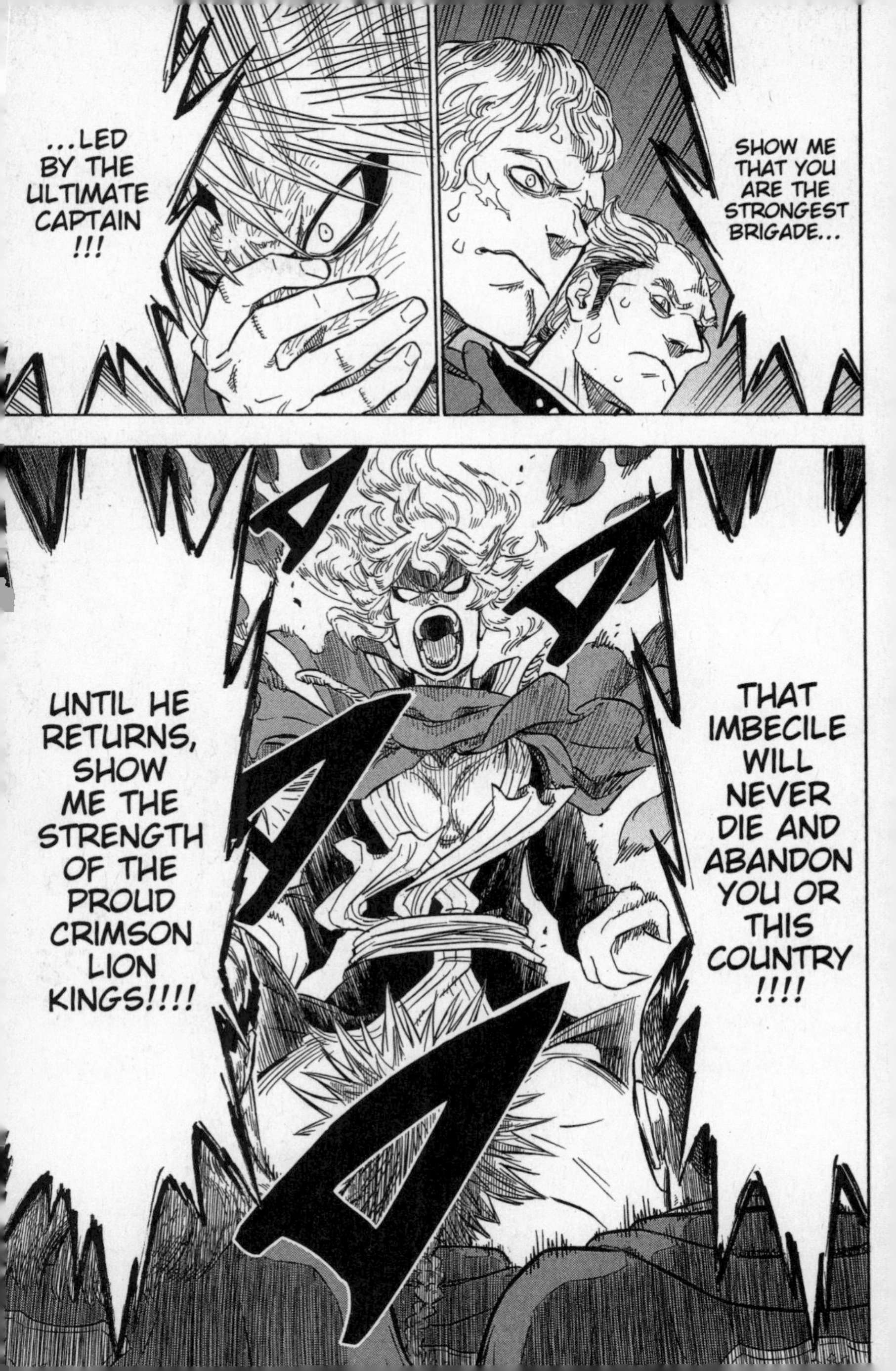
SHOW ME THAT YOU ARE THE STRONGEST BRIGADE...
...LED BY THE ULTIMATE CAPTAIN!!!
THAT IMBECILE WILL NEVER DIE AND ABANDON YOU OR THIS COUNTRY!!!!
UNTIL HE RETURNS, SHOW ME THE STRENGTH OF THE PROUD CRIMSON LION KINGS!!!!
AAAA

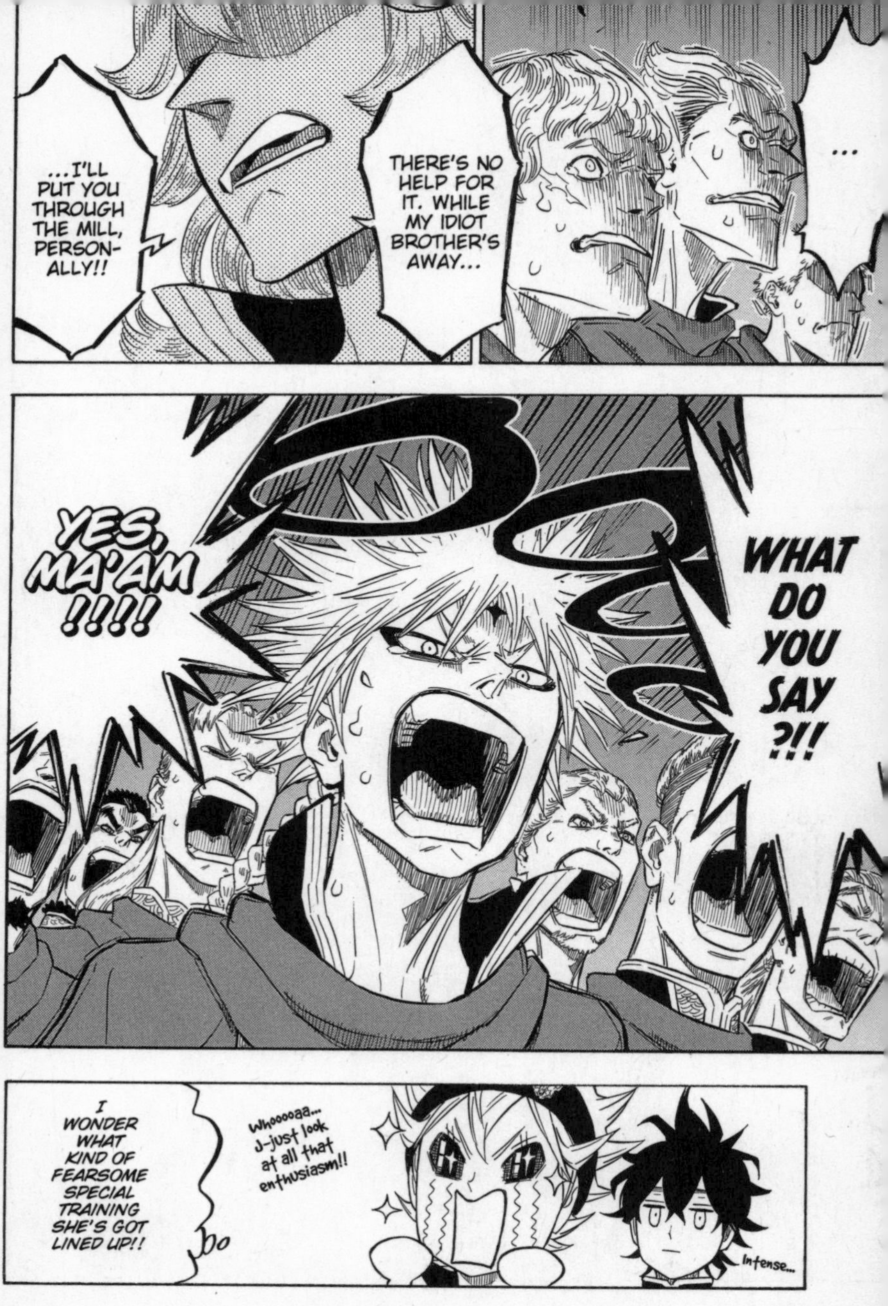
...
THERE'S NO HELP FOR IT. WHILE MY IDIOT BROTHER'S AWAY...
...I'LL PUT YOU THROUGH THE MILL, PERSON-ALLY!!
WHAT DO YOU SAY?!!
YES, MA'AM!!!!
Whoooaa... J-just look at all that enthusiasm!!
I WONDER WHAT KIND OF FEARSOME SPECIAL TRAINING SHE'S GOT LINED UP!!
Do
Intense...

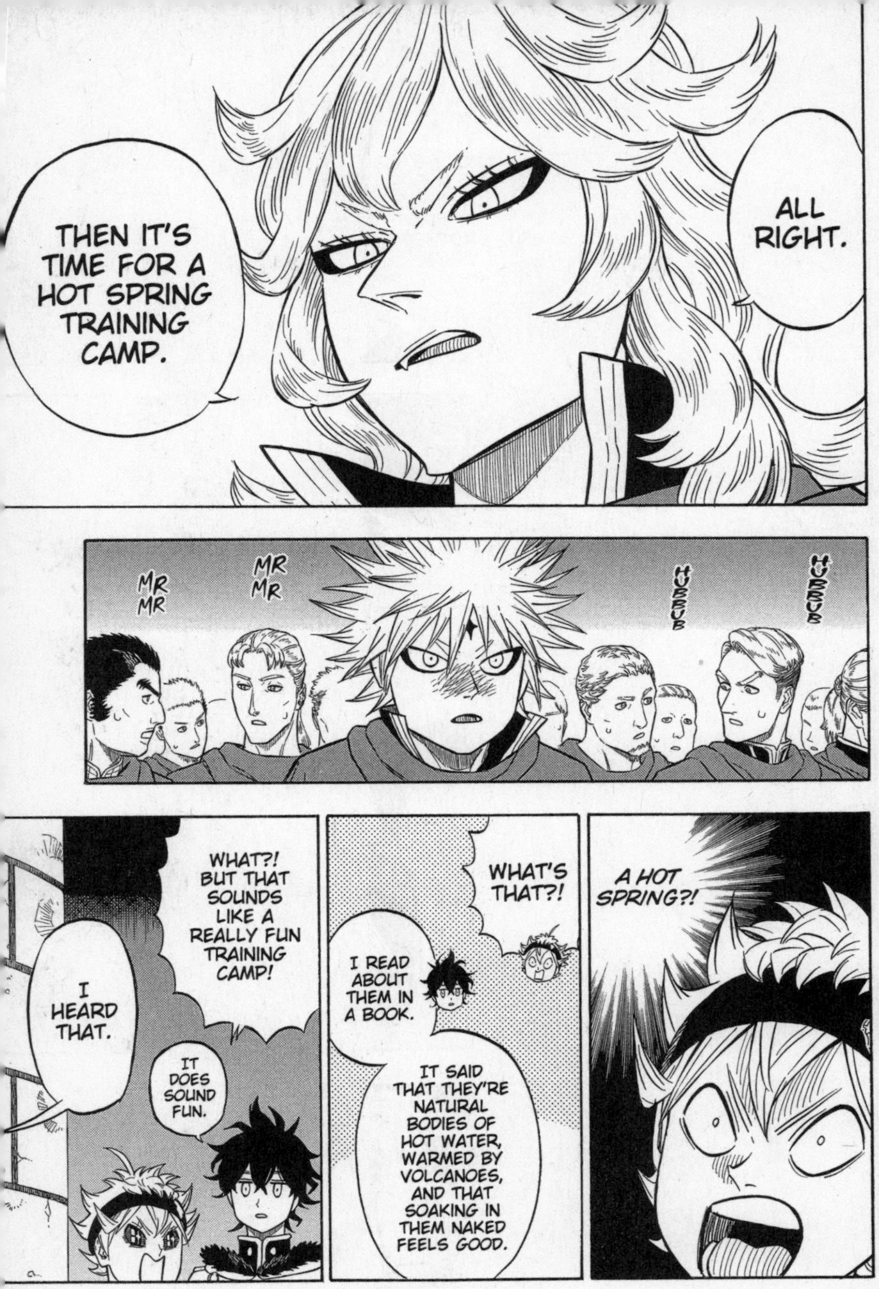
ALL RIGHT.
THEN IT'S TIME FOR A HOT SPRING TRAINING CAMP.
HUBBUB
HUBBUB
MR MR
MR MR
A HOT SPRING?!
WHAT'S THAT?!
I READ ABOUT THEM IN A BOOK.
IT SAID THAT THEY'RE NATURAL BODIES OF HOT WATER, WARMED BY VOLCANOES, AND THAT SOAKING IN THEM NAKED FEELS GOOD.
WHAT?! BUT THAT SOUNDS LIKE A REALLY FUN TRAINING CAMP!
I HEARD THAT.
IT DOES SOUND FUN.

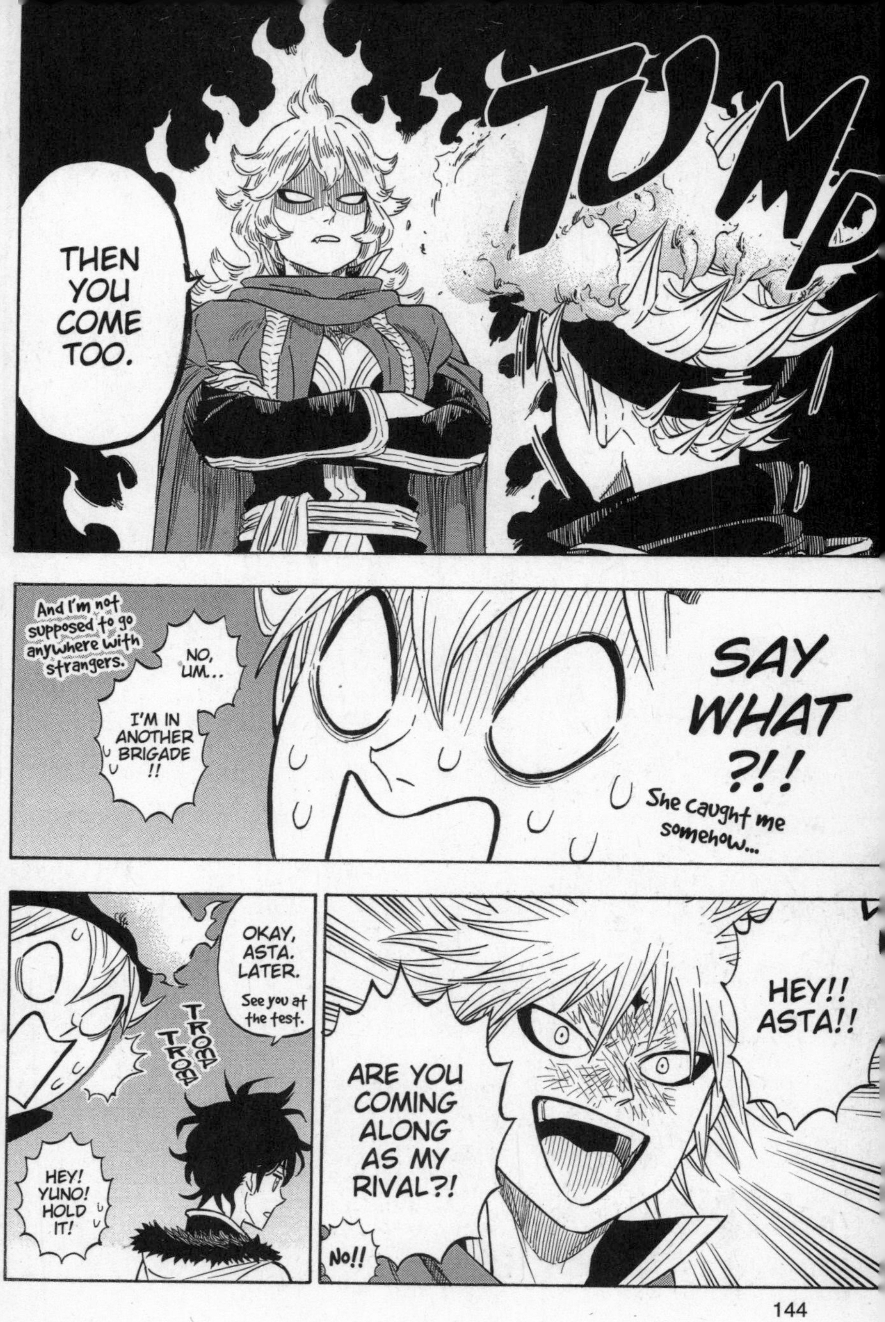
TUMP
THEN YOU COME TOO.
SAY WHAT?!!
She caught me somehow...
NO, UM...
I'M IN ANOTHER BRIGADE!!
And I'm not supposed to go anywhere with strangers.
HEY!! ASTA!!
ARE YOU COMING ALONG AS MY RIVAL?!
No!!
OKAY, ASTA. LATER.
See you at the test.
TROMA TROMA
HEY! YUNO! HOLD IT!

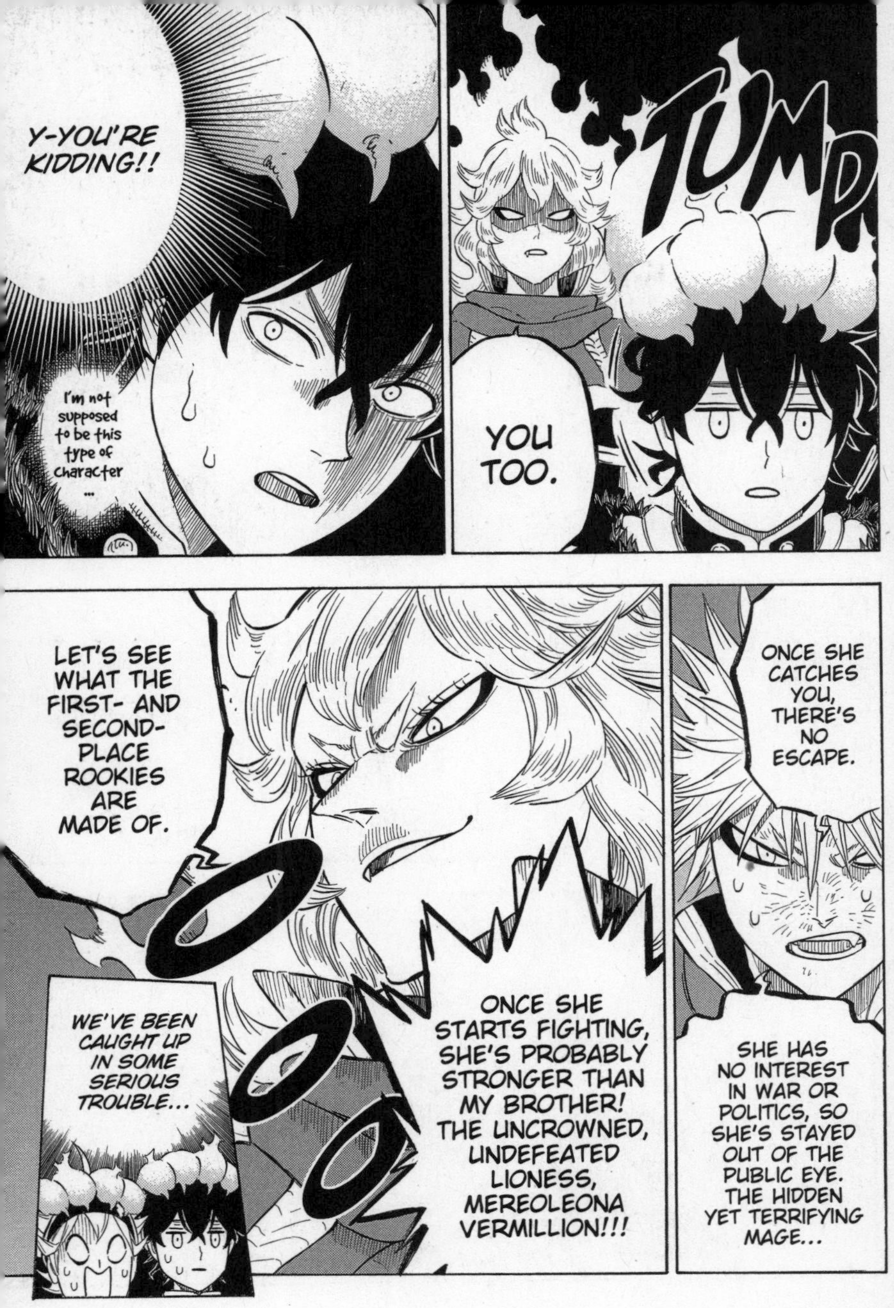
TUMP
YOU TOO.
Y-YOU'RE KIDDING!!
I'm not supposed to be this type of character ...
ONCE SHE CATCHES YOU, THERE'S NO ESCAPE.
SHE HAS NO INTEREST IN WAR OR POLITICS, SO SHE'S STAYED OUT OF THE PUBLIC EYE. THE HIDDEN YET TERRIFYING MAGE...
LET'S SEE WHAT THE FIRST- AND SECOND-PLACE ROOKIES ARE MADE OF.
ONCE SHE STARTS FIGHTING, SHE'S PROBABLY STRONGER THAN MY BROTHER! THE UNCROWNED, UNDEFEATED LIONESS, MEREOLEONA VERMILLION!!!
WE'VE BEEN CAUGHT UP IN SOME SERIOUS TROUBLE...

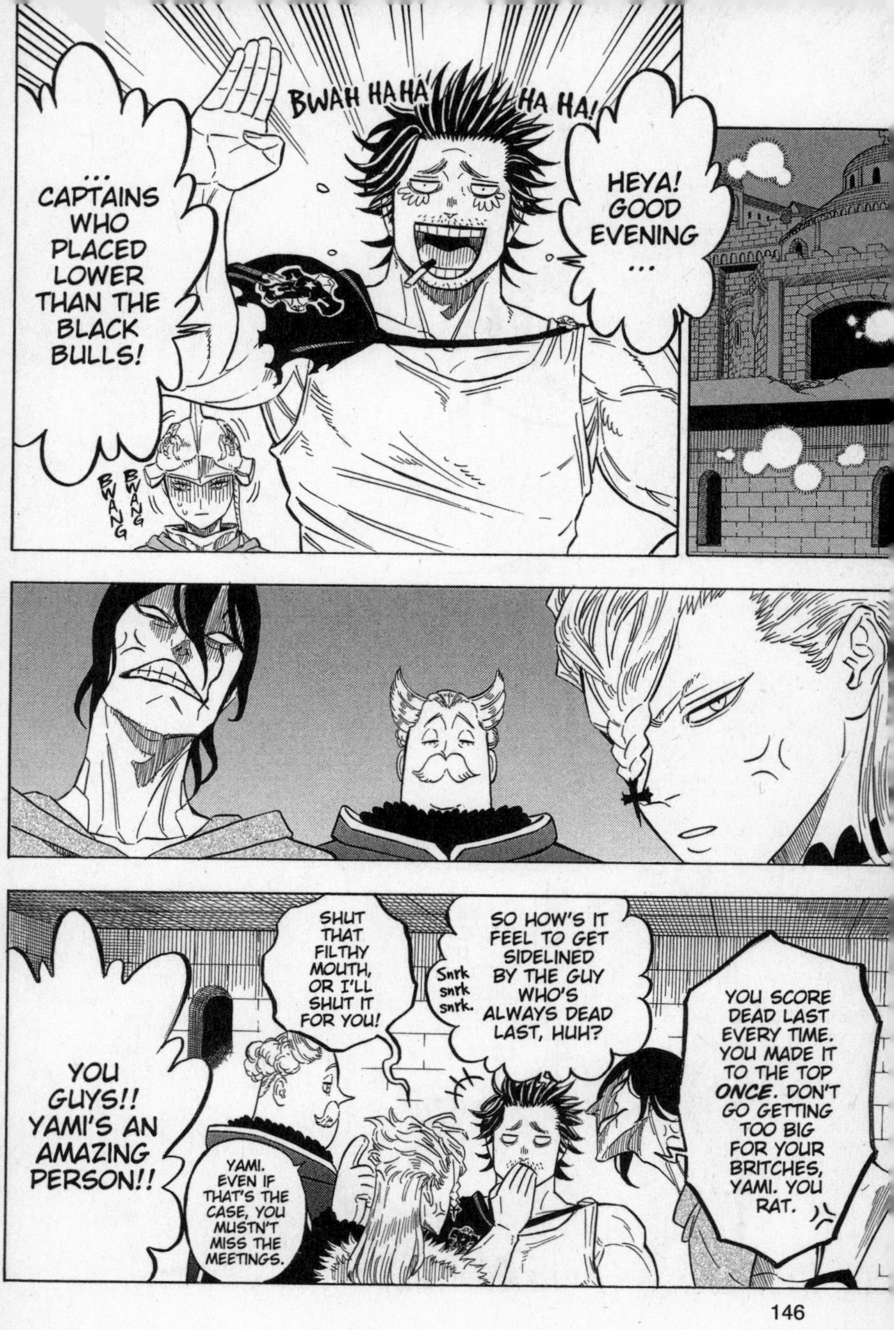
HEYA! GOOD EVENING ...
BWAH HA HA HA HA!
... CAPTAINS WHO PLACED LOWER THAN THE BLACK BULLS!
BWANG BWANG
YOU SCORE DEAD LAST EVERY TIME. YOU MADE IT TO THE TOP *ONCE*. DON'T GO GETTING TOO BIG FOR YOUR BRITCHES, YAMI. YOU RAT.
SO HOW'S IT FEEL TO GET SIDELINED BY THE GUY WHO'S ALWAYS DEAD LAST, HUH?
Snrk snrk snrk.
SHUT THAT FILTHY MOUTH, OR I'LL SHUT IT FOR YOU!
YAMI. EVEN IF THAT'S THE CASE, YOU MUSTN'T MISS THE MEETINGS.
YOU GUYS!! YAMI'S AN AMAZING PERSON!!

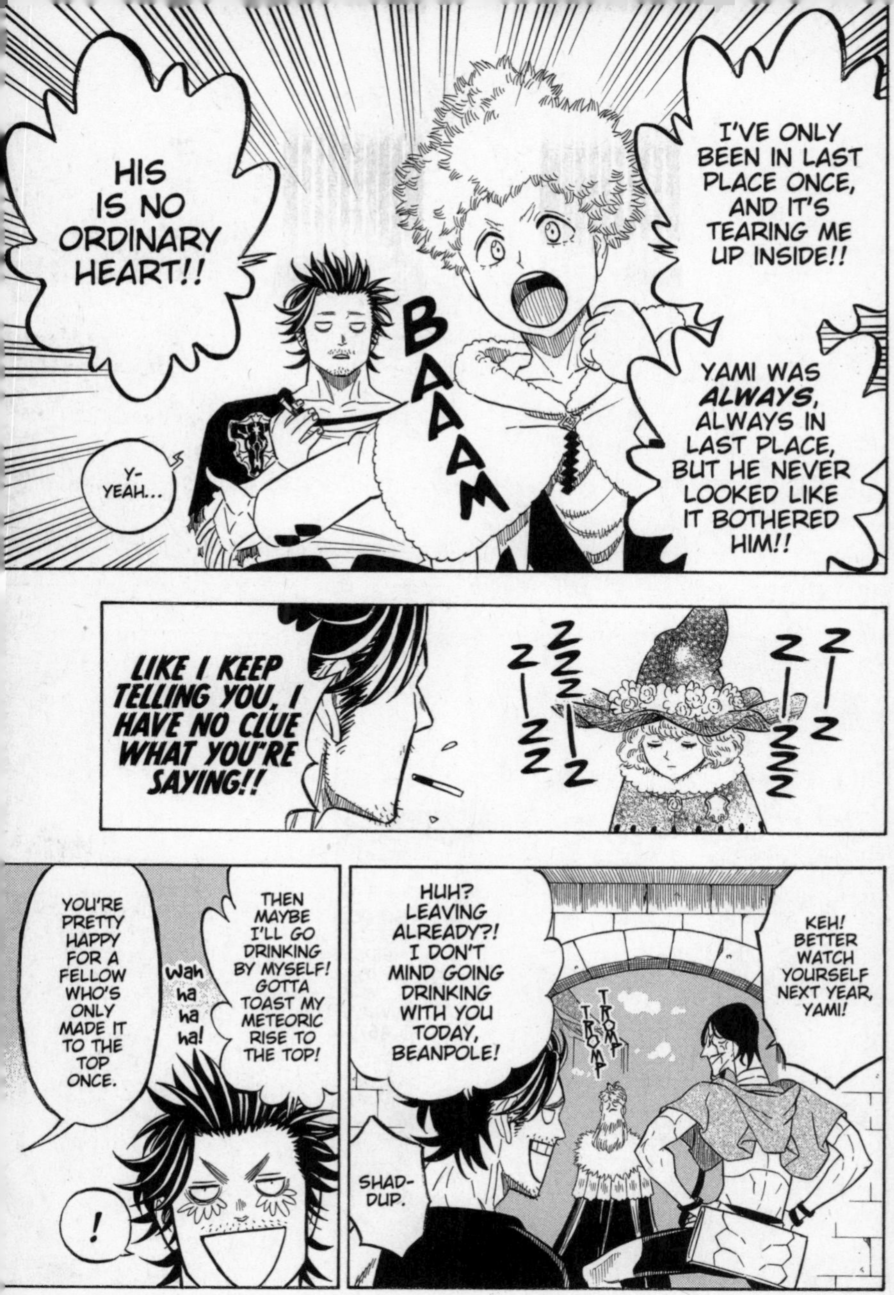
I'VE ONLY BEEN IN LAST PLACE ONCE, AND IT'S TEARING ME UP INSIDE!!
YAMI WAS ***ALWAYS***, ALWAYS IN LAST PLACE, BUT HE NEVER LOOKED LIKE IT BOTHERED HIM!!
BAAAM
HIS IS NO ORDINARY HEART!!
Y-YEAH...
Z-ZZZ Z-ZZZ
LIKE I KEEP TELLING YOU, I HAVE NO CLUE WHAT YOU'RE SAYING!!
KEH! BETTER WATCH YOURSELF NEXT YEAR, YAMI!
TROMP TROMP
HUH? LEAVING ALREADY?! I DON'T MIND GOING DRINKING WITH YOU TODAY, BEANPOLE!
SHAD-DUP.
THEN MAYBE I'LL GO DRINKING BY MYSELF! GOTTA TOAST MY METEORIC RISE TO THE TOP!
Wah ha ha ha!
YOU'RE PRETTY HAPPY FOR A FELLOW WHO'S ONLY MADE IT TO THE TOP ONCE.
!

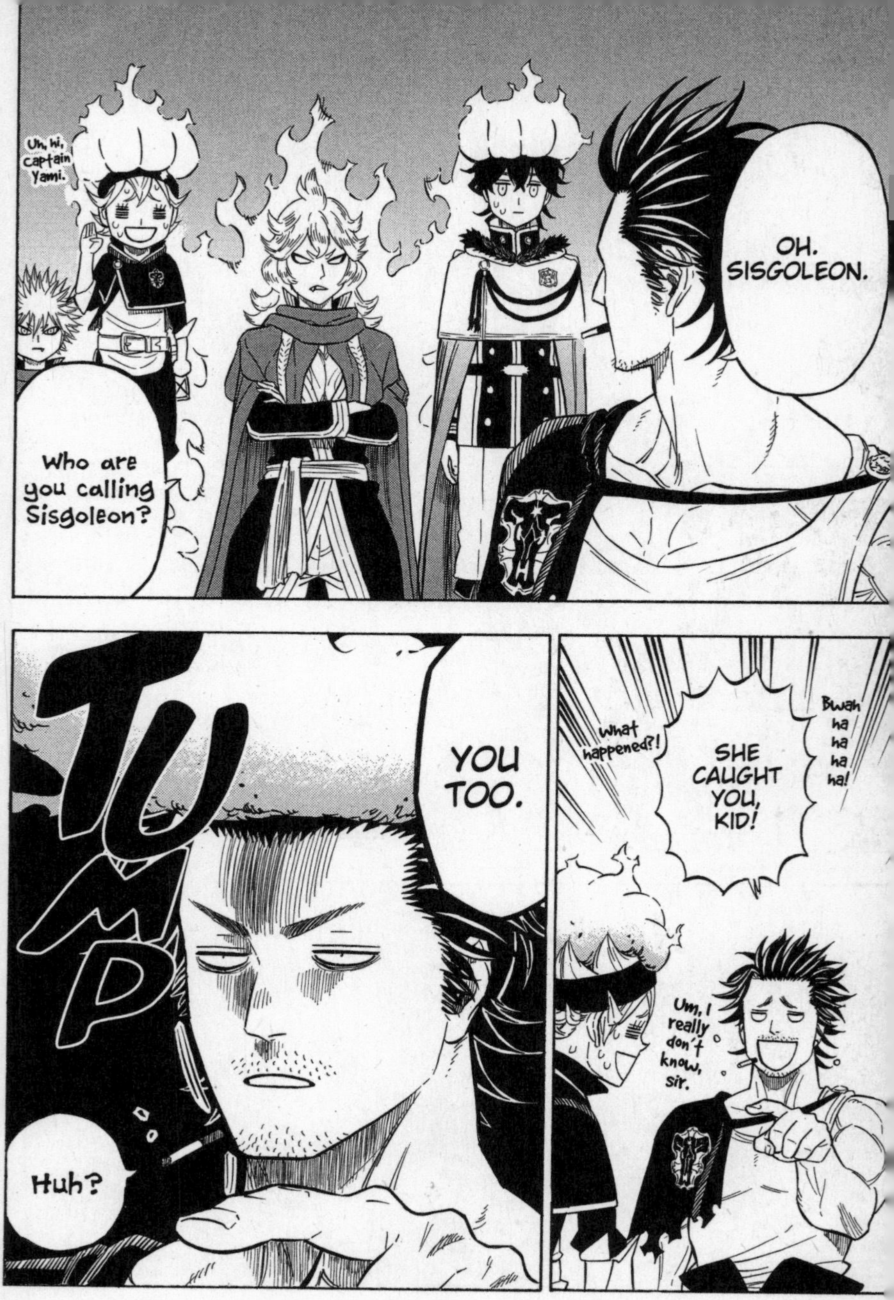

OH. SISGOLEON.
Uh, hi, captain Yami.
Who are you calling Sisgoleon?
Bwah ha ha ha ha!
SHE CAUGHT YOU, KID!
what happened?!
Um, I really don't know, sir.
YOU TOO.
TUMP
Huh?

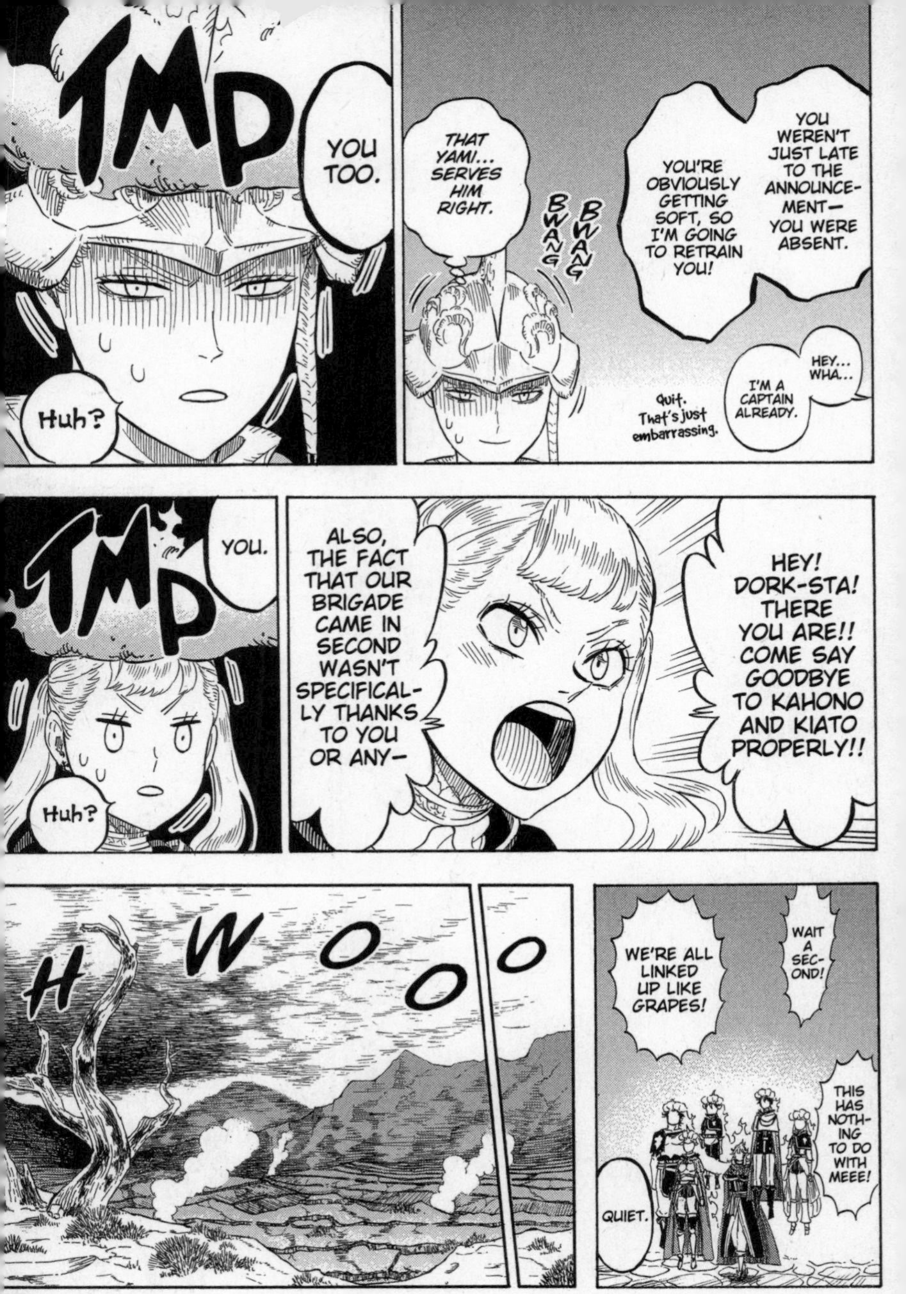
YOU WEREN'T JUST LATE TO THE ANNOUNCEMENT— YOU WERE ABSENT.
YOU'RE OBVIOUSLY GETTING SOFT, SO I'M GOING TO RETRAIN YOU!
HEY... WHA...
I'M A CAPTAIN ALREADY.
BWANG BWANG
Quit. That's just embarrassing.
THAT YAMI... SERVES HIM RIGHT.
YOU TOO.
TMP
Huh?
HEY! DORK-STA! THERE YOU ARE!! COME SAY GOODBYE TO KAHONO AND KIATO PROPERLY!!
ALSO, THE FACT THAT OUR BRIGADE CAME IN SECOND WASN'T SPECIFICAL-LY THANKS TO YOU OR ANY—
YOU.
TMP
Huh?
WAIT A SEC-OND!
WE'RE ALL LINKED UP LIKE GRAPES!
THIS HAS NOTHING TO DO WITH MEEE!
QUIET.
HWOOO

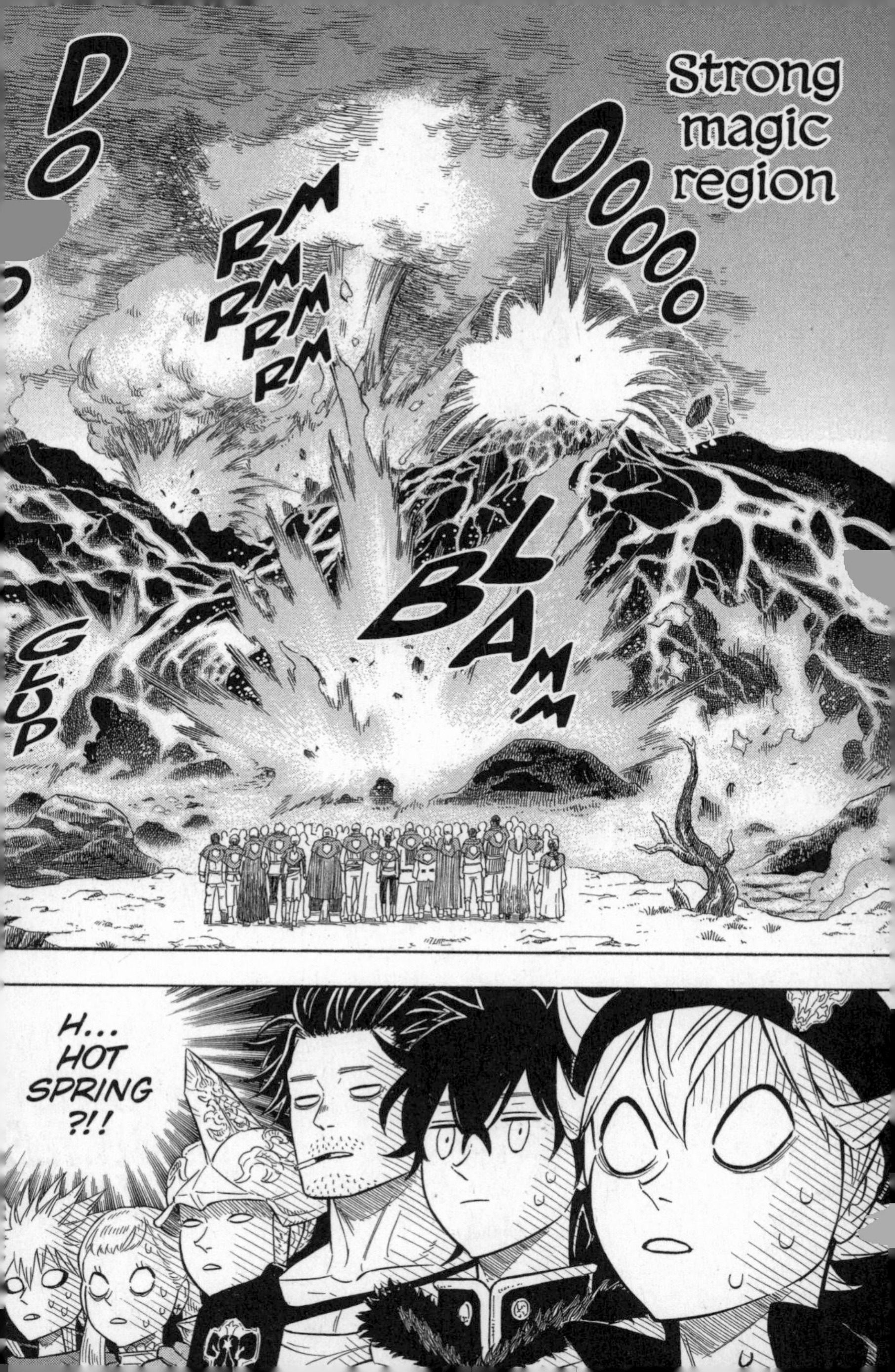
Strong magic region
OOOOO
RMRMRMRMRM
BLAMM
DO
GLUP
H... HOT SPRING ?!!

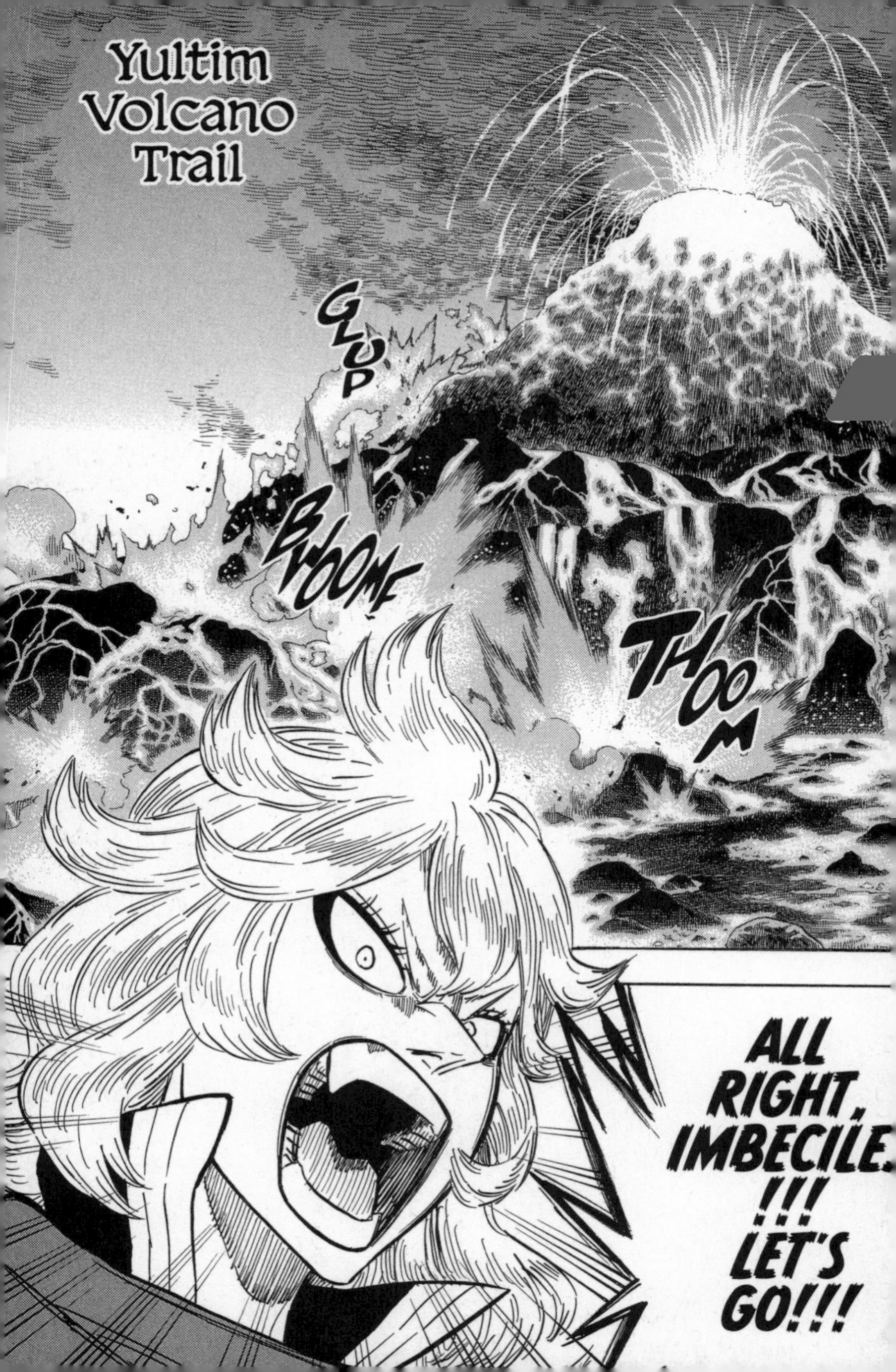
Yultim Volcano Trail
GLUP
BWOOME
THOOM
ALL RIGHT, IMBECILE!!! LET'S GO!!!

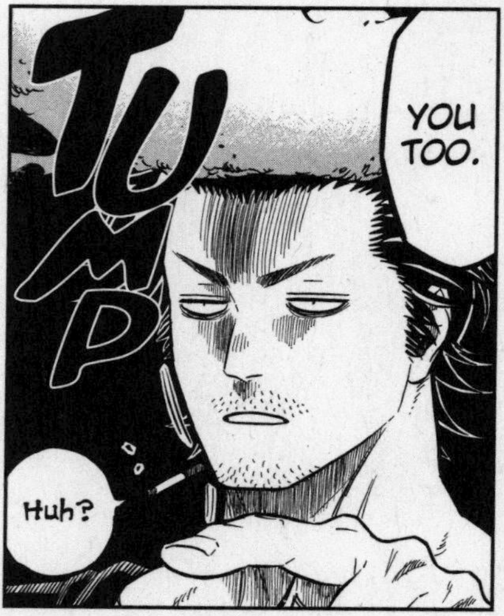
YOU TOO.
TUMP
Huh?

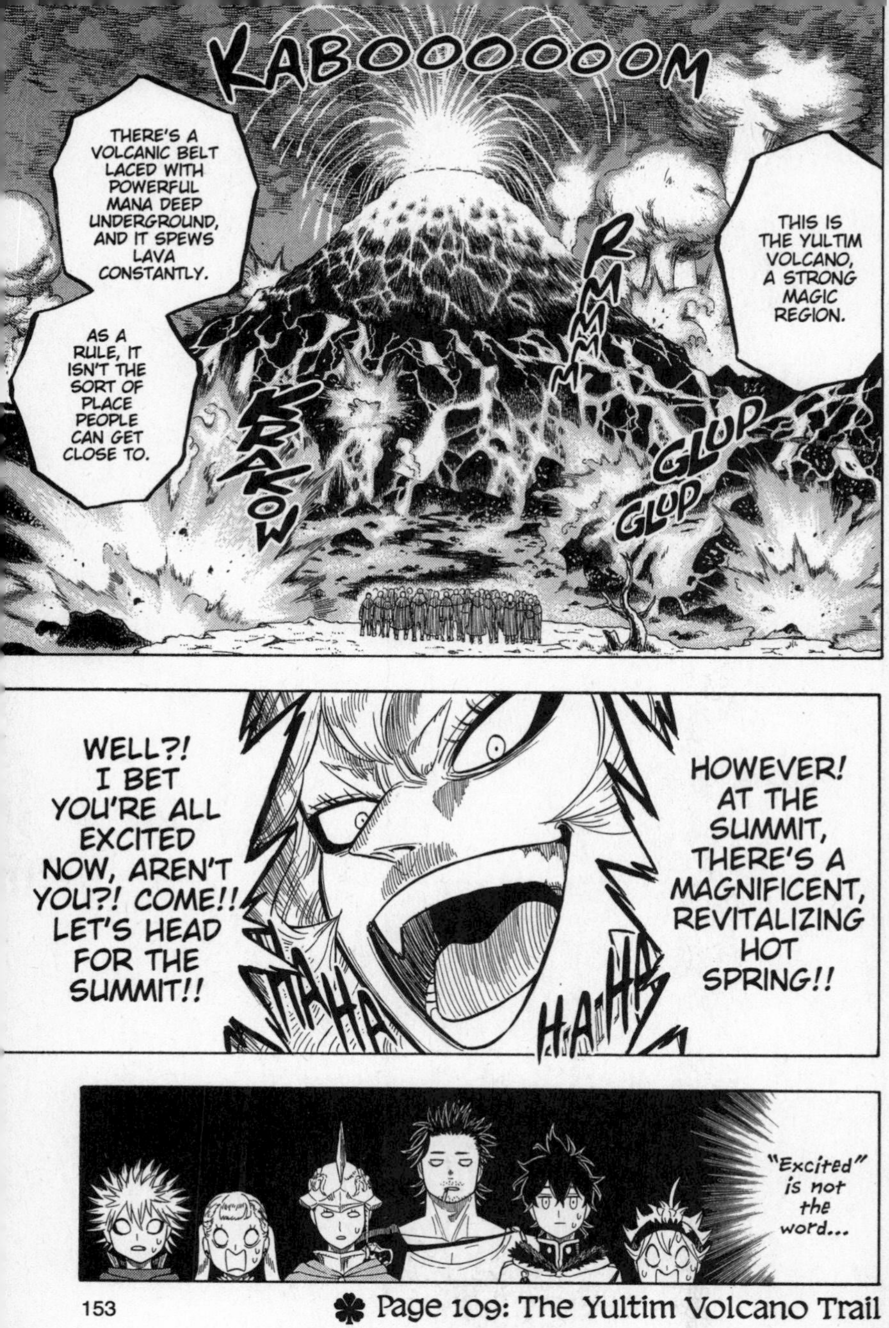
KABOOOOOOOM
THIS IS THE YULTIM VOLCANO, A STRONG MAGIC REGION.
RMMMMMM
THERE'S A VOLCANIC BELT LACED WITH POWERFUL MANA DEEP UNDERGROUND, AND IT SPEWS LAVA CONSTANTLY.
GLUP GLUP
KRAKOW
AS A RULE, IT ISN'T THE SORT OF PLACE PEOPLE CAN GET CLOSE TO.
HOWEVER! AT THE SUMMIT, THERE'S A MAGNIFICENT, REVITALIZING HOT SPRING!!
WELL?! I BET YOU'RE ALL EXCITED NOW, AREN'T YOU?! COME!! LET'S HEAD FOR THE SUMMIT!!
HA HA HA
HA HA HA
"Excited" is not the word...

Page 109: The Yultim Volcano Trail

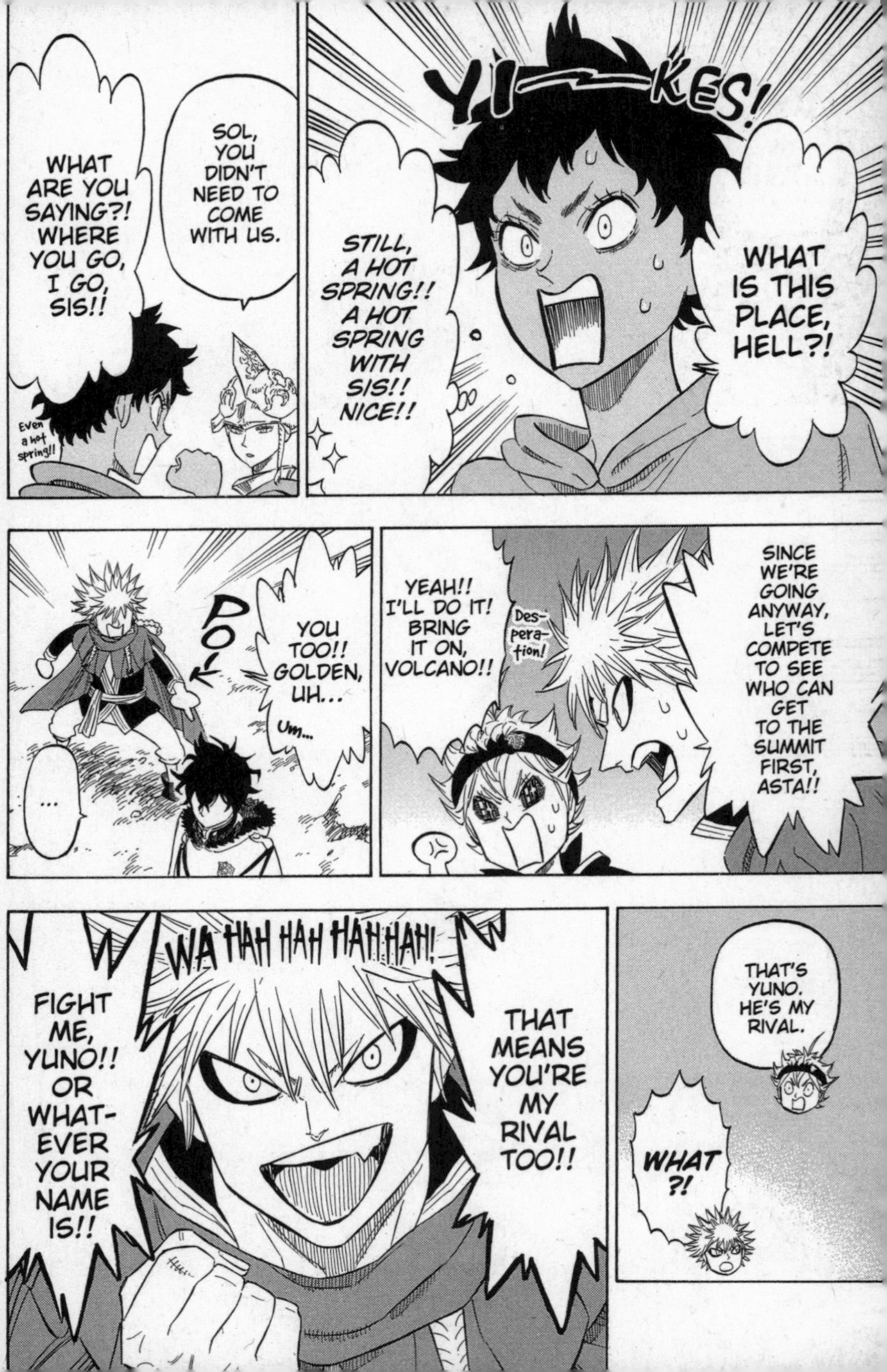
YI—KES!
WHAT IS THIS PLACE, HELL?!
STILL, A HOT SPRING!! A HOT SPRING WITH SIS!! NICE!!
SOL, YOU DIDN'T NEED TO COME WITH US.
WHAT ARE YOU SAYING?! WHERE YOU GO, I GO, SIS!!
Even a hot spring!!
SINCE WE'RE GOING ANYWAY, LET'S COMPETE TO SEE WHO CAN GET TO THE SUMMIT FIRST, ASTA!!
Desperation!
YEAH!! I'LL DO IT! BRING IT ON, VOLCANO!!
YOU TOO!! GOLDEN, UH...
Um...
PO!
...
THAT'S YUNO. HE'S MY RIVAL.
WHAT?!
WA HAH HAH HAH HAH!
THAT MEANS YOU'RE MY RIVAL TOO!!
FIGHT ME, YUNO!! OR WHATEVER YOUR NAME IS!!

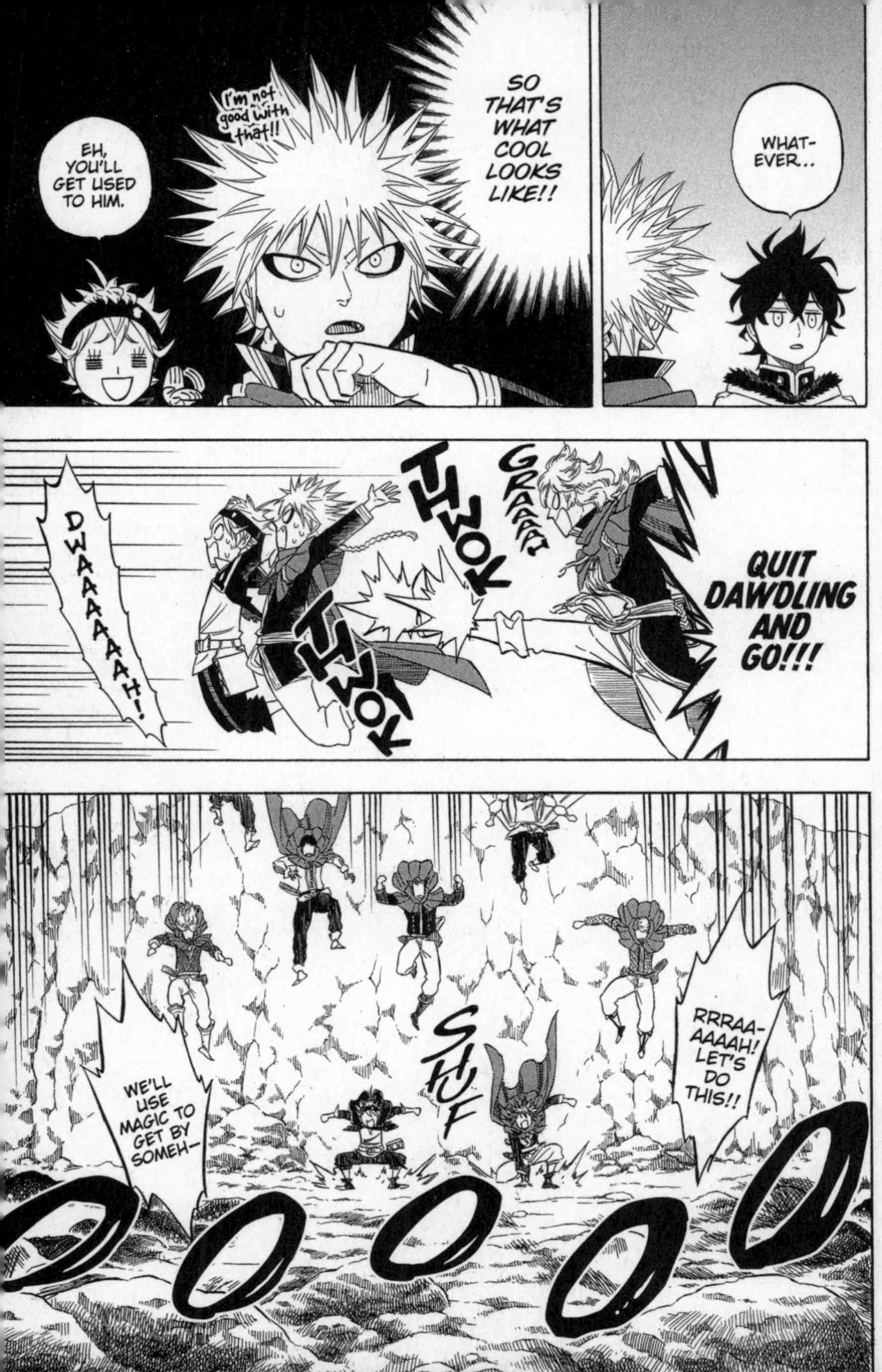
WHAT-EVER...
SO THAT'S WHAT COOL LOOKS LIKE!!
I'm not good with that!!
EH, YOU'LL GET USED TO HIM.
QUIT DAWDLING AND GO!!!
GRAAAA!
THWOK
THWOK
DWAAAAAAAAH!
RRRAA-AAAAH! LET'S DO THIS!!
SHUF
WE'LL USE MAGIC TO GET BY SOMEH-
OOOOOO

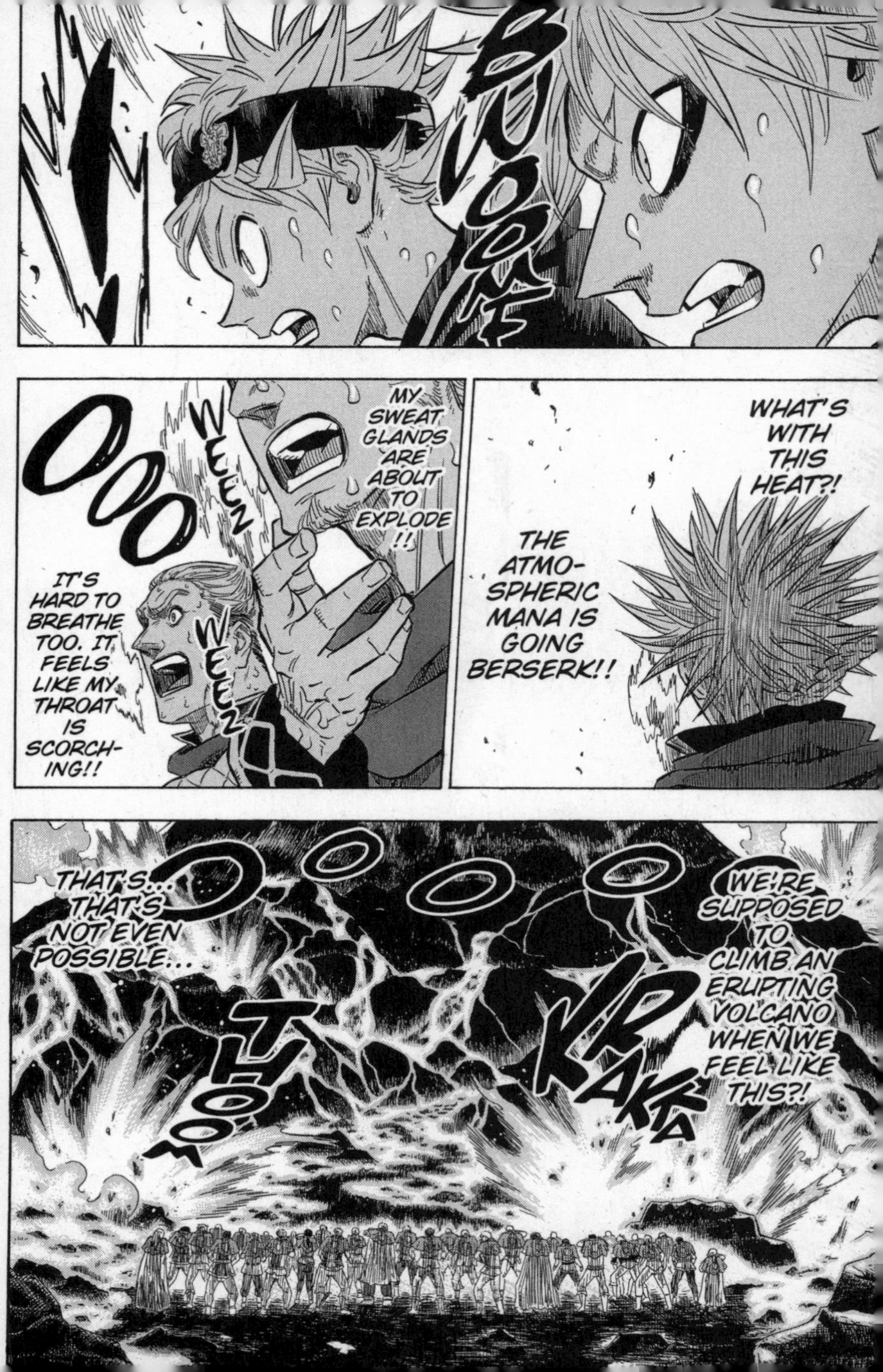
WHAT'S WITH THIS HEAT?!
THE ATMOSPHERIC MANA IS GOING BERSERK!!
MY SWEAT GLANDS ARE ABOUT TO EXPLODE!!
IT'S HARD TO BREATHE TOO. IT FEELS LIKE MY THROAT IS SCORCHING!!
WE'RE SUPPOSED TO CLIMB AN ERUPTING VOLCANO WHEN WE FEEL LIKE THIS?!
THAT'S... THAT'S NOT EVEN POSSIBLE...

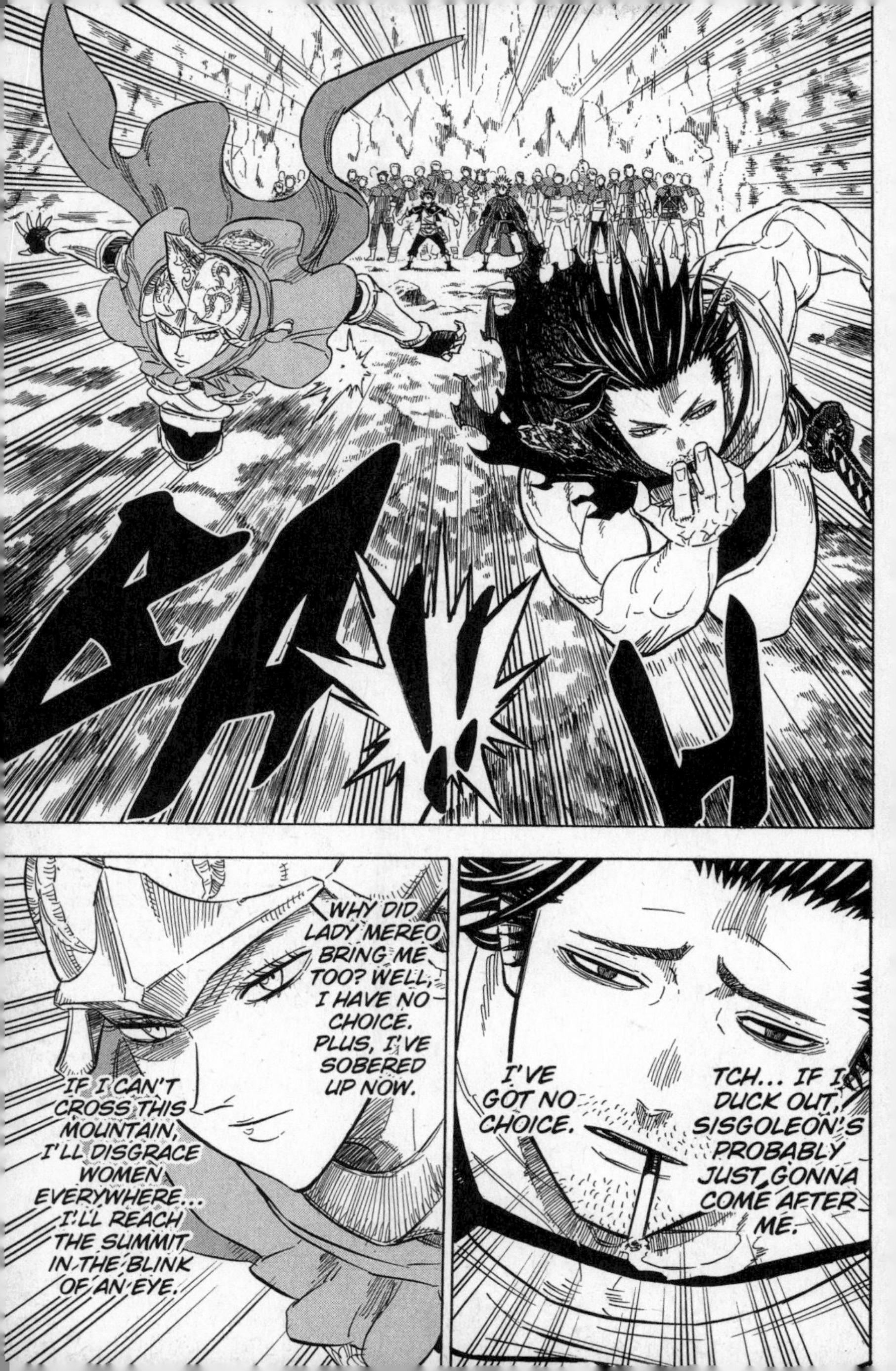
BAM!
TCH... IF I DUCK OUT, SISGOLEON'S PROBABLY JUST GONNA COME AFTER ME.
I'VE GOT NO CHOICE.
WHY DID LADY MEREO BRING ME TOO? WELL, I HAVE NO CHOICE. PLUS, I'VE SOBERED UP NOW.
IF I CAN'T CROSS THIS MOUNTAIN, I'LL DISGRACE WOMEN EVERYWHERE... I'LL REACH THE SUMMIT IN THE BLINK OF AN EYE.

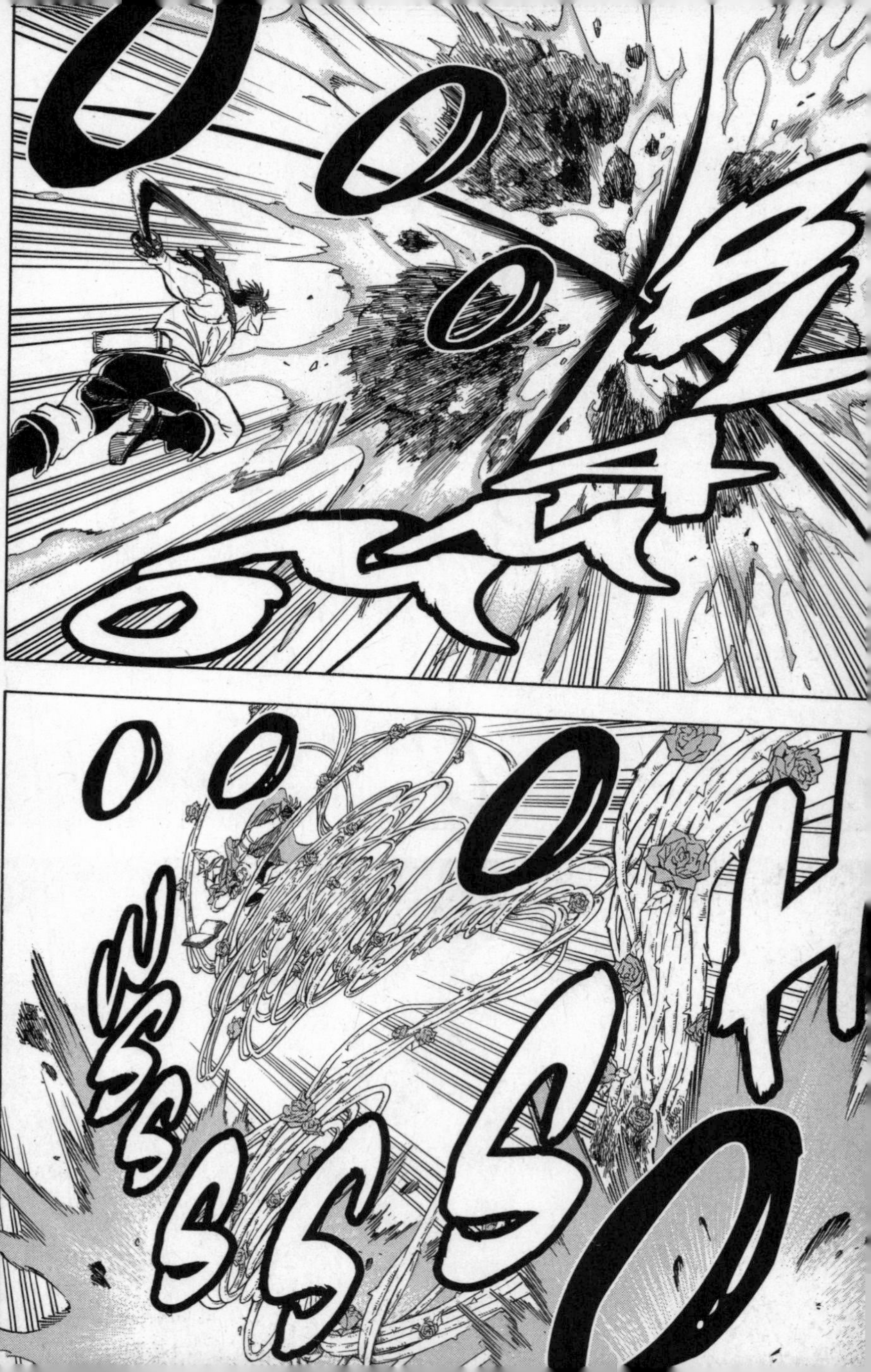

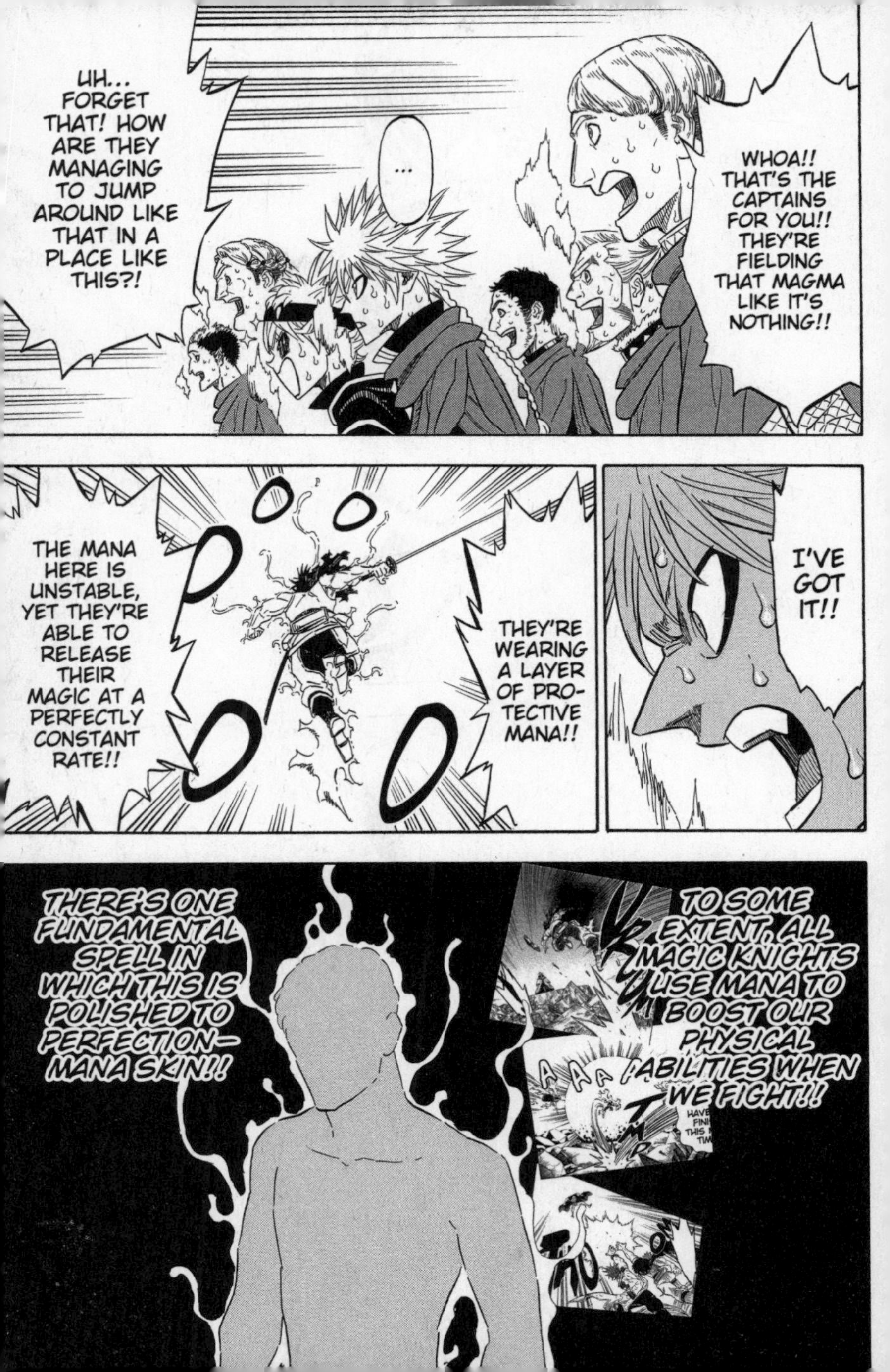
WHOA!! THAT'S THE CAPTAINS FOR YOU!! THEY'RE FIELDING THAT MAGMA LIKE IT'S NOTHING!!
...
UH... FORGET THAT! HOW ARE THEY MANAGING TO JUMP AROUND LIKE THAT IN A PLACE LIKE THIS?!
I'VE GOT IT!!
THEY'RE WEARING A LAYER OF PRO-TECTIVE MANA!!
THE MANA HERE IS UNSTABLE, YET THEY'RE ABLE TO RELEASE THEIR MAGIC AT A PERFECTLY CONSTANT RATE!!
TO SOME EXTENT, ALL MAGIC KNIGHTS USE MANA TO BOOST OUR PHYSICAL ABILITIES WHEN WE FIGHT!!
THERE'S ONE FUNDAMENTAL SPELL IN WHICH THIS IS POLISHED TO PERFECTION— MANA SKIN!!

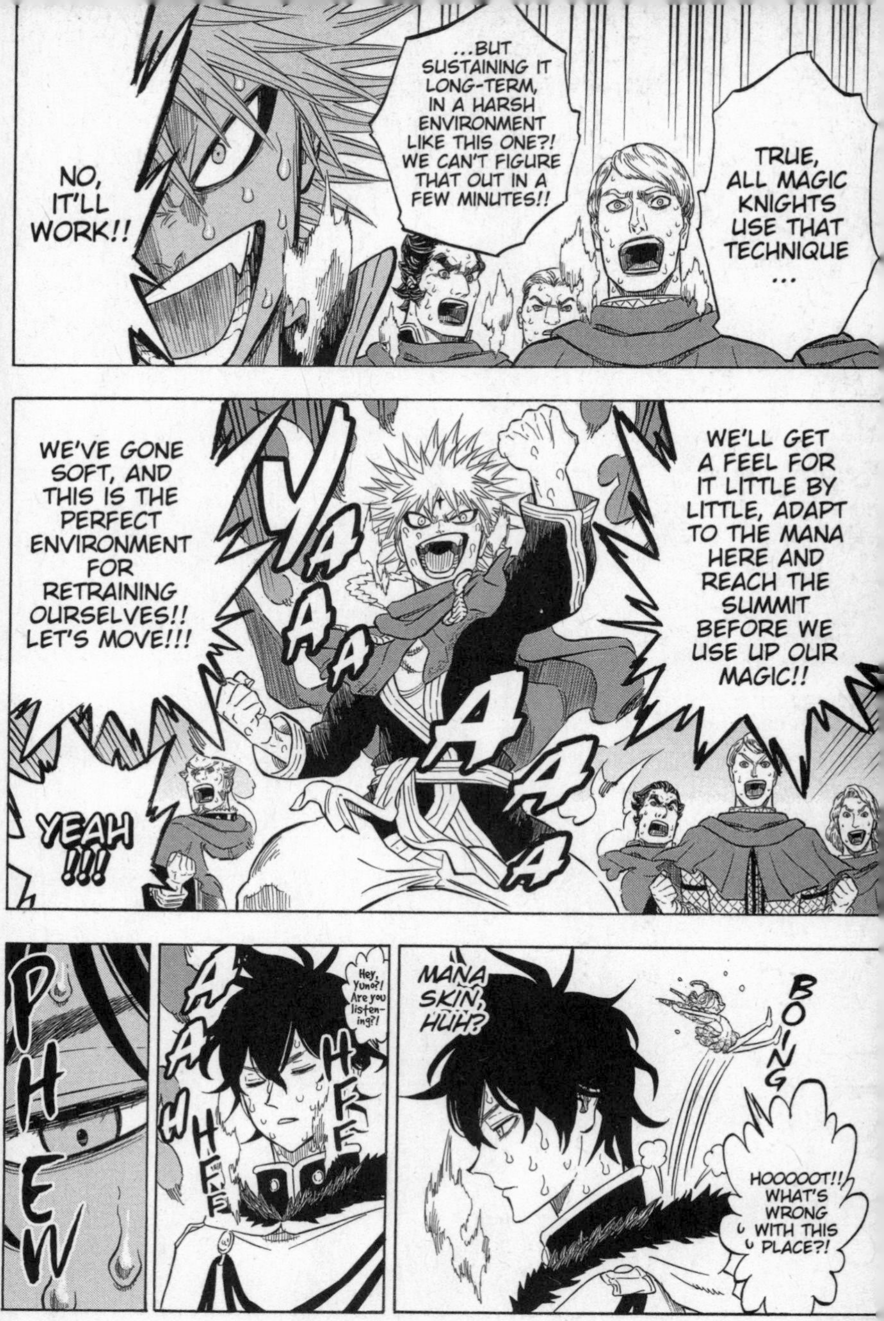
TRUE, ALL MAGIC KNIGHTS USE THAT TECHNIQUE ...
...BUT SUSTAINING IT LONG-TERM, IN A HARSH ENVIRONMENT LIKE THIS ONE?! WE CAN'T FIGURE THAT OUT IN A FEW MINUTES!!
NO, IT'LL WORK!!
WE'LL GET A FEEL FOR IT LITTLE BY LITTLE, ADAPT TO THE MANA HERE AND REACH THE SUMMIT BEFORE WE USE UP OUR MAGIC!!
WE'VE GONE SOFT, AND THIS IS THE PERFECT ENVIRONMENT FOR RETRAINING OURSELVES!! LET'S MOVE!!!
YAAAAAAAA
YEAH !!!
BOING
MANA SKIN, HUH?
HOOOOOT!! WHAT'S WRONG WITH THIS PLACE?!
Hey, Yuno?! Are you listening?!
AAH
HFF HFF
PHEW

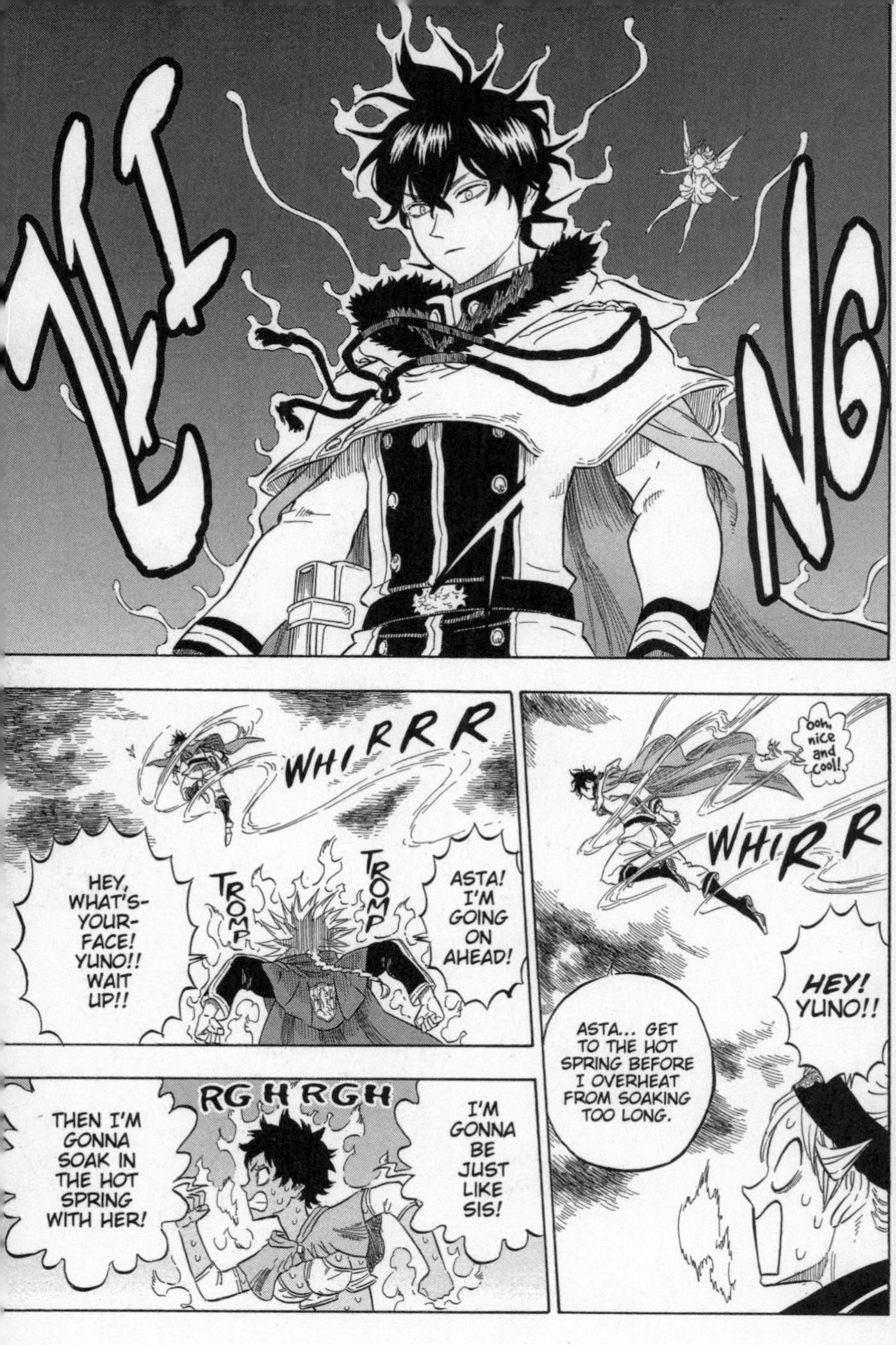
ZIIING
ooh, nice and cool!
WHIRR
HEY! YUNO!!
ASTA... GET TO THE HOT SPRING BEFORE I OVERHEAT FROM SOAKING TOO LONG.
WHIRRR
ASTA! I'M GOING ON AHEAD!
TROMP
TROMP
HEY, WHAT'S-YOUR-FACE! YUNO!! WAIT UP!!
RGHRGH
I'M GONNA BE JUST LIKE SIS!
THEN I'M GONNA SOAK IN THE HOT SPRING WITH HER!

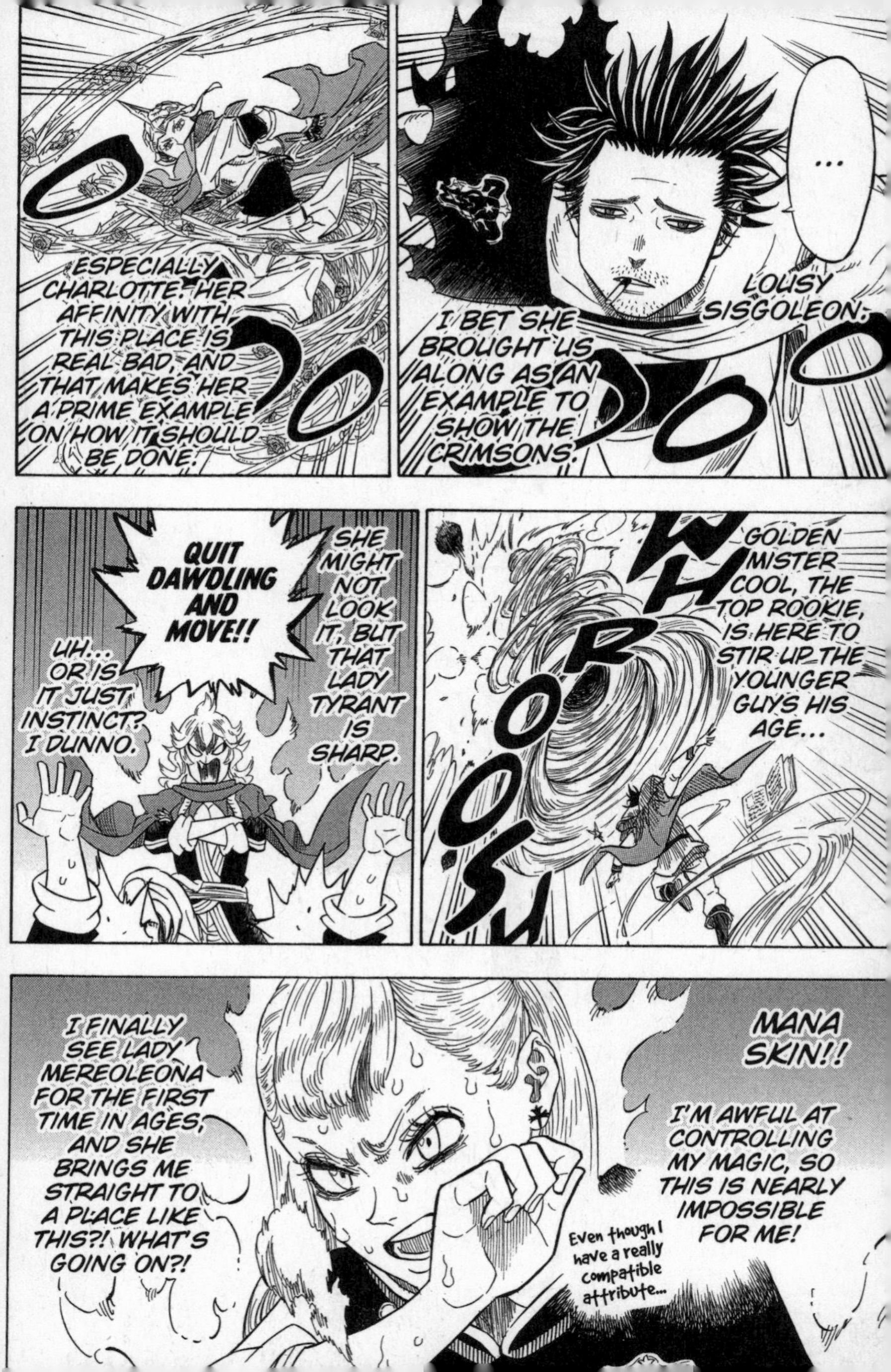
...
LOUSY SISGOLEON.
I BET SHE BROUGHT US ALONG AS AN EXAMPLE TO SHOW THE CRIMSONS.
ESPECIALLY CHARLOTTE. HER AFFINITY WITH THIS PLACE IS REAL BAD, AND THAT MAKES HER A PRIME EXAMPLE ON HOW IT SHOULD BE DONE.
GOLDEN MISTER COOL, THE TOP ROOKIE, IS HERE TO STIR UP THE YOUNGER GUYS HIS AGE...
WHROOOSH
SHE MIGHT NOT LOOK IT, BUT THAT LADY TYRANT IS SHARP.
QUIT DAWDLING AND MOVE!!
UH... OR IS IT JUST INSTINCT? I DUNNO.
MANA SKIN!!
I'M AWFUL AT CONTROLLING MY MAGIC, SO THIS IS NEARLY IMPOSSIBLE FOR ME!
Even though I have a really compatible attribute...
I FINALLY SEE LADY MEREOLEONA FOR THE FIRST TIME IN AGES, AND SHE BRINGS ME STRAIGHT TO A PLACE LIKE THIS?! WHAT'S GOING ON?!

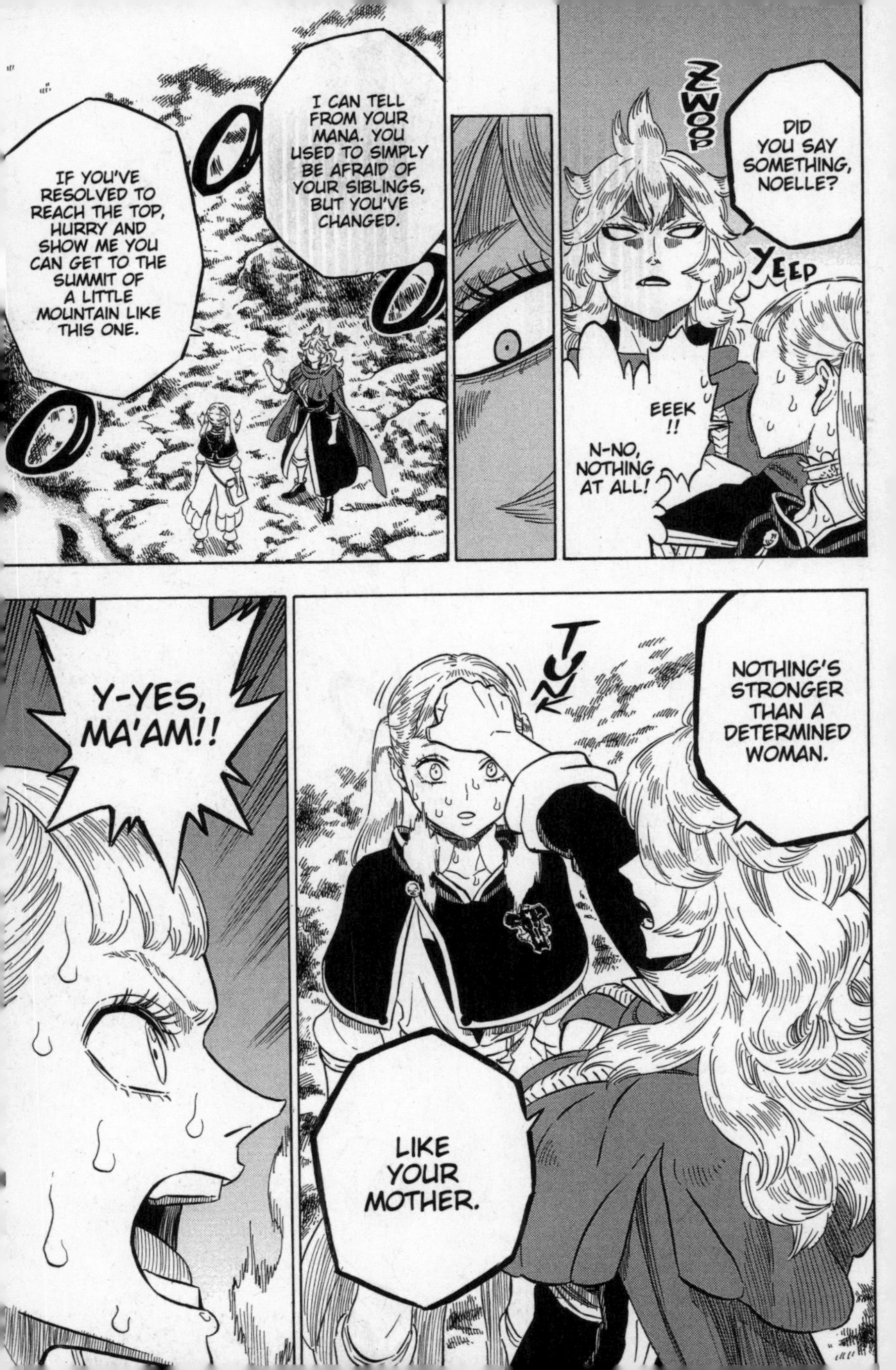
ZWOOP
DID YOU SAY SOMETHING, NOELLE?
YEEP
EEEK!!
N-NO, NOTHING AT ALL!
I CAN TELL FROM YOUR MANA. YOU USED TO SIMPLY BE AFRAID OF YOUR SIBLINGS, BUT YOU'VE CHANGED.
IF YOU'VE RESOLVED TO REACH THE TOP, HURRY AND SHOW ME YOU CAN GET TO THE SUMMIT OF A LITTLE MOUNTAIN LIKE THIS ONE.
TUNK
NOTHING'S STRONGER THAN A DETERMINED WOMAN.
LIKE YOUR MOTHER.
Y-YES, MA'AM!!

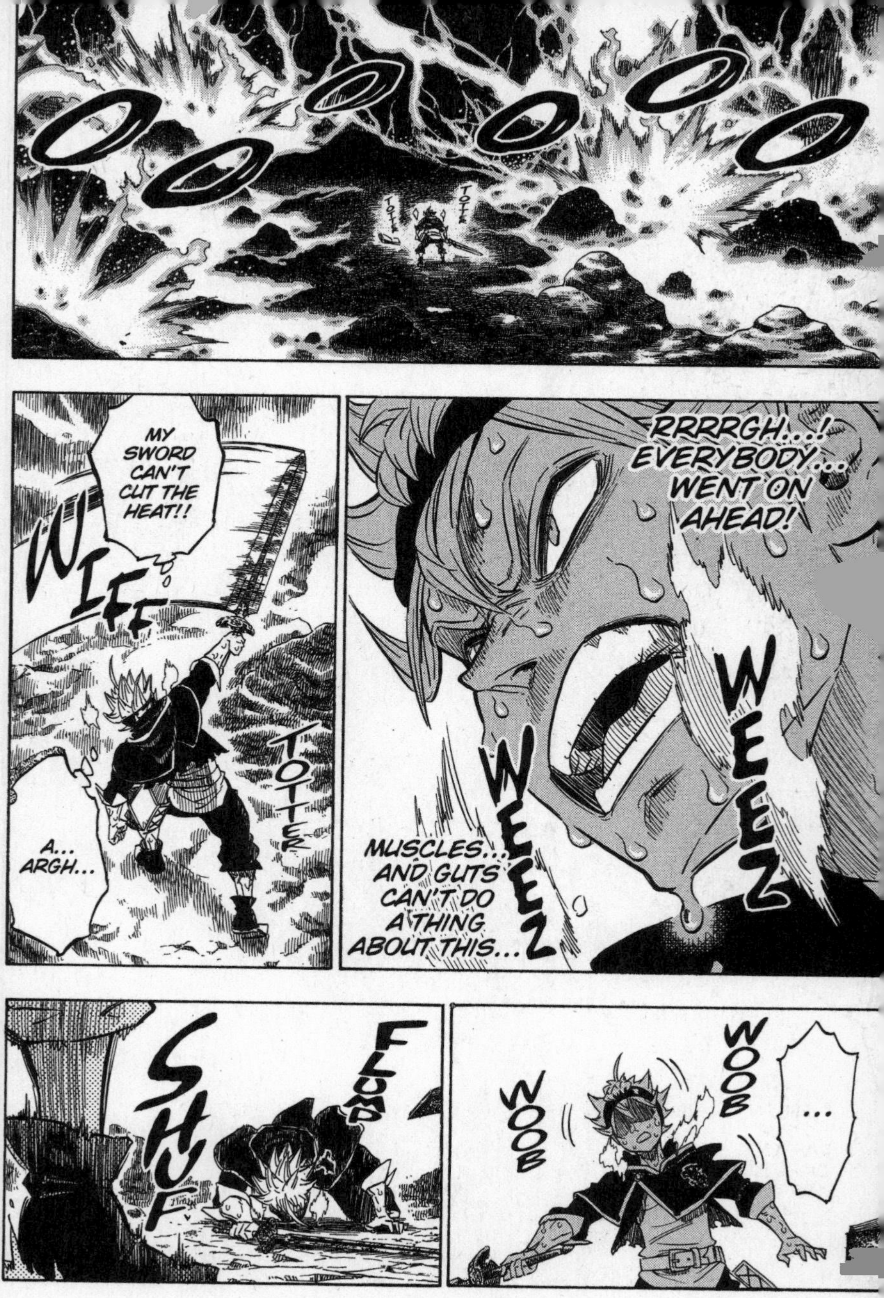
TOTTER
TOTTER
RRRRGH...! EVERYBODY... WENT ON AHEAD!
WEEZ
WEEZ
MUSCLES... AND GUTS CAN'T DO A THING ABOUT THIS...
MY SWORD CAN'T CUT THE HEAT!!
WIFF
TOTTER
A... ARGH...
WOOB
WOOB
...
FLUMP
SHUF

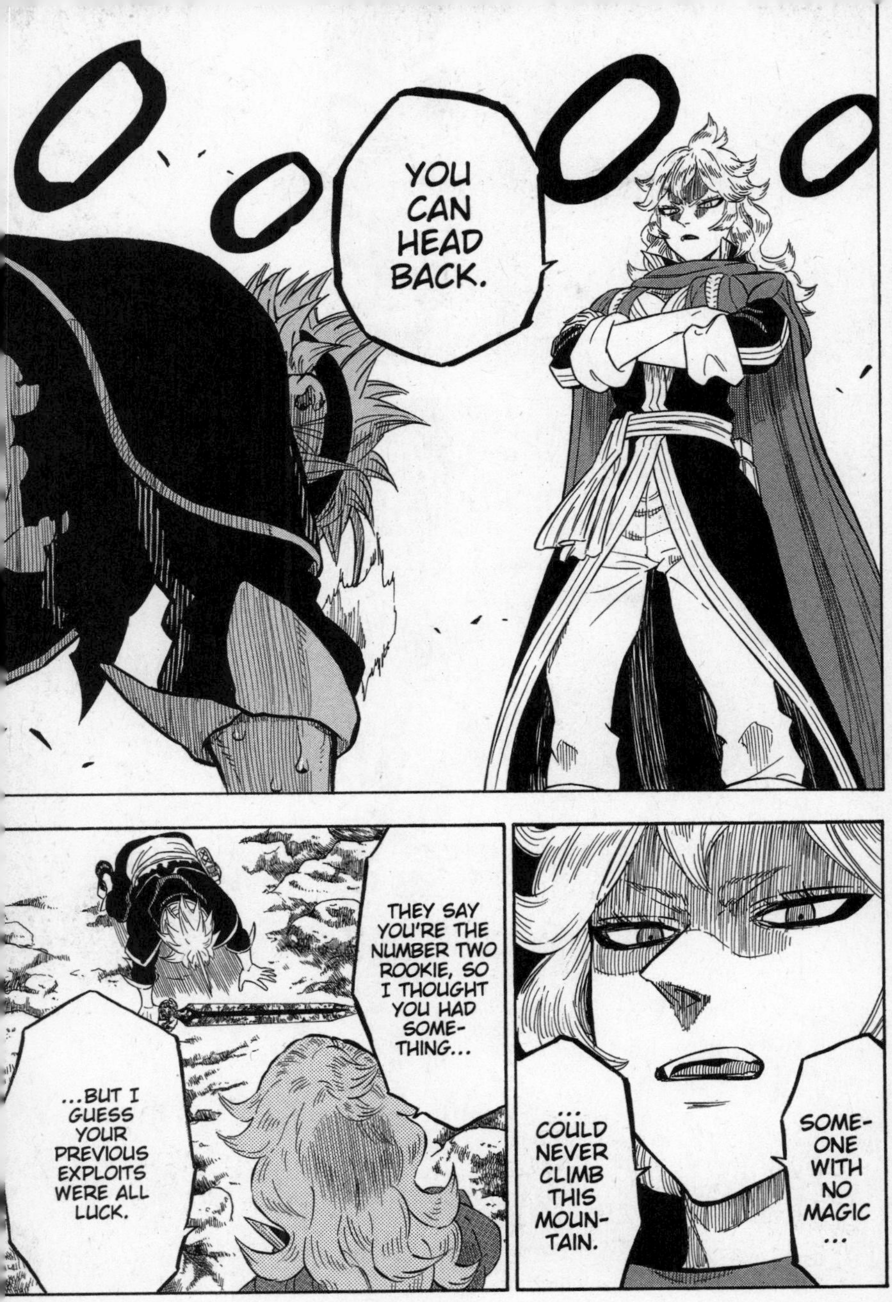
YOU CAN HEAD BACK.
SOMEONE WITH NO MAGIC...
...COULD NEVER CLIMB THIS MOUNTAIN.
THEY SAY YOU'RE THE NUMBER TWO ROOKIE, SO I THOUGHT YOU HAD SOMETHING...
...BUT I GUESS YOUR PREVIOUS EXPLOITS WERE ALL LUCK.

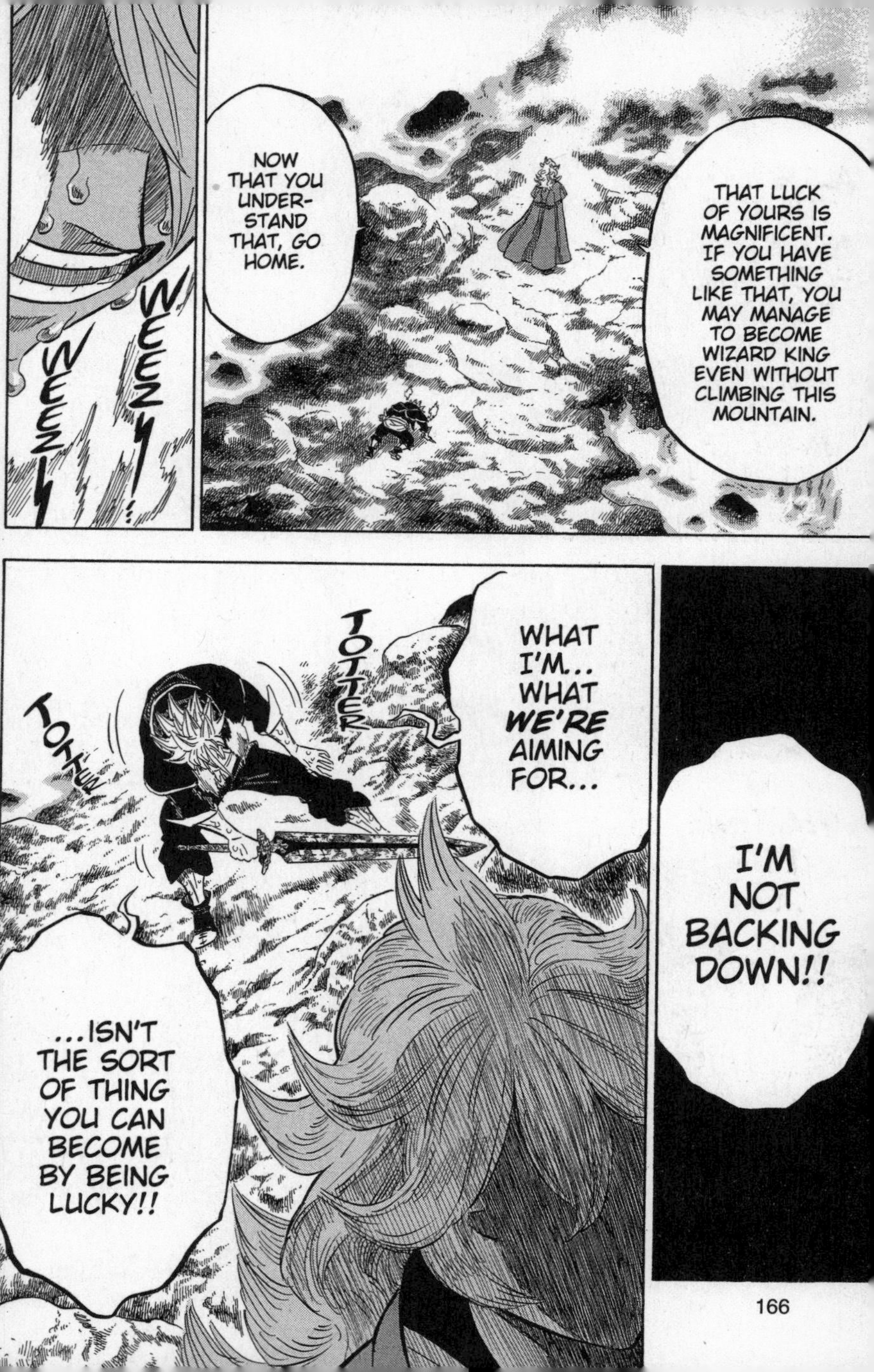
THAT LUCK OF YOURS IS MAGNIFICENT. IF YOU HAVE SOMETHING LIKE THAT, YOU MAY MANAGE TO BECOME WIZARD KING EVEN WITHOUT CLIMBING THIS MOUNTAIN.
NOW THAT YOU UNDER-STAND THAT, GO HOME.
WEEZY!!
WEEZY
I'M NOT BACKING DOWN!!
TOTTER
TOTTER
WHAT I'M... WHAT *WE'RE* AIMING FOR...
...ISN'T THE SORT OF THING YOU CAN BECOME BY BEING LUCKY!!

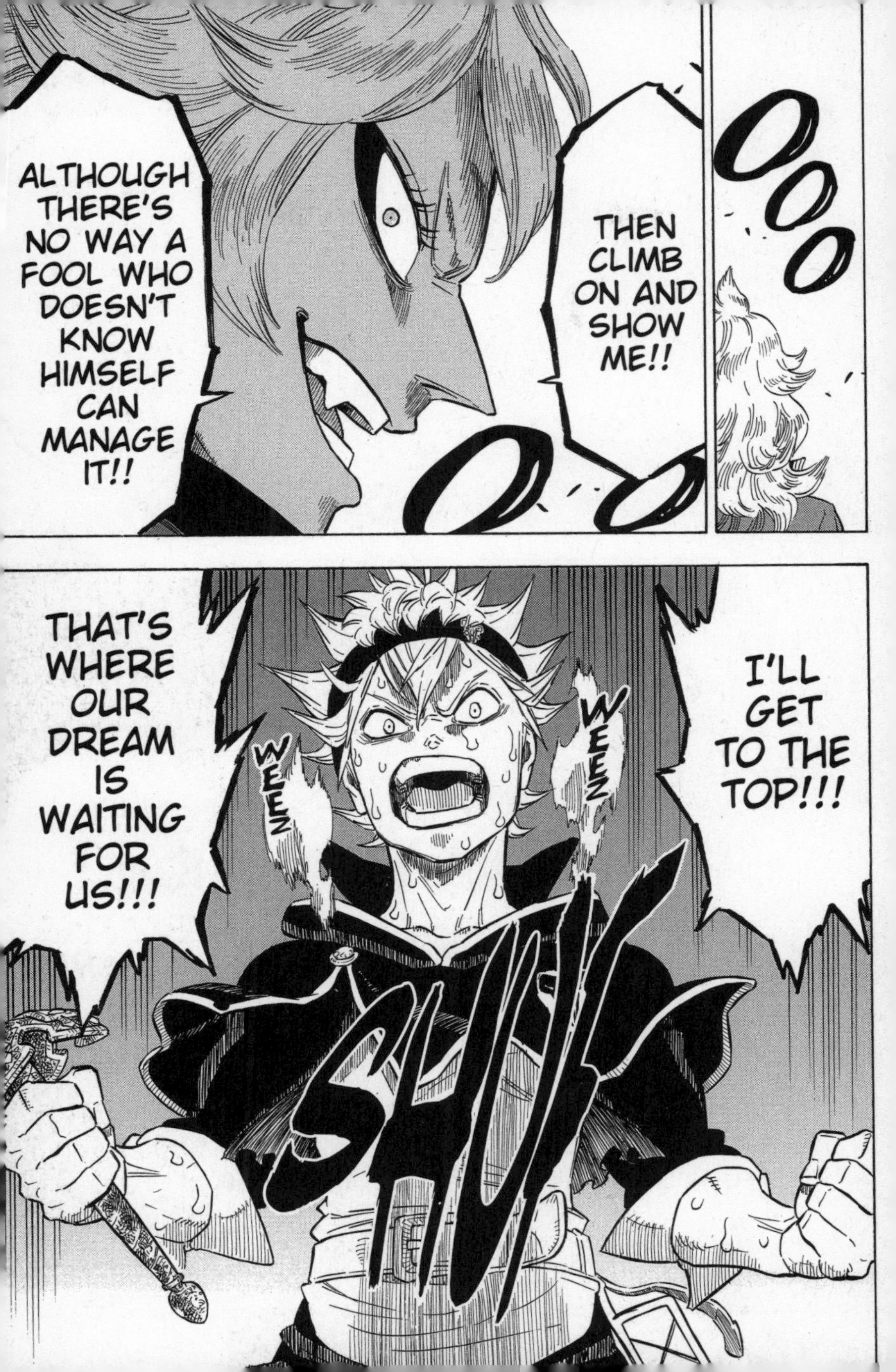
OOOOO
THEN CLIMB ON AND SHOW ME!!
ALTHOUGH THERE'S NO WAY A FOOL WHO DOESN'T KNOW HIMSELF CAN MANAGE IT!!
I'LL GET TO THE TOP!!!
WEEZ
THAT'S WHERE OUR DREAM IS WAITING FOR US!!!
WEEZ

Mereoleona
Vermillion

Age: 32   Height: 178 cm
Birthday: July 26   Sign: Leo   Blood Type: O
Likes: Drinking liquor in hot springs,
cooking wild game

Character   Profile

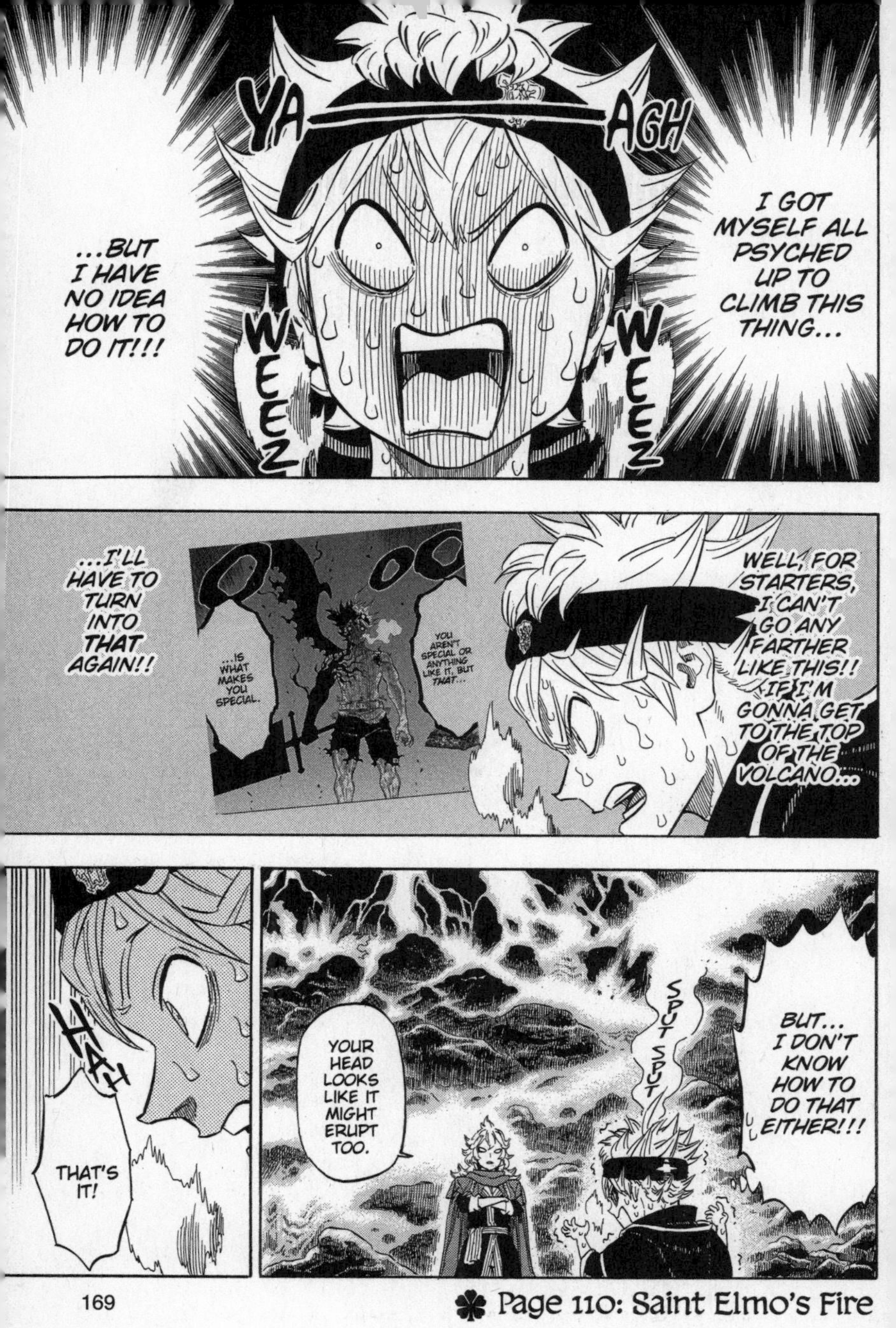
YA
AGH
I GOT MYSELF ALL PSYCHED UP TO CLIMB THIS THING...
...BUT I HAVE NO IDEA HOW TO DO IT!!!
WEEZ
WEEZ
WELL, FOR STARTERS, I CAN'T GO ANY FARTHER LIKE THIS!! IF I'M GONNA GET TO THE TOP OF THE VOLCANO...
YOU AREN'T SPECIAL OR ANYTHING LIKE IT, BUT THAT...
...IS WHAT MAKES YOU SPECIAL.
...I'LL HAVE TO TURN INTO THAT AGAIN!!
BUT... I DON'T KNOW HOW TO DO THAT EITHER!!!
SPUT SPUT
YOUR HEAD LOOKS LIKE IT MIGHT ERUPT TOO.
HA!
THAT'S IT!

Page 110: Saint Elmo's Fire

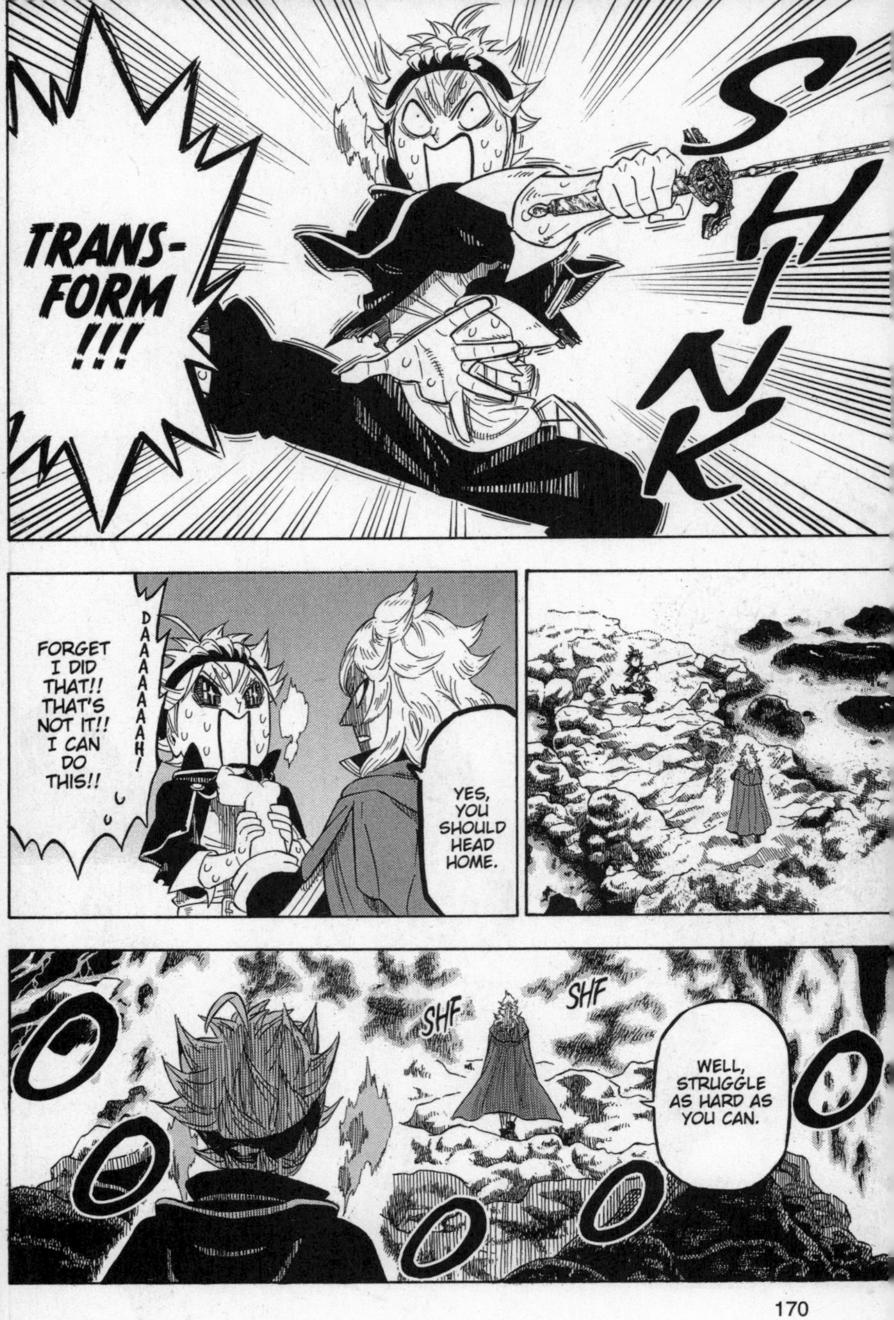
SHINK
TRANS-FORM!!!
DAAAAAAAAAH!
FORGET I DID THAT!! THAT'S NOT IT!! I CAN DO THIS!!
YES, YOU SHOULD HEAD HOME.
WELL, STRUGGLE AS HARD AS YOU CAN.
SHF
SHF
OOOOOO

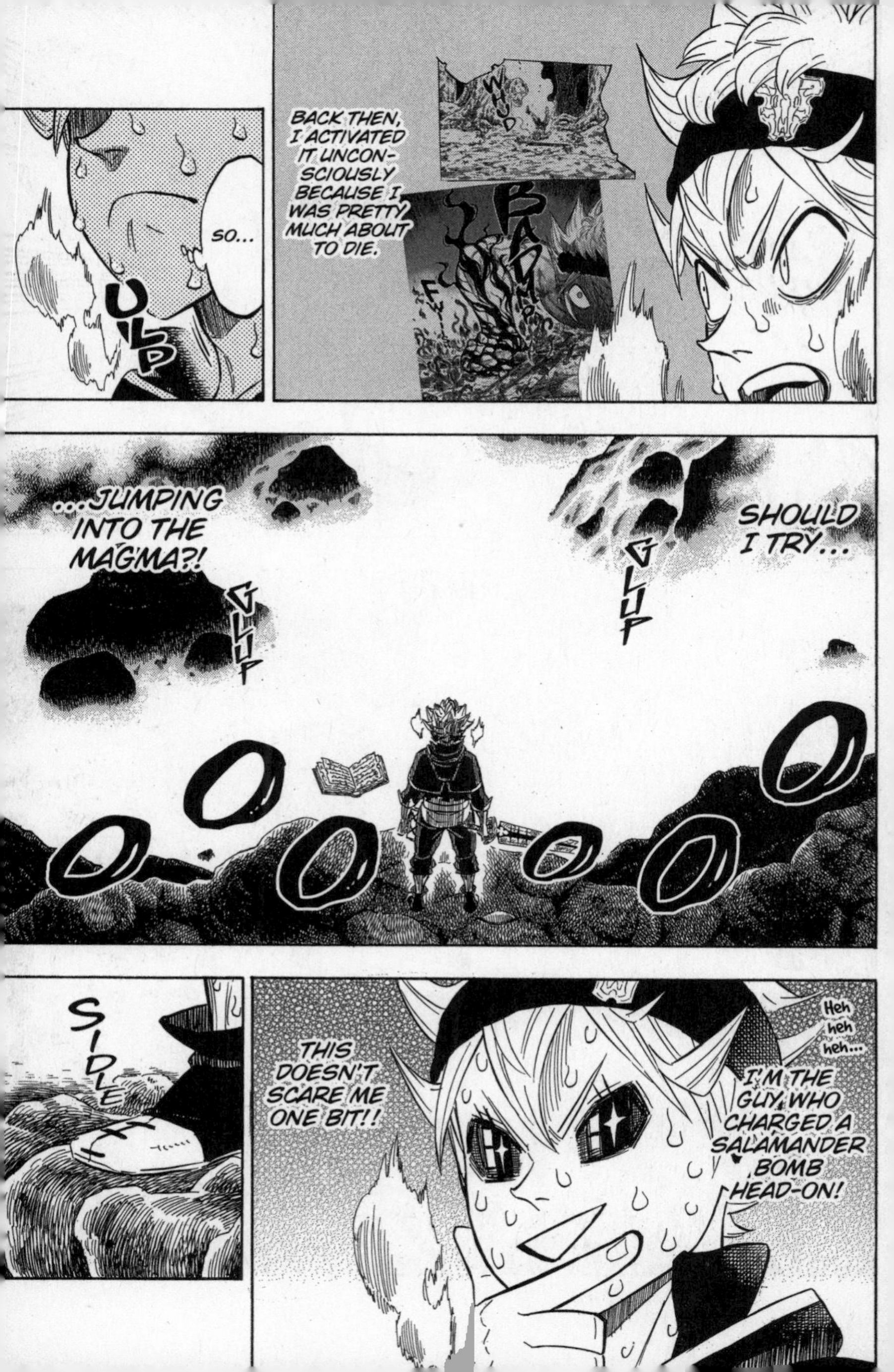
BACK THEN, I ACTIVATED IT UNCONSCIOUSLY BECAUSE I WAS PRETTY MUCH ABOUT TO DIE.
WHUD
BADUMP
SO...
ULP
SHOULD I TRY...
GLUP
...JUMPING INTO THE MAGMA?!
GLUP
Heh heh heh...
I'M THE GUY WHO CHARGED A SALAMANDER BOMB HEAD-ON!
THIS DOESN'T SCARE ME ONE BIT!!
SIDLE

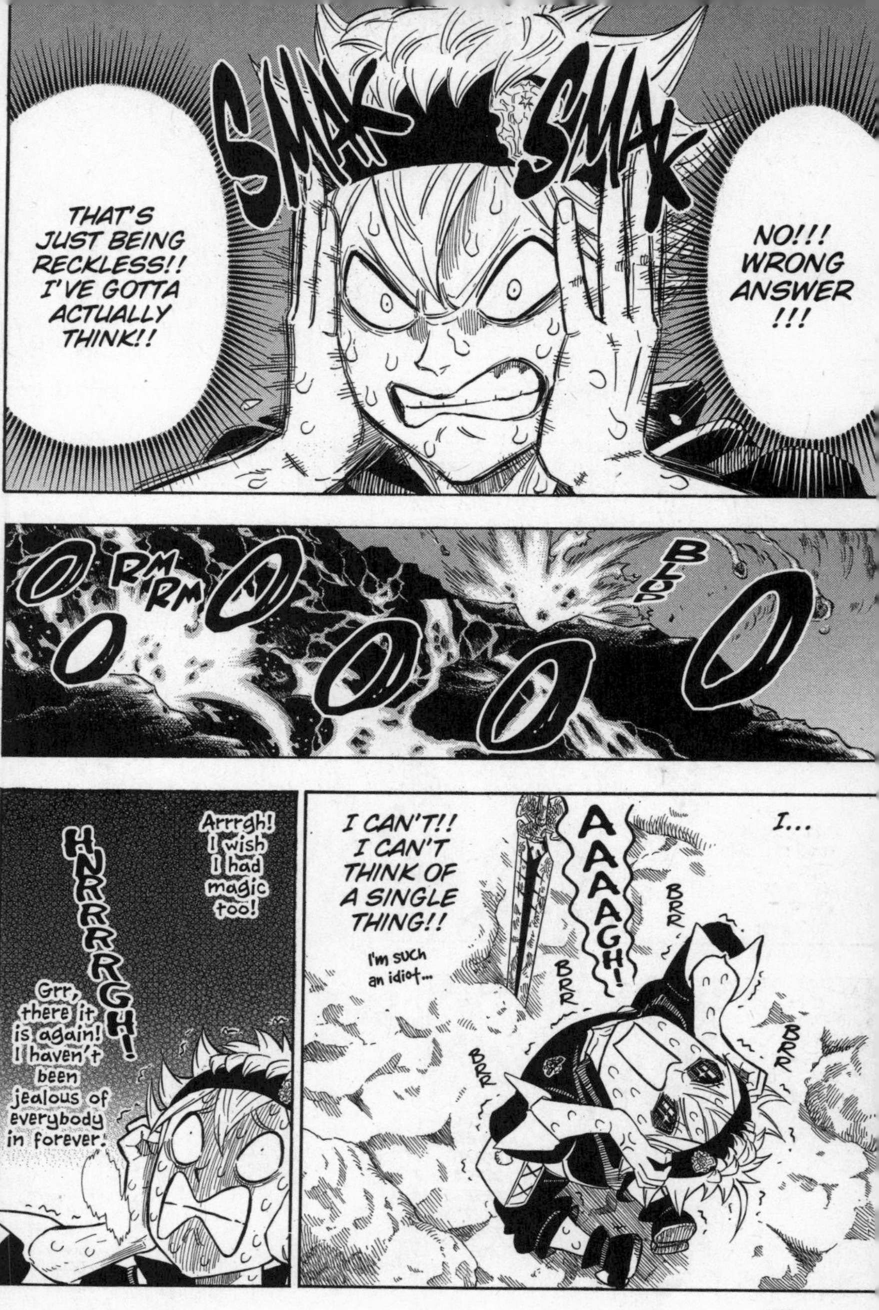
SMAK SMAK
NO!!! WRONG ANSWER !!!
THAT'S JUST BEING RECKLESS!! I'VE GOTTA ACTUALLY THINK!!
BLOP
ORMRMOOOOOO
I...
AAAAGH!
I CAN'T!! I CAN'T THINK OF A SINGLE THING!!
I'm such an idiot...
BRR
BRR
BRR
BRR
HNRRRRRGH!
Arrrgh! I wish I had magic too!
Grr, there it is again! I haven't been jealous of everybody in forever.

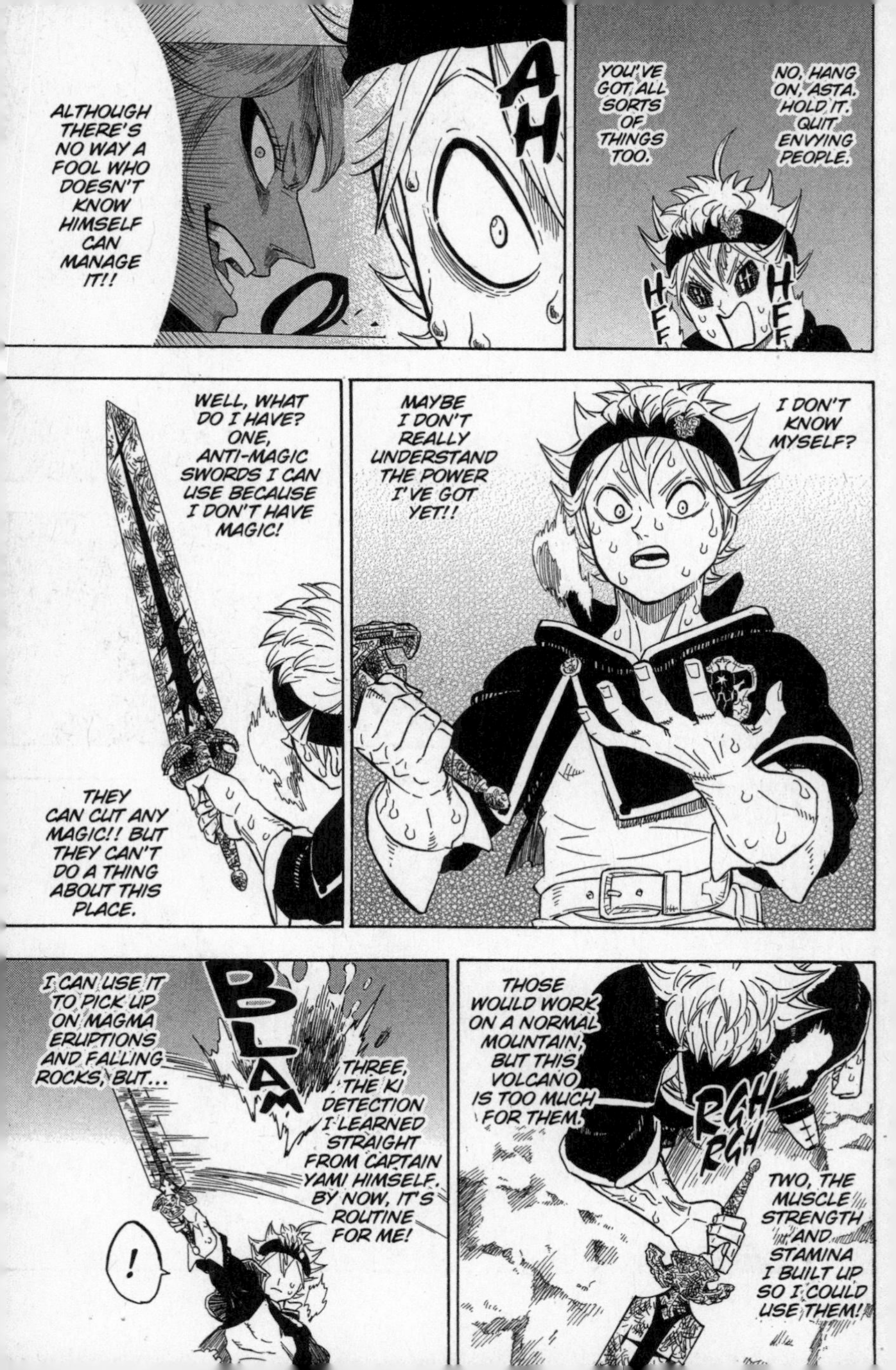
NO, HANG ON, ASTA. HOLD IT. QUIT ENVYING PEOPLE.
YOU'VE GOT ALL SORTS OF THINGS TOO.
HFF HFF
AH
ALTHOUGH THERE'S NO WAY A FOOL WHO DOESN'T KNOW HIMSELF CAN MANAGE IT!!
I DON'T KNOW MYSELF?
MAYBE I DON'T REALLY UNDERSTAND THE POWER I'VE GOT YET!!
WELL, WHAT DO I HAVE? ONE, ANTI-MAGIC SWORDS I CAN USE BECAUSE I DON'T HAVE MAGIC!
THEY CAN CUT ANY MAGIC!! BUT THEY CAN'T DO A THING ABOUT THIS PLACE.
TWO, THE MUSCLE STRENGTH AND STAMINA I BUILT UP SO I COULD USE THEM!
RGH RGH
THOSE WOULD WORK ON A NORMAL MOUNTAIN, BUT THIS VOLCANO IS TOO MUCH FOR THEM.
BLAM
THREE, THE KI DETECTION I LEARNED STRAIGHT FROM CAPTAIN YAMI HIMSELF. BY NOW, IT'S ROUTINE FOR ME!
I CAN USE IT TO PICK UP ON MAGMA ERUPTIONS AND FALLING ROCKS, BUT...
!

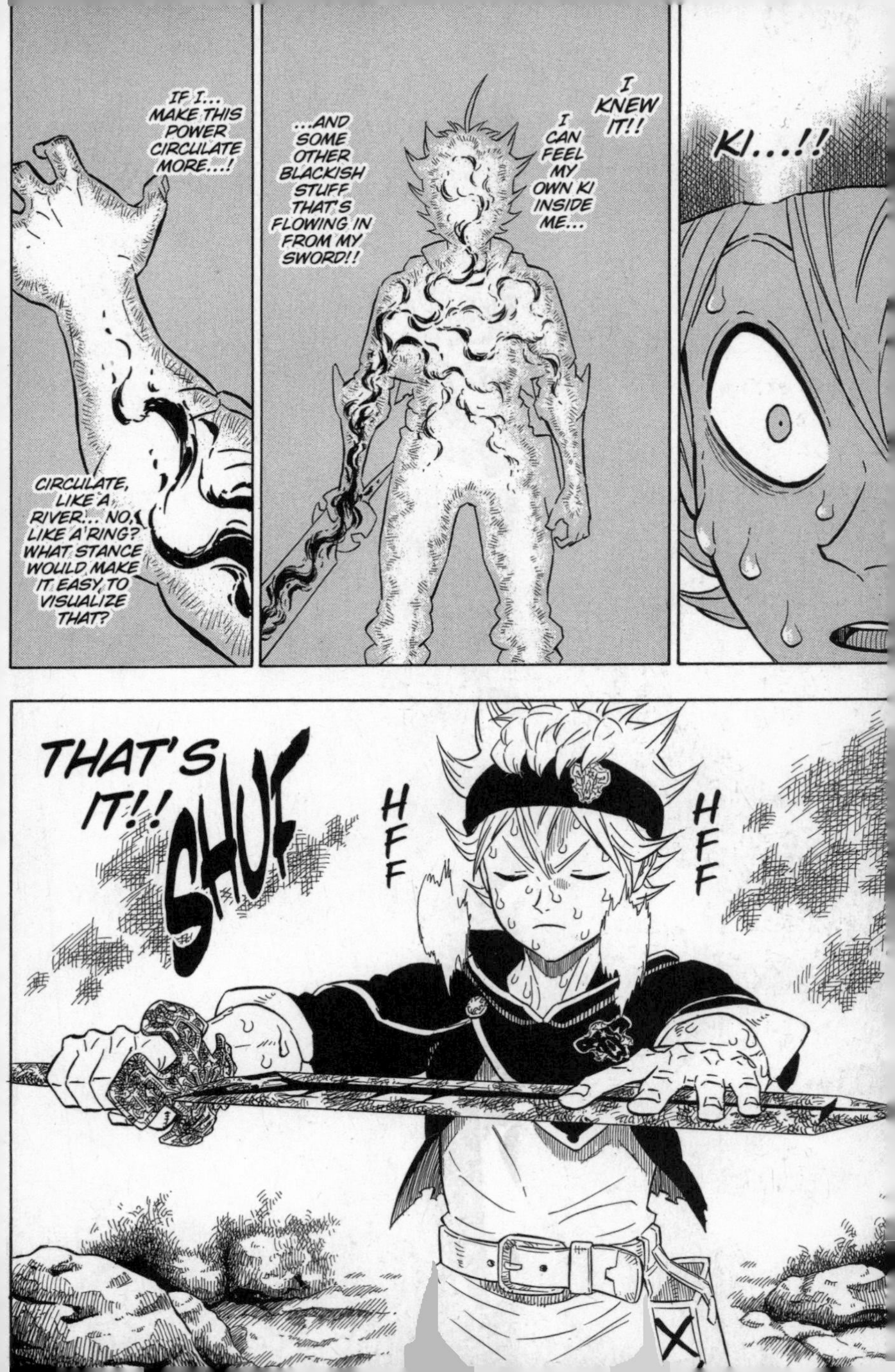
KI...!!
I KNEW IT!!
I CAN FEEL MY OWN KI INSIDE ME...
...AND SOME OTHER BLACKISH STUFF THAT'S FLOWING IN FROM MY SWORD!!
IF I... MAKE THIS POWER CIRCULATE MORE...!
CIRCULATE, LIKE A RIVER... NO, LIKE A RING? WHAT STANCE WOULD MAKE IT EASY TO VISUALIZE THAT?
HFF
HFF
THAT'S IT!!
SHUF

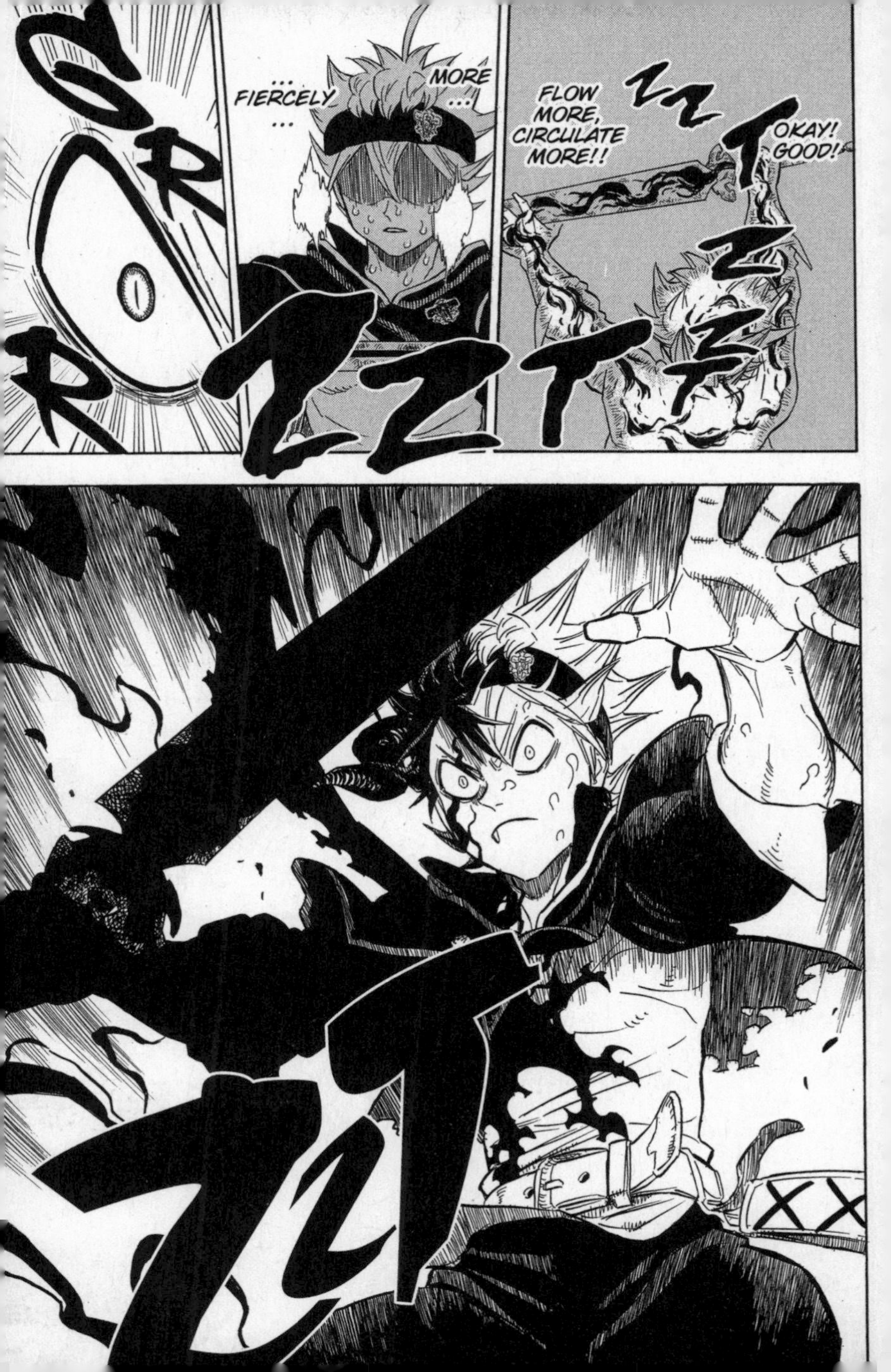
OKAY! GOOD!
FLOW MORE, CIRCULATE MORE!!
MORE ...
... FIERCELY ...

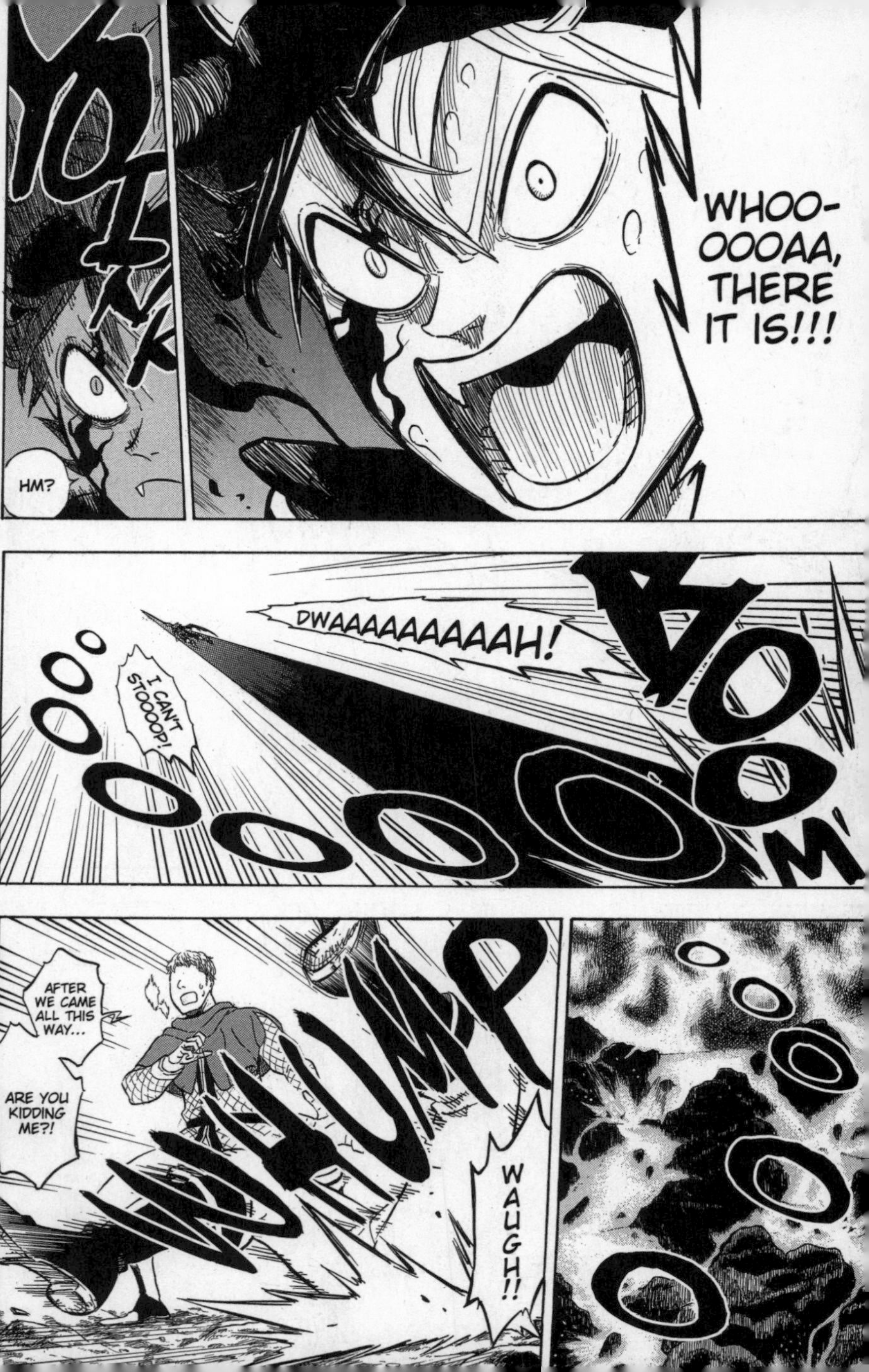
WHOOO-OOOAA, THERE IT IS!!!
HM?
DWAAAAAAAAAAH!
I CAN'T STOOOOP!
WAUGH!!
WHUMP
AFTER WE CAME ALL THIS WAY...
ARE YOU KIDDING ME?!

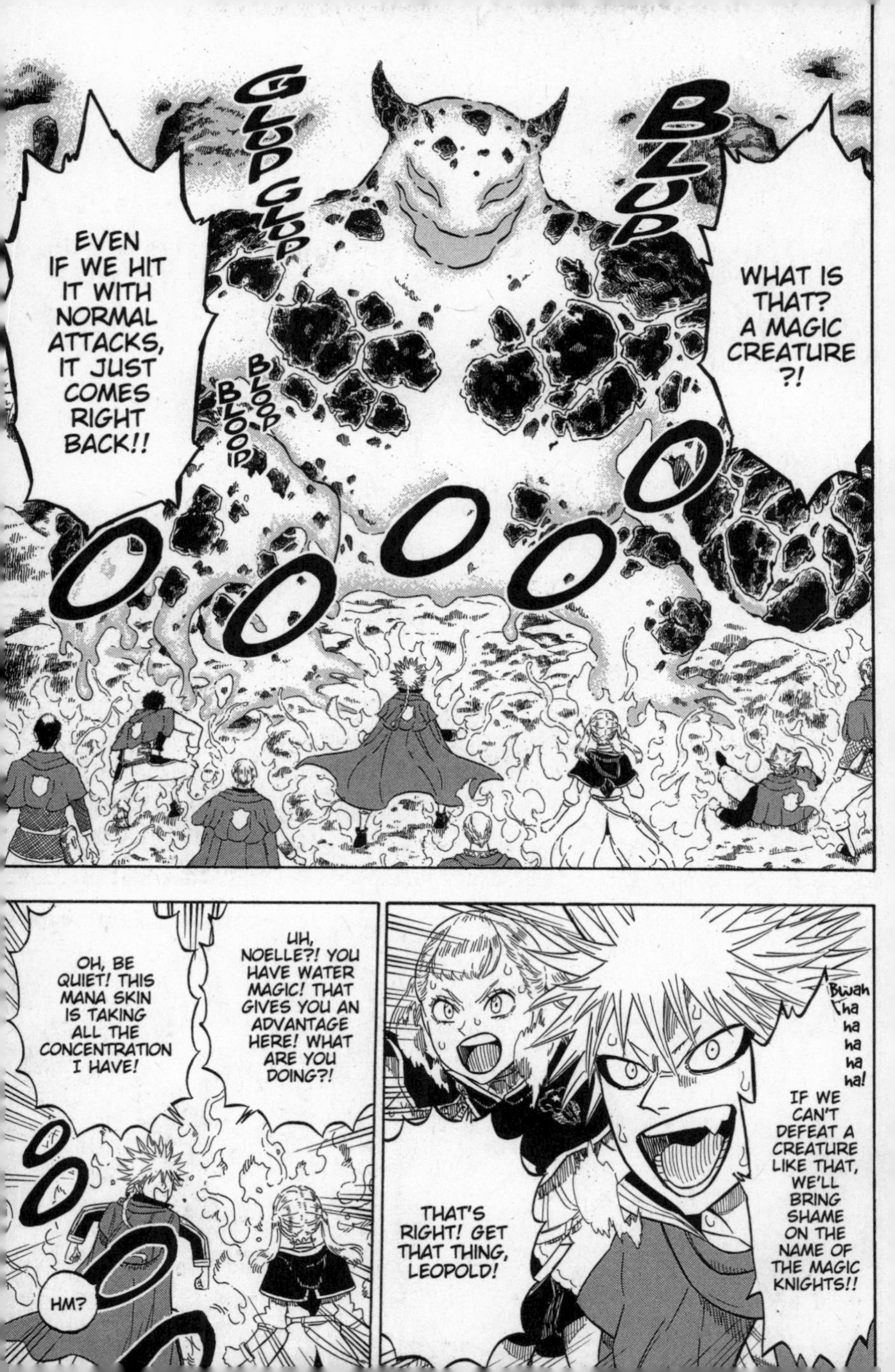
BLUP
WHAT IS THAT? A MAGIC CREATURE?!
GLUP GLUP
EVEN IF WE HIT IT WITH NORMAL ATTACKS, IT JUST COMES RIGHT BACK!!
BLOOP BLOOP
OOOOOOO
Bwah ha ha ha ha ha!
IF WE CAN'T DEFEAT A CREATURE LIKE THAT, WE'LL BRING SHAME ON THE NAME OF THE MAGIC KNIGHTS!!
THAT'S RIGHT! GET THAT THING, LEOPOLD!
UH, NOELLE?! YOU HAVE WATER MAGIC! THAT GIVES YOU AN ADVANTAGE HERE! WHAT ARE YOU DOING?!
OH, BE QUIET! THIS MANA SKIN IS TAKING ALL THE CONCENTRATION I HAVE!
HM?

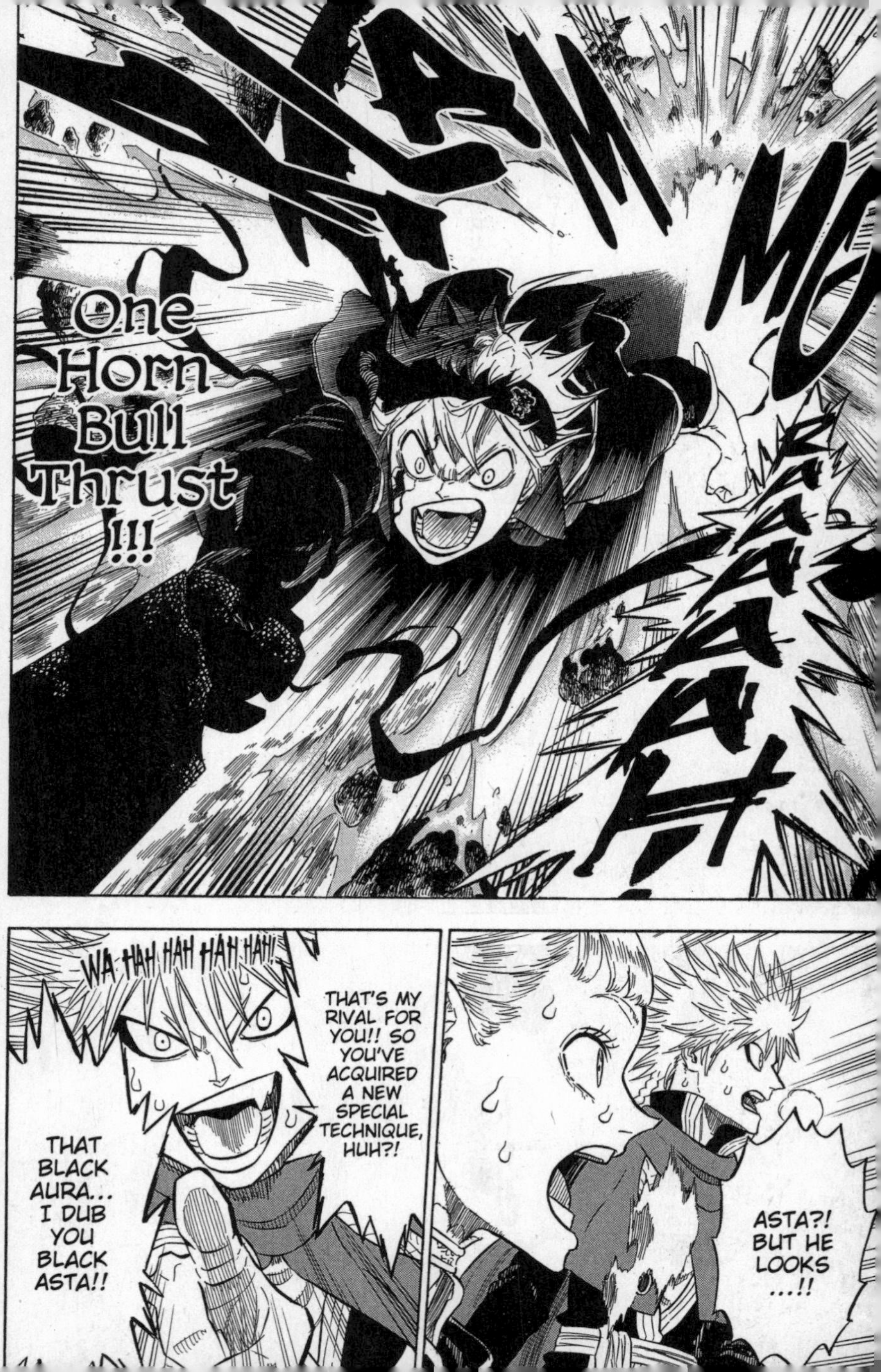
One Horn Bull Thrust !!!
ASTA?! BUT HE LOOKS ...!!
WA HAH HAH HAH HAH!
THAT'S MY RIVAL FOR YOU!! SO YOU'VE ACQUIRED A NEW SPECIAL TECHNIQUE, HUH?!
THAT BLACK AURA... I DUB YOU BLACK ASTA!!

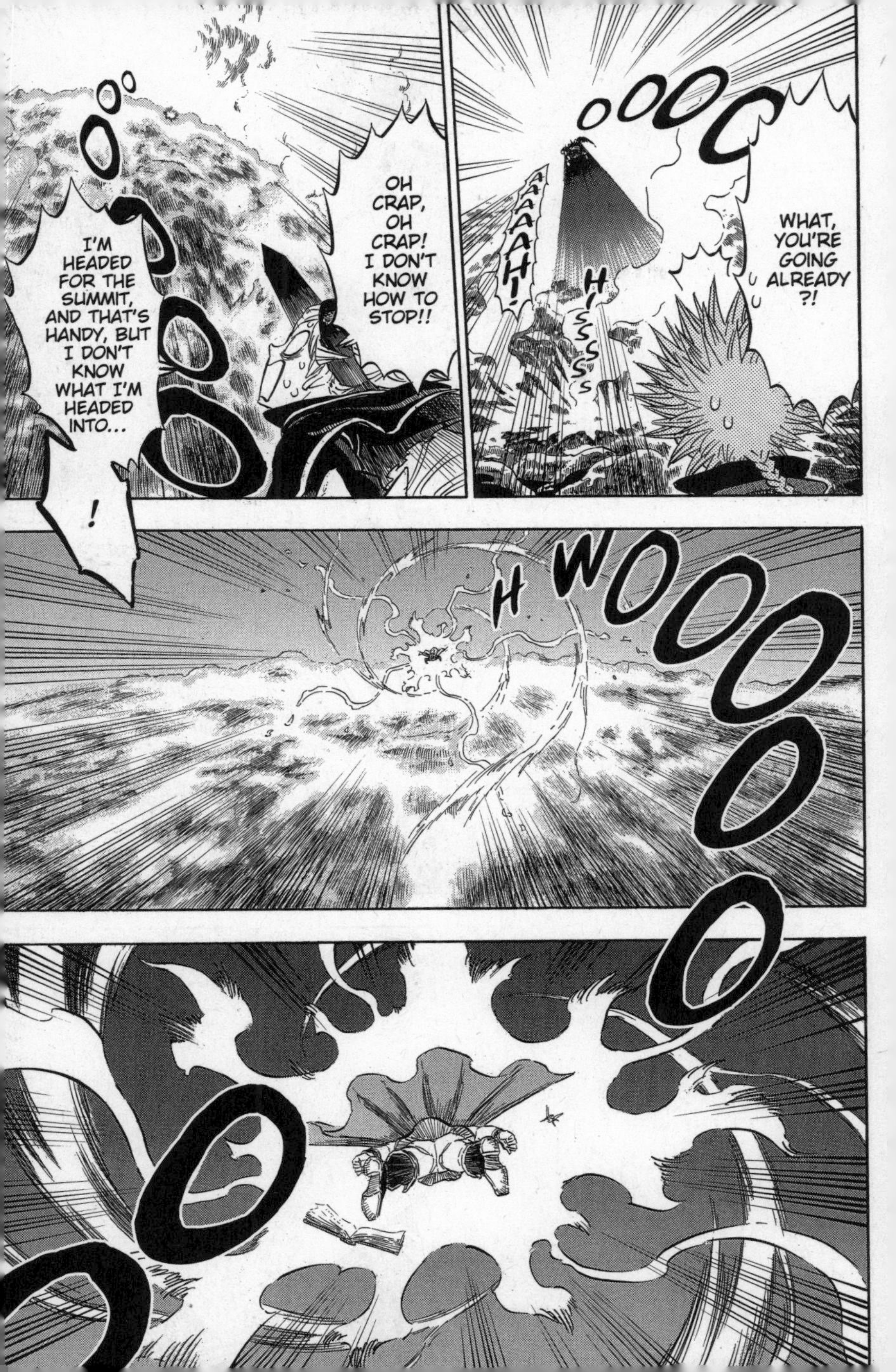
OOOC
WHAT, YOU'RE GOING ALREADY?!
AAAAAH!
HISSSS
OH CRAP, OH CRAP! I DON'T KNOW HOW TO STOP!!
I'M HEADED FOR THE SUMMIT, AND THAT'S HANDY, BUT I DON'T KNOW WHAT I'M HEADED INTO...
!
HWOOOOOO

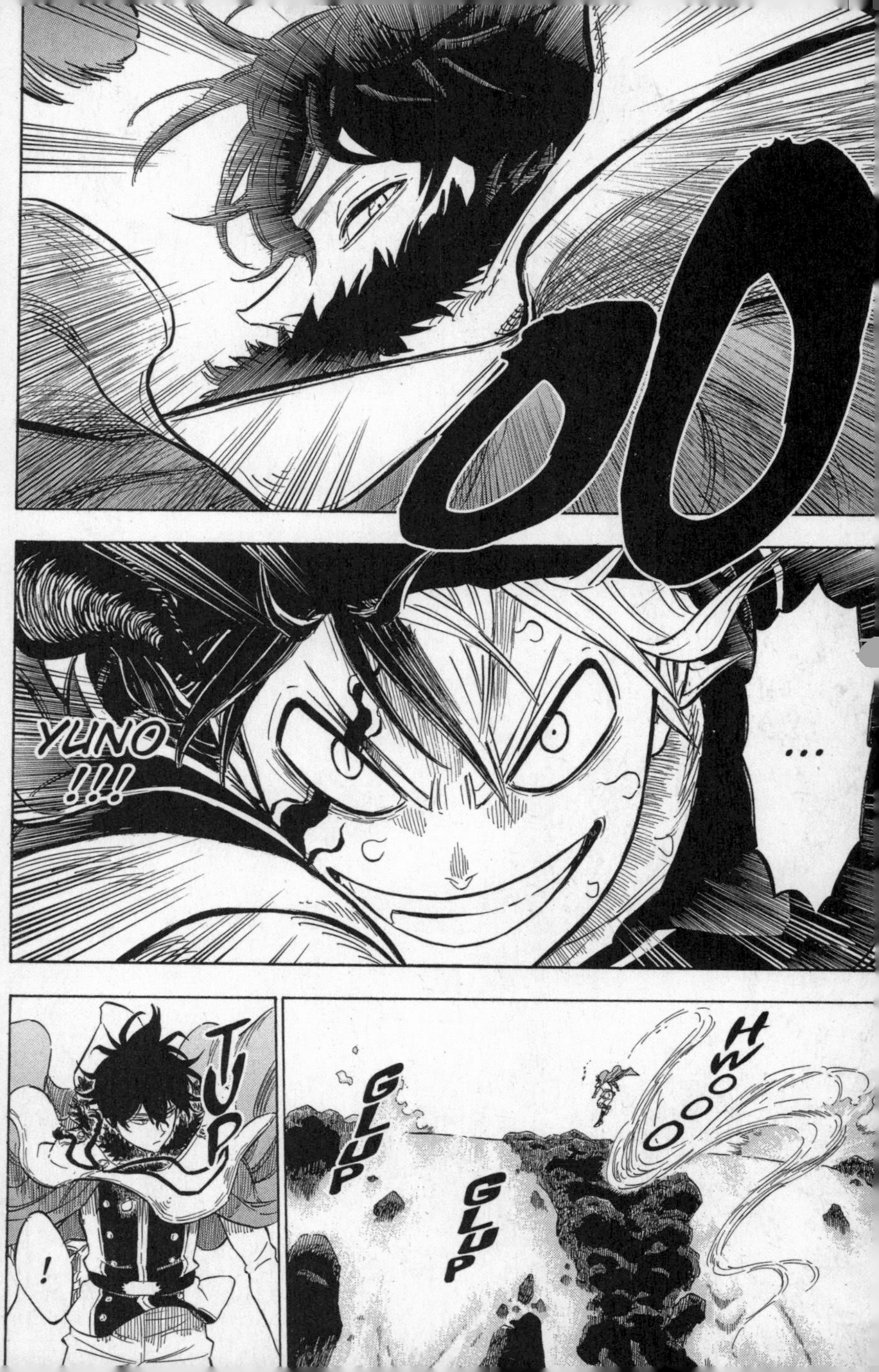
...
YUNO !!!
HWOOOO
GLUP
GLUP
TUP
!

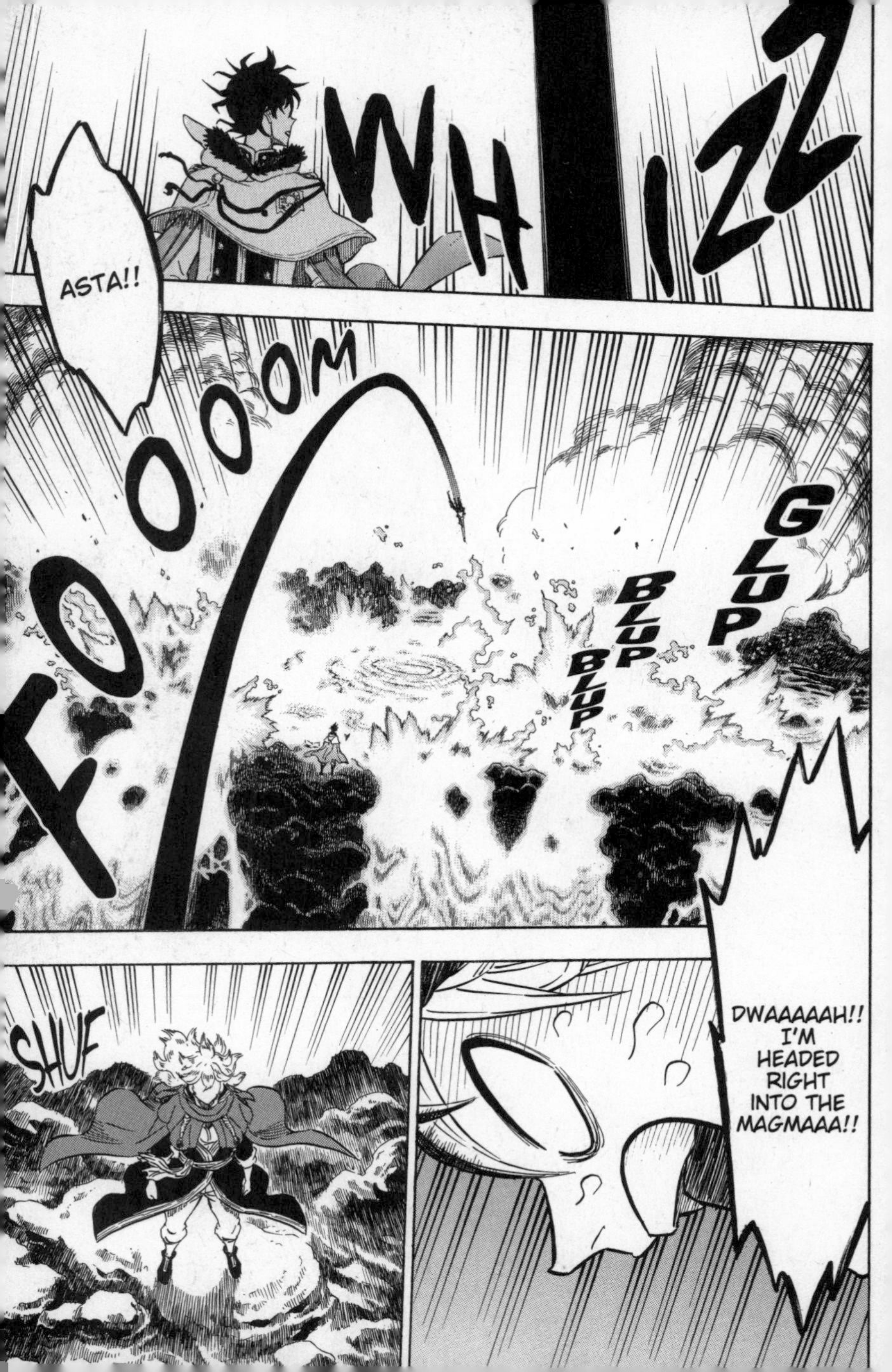
WHIZZ
ASTA!!
GLUP
BLUP
BLUP
FOOOOM
DWAAAAAH!! I'M HEADED RIGHT INTO THE MAGMAAA!!
SHUF

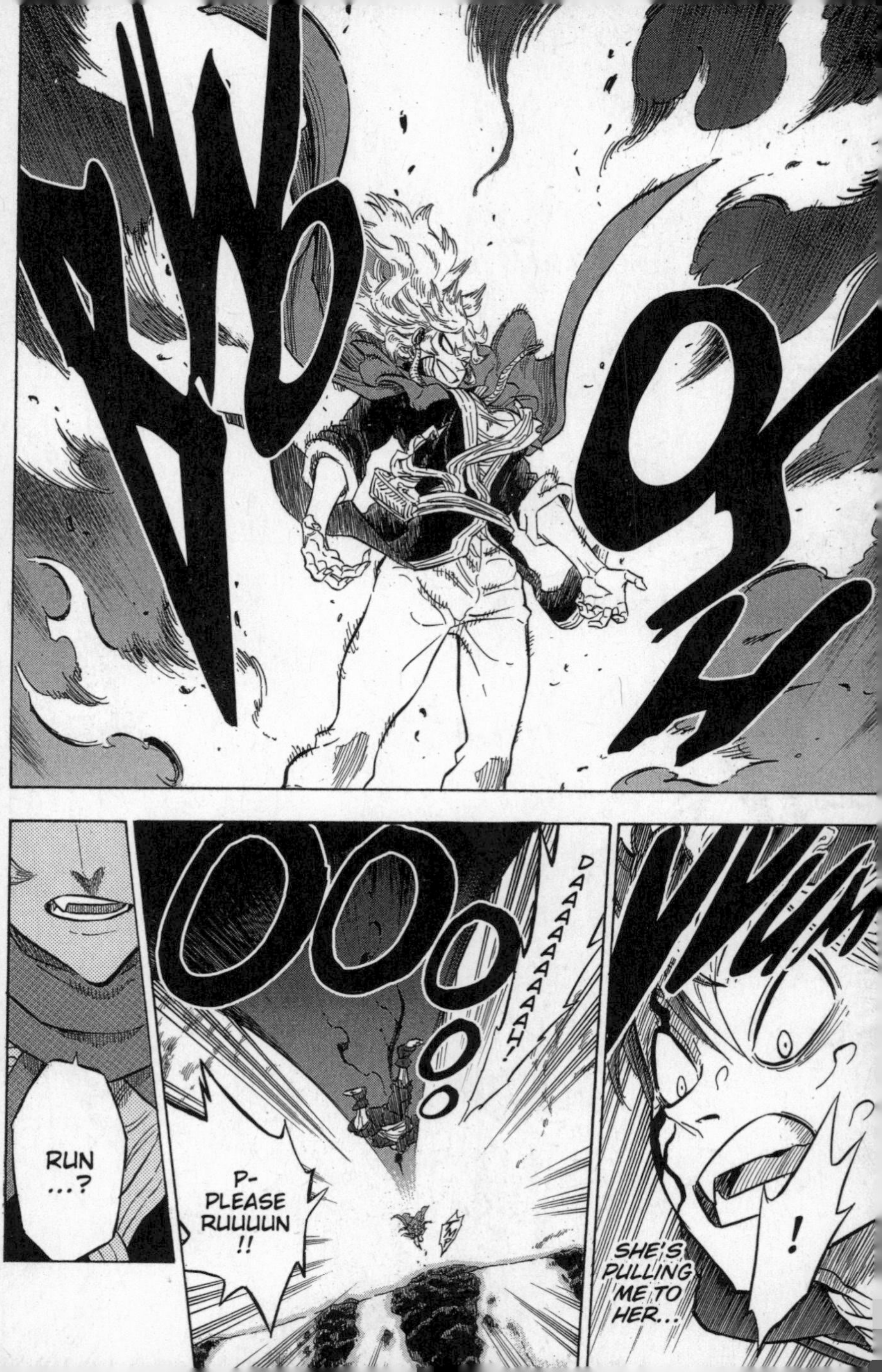

SHE'S PULLING ME TO HER...
!
P-PLEASE RUUUUN!!
RUN ...?

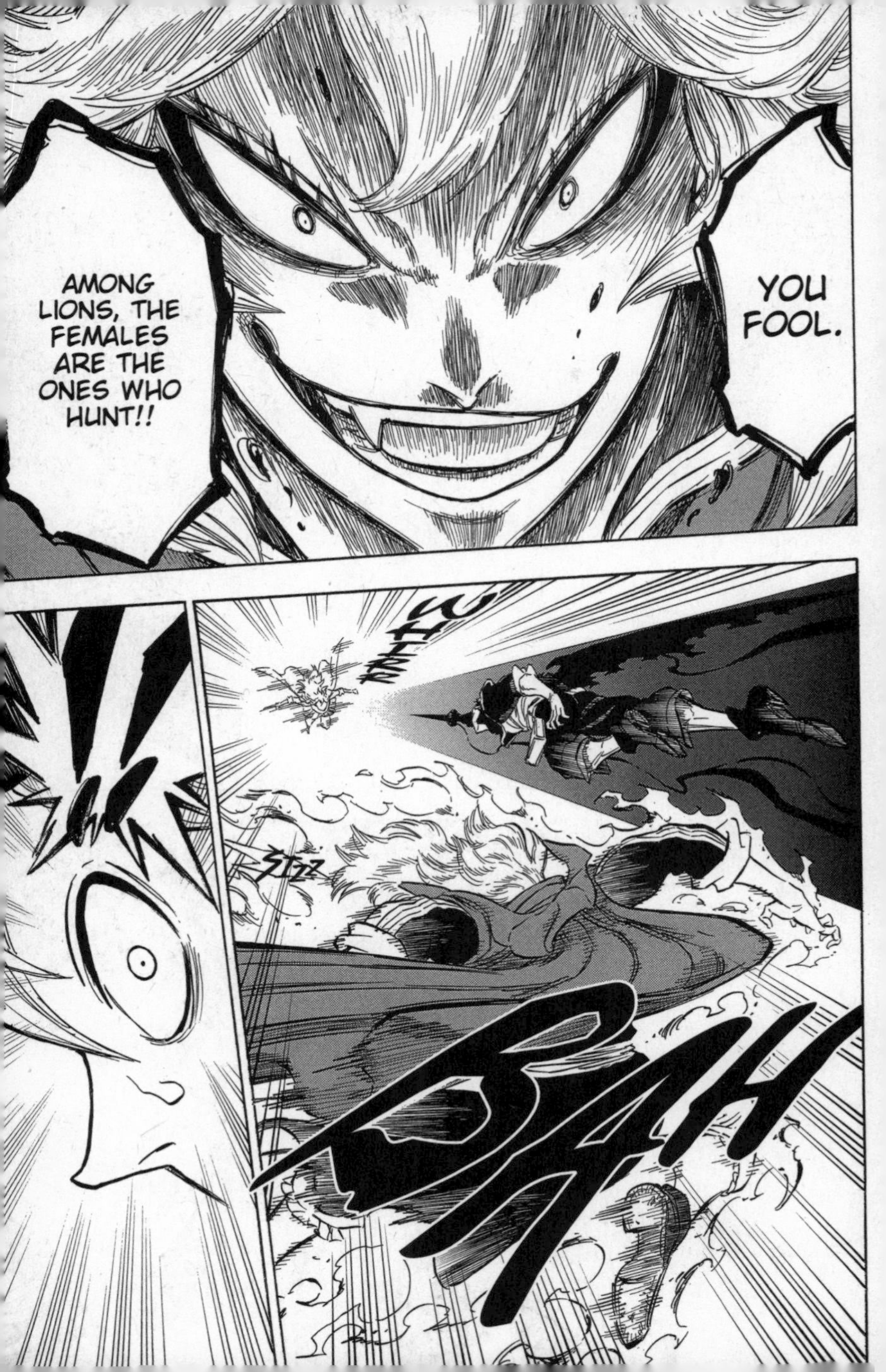
YOU FOOL.
AMONG LIONS, THE FEMALES ARE THE ONES WHO HUNT!!
WHIRR
SIZZ
BAM
!

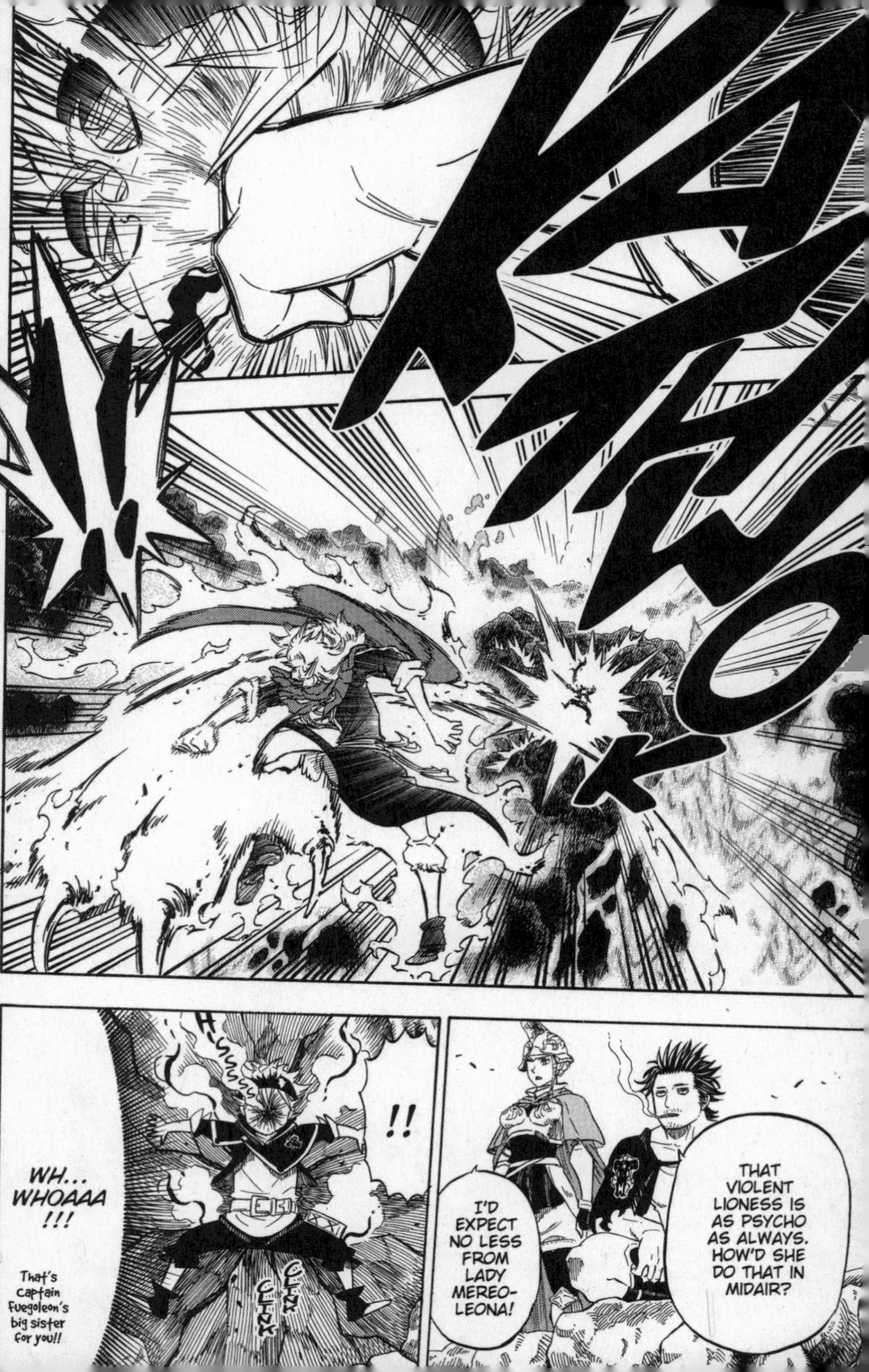
THAT VIOLENT LIONESS IS AS PSYCHO AS ALWAYS. HOW'D SHE DO THAT IN MIDAIR?
I'D EXPECT NO LESS FROM LADY MEREO-LEONA!
H-SSSSS
!!
WH... WHOAAA!!!
CLINK
CLINK
That's captain Fuegoleon's big sister for you!!

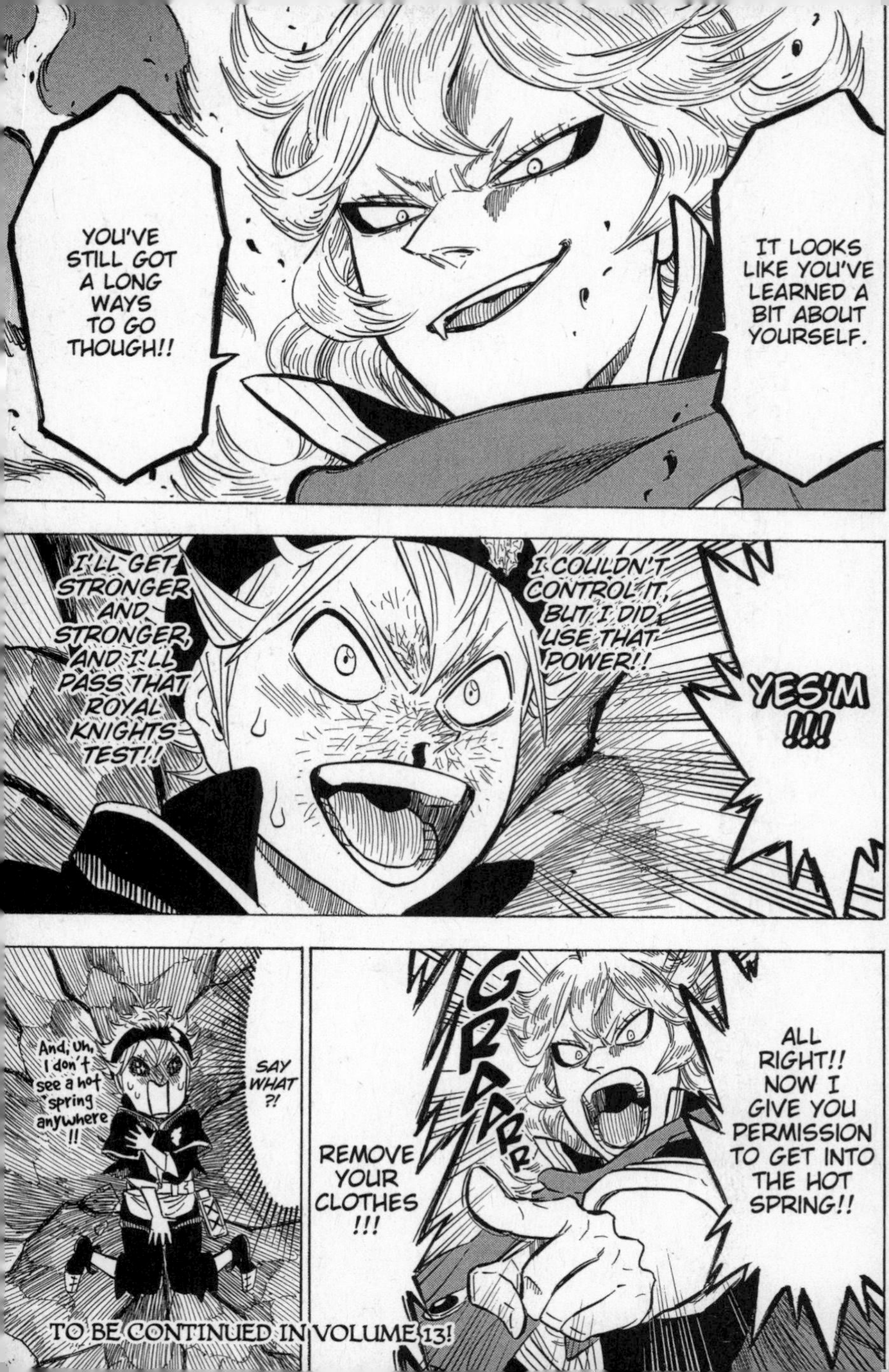
IT LOOKS LIKE YOU'VE LEARNED A BIT ABOUT YOURSELF.
YOU'VE STILL GOT A LONG WAYS TO GO THOUGH!!
YES'M!!!
I COULDN'T CONTROL IT, BUT I DID USE THAT POWER!!
I'LL GET STRONGER AND STRONGER, AND I'LL PASS THAT ROYAL KNIGHTS TEST!!
ALL RIGHT!! NOW I GIVE YOU PERMISSION TO GET INTO THE HOT SPRING!!
GRRRRR
REMOVE YOUR CLOTHES!!!
SAY WHAT?!
And, uh, I don't see a hot spring anywhere!!
TO BE CONTINUED IN VOLUME 13!

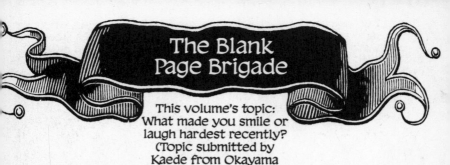

The Blank Page Brigade

This volume's topic:
What made you smile or laugh hardest recently?
(Topic submitted by Kaede from Okayama Prefecture!)

Running into a friend from a long time ago.

Hayato Gotō

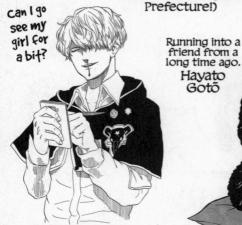

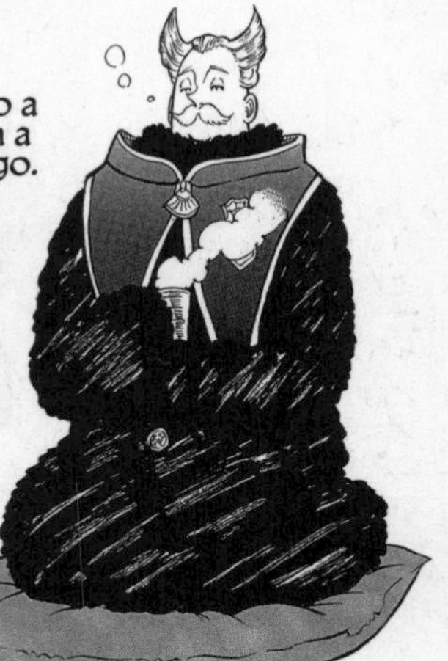

Can I go see my girl for a bit?

I laughed because a hedgehog video on YouTube was way too cute.

Kazuhiro Wakao

A MAGIC EGGPLANT THAT GREW NICE AND BIG...
...IN THE ASHES FROM YULTIM VOLCANO!!

I did a Dylan McKay imitation all alone in the bath and cracked myself up.

Yōtarō Hayakawa

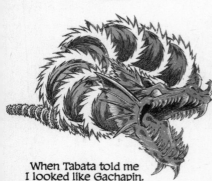

When Tabata told me I looked like Gachapin.

Suzuki

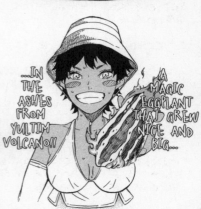

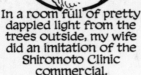

In the morning, when Mr. Tabata was sleeping, his beloved doggy was sacked out on top of his stomach.

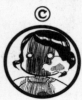

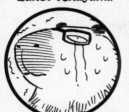

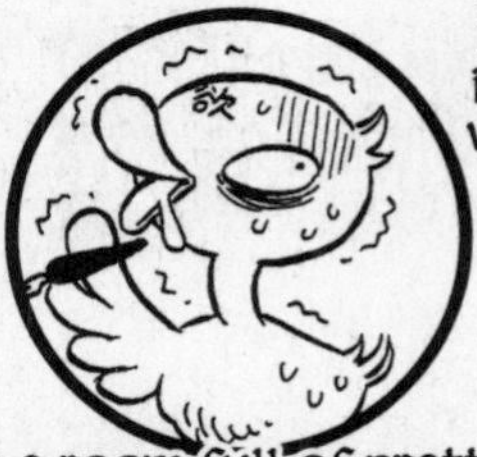

In a room full of pretty dappled light from the trees outside, my wife did an imitation of the Shiromoto Clinic commercial.

Captain Tabata

When I went into a ramen shop near the office, and almost everyone in the place was a *Jump* editorial department member.

Editor Katayama

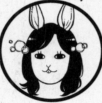

I fell into an irrigation canal in the middle of the night.

Designer Iwai

When Tabata Sensei's dog Amelie started to let me play with her.

Comics Editor Koshimura

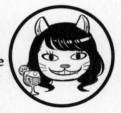

AFTERWORD

Between this, that and the other, the *Black Clover* anime will begin airing in October of 2017!! Hooraaaaay!!

A TV anime... A TV anime, huh...

The first anime I remember seeing was *Dragon Ball*. Goku was fighting a white-hot battle with Freeza, and it was just way too awesome!!

A little while later, a friend of mine brought an issue of *Jump* to daycare. When I saw *Dragon Ball* in it, I learned that that was what the *Dragon Ball* on TV was based on, and that there was a job called "manga creator," and that's when I decided I'd be one. Wow... And they're still airing that anime... *Dragon Ball* is just too incredible!!!

Between this, that and the other, I'm looking forward to the *Black Clover* TV anime!!

Black Clover Side Story:

Royal Clover Academy

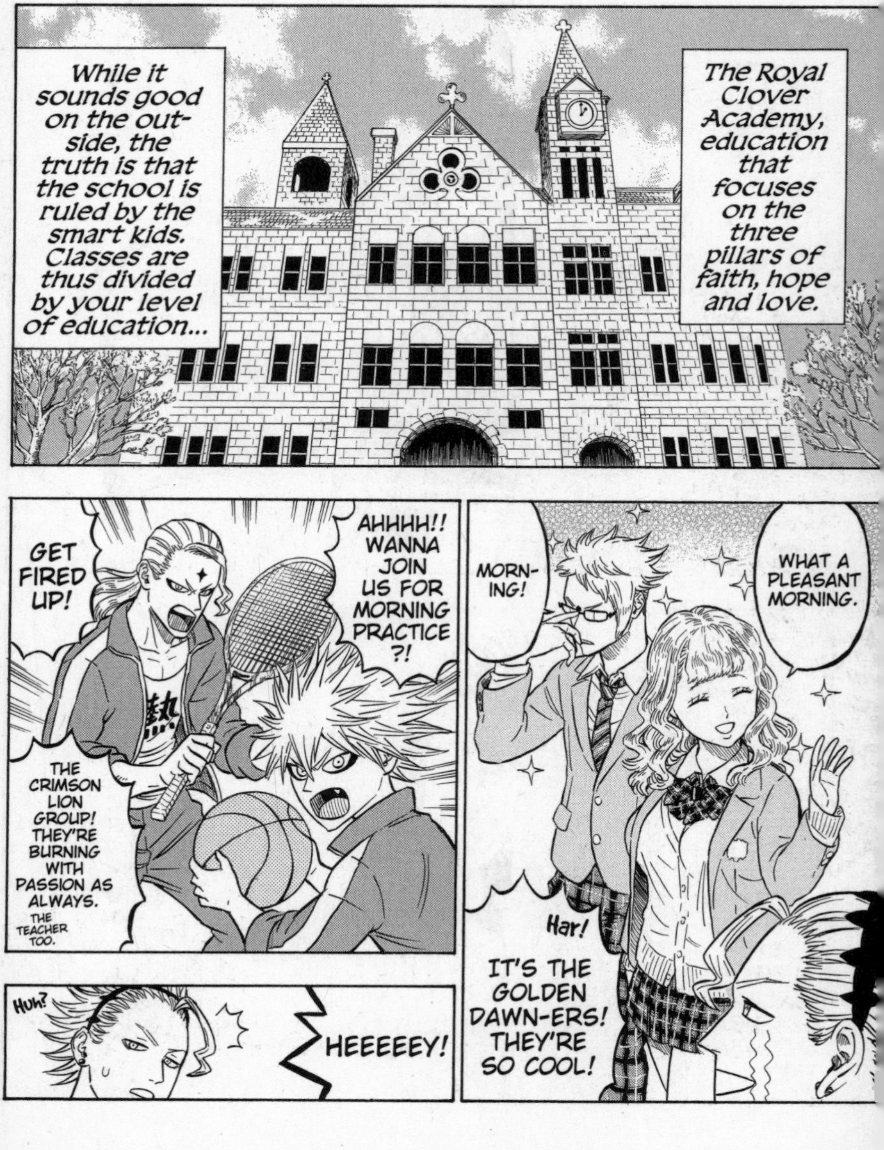
The Royal Clover Academy, education that focuses on the three pillars of faith, hope and love.
While it sounds good on the out-side, the truth is that the school is ruled by the smart kids. Classes are thus divided by your level of education...
WHAT A PLEASANT MORNING.
MORNING!
Har!
IT'S THE GOLDEN DAWN-ERS! THEY'RE SO COOL!
AHHHH!! WANNA JOIN US FOR MORNING PRACTICE?!
GET FIRED UP!
THE CRIMSON LION GROUP! THEY'RE BURNING WITH PASSION AS ALWAYS.
THE TEACHER TOO.
HEEEEEY!
Huh?

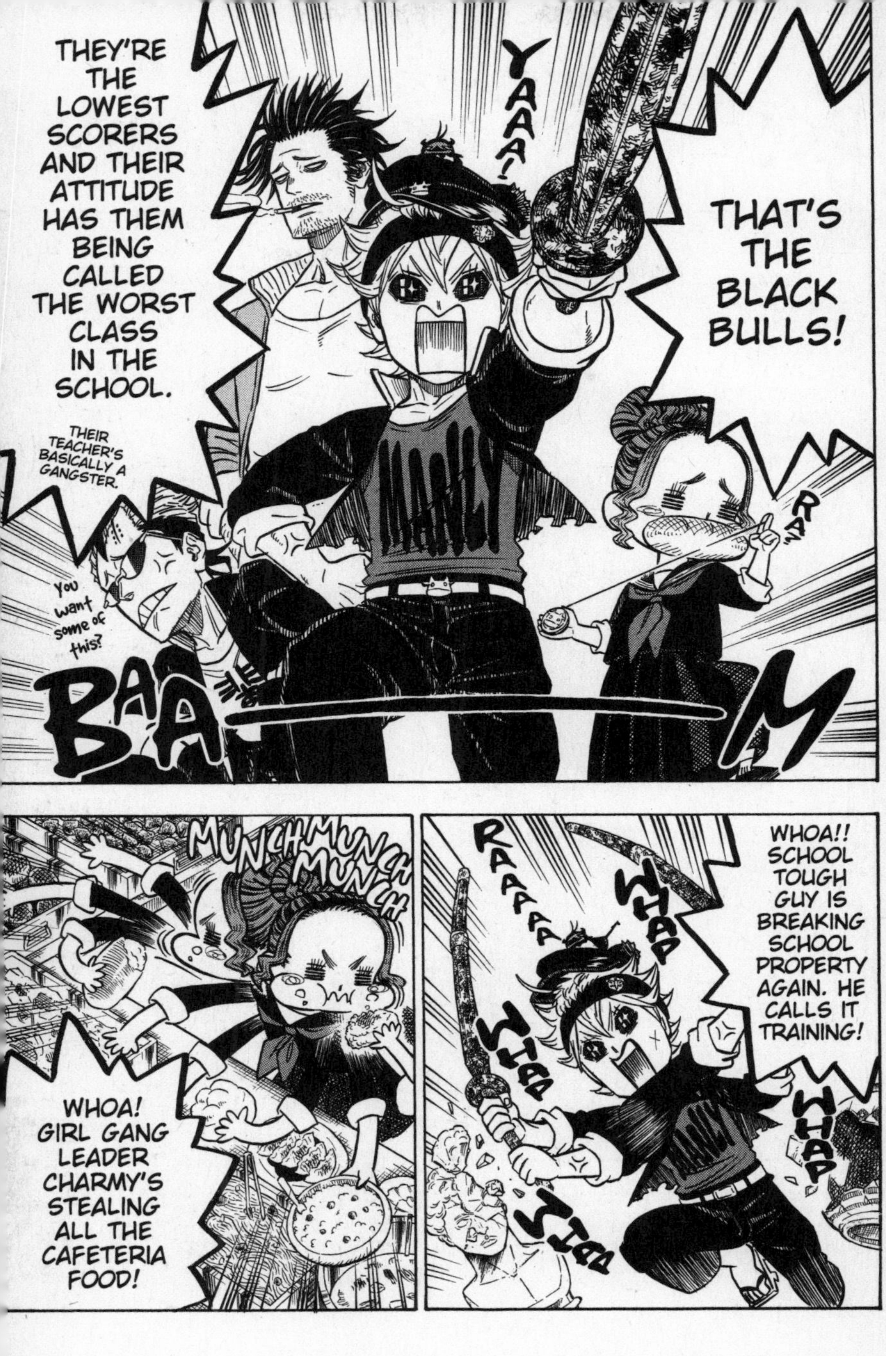
YAAA!
THAT'S THE BLACK BULLS!
THEY'RE THE LOWEST SCORERS AND THEIR ATTITUDE HAS THEM BEING CALLED THE WORST CLASS IN THE SCHOOL.
THEIR TEACHER'S BASICALLY A GANGSTER.
RA
You want some of this?
BAAM
WHOA!! SCHOOL TOUGH GUY IS BREAKING SCHOOL PROPERTY AGAIN. HE CALLS IT TRAINING!
WHAP
RAAAAAA
WHAP
MUNCH MUNCH MUNCH MUNCH
WHOA! GIRL GANG LEADER CHARMY'S STEALING ALL THE CAFETERIA FOOD!

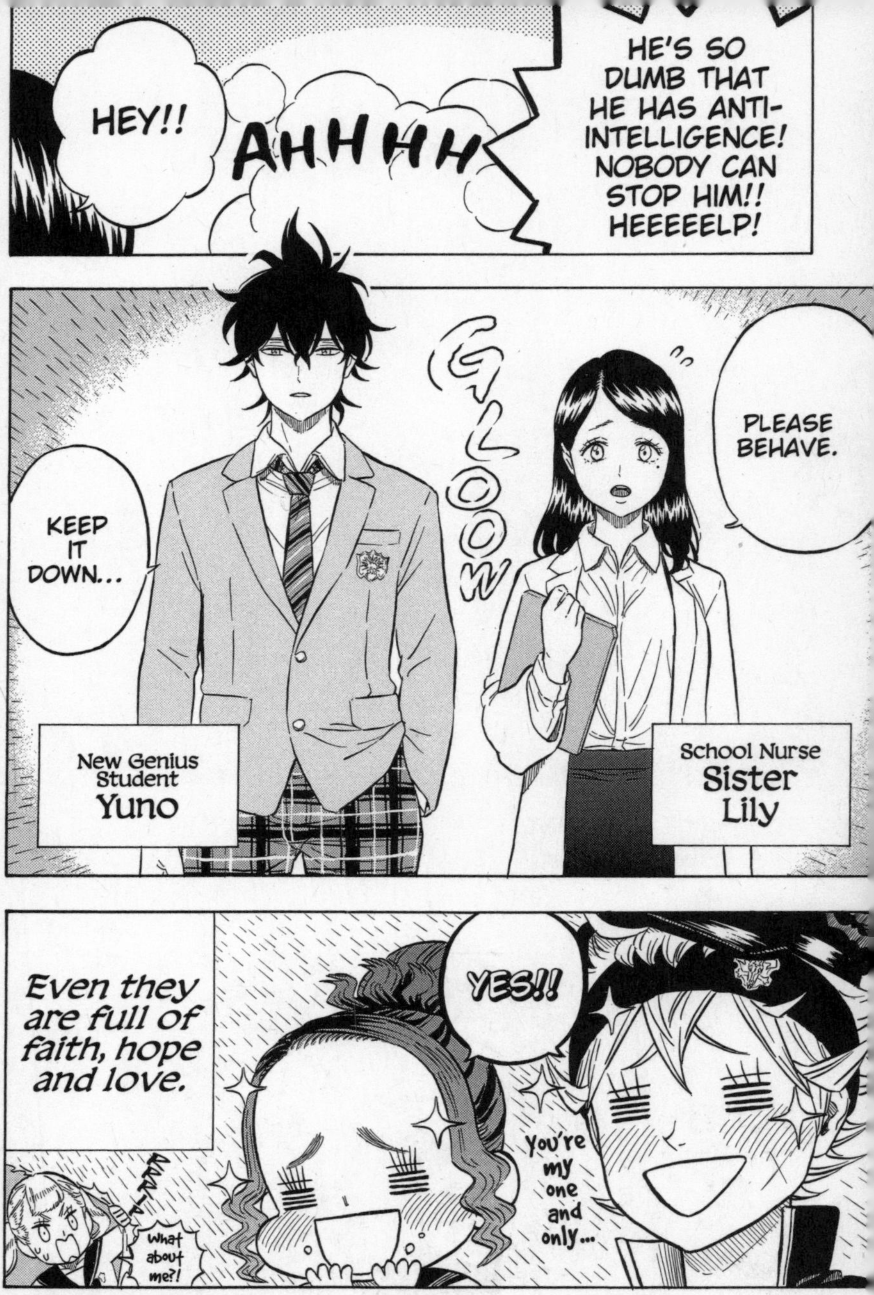
HE'S SO DUMB THAT HE HAS ANTI-INTELLIGENCE! NOBODY CAN STOP HIM!! HEEEEELP!
AHHHH
HEY!!
PLEASE BEHAVE.
GLOOW
School Nurse Sister Lily
KEEP IT DOWN...
New Genius Student Yuno
YES!!
You're my one and only...
Even they are full of faith, hope and love.
What about me?!

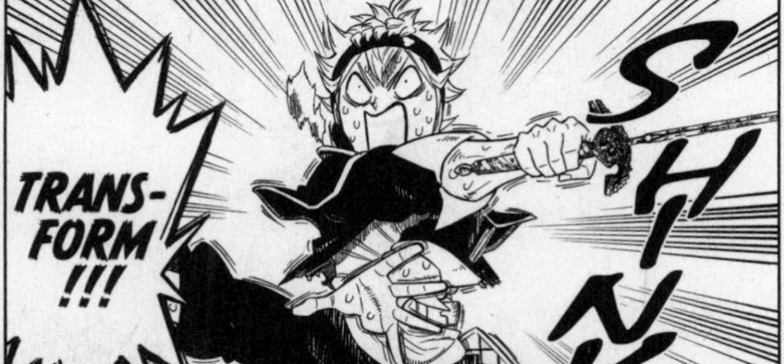
SHINK
TRANS-FORM!!!

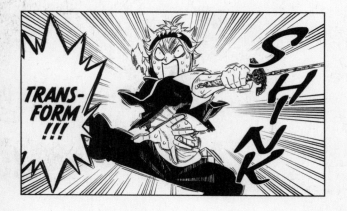

Presenting a special
illustration of Yami and Yuno. A
rather unexpected combination...

Special Bonus Materials

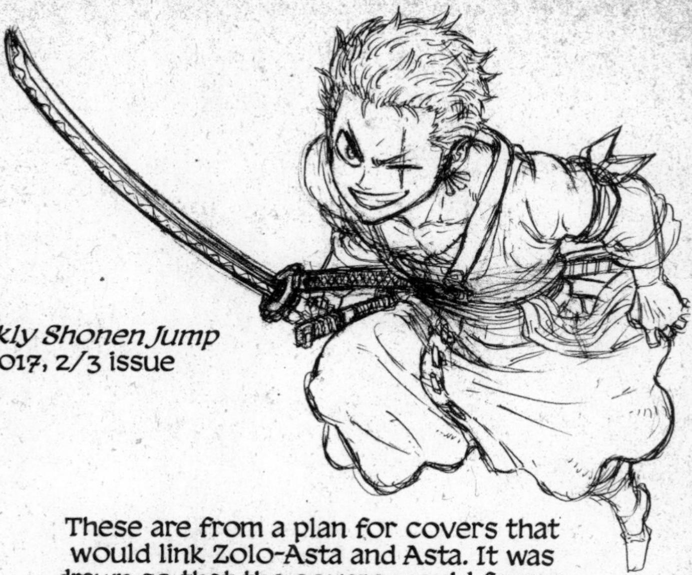

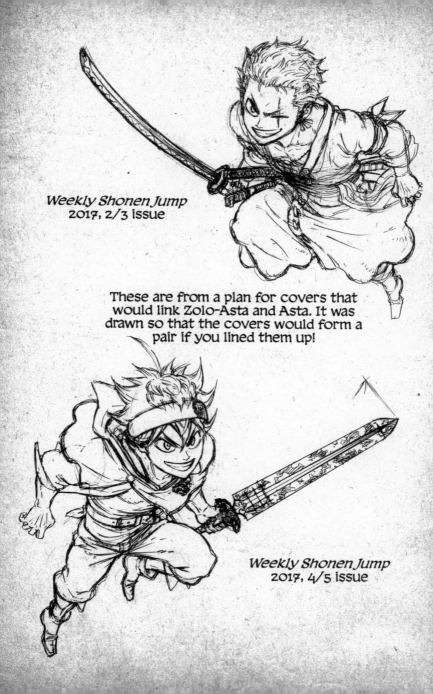

Weekly Shonen Jump
2017, 2/3 issue

These are from a plan for covers that would link Zolo-Asta and Asta. It was drawn so that the covers would form a pair if you lined them up!

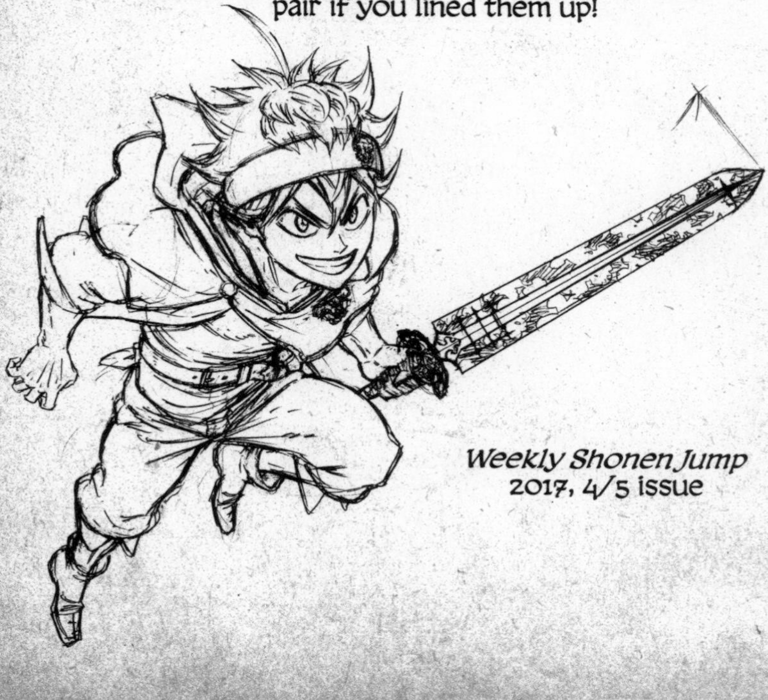

Weekly Shonen Jump
2017, 4/5 issue

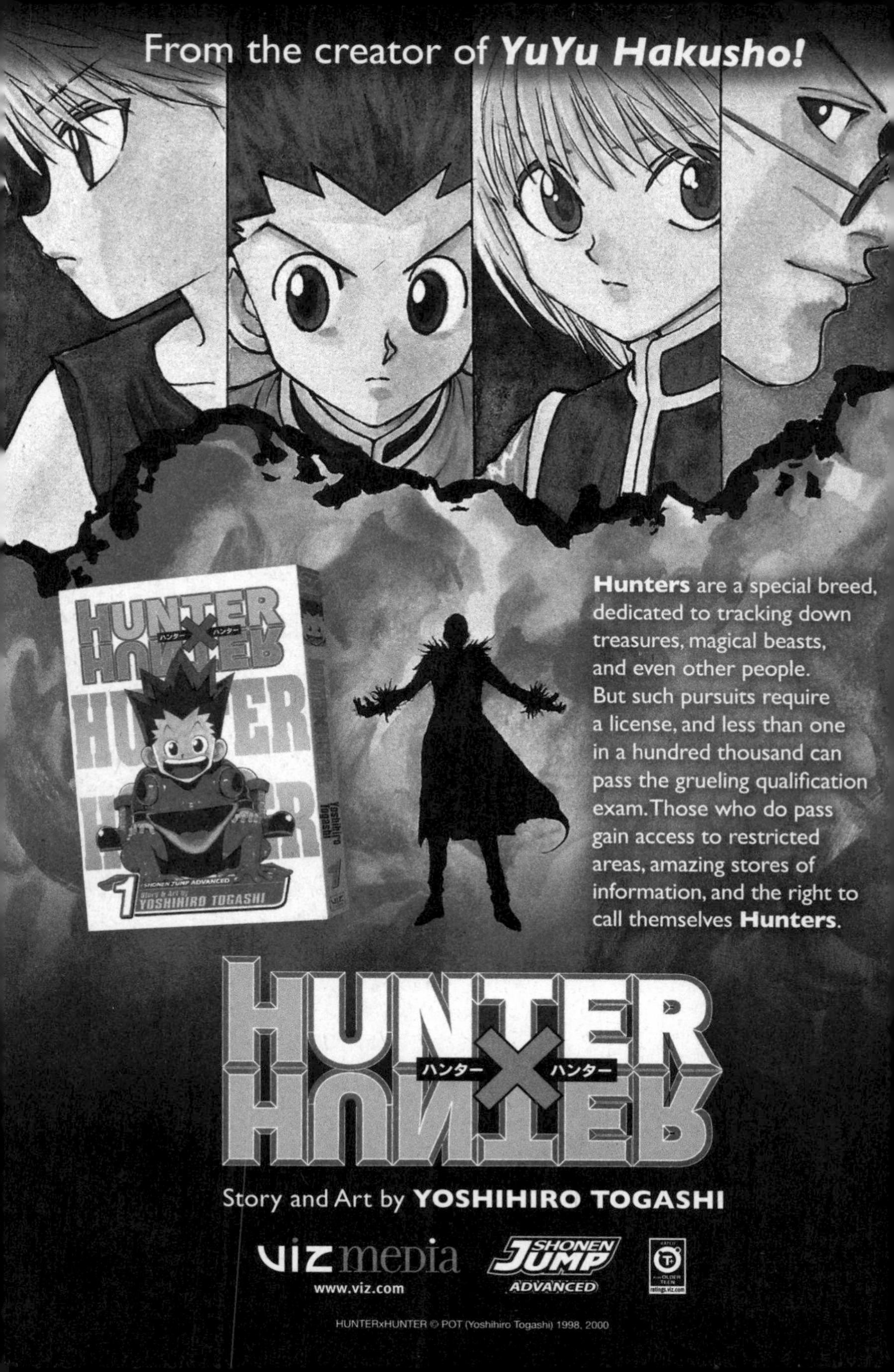
From the creator of YuYu Hakusho!
HUNTER × HUNTER
ハンター ハンター
SHONEN JUMP ADVANCED
Story & Art by YOSHIHIRO TOGASHI
Yoshihiro Togashi
Hunters are a special breed, dedicated to tracking down treasures, magical beasts, and even other people. But such pursuits require a license, and less than one in a hundred thousand can pass the grueling qualification exam. Those who do pass gain access to restricted areas, amazing stores of information, and the right to call themselves Hunters.
HUNTER × HUNTER
ハンター ハンター
Story and Art by YOSHIHIRO TOGASHI
VIZ media
www.viz.com
SHONEN JUMP ADVANCED
OLDER TEEN
ratings.viz.com
HUNTERxHUNTER © POT (Yoshihiro Togashi) 1998, 2000

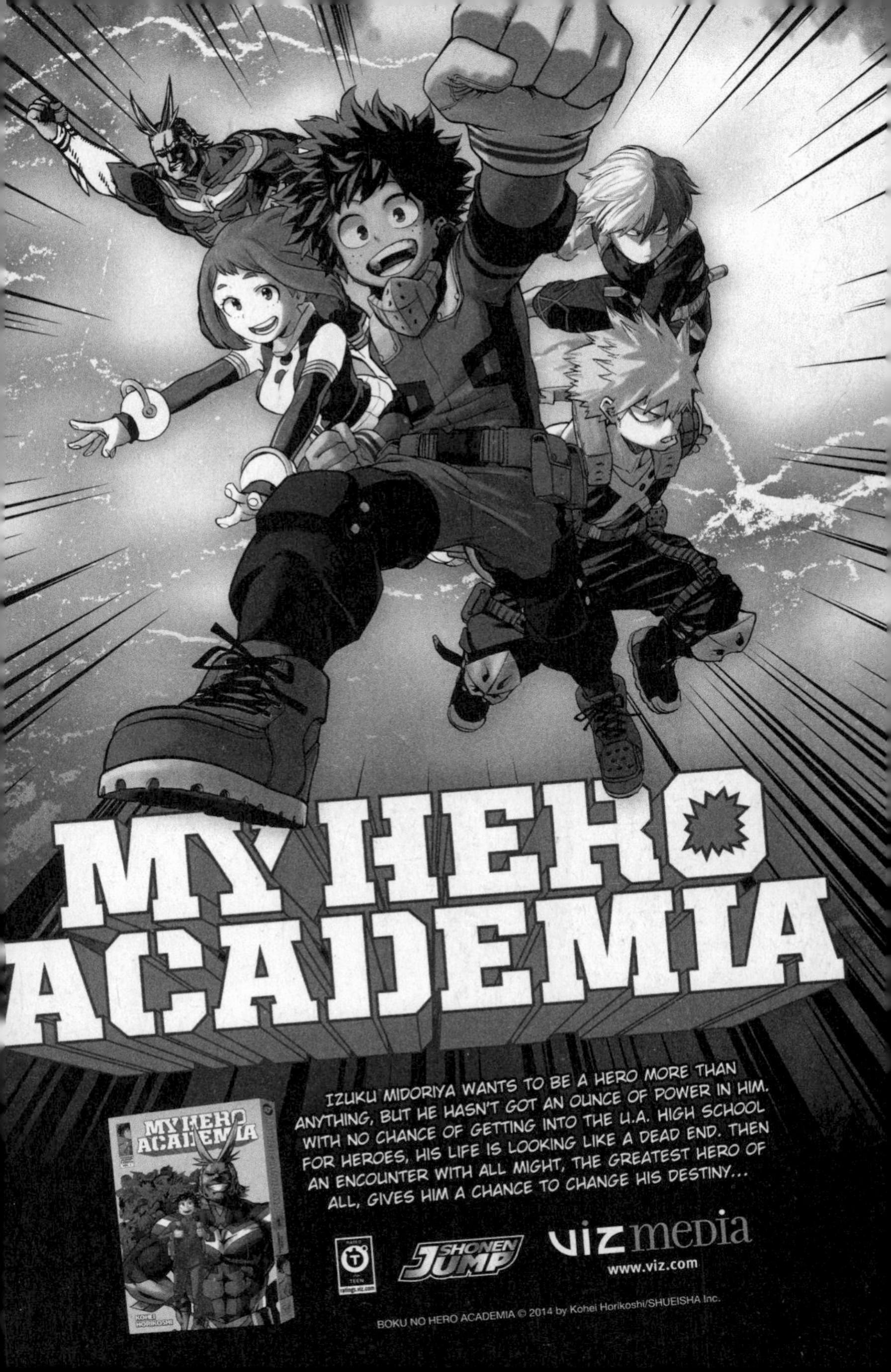
MY HERO ACADEMIA
IZUKU MIDORIYA WANTS TO BE A HERO MORE THAN ANYTHING, BUT HE HASN'T GOT AN OUNCE OF POWER IN HIM. WITH NO CHANCE OF GETTING INTO THE U.A. HIGH SCHOOL FOR HEROES, HIS LIFE IS LOOKING LIKE A DEAD END. THEN AN ENCOUNTER WITH ALL MIGHT, THE GREATEST HERO OF ALL, GIVES HIM A CHANCE TO CHANGE HIS DESTINY…
MY HERO ACADEMIA
KOHEI HORIKOSHI
TEEN
ratings.viz.com
SHONEN JUMP
viz media
www.viz.com
BOKU NO HERO ACADEMIA © 2014 by Kohei Horikoshi/SHUEISHA Inc.

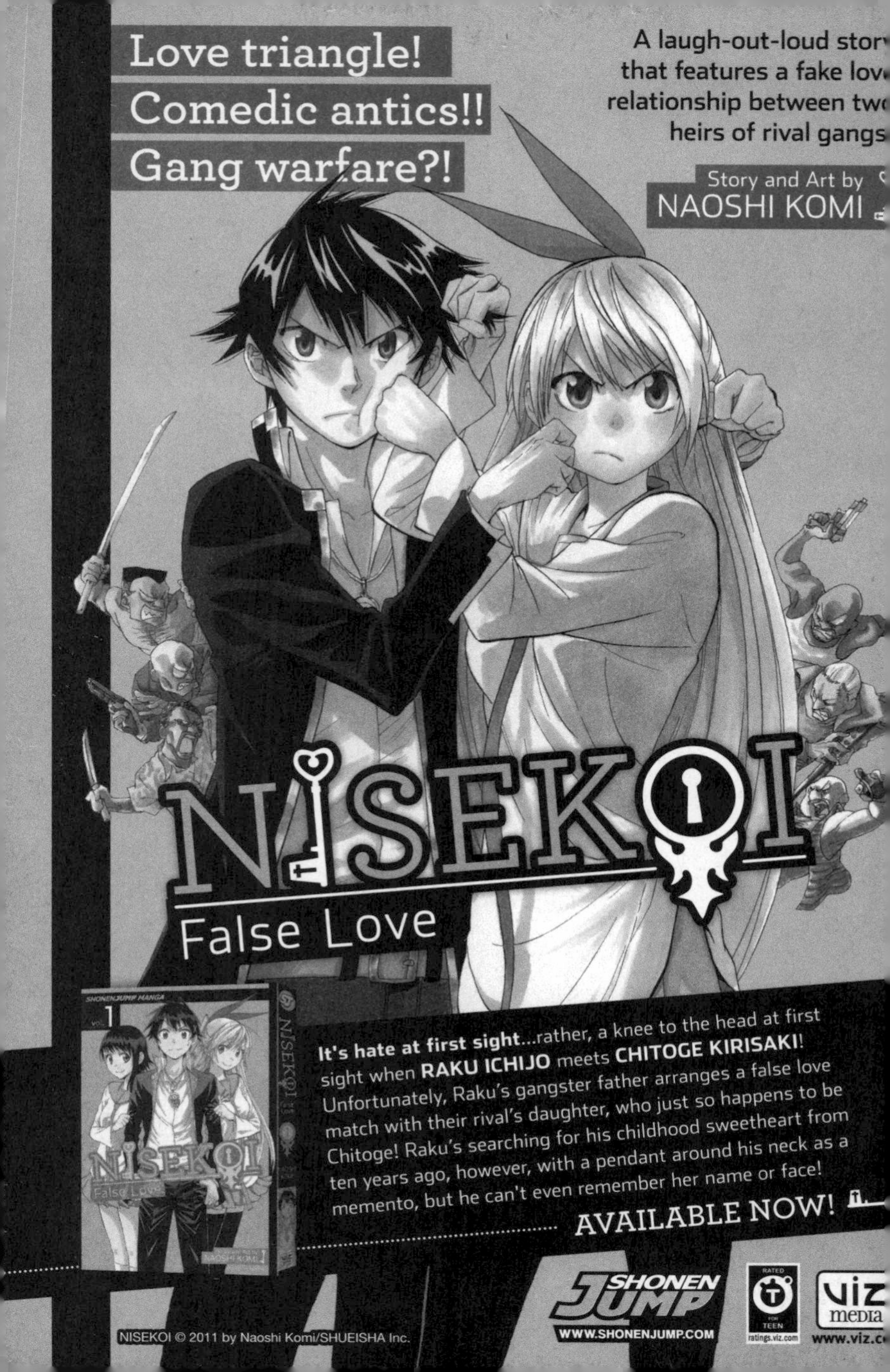
Love triangle!
Comedic antics!!
Gang warfare?!
A laugh-out-loud stor
that features a fake lov
relationship between tw
heirs of rival gangs
Story and Art by
NAOSHI KOMI
NISEKOI
False Love
SHONENJUMP MANGA
vol. 1
NISEKOI
False Love
NAOSHI KOMI
It's hate at first sight...rather, a knee to the head at first sight when RAKU ICHIJO meets CHITOGE KIRISAKI! Unfortunately, Raku's gangster father arranges a false love match with their rival's daughter, who just so happens to be Chitoge! Raku's searching for his childhood sweetheart from ten years ago, however, with a pendant around his neck as a memento, but he can't even remember her name or face!
AVAILABLE NOW!
SHONEN JUMP
WWW.SHONENJUMP.COM
RATED T FOR TEEN
ratings.viz.com
viz media
www.viz.c
NISEKOI © 2011 by Naoshi Komi/SHUEISHA Inc.

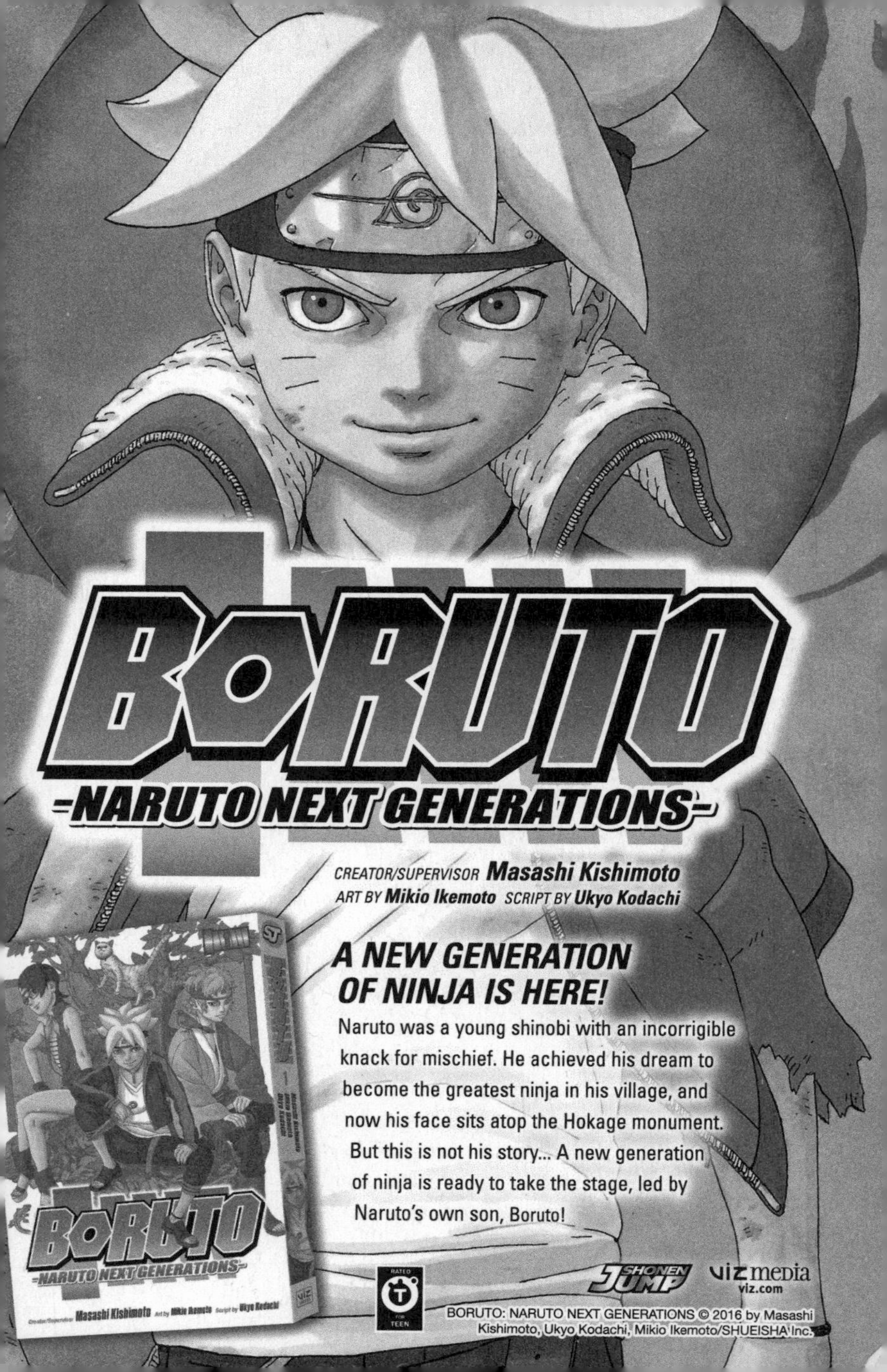
BORUTO
-NARUTO NEXT GENERATIONS-
CREATOR/SUPERVISOR Masashi Kishimoto
ART BY Mikio Ikemoto SCRIPT BY Ukyo Kodachi
A NEW GENERATION OF NINJA IS HERE!
Naruto was a young shinobi with an incorrigible knack for mischief. He achieved his dream to become the greatest ninja in his village, and now his face sits atop the Hokage monument. But this is not his story... A new generation of ninja is ready to take the stage, led by Naruto's own son, Boruto!
RATED T FOR TEEN
SHONEN JUMP
viz media
viz.com
BORUTO: NARUTO NEXT GENERATIONS © 2016 by Masashi Kishimoto, Ukyo Kodachi, Mikio Ikemoto/SHUEISHA Inc.

Stop

YOU'RE READING
THE WRONG WAY!

BLACK CLOVER
reads from right to left, starting
in the upper-right corner. Japanese
is read from right to left, meaning
that action, sound effects, and
word-balloon order are completely
reversed from English order.

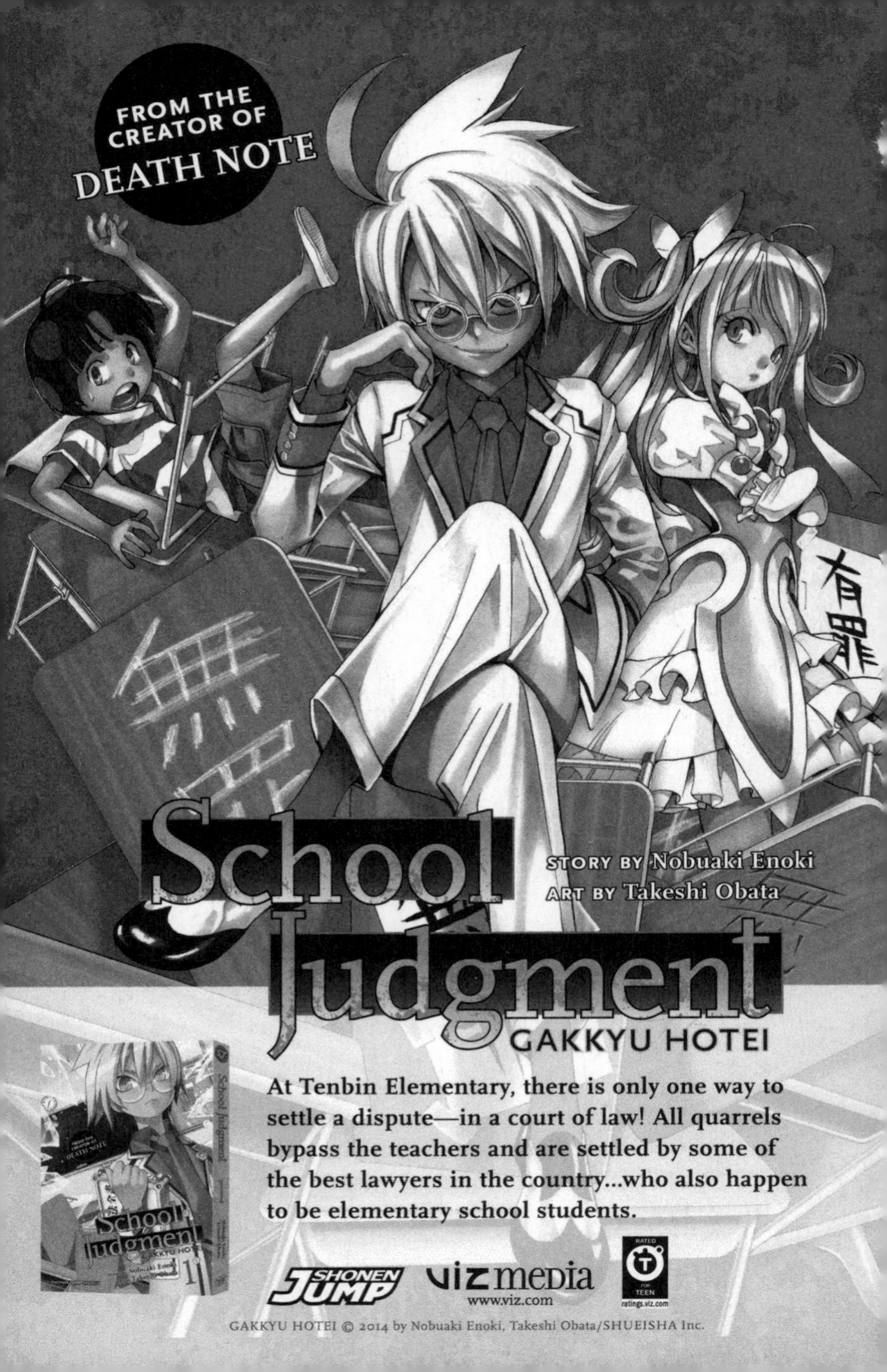

FROM THE CREATOR OF DEATH NOTE
School Judgment
STORY BY Nobuaki Enoki
ART BY Takeshi Obata
GAKKYU HOTEI
At Tenbin Elementary, there is only one way to settle a dispute—in a court of law! All quarrels bypass the teachers and are settled by some of the best lawyers in the country...who also happen to be elementary school students.
SHONEN JUMP
VIZ media
www.viz.com
RATED T FOR TEEN
ratings.viz.com
GAKKYU HOTEI © 2014 by Nobuaki Enoki, Takeshi Obata/SHUEISHA Inc.